3rd Joint Conference on Lexical and Computational Semantics

(SEM 2014)

Held with SemEval 2014 at COLING 2014

Dublin, Ireland
23 – 24 August 2014

ISBN: 978-1-63439-233-4

Printed from e-media with permission by:

Curran Associates, Inc.
57 Morehouse Lane
Red Hook, NY 12571

Some format issues inherent in the e-media version may also appear in this print version.

Printed by Curran Associates, Inc. (2014)

For permission requests, please contact the Association for Computational Linguistics at the address below.

Association for Computational Linguistics
209 N. Eighth Street
Stroudsburg, Pennsylvania 18360

Phone: 1-570-476-8006
Fax: 1-570-476-0860

acl@aclweb.org

Additional copies of this publication are available from:

Curran Associates, Inc.
57 Morehouse Lane
Red Hook, NY 12571 USA
Phone: 845-758-0400
Fax: 845-758-2634
Email: curran@proceedings.com
Web: www.proceedings.com

⋆SEM 2014: Joint Conference on Lexical and Computational Semantics

Building on the success of the previous editions of the **Joint Conference on Lexical and Computational Semantics (⋆SEM)** in Montreal 2012 and Atlanta 2013, ⋆SEM provides a forum of exchange for the growing number of NLP researchers working on different aspects of semantic processing, which have been scattered over a large array of small workshops and conferences. The 2014 edition of ⋆SEM takes place in Dublin on August 23 and 24 and is collocated with SemEval and COLING. On this occasion, ⋆SEM and SemEval chose to coordinate their programs by featuring a joint invited talk.

In this way, ⋆SEM aims to bring together the ACL SIGLEX and ACL SIGSEM communities that in present their top-tier research in computational semantics on this occasion. As in the previous editions of ⋆SEM, the acceptance rate was very competitive. We accepted 22 papers (14 long and 8 short papers) for publication at the conference, out of 49 long and 25 short paper submissions (resulting in an overall acceptance rate of 29.7%). This is on par with some of the most competitive conferences in computational linguistics. The papers cover a wide range of topics including formal and distributional semantics, lexical semantics, discourse semantics, as well as application-oriented themes. We are confident these various contributions will set the stage for an inspiring conference.

The ⋆SEM 2014 schedule consists of oral presentations for long papers and a poster session for short papers. Next to the accepted papers the ⋆SEM 2014 programme features the following highlights:

Day One, August 23th:

- In the morning, a joint ⋆SEM SemEval keynote address by **Mark Steedman**;
- In the afternoon, the poster session.

Day Two, August 24th:

- In the morning, a keynote address by **Timothy Baldwin**;
- Finally, at the end of the day, a ceremony for the ⋆SEM Best Paper Award.

As always, ⋆SEM 2014 would not have been possible without the considerable efforts of our area chairs and an impressive assortment of reviewers, drawn from the ranks of SIGLEX and SIGSEM, and the computational semantics community at large.

We hope you will enjoy ⋆SEM 2014, and look forward to engaging with all of you,

Johan Bos, University of Groningen, General Chair
Anette Frank, Heidelberg University, Program Co-Chair
Roberto Navigli, Sapienza University of Rome, Program Co-Chair

*SEM 2014 Chairs and Reviewers

General Chair

Johan Bos, University of Groningen

Program Co-Chairs

Anette Frank, Heidelberg University

Roberto Navigli, Sapienza University of Rome

Area Chairs

Anna Korhonen, University of Cambridge

Bernardo Magnini, Fondazione Bruno Kessler Trento

Katja Markert, University of Leeds

Gerard de Melo, Tsinghua University

Stephen Pulman, University of Oxford

Yannick Versley, Heidelberg University

Sabine Schulte im Walde, Stuttgart University

Publication Chairs

Valerio Basile, University of Groningen

Kilian Evang, University of Groningen

Program Committee

Omri Abend, Eneko Agirre, Marianna Apidianaki, Marco Baroni, Pierpaolo Basile, Beata Beigman Klebanov, Charley Beller, Sabine Bergler, Chris Biemann, Gemma Boleda, Paul Buitelaar, Md. Faisal Mahbub Chowdhury, Philipp Cimiano, Paul Cook, Ann Copestake, Walter Daelemans, Gerard de Melo, Mona Diab, Greg Durrett, Katrin Erk, Stefan Evert, Ingrid Falk, Richárd Farkas, Afsaneh Fazly, Vanessa Wei Feng, Anette Frank, Matthew Gerber, Claudio Giuliano, Edward Grefenstette, Sanda Harabagiu, Karl Moritz Hermann, Graeme Hirst, Nancy Ide, Diana Inkpen, Radu Ion, Daisuke Kawahara, Roman Kern, Manfred Klenner, Oleksandr Kolomiyets, Maria Koutsombogera, Alessandro Lenci, Omer Levy, Annie Louis, Bernardo Magnini, Suresh Manandhar, Katja Markert, Diana McCarthy, Pablo Mendes, Rada Mihalcea, Roser Morante, Preslav Nakov, Vivi Nastase, Roberto Navigli, Guenter Neumann, Hwee Tou Ng, Vincent Ng, Malvina Nissim, Tae-Gil Noh, Diarmuid Ó Séaghdha, Sebastian Padó, Martha Palmer, Rebecca J. Passonneau, Massimo Poesio, Allan Ramsay, Aarne Ranta, Jonathon Read, Josef Ruppenhofer, Felix Sasaki, Yves Scherrer, Aitor Soroa, Caroline Sporleder, Mark Steedman, Mark Stevenson, Michael Strube, Lin Sun, Stefan Thater, Peter Turney, Tim Van de Cruys, Lonneke van der Plas, Marieke van Erp, Eva Maria Vecchi, Aline Villavicencio, Vinod Vydiswaran, Janyce Wiebe, Fei Xia, Annie Zaenen, Luke Zettlemoyer, Michael Zock

Table of Contents

Conference Program

Saturday, August 23

9:00-9:30 Welcome

9:30-10:30 Joint *SEM and SemEval keynote by Mark Steedman
Robust Semantics for NLP

10:30-11:00 Coffee break

11:00–11:30 *More or less supervised supersense tagging of Twitter*
Anders Johannsen, Dirk Hovy, Héctor Martínez Alonso, Barbara Plank and Anders Søgaard

11:30–12:00 *Generating a Word-Emotion Lexicon from #Emotional Tweets*
Anil Bandhakavi, Nirmalie Wiratunga, Deepak P and Stewart Massie

12:00–12:30 *Improvement of a Naive Bayes Sentiment Classifier Using MRS-Based Features*
Jared Kramer and Clara Gordon

12:30-14:00 Lunch break

14:00–14:30 *Sense and Similarity: A Study of Sense-level Similarity Measures*
Nicolai Erbs, Iryna Gurevych and Torsten Zesch

14:30–15:00 *An Iterative 'Sudoku Style' Approach to Subgraph-based Word Sense Disambiguation*
Steve L. Manion and Raazesh Sainudiin

15:00-15:30 Coffee break

15:30-17:30 Poster session with lightning talks intro

Exploring ESA to Improve Word Relatedness
Nitish Aggarwal, Kartik Asooja and Paul Buitelaar

Identifying semantic relations in a specialized corpus through distributional analysis of a cooccurrence tensor
Gabriel Bernier-Colborne

Learning the Peculiar Value of Actions
Daniel Dahlmeier

Saturday, August 23 (continued)

An analysis of textual inference in German customer emails
Kathrin Eichler, Aleksandra Gabryszak and Günter Neumann

Text Summarization through Entailment-based Minimum Vertex Cover
Anand Gupta, Manpreet Kaur, Shachar Mirkin, Adarsh Singh and Aseem Goyal

Semantic Roles in Grammar Engineering
Wojciech Jaworski and Adam Przepiórkowski

Semantic Role Labelling with minimal resources: Experiments with French
Rasoul Kaljahi, Jennifer Foster and Johann Roturier

Compositional Distributional Semantics Models in Chunk-based Smoothed Tree Kernels
Nghia The Pham, Lorenzo Ferrone and Fabio Massimo Zanzotto

Sunday, August 24

9:00-10:00 Keynote by Timothy Baldwin
Robust Semantics for NLP

10:00–10:30 *Generating Simulations of Motion Events from Verbal Descriptions*
James Pustejovsky and Nikhil Krishnaswamy

10:30-11:00 Coffee break

11:00–11:30 *See No Evil, Say No Evil: Description Generation from Densely Labeled Images*
Mark Yatskar, Michel Galley, Lucy Vanderwende and Luke Zettlemoyer

11:30–12:00 *Extracting Latent Attributes from Video Scenes Using Text as Background Knowledge*
Anh Tran, Mihai Surdeanu and Paul Cohen

12:00–12:30 *Using Text Segmentation Algorithms for the Automatic Generation of E-Learning Courses*
Can Özmen, Alexander Streicher and Andrea Zielinski

12:30-14:00 Lunch break

14:00–14:30 *Cognitive Compositional Semantics using Continuation Dependencies*
William Schuler and Adam Wheeler

Sunday, August 24 (continued)

14:30–15:00 *Vagueness and Learning: A Type-Theoretic Approach*
Raquel Fernandez and Staffan Larsson

15:00-15:30 Coffee break

15:30–16:00 *Contrasting Syntagmatic and Paradigmatic Relations: Insights from Distributional Semantic Models*
Gabriella Lapesa, Stefan Evert and Sabine Schulte im Walde

16:00–16:30 *Dead parrots make bad pets: Exploring modifier effects in noun phrases*
Germán Kruszewski and Marco Baroni

16:30–17:00 *Syntactic Transfer Patterns of German Particle Verbs and their Impact on Lexical Semantics*
Stefan Bott and Sabine Schulte im Walde

17:00-17:30 Best Paper Award and Closing

Invited Talks

Robust Semantics for NLP
Mark Steedman, University of Edinburgh

The paper presents a robust semantics for NLP applications that combines a (fairly) standard treatment of logical operators such as negation and quantification (Steedman 2012) with a paraphrase- and entailment–based semantics of relational terms derived from text data (Lewis and Steedman 2013a; 2013b). I'll consider the extension of the latter component to temporal and causal entailment using text-based methods, building on Lewis and Steedman 2014.

Lexical Semantic Analysis of Social Media
Timothy Baldwin, University of Melbourne

There has recently been a proliferation of research on Twitter and other social media, but is social media simply a fad? I argue that it is an inherently different text source to those conventionally targeted in computational linguistics, with unique challenges and opportunities for sub-fields including computational lexical semantics. In doing so, I draw on recent work on user-level sense distributions and novel senses, and point to unique features of social media which open up new challenges and opportunities for the field.

More or less supervised supersense tagging of Twitter

Anders Johannsen, Dirk Hovy, Héctor Martínez Alonso, Barbara Plank, Anders Søgaard
Center for Language Technology
University of Copenhagen, Denmark
Njalsgade 140
ajohannsen@hum.ku.dk, dirk@cst.dk, alonso@hum.ku.dk
plank@cst.dk, soegaard@hum.ku.dk

Abstract

We present two Twitter datasets annotated with coarse-grained word senses (supersenses), as well as a series of experiments with three learning scenarios for supersense tagging: weakly supervised learning, as well as unsupervised and supervised domain adaptation. We show that (a) off-the-shelf tools perform poorly on Twitter, (b) models augmented with embeddings learned from Twitter data perform much better, and (c) errors can be reduced using type-constrained inference with distant supervision from WordNet.

1 Introduction

Supersense tagging (SST, Ciaramita and Altun, 2006) is the task of assigning high-level ontological classes to open-class words (here, nouns and verbs). It is thus a coarse-grained word sense disambiguation task. The labels are based on the lexicographer file names for Princeton WordNet (Fellbaum, 1998). They include 15 senses for verbs and 26 for nouns (see Table 1). While WordNet also provides catch-all supersenses for adjectives and adverbs, these are grammatically, not semantically motivated, and do not provide any higher-level abstraction (recently, however, Tsvetkov et al. (2014) proposed a semantic taxonomy for adjectives). They will not be considered in this paper.

Coarse-grained categories such as supersenses are useful for downstream tasks such as question-answering (QA) and open relation extraction (RE). SST is different from NER in that it has a larger set of labels and in the absence of strong orthographic cues (capitalization, quotation marks, etc.). Moreover, supersenses can be applied to any of the lexical parts of speech and not only proper names. Also, while high-coverage gazetteers can be found for named entity recognition, the lexical resources available for SST are very limited in coverage.

Twitter is a popular micro-blogging service, which, among other things, is used for knowledge sharing among friends and peers. Twitter posts (tweets) announce local events, say talks or concerts, present facts about pop stars or programming languages, or simply express the opinions of the author on some subject matter.

Supersense tagging is relevant for Twitter, because it can aid e.g. QA and open RE. If someone posts a message saying that some LaTeX module now supports "drawing trees", it is important to know whether the post is about drawing natural objects such as oaks or pines, or about drawing tree-shaped data representations.

This paper is, to the best of our knowledge, the first work to address the problem of SST for Twitter. While there exist corpora of newswire and literary texts that are annotated with supersenses, e.g., SEMCOR (Miller et al., 1994), no data is available for microblogs or related domains. This paper introduces two new data sets.

Furthermore, most, if not all, of previous work on SST has relied on gold standard part-of-speech (POS) tags as input. However, in a domain such as Twitter, which has proven to be challenging for POS tagging (Foster et al., 2011; Ritter et al., 2011), results obtained under the assumption of available perfect POS information are almost meaningless for any real-life application.

In this paper, we instead use predicted POS tags and investigate experimental settings in which one or more of the following resources are available to us:

- a large corpus of unlabeled Twitter data;
- Princeton WordNet (Fellbaum, 1998);
- SEMCOR (Miller et al., 1994); and
- a small corpus of Twitter data annotated with supersenses.

We approach SST of Twitter using various degrees of supervision for both learning and domain adaptation (here, from newswire to Twitter). In

*Proceedings of the Third Joint Conference on Lexical and Computational Semantics (*SEM 2014)*, pages 1–11,
Dublin, Ireland, August 23-24 2014.

weakly supervised learning, only *unlabeled* data and the lexical resource WordNet are available to us. While the quality of lexical resources varies, this is the scenario for most languages. We present an approach to weakly supervised SST based on type-constrained EM-trained second-order HMMs (HMM2s) with continuous word representations.

In contrast, when using *supervised* learning, we can distinguish between two degrees of supervision for domain adaptation. For some languages, e.g., Basque, English, Swedish, sense-annotated resources exist, but these corpora are all limited to newswire or similar domains. In such languages, **unsupervised domain adaptation** (DA) techniques can be used to exploit these resources. The setting does not presume labeled data from the target domain. We use discriminative models for unsupervised domain adaptation, training on SEMCOR and testing on Twitter.

Finally, we annotated data sets for Twitter, making **supervised domain adaptation** (SU) experiments possible. For supervised domain adaptation, we use the annotated training data sets from both the newswire and the Twitter domain, as well as WordNet.

For both unsupervised domain adaptation and supervised domain adaptation, we use structured perceptron (Collins, 2002), i.e., a discriminative HMM model, and search-based structured prediction (SEARN) (Daume et al., 2009). We augment both the EM-trained HMM2, discriminative HMMs and SEARN with type constraints and continuous word representations. We also experimented with conditional random fields (Lafferty et al., 2001), but obtained worse or similar results than with the other models.

Contributions In this paper, we present two Twitter data sets with manually annotated supersenses, as well as a series of experiments with these data sets. These experiments cover existing approaches to related tasks, as well as some new methods. In particular, we present type-constrained extensions of discriminative HMMs and SEARN sequence models with continuous word representations that perform well. We show that when no in-domain labeled data is available, type constraints improve model performance considerably. Our best models achieve a weighted average F1 score of 57.1 over nouns and verbs on our main evaluation data set, i.e., a 20% error reduction over the most frequent sense baseline. The two annotated Twitter data sets are publicly released for download at `https://github.com/coastalcph/supersense-data-twitter`.

n.Tops	n.object	v.cognition
n.act	n.person	v.communication
n.animal	n.phenomenon	v.competition
n.artifact	n.plant	v.consumption
n.attribute	n.possession	v.contact
n.body	n.process	v.creation
n.cognition	n.quantity	v.emotion
n.communication	n.relation	v.motion
n.event	n.shape	v.perception
n.feeling	n.state	v.possession
n.food	n.substance	v.social
n.group	n.time	v.stative
n.location	v.body	v.weather
n.motive	v.change	

Table 1: The 41 noun and verb supersenses in WordNet

2 More or less supervised models

This sections covers the varying degree of supervision of our systems as well as the usage of type constraints as distant supervision.

2.1 Distant supervision

Distant supervision in these experiments was implemented by only allowing a system to predict a certain supersense for a given word if that supersense had either been observed in the training data, or, for unobserved words, if the sense was the most frequent sense in WordNet. If the word did not appear in the training data nor in WordNet, no filtering was applied. We refer to the distant-supervision strategy as *type constraints*.

Distant supervision was implemented differently in SEARN and the HMM model. SEARN decomposes sequential labelling into a series of binary classifications. To constrain the labels we simply pick the top-scoring sense for each token from the allowed set. Structured perceptron uses Viterbi decoding. Here we set the emission probabilities for disallowed senses to negative infinity and decode as usual.

2.2 Weakly supervised HMMs

The HMM2 model is a second-order hidden Markov model (Mari et al., 1997; Thede and Harper, 1999) using logistic regression to estimate emission probabilities. In addition we constrain

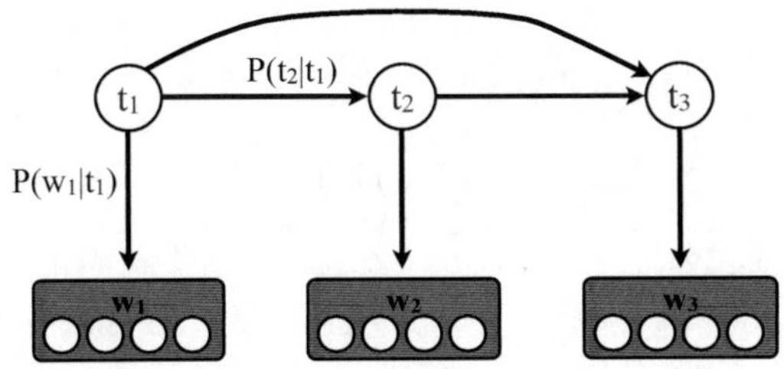

Figure 1: HMM2 with continuous word representations

the inference space of the HMM2 tagger using type-level tag constraints derived from WordNet, leading to roughly the model proposed by Li et al. (2012), who used Wiktionary as a (part-of-speech) tag dictionary. The basic feature model of Li et al. (2012) is augmented with continuous word representation features as shown in Figure 1, and our logistic regression model thus works over a combination of discrete and continuous variables when estimating emission probabilities. We do 50 passes over the data as in Li et al. (2012).

We introduce two simplifications for the HMM2 model. First, we only use the most frequent senses ($k = 1$) in WordNet as type constraints. The most frequent senses seem to better direct the EM search for a local optimum, and we see dramatic drops in performance on held-out data when we include more senses for the words covered by WordNet. Second, motivated by computational concerns, we only train and test on sequences of (predicted) nouns and verbs, leaving out all other word classes. Our supervised models performed slightly worse on shortened sequences, and it is an open question whether the HMM2 models would perform better if we could train them on full sentences.

2.3 Structured perceptron and SEARN

We use two approaches to supervised sequential labeling, structured perceptron (Collins, 2002) and search-based structured prediction (SEARN) (Daume et al., 2009). The structured perceptron is a in-house reimplementation of Ciaramita and Altun (2006).[1] SEARN performed slightly better than structured perceptron, so we use it as our in-house baseline in the experiments below. In this section, we briefly explain the two approaches.

[1]https://github.com/coastalcph/rungsted

2.3.1 Structured perceptron (HMM)

Structured perceptron learning was introduced in Collins (2002) and is an extension of the online perceptron learning algorithm (Rosenblatt, 1958) with averaging (Freund and Schapire, 1999) to structured learning problems such as sequence labeling.

In structured perceptron for sequential labeling, where we learn a function from sequences of data points $x_1 \dots x_n$ to sequences of labels $y_1 \dots y_n$, we begin with a random weight vector $\mathbf{w}_0$ initialized to all zeros. This weight vector is used to assign weights to transitions between labels, i.e., the discriminative counterpart of $P(y_{i+1} \mid y_i)$, and emissions of tokens given labels, i.e., the counterpart of $P(x_i \mid y_i)$. We use Viterbi decoding to derive a best path $\hat{\mathbf{y}}$ through the corresponding $m \times n$ lattice (with m the number of labels). Let the feature mapping $\Phi(\mathbf{x}, \mathbf{y})$ be a function from a pair of sequences $\langle \mathbf{x}, \mathbf{y} \rangle$ to all the features that fired to make $\mathbf{y}$ the best path through the lattice for $\mathbf{x}$. Now the structured update for a sequence of data points is simply $\alpha(\Phi(\mathbf{x}, \mathbf{y}) - \Phi(\mathbf{x}, \hat{\mathbf{y}}))$, i.e., a fixed positive update of features that fired to produce the correct sequence of labels, and a fixed negative update of features that fired to produce the best path under the model. Note that if $\mathbf{y} = \hat{\mathbf{y}}$, no features are updated.

2.3.2 SEARN

SEARN is a way of decomposing structured prediction problems into search and history-based classification. In sequential labeling, we decompose the sequence of m tokens into m classification problems, conditioning our labeling of the ith token on the history of $i - 1$ previous decisions. The cost of a mislabeling at training time is defined by a cost function over output structures. We use Hamming loss rather than F_1 as our cost function, and we then use stochastic gradient descent with quantile loss as a our cost-sensitive learning algorithm. We use a publicly available implementation.[2]

3 Experiments

We experiment with weakly supervised learning, unsupervised domain adaptation, as well as supervised domain adaptation, i.e., where our models are induced from hand-annotated newswire *and* Twitter data. Note that in all our experiments,

[2]http://hunch.net/~vw/

we use *predicted POS tags* as input to the system, in order to produce a realistic estimate of SST performance.

3.1 Data

Our experiments rely on combinations of available resources and newly annotated Twitter data sets made publicly available with this paper.

3.1.1 Available resources

Princeton WordNet (Fellbaum, 1998) is the main resource for SST. The lexicographer file names provide the label alphabet of the task, and the taxonomy defined therein is used not only in the baselines, but also as a feature in the discriminative models. We use the WordNet 3.0 distribution.

SEMCOR (Miller et al., 1994) is a sense-annotated corpus composed of 80% newswire and 20% literary text, using the sense inventory from WordNet. SEMCOR comprises $23k$ distinct lemmas in $234k$ instances. We use the texts which have full annotations, leaving aside the verb-only texts (see Section 6).

We use a distributional semantic model in order to incorporate distributional information as features in our system. In particular, we use the neural-network based models from (Mikolov et al., 2013), also referred as *word embeddings*. This model makes use of skip-grams (n-grams that do not need to be consecutive) within a word window to calculate continuous-valued vector representations from a recurrent neural network. These distributional models have been able to outperform state of the art in the SemEval-2012 Task 2 (Measuring degrees of relational similarity). We calculate the embeddings from an in-house corpus of $57m$ English tweets using a window size 5 and yielding vectors of 100 dimensions.

We also use the first $20k$ tweets of the $57m$ tweets to train our HMM2 models.

3.1.2 Annotation

While an annotated newswire corpus and a high-quality lexical resource already enable us to train, we also need at least a small sample of annotated tweets data to evaluate SST for Twitter. Furthermore, if we want to experiment with supervised SST, we also need sufficient annotated Twitter data to learn the distribution of sense tags.

This paper presents two data sets: (a) supersense annotations for the POS+NER-annotated data set described in Ritter et al. (2011), which we use for training, development and evaluation, using the splits proposed in Derczynski et al. (2013), and (b) supersense annotations for a sample of 200 tweets, which we use for additional, out-of-sample evaluation. We call these data sets RITTER-{TRAIN,DEV,EVAL} and IN-HOUSE-EVAL, respectively. The IN-HOUSE-EVAL dataset was downloaded in 2013 and is a sample of tweets that contain links to external homepages but are otherwise unbiased. It was previously used (with part-of-speech annotation) in (Plank et al., 2014). Both data sets are made publicly available with this paper.

Supersenses are annotated with in spans defined by the BIO (Begin-Inside-Other) notation. To obtain the Twitter data sets, we carried out an annotation task. We first pre-annotated all data sets with WordNet's most frequent senses. If the word was not in WordNet and a noun, we assigned it the sense *n.person*. All other words were labeled *O*.

Chains of nouns were altered to give every element the sense of the head noun, and the BI tags adjusted, i.e.:

Empire/B-n.loc State/B-n.loc Building/B-n.artifact

was changed to

Empire/B-n.artifact State/I-n.artifact Building/I-n.artifact

For the RITTER data, three paid student annotators worked on different subsets of the pre-annotated data. They were asked to correct mistakes in both the BIO notation and the assigned supersenses. They were free to chose from the full label set, regardless of the pre-annotation. While the three annotators worked on separate parts, they overlapped on a small part of RITTER-TRAIN (841 tokens). On this subset, we computed agreement scores and annotation difficulties. The average raw agreement was 0.86 and Cohen's κ 0.77. The majority of tokens received the *O* label by all annotators; this happended in 515 out of 841 cases. Excluding these instances to evaluate the performance on the more difficult content words, raw agreement dropped to 0.69 and Cohen's κ to 0.69.

The IN-HOUSE-EVAL data set was annotated by two different annotators, namely two of the authors of this article. Again, for efficiency reasons they worked on different subsets of the data, with an overlapping portion. Their average raw agreement was 0.65 and their Cohen's κ 0.62. For this data set, we also compute F_1, defined as usual as the harmonic mean of recall and precision. To compute this, we set one of the annotators as gold data and the other as predicted data. However, since F_1 is symmetrical, the order does not matter. The annotation F_1 gives us another estimate of annotation difficulty. We present the figures in Table 3.

3.2 Baselines

For most word sense disambiguation studies, predicting the most frequent sense (MFS) of a word has been proven to be a strong baseline. Following this, our MFS baseline simply predicts the supersense of the most frequent WordNet sense for a tuple of a word and a part of speech. We use the part of speech predicted by the LAPOS tagger (Tsuruoka et al., 2011). Any word not in WordNet is labeled as *noun.person*, which is the most frequent sense overall in the training data. After tagging, we run a script to correct the BI tag prefixes, as described above for the annotation ask.

We also compare to the performance of existing SST systems. In particular we use SenseLearner (Mihalcea and Csomai, 2005) as a baseline, which produces estimates of the WordNet sense for each word. For these predictions, we retrieve the corresponding supersense. Finally, we use a publicly available reimplementation of Ciaramita and Altun (2006) by Michael Heilman, which reaches comparable performance on gold-tagged SEMCOR.[3]

3.3 Model parameters

We use the feature model of Paaß and Reichartz (2009) in all our models, except the weakly supervised models. For the structured perceptron we set the number of passes over the training data on the held-out development data. The weakly supervised models use the default setting proposed in Li et al. (2012). We have used the standard online setup for SEARN, which only takes one pass over the data.

The type of embedding is the same in all our experiments. For a given word the embedding feature is a 100 dimensional vector, which combines the embedding of the word with the embedding of adjacent words. The feature combination $f_{\mathbf{e}}$ for a word w_t is calculated as:

$$\mathrm{f}_{\mathbf{e}}(w_t) = \frac{1}{2}(\mathbf{e}(w_{t-1}) + \mathbf{e}(w_{t+1})) - 2\mathbf{e}(w_t),$$

where the factor of two is chosen heurestically to give more weight to the current word.

We also set a parameter k on development data for using the k-most frequent senses inWordNet as type constraints. Our supervised models are trained on SEMCOR+RITTER-TRAIN or simply RITTER-TRAIN, depending on what gave us the best performance on the held-out data.

4 Results

The results are presented in Table 2. We distinguish between three settings with various degrees of supervision: weakly supervised, which uses no domain annotated information, but solely relies on embeddings trained on unlabeled Twitter data; unsupervised domain adaptation (DA), which uses SemCor for supervised training; and supervised domain adaptation (SU), which uses annotated Twitter data in addition to the SemCor data for training.

In each of the two domain adaptation settings, SEARN and HMM are evaluated with type constraints as distant supervision, and without for comparison. SEARN without embeddings or distant supervision serves as an in-house baseline.

In Table 3 we present the WordNet token coverage of predicted nouns and verbs in the development and evaluation data, as well as the inter-annotator agreement F_1 scores.

All the results presented in Table 2 are (weighted averaged) F_1 measures obtained on predicted POS tags. Note that these results are considerably lower than results on supersense tagging newswire (up to 80 F_1) that assume gold standard POS tags (Ciaramita and Altun, 2006; Paaß and Reichartz, 2009).

The re-implementation of the state-of-the-art system improves slightly upon the most frequent sense baseline. SenseLearner does not seem to capture the relevant information and does not reach baseline performance. In other words, there is no off-the-shelf tool for supersense tagging of Twitter that does much better than assigning the most frequent sense to predicted nouns and verbs.

Our weakly supervised model performs worse than the most frequent sense baseline. This is a negative result. It is, however, well-known from the word sense disambiguation literature that the MFS is a very strong baseline. Moreover, the EM learning problem is hard because of the large label set and weak distributional evidence for super-

[3] http://www.ark.cs.cmu.edu/mheilman/questions/SupersenseTagger-10-01-12.tar.gz

	RITTER DEV	RITTER EVAL	IN-HOUSE EVAL
Wordnet noun-verb token coverage	83.72	70.22	41.18
Inter-annotator agreement (F1)	81.01	69.15	61.57

Table 3: Properties of dataset.

senses.

The unsupervised domain adaptation and fully supervised systems perform considerably better than this baseline across the board. In the unsupervised domain adaptation setup, we see huge improvements from using type constraints as distant supervision. In the supervised setup, we only see significant improvements adding type constraints for the structured perceptron (HMM), but not for search-based structured prediction (SEARN).

For all the data sets, there is still a gap between model performance and human inter-annotator agreement levels (see Table 3), leaving some room for improvements. We hope that the release of the data sets will help further research into this.

4.1 Coarse-grained evaluation

We also experimented with the more coarse-grained classes proposed by Yuret and Yatbaz (2010). Here our best model obtained an F_1 score for mental concepts (nouns) of 72.3%, and 62.6% for physical concepts, on RITTER-DEV. The overall F_1 score for verbs is 85.6%. The overall F_1 is 75.5%. Note that this result is not directly comparable to the figure (72.9%) reported in Yuret and Yatbaz (2010), since they use different data sets, exclude verbs and make different assumptions, e.g., relying on gold POS tags.

5 Error analysis

We have seen that inter-annotator agreements on supersense annotation are reliable at above .60 but far from perfect. The Hinton diagram in Table 2 presents the confusion matrix between our annotators on IN-HOUSE-EVAL.

Errors in the prediction primarily stem from two sources: out-of-vocabulary words and incorrect POS tags. Figure 3 shows the distribution of senses over the words that were not contained in either the training data, WordNet, or the Twitter data used to learn the embeddings. The distribution follows a power law, with the most frequent sense being *noun.person*, followed by *noun.group*, and *noun.artifact*. The first two are related to NER categories, namely *PER* and *ORG*, and can be expected, since Twitter users frequently talk about new actors, musicians, and bands. Nouns of communication are largely related to films, but also include Twitter, Facebook, and other forms of social media. Note that verbs occur only towards the tail end of the distribution, i.e., there are very few unknown verbs, even in Twitter.

Overall, our models perform best on labels with low lexical variability, such as quantities, states and times for nouns, as well as consumption, possession and stative for verbs. This is unsurprising, since these classes have lower out-of-vocabulary rates.

With regards to the differences between source (SEMCOR) and target (Twitter) domains, we observe that the distribution of supersenses is always headed by the same noun categories like *noun.person* or *noun.group*, but the frequency of out-of-vocabulary stative verbs plummets in the target domain, as some semantic types are more closed class than others. There are for instance fewer possibilities for creating new time units (noun.time) or stative verbs like *be* than people or company names (*noun.person* or *noun.group*, respectively).

The weakly supervised model HMM2 has higher precision (57% on RITTER-DEV) than recall (48.7%), which means that it often predicts words to not belong to a semantic class. This suggests an alternative strategy, which is to train a model on sequences of purely non-*O* instances. This would force the model to only predict *O* on words that do not appear in the reduced sequences.

One important source of error seems to be unreliable part-of-speech tagging. In particular we predict the wrong POS for 20-35% of the verbs across the data sets, and for 4-6.5% of the nouns. In the SEMCOR data, for comparability, we have wrongly predicted tags for 6-8% of the annotated tokens. Nevertheless, the error propagation of wrongly predicted nouns and verbs is partially compensated by our systems, since they are trained on imperfect input, and thus it becomes possible for the systems to predict a noun supersense for a verb and viceversa. In our data we have found e.g. that the noun *Thanksgiving* was incorrectly tagged as a verb, but its supersense was correctly predicted to be *noun.time*, and that the verb *guess* had been mistagged as noun but the system

	Resources				Results		
	Token-level		Type-level		RITTER		IN-HOUSE
	SemCor	Twitter	Embeddings	Type constraints	DEV	EVAL	EVAL
General baselines							
MFS	-	-	-	+	47.54	44.98	38.65
SENSELEARNER	+	-	-	-	14.61	26.24	22.81
HEILMAN	+	-	-	-	*48.96*	*45.03*	*39.65*
Weakly supervised systems							
HMM2	-	-	-	+	47.09	42.12	26.99
Unsupervised domain adaptation systems (DA)							
SEARN (Baseline)	+	-	-	-	48.31	42.34	34.30
SEARN	+	-	+	-	52.45	48.30	40.22
SEARN	+	-	+	+	56.59	**50.89**	40.50
HMM	+	-	+	-	52.40	47.90	40.51
HMM	+	-	+	+	**57.14**	**50.98**	**41.84**
Supervised domain adaptation systems (SU)							
SEARN (Baseline)	+	+	-	-	58.30	*52.12*	36.86
SEARN	+	+	+	-	**63.05**	57.09	42.37
SEARN	+	+	+	+	62.72	**57.14**	**42.42**
HMM	+	+	+	-	57.20	49.26	39.88
HMM	+	+	+	+	60.66	51.40	41.60

Table 2: Weighted F1 average over 41 supersenses.

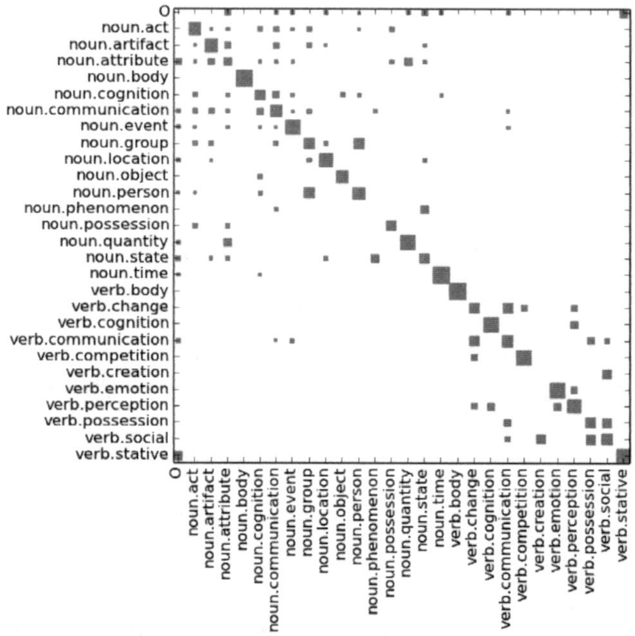

Figure 2: Inter-annotator confusion matrix on TWITTER-EVAL.

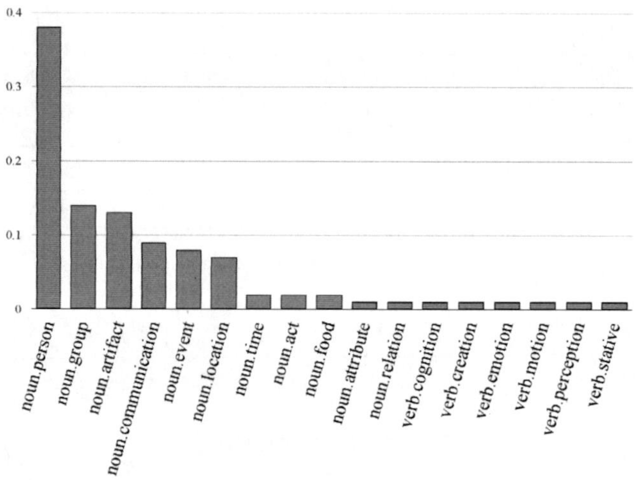

Figure 3: Sense distribution of OOV words.

still predicted the correct *verb.cognition* as supersense.

6 Related Work

There has been relatively little previous work on supersense tagging, and to the best of our knowledge, all of it has been limited to English newswire and literature (SEMCOR and SENSEVAL).

The task of supersense tagging was first introduced by Ciaramita and Altun (2006), who used a structured perceptron trained and evaluated on SEMCOR via 5-fold cross validation. Their evaluation included a held-out development set on each fold that was used to estimate the number of epochs. They used additional training data containing only verbs. More importantly, they relied on gold standard POS tags. Their overall F_1 score on SEMCOR was 77.1. Reichartz and Paaß (Reichartz and Paaß, 2008; Paaß and Reichartz, 2009) extended this work, using a CRF model as well as LDA topic features. They report an F_1 score of 80.2, again relying on gold standard POS features. Our implementation follows their setup and feature model, but we rely on *predicted* POS features, not gold standard features.

Supersenses provide information similar to higher-level distributional clusters, but more interpretable, and have thus been used as high-level features in various tasks, such as preposition sense disambiguation, noun compound interpretation, and metaphor detection (Ye and Baldwin, 2007; Tratz and Hovy, 2010; Tsvetkov et al., 2013). Princeton WordNet only provides a fully developed taxonomy of supersenses for verbs and nouns, but Tsvetkov et al. (2014) have recently proposed an extension of the taxonomy to cover adjectives. Outside of English, supersenses have been annotated for Arabic Wikipedia articles by Schneider et al. (2012).

In addition, a few researchers have tried to solve coarse-grained word sense disambiguation problems that are very similar to supersense tagging. Kohomban and Lee (2005) and Kohomban and Lee (2007) also propose to use lexicographer file identifers from Princeton WordNet senses (supersenses) and, in addition, discuss how to retrieve fine-grained senses from those predictions. They evaluate their model on all-words data from SENSEEVAL-2 and SENSEEVAL-3. They use a classification approach rather than structured prediction.

Yuret and Yatbaz (2010) present a weakly unsupervised approach to this problem, still evaluating on SENSEVAL-2 and SENSEVAL-3. They focus only on nouns, relying on gold part-of-speech, but also experiment with a coarse-grained mapping, using only three high level classes.

For Twitter, we are aware of little previous work on word sense disambiguation. Gella et al. (2014) present lexical sample word sense disambiguation annotation of 20 target nouns on Twitter, but no experimental results with this data. There has also been related work on disambiguation to Wikipedia for Twitter (Cassidy et al., 2012).

In sum, existing work on supersense tagging and coarse-grained word sense disambiguation for English has to the best of our knowledge all focused on newswire and literature. Moreover, they all rely on gold standard POS information, making previous performance estimates rather optimistic.

7 Conclusion

In this paper, we present two Twitter data sets with manually annotated supersenses, as well as a series of experiments with these data sets. The data is publicly available for download.

In this article we have provided, to the best of our knowledge, the first supersense tagger for Twitter. We have shown that off-the-shelf tools perform poorly on Twitter, and we offer two strategies—namely distant supervision and the usage of embeddings as features—that can be combined to improve SST for Twitter.

We propose that distant supervision implemented as type constraints during decoding is a viable method to limit the mispredictions of supersenses by our systems, thereby enforcing predicted senses that a word has in WordNet. This approach compensates for the size limitations of the training data and mitigates the out-of-vocabulary effect, but is still subject to the coverage of WordNet; which is far from perfect for words coming from high-variability sources such as Twitter.

Using distributional semantics as features in form of word embeddings also improves the prediction of supersenses, because it provides semantic information for words, regardless of whether they have been observed the training data. This method does not require a hand-created knowledge base like WordNet, and is a promising technique for domain adaptation of supersense tagging.

References

Taylor Cassidy, Heng Ji, Lev-Arie Ratinov, Arkaitz Zubiaga, and Hongzhao Huang. 2012. Analysis and enhancement of wikification for microblogs with context expansion. In *COLING*, volume 12, pages 441–456.

Massimiliano Ciaramita and Yasemin Altun. 2006. Broad-coverage sense disambiguation and information extraction with a supersense sequence tagger. In *Proc. of EMNLP*, pages 594–602, Sydney, Australia, July.

Michael Collins. 2002. Discriminative training methods for hidden markov models: Theory and experiments with perceptron algorithms. In *EMNLP*.

Hal Daume, John Langford, and Daniel Marcu. 2009. Search-based structured prediction. *Machine Learning*, pages 297–325.

Leon Derczynski, Alan Ritter, Sam Clark, and Kalina Bontcheva. 2013. Twitter part-of-speech tagging for all: overcoming sparse and noisy data. In *RANLP*.

Christiane Fellbaum. 1998. *WordNet: an electronic lexical database*. MIT Press USA.

Jennifer Foster, Ozlem Cetinoglu, Joachim Wagner, Josef Le Roux, Joakim Nivre, Deirde Hogan, and Josef van Genabith. 2011. From news to comments: Resources and benchmarks for parsing the language of Web 2.0. In *IJCNLP*.

Yoav Freund and Robert Schapire. 1999. Large margin classification using the perceptron algorithm. *Machine Learning*, 37:277–296.

Spandana Gella, Paul Cook, and Timothy Baldwin. 2014. One sense per tweeter and other lexical semantic tales of Twitter. In *EACL*.

Upali Kohomban and Wee Lee. 2005. Learning semantic classes for word sense disambiguation. In *ACL*.

Upali Kohomban and Wee Lee. 2007. Optimizing classifier performance in word sense disambiguation by redefining word sense classes. In *IJCAI*.

John Lafferty, Andrew McCallum, and Fernando Pereira. 2001. Conditional random fields: probabilistic models for segmenting and labeling sequence data. In *ICML*.

Shen Li, João Graça, and Ben Taskar. 2012. Wiki-ly supervised part-of-speech tagging. In *EMNLP*.

Jean-Francois Mari, Jean-Paul Haton, and Abdelaziz Kriouile. 1997. Automatic word recognition based on second-order hidden Markov models. *IEEE Transactions on Speech and Audio Processing*, 5(1):22–25.

Rada Mihalcea and Andras Csomai. 2005. Senselearner: Word sense disambiguation for all words in unrestricted text. In *Proceedings of the ACL 2005 on Interactive poster and demonstration sessions*, pages 53–56. Association for Computational Linguistics.

Tomas Mikolov, Ilya Sutskever, Kai Chen, Gregory Corrado, and Jeffrey Dean. 2013. Distributed representations of words and phrases and their compositionality. In *NIPS*.

George A. Miller, Martin Chodorow, Shari Landes, Claudia Leacock, and Robert G. Thomas. 1994. Using a semantic concordance for sense identification. In *Proceedings of the workshop on Human Language Technology*, pages 240–243. Association for Computational Linguistics.

Gerhard Paaß and Frank Reichartz. 2009. Exploiting semantic constraints for estimating supersenses with CRFs. In *Proc. of the Ninth SIAM International Conference on Data Mining*, pages 485–496, Sparks, Nevada, May.

Barbara Plank, Dirk Hovy, and Anders Søgaard. 2014. Learning part-of-speech taggers with inter-annotator agreement loss. In *Proceedings of EACL*.

Frank Reichartz and Gerhard Paaß. 2008. Estimating Supersenses with Conditional Random Fields. In *Proceedings of ECMLPKDD*.

Alan Ritter, Sam Clark, Mausam, and Oren Etzioni. 2011. Named entity recognition in tweets: an experimental study. In *EMNLP*.

Frank Rosenblatt. 1958. The perceptron: a probabilistic model for information storage and organization in the brain. *Psychological Review*, 65(6):386–408.

Nathan Schneider, Behrang Mohit, Kemal Oflazer, and Noah A Smith. 2012. Coarse lexical semantic annotation with supersenses: an arabic case study. In *Proceedings of the 50th Annual Meeting of the Association for Computational Linguistics*, pages 253–258. Association for Computational Linguistics.

Scott Thede and Mary Harper. 1999. A second-order hidden Markov model for part-of-speech tagging. In *ACL*.

Stephen Tratz and Eduard Hovy. 2010. Isi: automatic classification of relations between nominals using a maximum entropy classifier. In *Proceedings of the 5th International Workshop on Semantic Evaluation*, pages 222–225. Association for Computational Linguistics.

Yoshimasa Tsuruoka, Yusuke Miyao, and Jun'ichi Kazama. 2011. Learning with lookahead: can history-based models rival globally optimized models? In *CoNLL*.

Yulia Tsvetkov, Elena Mukomel, and Anatole Gershman. 2013. Cross-lingual metaphor detection using common semantic features. *Meta4NLP 2013*, page 45.

Yulia Tsvetkov, Nathan Schneider, Dirk Hovy, Archna Bhatia, Manaal Faruqui, and Chris Dyer. 2014. Augmenting english adjective senses with supersenses. In *Proc. of LREC*.

Patrick Ye and Timothy Baldwin. 2007. Melb-yb: Preposition sense disambiguation using rich semantic features. In *Proceedings of the 4th International Workshop on Semantic Evaluations*, pages 241–244. Association for Computational Linguistics.

Deniz Yuret and Mehmet Yatbaz. 2010. The noisy channel model for unsupervised word sense disambiguation. *Computational Linguistics*, 36:111–127.

Generating a Word-Emotion Lexicon from #Emotional Tweets

Anil Bandhakavi[1] **Nirmalie Wiratunga**[1] **Deepak P**[2] **Stewart Massie**[1]

[1] IDEAS Research Institute, Robert Gordon University, Scotland, UK
[2] IBM Research - India, Bangalore, India
{a.s.bandhakavi,n.wiratunga}@rgu.ac.uk
deepaksp@acm.org, s.massie@rgu.ac.uk

Abstract

Research in emotion analysis of text suggest that emotion lexicon based features are superior to corpus based n-gram features. However the static nature of the general purpose emotion lexicons make them less suited to social media analysis, where the need to adopt to changes in vocabulary usage and context is crucial. In this paper we propose a set of methods to extract a word-emotion lexicon automatically from an emotion labelled corpus of tweets. Our results confirm that the features derived from these lexicons outperform the standard Bag-of-words features when applied to an emotion classification task. Furthermore, a comparative analysis with both manually crafted lexicons and a state-of-the-art lexicon generated using Point-Wise Mutual Information, show that the lexicons generated from the proposed methods lead to significantly better classification performance.

1 Introduction

Emotion mining or affect sensing is the computational study of natural language expressions in order to quantify their associations with different emotions (e.g. anger, fear, joy, sadness and surprise). It has a number of applications for the industry, commerce and government organisations, but uptake has arguably been slow. This in part is due to the challenges involved with modelling subjectivity and complexity of the emotive content. However, use of qualitative metrics to capture emotive strength and extraction of features from these metrics has in recent years shown promise (Shaikh, 2009). A general-purpose emotion lexicon (GPEL) is a commonly used resource that allows qualitative assessment of a piece of emotive text. Given a word and an emotion, the lexicon provides a score to quantify the strength of emotion expressed by that word. Such lexicons are carefully crafted and are utilised by both supervised and unsupervised algorithms to directly aggregate an overall emotion score or indirectly derive features for emotion classification tasks (Mohammad, 2012a), (Mohammad, 2012b).

Socio-linguistics suggest that social media is a popular means for people to converse with individuals, groups and the world in general (Boyd et al., 2010). These conversations often involve usage of non-standard natural language expressions which consistently evolve. Twitter and Facebook were credited for providing momentum for the 2011 Arab Spring and Occupy Wall street movements (Ray, 2011),(Skinner, 2011). Therefore efforts to model social conversations would provide valuable insights into how people influence each other through emotional expressions. Emotion analysis in such domains calls for automated discovery of lexicons. This is so since learnt lexicons can intuitively capture the evolving nature of vocabulary in such domains better than GPELs.

In this work we show how an emotion labelled corpus can be leveraged to generate a word-emotion lexicon automatically. Key to this is the availability of a labelled corpus which may be obtained using a distance-supervised approach to labelling (Wang et al., 2012). In this paper we propose three lexicon generation methods and evaluate the quality of these by deploying them in an emotion classification task. We show through our experiments that the word-emotion lexicon generated using the proposed methods in this paper significantly outperforms GPELs such as WordnetAffect, NRC word-emotion association lexicon and a leaxicon learnt using Point-wise Mutual Information (PMI). Additionally, our lexicons also outperform the traditional Bag-of-Words representation.

The rest of the paper is organised as follows: In

*Proceedings of the Third Joint Conference on Lexical and Computational Semantics (*SEM 2014)*, pages 12–21,
Dublin, Ireland, August 23-24 2014.

Section 2 we present the related work. In Section 3 we outline the problem. In Section 4 we formulate the different methods proposed to generate the word-emotion lexicons. In Section 5 we discuss experimental results followed by conclusions and future work in Section 6.

2 Related Work

Computational emotion analysis, draws from cognitive and physiology studies to establish the key emotion categories; and NLP and text mining research to establish features designed to represent emotive content. Emotion analysis has been applied in a variety of domains: fairy tales (Francisco and Gervas, 2006; Alm et al., 2005); blogs (Mihalcea and Liu, 2006; Neviarouskaya et al., 2010), novels (John et al., 2006), chat messages (E.Holzman and William M, 2003; Ma et al., 2005; Mohammad and Yang, 2011) and emotional events on social media content(Kim et al., 2009). Comparative studies on emotive word distributions on micro-blogs and personal content (e.g. love letters, suicide notes) have shown that emotions such as *disgust* are expressed well in tweets. Further, expression of emotion in tweets and love letters have been shown to have similarities(K. Roberts and Harabagiu, 2012).

Emotion classification frameworks provide insights into human emotion expressions (Ekman, 1992; Plutchik, 1980; Parrott, 2001). The emotions proposed by (Ekman, 1992) are popular in emotion classification tasks (Mohammad, 2012b; Aman and Szpakowicz, 2008). Recently there has also been interest in extending this basic emotion framework to model more complex emotions (such as politeness, rudeness, deception, depression, vigour and confusion) (Pearl and Steyvers, 2010; Bollen et al., 2009). A common theme across these approaches involves the selection of emotion-rich features and learning of relevant weights to capture emotion strength (Mohammad, 2012a; Qadir and Riloff, 2013).

Usefulness of a lexicon: Lexicons such as Wordnet Affect (Strapparava and Valitutti, 2004) and NRC (Saif M. Mohammad, 2013)) are very valuable resources from which emotion features can be derived for text representation. These are manually crafted and typically contain emotion-rich formal vocabulary. Hybrid approaches that combine features derived from these static lexicons with n-grams have resulted in better performance than either alone (Mohammad, 2012b),(Aman and Szpakowicz, 2008). However the informal and dynamic nature of social media content makes it harder to adopt these lexicons for emotion analysis. An alternative strategy is to derive features from a dynamic (i.e., learnt) lexicon. Here association metrics such as Pointwise Mutual Information (PMI) can be used to model emotion polarity between a word and emotion labelled content (Mohammad, 2012a). Such approaches will be used as baselines to compare against our proposed lexicon generation strategies. There are other lexicon generation methods proposed by Rao .et. al (Yanghui Rao and Chen, 2013) and Yang .et. al (Yang et al., 2007). We do not consider these in our comparative evaluation since these methods require rated emotion labels and emoticon classes respectively.

Lexicon generation, relies on the availability of a labelled corpus from which the word-emotion distributions can be discovered. For this purpose we exploit a distance-supervised approach where indirect cues are used to unearth implicit (or distant) labels that are contained in the corpus (Alec Go and Huang, 2009). We adopt the approach as in (Wang et al., 2012) to corpus labelling where social media content, and in particular Twitter content is sampled for a predefined set of hashtag cues (P. Shaver, 1987) . Here each set of cues represent a given emotion class. Distant-supervision is particularly suited to Twitter-like platforms because people use hashtags to extensively convey or emphasis the emotion behind their tweets (e.g., That was my best weekend ever.#happy!! #satisfied!). Also given that tweets are length restricted (140 characters), modelling the emotional orientation of words in a Tweet is easier compared to longer documents that are likely to capture complex and mixed emotions. This simplicity and access to sample data has made Twitter one of the most popular domains for emotion analysis research (Wang et al., 2012; Qadir and Riloff, 2013).

3 Problem Definition

We now outline the problem formally. We start with a set of documents $\mathcal{D} = \{d_1, d_2, \ldots, d_n\}$ where each document d_i has an associated label C_{d_i} indicating the emotion class to which d_i belongs. We consider the case where the documents are tweets. For example, a tweet d_i *nice sunday*

#awesome may have a label *joy* indicating that the tweet belongs to the *joy* emotion class. We also assume that the labels C_{d_i} come from a pre-defined set of six emotion classes *anger, fear, joy, sad, surprise, love*. Since our techniques are generic and do not depend on the number of emotion classes, we will denote the emotion classes as $\{C_j\}_{j=1}^{N}$. Let there be K words extracted from the training documents, denoted as $\{w_i\}_{i=1}^{K}$. Our task is to derive a lexicon Lex that quantifies the emotional valence of words (from the tweets in $\mathcal{D}$) to emotion classes. In particular, the lexicon may be thought of as a 2d-associative array where $Lex[w][c]$ indicates the emotional valence of the word w to the emotion class c. When there is no ambiguity, we will use $Lex(i, j)$ to refer to the emotional valence of word w_i to the emotion class C_j. We will quantify the goodness of the lexicons that are generated using various methods by measuring their performance in an emotion classification task.

4 Lexicon Generation Methods

We now outline the various methods for lexicon generation. We first start off with a simple technique for learning lexicons based on just term frequencies (which we will later use as a baseline technique), followed by more sophisticated methods that are based on conceptual models on how tweets are generated.

4.1 Term Frequency based Lexicon

A simple way to measure the emotional valence of the word w_i to the emotion class C_j is to compute the probability of occurrence of w_i in a tweet labelled as C_j, normalized by its probability across all classes. This leads to:

$$Lex(i, j) = \frac{p(w_i|C_j)}{\sum_{k=1}^{N} p(w_i|C_k)} \quad (1)$$

where the conditional probability is simply computed using term frequencies.

$$p(w_i|C_j) = \frac{freq(w_i, C_j)}{freq(C_j)} \quad (2)$$

where $freq(w_i, C_j)$ is the *number of times w_i occurs in documents labeled with class C_j*. $freq(C_j)$ is the *total number of documents in C_j*.

4.2 Iterative methods for Lexicon Generation

The formulation in the previous section generates a word-emotion matrix L by observing the term frequencies within a class. However term frequencies alone do not capture the term-class associations, because not all frequently occurring terms exhibit the characteristics of a class. For example, a term *sunday* that occurs in a tweet *nice sunday #awesome* labelled *joy* is evidently not indicative of the class *joy*; however, the frequency based computation increments the weight of *sunday* wrt the class *joy* by virtue of this occurrence. In the following sections, we propose generative models that seek to remedy such problems of the simple term frequency based lexicon.

4.2.1 Generative models for Documents

As discussed above, though a document is labelled with an emotion class, not all terms relate strongly to the labelled emotion. Some documents may have terms conveying a different emotion than what the document is labelled with, since the label is chosen based on the most prominent emotion in the tweet. Additionally, some words could be emotion-neutral (e.g., *sunday* in our example tweet) and could be conveying non-emotional information. We now describe two generative models that account for such considerations, and then outline methods to learn lexicons based on them.

Mixture of Classes Model: Let L_{C_k} be the unigram language model (Liu and Croft, 2005) that expresses the lexical character for the emotion class C_k; though microblogs are short text fragments, language modeling approaches have been shown to be effective in similarity assesment between them (Deepak and Chakraborti, 2012). We model a document d_i to be generated from across the emotion class language models:

1. For each word w_j in document d_i,
   (a) Lookup the unit vector $[\lambda_{d_{ij}}^{(1)}, \ldots, \lambda_{d_{ij}}^{(N)}]$; This unit vector defines a probability distribution over the language models.
   (b) Choose a language model L from among the K LMs, in accordance with the vector
   (c) Sample w_j in accordance with the multinomial distribution L

If d_i is labelled with the emotion class C_{d_i}, it is likely that the value of $\lambda_{d_{ij}}^{(n)}$ is high for words in d_i since it is likely that majority of the words are sampled from the $L_{C_{d_i}}$ language model. The posterior probability in accordance with this model can then be intuitively formulated as:

$$P(d_i, C_{d_i}|\theta) = \prod_{w_j \in d_i} \sum_{x=1}^{N} \lambda_{d_{ij}}^{(x)} \times L_{C_x}(w_j) \quad (3)$$

where θ is the parameters $\{L_{C_j}\}_{j=1}^{N}$, λ and C_{d_i} is the class label for document d_i.

Class and Neutral Model: We now introduce another model where the words in a document are assumed to be sampled from either the language model of the corresponding (i.e., labelled) emotion class or from the *neutral language model*, L_C. Thus, the generative model for a document d_i labelled with emotion class C_{d_i} would be as follows:

1. For each word w_j in document d_i,
   (a) Lookup the weight $\mu_{d_{ij}}$; this parameter determines the mix of the labelled emotion class and the neutral class, for w_j in d_i
   (b) Choose L_{C_k} with a probability of $\mu_{d_{ij}}$, and L_C with a probability of $1.0 - \mu_{d_{ij}}$
   (c) Sample w_j in accordance with the multinomial distribution of the chosen language model

The posterior probability in accordance with this model can be intuitively formulated as :

$$P(d_i, C_{d_i}|\theta) = \prod_{w_j \in d_i} \mu_{d_{ij}} \times L_{C_{d_i}}(w_j) + (1 - \mu_{d_{ij}}) \times L_C(w_j) \quad (4)$$

where θ is the parameters $\{L_{C_j}\}_{j=1}^{N}, L_C, \mu$.

Equation 3 models a document to exhibit characteristics of many classes with different levels of magnitude. Equation 4 models a document to be a composition of terms that characterise one class and other general terms; a similar formulation where a document is modeled using a mix of two models has been shown to be useful in characterizing problem-solution documents (Deepak et al., 2012; Deepak and Visweswariah, 2014). The central idea of the expectation maximization (EM) algorithm is to maximize the probability of the data, given the language models $\{L_{C_j}\}_{j=1}^{N}$ and L_C. The term weights are estimated from the language models (E-step) and the language models are re-estimated (M-step) using the term weights from the E-step. Thus the maximum likelihood estimation process in EM alternates between the E-step and the M-step. In the following sections we detail the EM process for the two generative models separately. We compare and contrast the two variants of the EM algorithm in Table 1.

4.2.2 EM with Mixture of Classes Model

We will use a matrix based representation for the language model and the lexicon, to simplify the illustration of the EM steps. Under the matrix notation, $L^{(p)}$ denotes the $K \times N$ matrix at the pth iteration where the ith column is the language model corresponding to the ith class, i.e., L_{C_i}. The pth E-step estimates the various $\lambda_{d_{ij}}$ vectors for all documents based on the language models in $L^{(p-1)}$, whereas the M-step re-learns the language models based on the λ values from the E-step. The steps are detailed as follows:

E-Step: The $\lambda_{d_{ij}}^{(n)}$ is simply estimated to the fractional support for the jth word in the ith document (denoted as w_{ij}) from the nth class language model:

$$\lambda_{d_{ij}}^{(n)} = \frac{L_{C_n}^{(p-1)}(w_{ij})}{\sum_x L_{C_x}^{(p-1)}(w_{ij})} \quad (5)$$

M-Step: As mentioned before in Table 1 this step learns the language models from the λ estimates of the previous step. As an example, if a word w is estimated to have come from the *joy* language model with a weight (i.e., λ) 0.5, it would contribute 0.5 as its count to the *joy* language model. Thus, every occurrence of a word is split across language models using their corresponding λ estimates:

$$L_{C_n}^{(p)}[w] = \frac{\sum_i \sum_j I(w_{ij} = w) \times \lambda_{d_{ij}}^{(n)}}{\sum_i \sum_j \lambda_{d_{ij}}^{(n)}} \quad (6)$$

where the indicator function $I(w_{ij} = w)$ evaluates to 1 if $w_{ij} = w$ is satisfied and 0 otherwise.

After any M-Step, the lexicon can be obtained by normalizing the $L^{(p)}$ language models so that the weights for each word adds up to 1.0. i.e.,

$$Lex^{(p)}(i,j) = \frac{L_{C_j}^{(p)}[w_i]}{\sum_{x=1}^{K} L_{C_x}^{(p)}[w_i]} \quad (7)$$

In the above equation, the suffix (i, j) refers to the ith word in the jth class, confirming to our 2d-array representation of the language models.

Table 1: EM Algorithm variants

States	EM with mixture of classes model	EM with class and neutral model
INPUT	Training data T	Training data T
OUTPUT	Word-Emotion Lexicon	Word-Emotion Lexicon
Initialisation	Learn the initial language models $\{L_{C_j}\}_{j=1}^{N}$	Learn the initial language models $\{L_{C_j}\}_{j=1}^{N}$ and L_C
Convergence	While not converged or #Iterations $< \delta$, a threshold	While not converged or #Iterations $< \delta$, a threshold
E-step	Estimate the $\lambda_{d_{ij}}s$ based on the current estimate of $\{L_{C_j}\}_{j=1}^{N}$ (Sec 4.2.2)	Estimate $\mu_{d_{ij}}$ based on the current estimate of $\{L_{C_j}\}_{j=1}^{N}$ and L_C (Sec 4.2.3)
M-step	Estimate the language models $\{L_{C_j}\}_{j=1}^{N}$ using $\lambda_{d_{ij}}s$ (Sec 4.2.2)	Estimate the language models $\{L_{C_j}\}_{j=1}^{N}$ and L_C using $\mu_{d_{ij}}$ (Sec 4.2.3)
Lexicon Induction	Induce a word-emotion lexicon from $\{L_{C_j}\}_{j=1}^{N}$ (Sec 4.2.2)	Induce a word-emotion lexicon from $\{L_{C_j}\}_{j=1}^{N}$ and L_C (Sec 4.2.3)

4.2.3 EM with Class and Neutral Model

The main difference in this case, when compared to the previous is that we need to estimate a neutral language model L_C in addition to the class specific models. We also have fewer parameters to learn since the $\mu_{d_{ij}}$ is a single value rather than a vector of N values as in the previous case.

E-Step: $\mu_{d_{ij}}$ is estimated to the relative weight of the word w_{ij} from across the language model of the corresponding class, and the neutral model:

$$\mu_{d_{ij}} = \frac{L_{C_{d_i}}^{(p-1)}(w_{ij})}{L_{C_{d_i}}^{(p-1)}(w_{ij}) + L_C^{(p-1)}(w_{ij})} \tag{8}$$

Where C_{d_i} denotes the class corresponding to the label of the document d_i.

M-Step: In a slight contrast from the M-Step for the earlier case as shown in Table 1, a word estimated to have a weight (i.e., μ value) of 0.2 would contribute 20% of its count to the corresponding class' language model, while the remaining would go to the neutral language model L_C. Since the class-specific and neutral language models are estimated differently, we have two separate equations:

$$L_{C_n}^{(p)}[w] = \frac{\sum_{i,label(d_i)=C_n} \sum_j I(w_{ij} = w) \times \mu_{d_{ij}}}{\sum_{i,label(d_i)=C_n} \sum_j \mu_{d_{ij}}} \tag{9}$$

$$L_C^{(p)}[w] = \frac{\sum_i \sum_j I(w_{ij} = w) \times (1.0 - \mu_{d_{ij}})}{\sum_i \sum_j (1.0 - \mu_{d_{ij}})} \tag{10}$$

where $label(d_i) = C_n$ As is obvious, the class-specific language models are contributed to by the documents labelled with the class whereas the neutral language model has contributions from all documents. The normalization to achieve the lexicon is exactly the same as in the mixture of classes case, and hence, is omitted here.

4.2.4 EM Initialization

In the case of iterative approaches like EM, the initialization is often considered crucial. In our case, we initialize the unigram class language models by simply aggregating the scores of the words in tweets labelled with the respective class. Thus, the *joy* language model would be the initialized to be the maximum likelihood model to explain the documents labelled *joy*. In the case of the *class and neutral* generative model, we additionally build the neutral language model by aggregating counts across all the documents in the corpus (regardless of what their emotion label is).

5 Experiments

In this section we detail our experimental evaluation. We begin with the details about the Twitter data used in our experiments. We then discuss how we created the folds for a cross validation experiment. Thereafter we detail the classification task used to evaluate the word-emotion lexicon. Finally we discuss the performance of our proposed methods for lexicon generation in comparison with other manually crafted lexicons, PMI based method for lexicon generation and the standard BoW in an emotion classification task.

5.1 Twitter Dataset

The data set used in our experiments was a corpus of emotion labelled tweets harnessed by (Wang et al., 2012). The data set was available in the form of tweet ID's and the corresponding emotion label. The emotion labels comprised namely : *anger, fear, joy, sadness, surprise, love and thankfulness.* We used the Twitter search API[1] to obtain the tweets by searching with the corresponding tweet ID. After that we decided to consider only tweets that belong to the primary set of emotions defined by Parrott (Parrott, 2001). The emotion classes in our case included *anger, fear, joy, sadness, surprise and love.* We had a collection of 0.28 million tweets which we used to carry out a 10 fold cross-validation experiment.

We decided to generate the folds manually,in order to compare the performance of the different algorithms used in our experiments. We split the collection of 0.28 million tweets into 10 equal size sets to generate 10 folds with different training and test sets in each fold. Also all the folds in our experiments were obtained by stratified sampling, ensuring that we had documents representing all the classes in both the training and test sets. We used the training data in each fold to generate the word-emotion lexicon and measured the performance of it on the test data in an emotion classification task. Table 2 shows the average distribution of the different classes namely: *anger, fear, joy, sadness, surprise and love* over the 10 folds. Observe that emotions such as *joy* and *sadness* had a very high number of representative documents . Emotions such as *anger,love* and *fear* were the next most represented emotions. The emotion *surprise* had very few representative documents compared to that of the other emotions.

5.2 Evaluating the word-emotion lexicon

We adopted an emotion classification task in order to evaluate the quality of the word-emotion lexicon generated using the proposed methods. Also research in emotion analysis of text suggest that

[1] https://dev.twitter.com/docs/using-search

Table 2: Average distribution of emotions across the folds

Emotion	Training	Test
Anger	58410	6496
Fear	13692	1548
Joy	74108	8235
Sadness	63711	7069
Surprise	2533	282
Love	31127	3464
Total	243855	27095

lexicon based features were effective compared to that of n-gram features in an emotion classification of text (Aman and Szpakowicz, 2008; Mohammad, 2012a). Therefore we decided to use the lexicon to derive features for text representation. We followed a similar procedure as in (Mohammad, 2012a) to define integer valued features for text representation. We define one feature for each emotion to capture the number of words in a training/test document that are associated with the corresponding emotion. The feature vector for a training/test document was constructed using the word-emotion lexicon. Given a training/test document d we construct the corresponding feature vector $d' =< count(e_1), count(e_2), \ldots, count(e_m)) >$ of length m (in our case m is 6), wherein $count(e_i)$ represents the *number of words* in d that exhibit emotion e_i. $count(e_i)$ is computed as:

$$count(e_i) = \sum_{w \in d} I(\max_{j=1,\ldots,m} Lex(w,j) = C_i) \quad (11)$$

where $I(\ldots)$ is the indicator function as used previously. For example if a document has 1 joy word, 2 love words and 1 surprise word the feature vector for the document would be $(0, 0, 1, 0, 1, 2)$. We used the different lexicon generation methods discussed in sections 4.1, 4.2.2 and 4.2.3 to construct the feature vectors for the documents. In the case of the lexicon generated as in section 4.2.3 the max in equation 11 is computed over $m + 1$ columns. We also used the lexicon generation method proposed in (Mohammad, 2012a) to construct the feature vectors. PMI was used in (Mohammad, 2012a) to generate a word-emotion lexicon which is as follows :

$$Lex(i,j) = \log \frac{freq(w_i, C_j) * freq(\neg C_j)}{freq(C_j) * freq(w_i, \neg C_j)} \quad (12)$$

where $freq(w_i, C_j)$ is the number of times n-gram w_i occurs in a document labelled with emotion C_j, $freq(w_i, \neg C_j)$ is the number of times n-gram w_i occurs in a document not labelled with emotion C_j. $freq(C_j)$ and $freq(\neg C_j)$ are the number of documents labelled with emotion C_j and $\neg C_j$ respectively.

Apart from the aforementioned automatically generated lexicons we also used manually crafted lexicons such as WordNet Affect (Strapparava and Valitutti, 2004) and the NRC word-emotion association lexicon (Saif M. Mohammad, 2013) to construct the feature vectors for the documents. Unlike the automatic lexicons, the general purpose lexicons do not offer numerical scores. Therefore we looked for presence/absence of words in the lexicons to obtain the feature vectors. Furthermore we also represented documents in the standard BoW representation. We performed feature selection using the metric Chisquare[2], to select the top 500 features to represent documents. Since tweets are very short we incorporated a binary representation for BoW instead of term frequency. For classification we used a multiclass SVM classifier [3] and all the experiments were conducted using the data mining software Weka[2]. We used standard metrics such as Precision, Recall and F-measure to compare the performance of the different algorithms. In the following section we analyse the experimental results for TF-lex (Sec 4.1), EMallclass-lex (Sec 4.2.2), EMclass-corpus-lex (Sec 4.2.3), PMI-lex (Mohammad, 2012a), WNA-lex (Strapparava and Valitutti, 2004), NRC-lex (Saif M. Mohammad, 2013) and BoW in an emotion classification task. Also in the case of EM based methods we experimented with different threshold limits δ shown in Table 1. We report the results only w.r.t $\delta = 1$ due to space limitations.

5.3 Results and Analysis

Table 3 shows the F-scores obtained for different methods for each emotion. Observe that the F-score for each emotion shown in Table 3 for a method is the average F-score obtained over the 10 test sets (one per fold). We carried a two tail paired t-test[4] between the baselines and our proposed methods to measure statistical significance for performance on the test set in each fold. From the t-test we observed that our proposed methods are statistically significant over the baselines with a confidence of 95% (i.e with p value 0.05). Also note that the best results obtained for an emotion are highlighted in bold. It is evident from the results that the manually crafted lexicons Worndnet Affect and the NRC word-emotion association lexicon are significantly outperformed by all the automatically generated lexicons for all emotions. Also the BoW model significantly outperforms the manually crafted lexicons suggesting that these lexicons are not sufficiently effective for emotion mining in a domain like Twitter.

When compared with BoW the PMI-lex proposed by (Mohammad, 2012a) achieves a 2% gain w.r.t emotion *love*, a 0.6% gain w.r.t emotion *joy* and 1.28% gain w.r.t emotion *sadness*. However in the case of emotions such as *fear* and *surprise* BoW achieves significant gains of 11.17% and 20.96% respectively. The results suggest that the PMI-lex was able to leverage the availability of adequate training examples to learn the patterns about emotions such as *anger, joy, sadness* and *love*. However given that not all emotions are widely expressed a lexicon generation method that relies heavily on abundant training data could be ineffective to mine less represented emotions.

Now we analyse the results obtained for the lexicons generated from our proposed methods and compare them with BoW and PMI-lex. From the results obtained for our methods in Table 3 it suggests that our methods achieve the best F-scores for 4 emotions namely *anger, fear, sadness and love* out of the 6 emotions. In particular the EM-class-corpus-lex method obtains the best F-score for 3 emotions namely *anger, sadness and love*. When compared with BoW and PMI-lex, EM-class-corpus-lex obtains a gain of 0.85% and 0.93% respectively w.r.t emotion *anger*, 1.85% and 0.57% respectively w.r.t emotion *sadness*, 18.67% and 16.88% respectively w.r.t emotion *love*. Our method TF-lex achieves a gain of 5.47% and 16.64% respectively over BoW and PMI-lex w.r.t emotion *fear*. Furthermore w.r.t emotion *surprise* all our proposed methods outperform PMI-lex. However BoW still obtains the best F-score for emotion *surprise*.

When we compared the results between our own methods EM-class-corpus-lex obtains the best F-scores for emotions *anger, joy, sadness and love*. We expected that modelling a document

[2] http://www.cs.waikato.ac.nz/ml/weka/

[3] http://www.csie.ntu.edu.tw/ cjlin/liblinear/

[4] http://office.microsoft.com/en-gb/excel-help/ttest-HP005209325.aspx

Table 3: Emotion classification results

Method	Average F-Score					
	Anger	**Fear**	**Joy**	**Sadness**	**Surprise**	**Love**
Baselines						
WNA-lex	25.82%	6.61%	12.94%	8.76%	0.76%	2.67%
NRC-lex	21.37%	3.97%	16.04%	8.87%	1.54%	7.22%
Bow	56.5%	13.56%	63.34%	50.57%	**21.65%**	20.52%
PMI-lex	56.42%	2.39%	**63.4%**	50.57%	0.69%	22.31%
Our Learnt Lexicons						
TF-lex	55.85%	**19.03%**	62.01%	50.54%	11.29%	37.69%
EMallclass-lex	56.64%	14.53%	61.89%	50.48%	12.33%	38.13%
EMclass-corpus-lex	**57.35%**	16.1%	62.74%	**51.14%**	12.05%	**39.19%**

to exhibit more than one emotion (EM-allclass-lex) would better distinguish the class boundaries. However given that tweets are very short it was observed that modelling a document as a mixture of emotion terms and general terms (EM-class-corpus-lex) yielded better results. However we expect EM-allclass-lex to be more effective in other domains such as blogs, discussion forums wherein the text size is larger compared to tweets.

Table 4 summarizes the overall F-scores obtained for the different methods. Note that the F-scores shown in Table 4 are the average overall F-scores over the 10 test sets. Again we conducted a two tail paired t-test[4] between the baselines and our proposed methods to measure the performance gains. It was observed that all our proposed methods are statistically significant over the baselines with a confidence of 95% (i.e with p value 0.05). In Table 4 we italicize all our best performing methods and highlight in bold the best among them. From the results it is evident that our proposed methods obtain significantly better F-scores over all the baselines with EM-class-corpus achieving the best F-score with a gain of 3.21%, 2.9%, 39.03% and 38.7% over PMI-lex, BoW, WNA-lex and NRC-lex respectively. Our findings reconfirm previous findings in the literature that emotion lexicon based features improve over corpus based n-gram features in a emotion classification task. Also our findings suggest that domain specific automatic lexicons are significantly better over manually crafted lexicons.

6 Conclusions and Future Work

We proposed a set of methods to automatically extract a word-emotion lexicon from an emotion labelled corpus. Thereafter we used the lexicons to derive features for text representation and showed that lexicon based features significantly outperform the standard BoW features in the emotion classification of tweets. Furthermore our lexicons achieve significant improvements over the general purpose lexicons and the PMI based automatic lexicon in the classification experiments. In future we intend to leverage the lexicons to design different text representations and also test them on emotional content from other domains. Automatically generating human-interpretable models (e.g., (Balachandran et al., 2012)) to accompany emotion classifier decisions is another interesting direction for future work.

Table 4: Overall F-scores

Method	Avg Overall F-score
Baselines	
WNA-lex	13.17%
NRC-lex	13.50%
Bow	49.30%
PMI-lex	48.99%
Our automatic lexicons	
TF-lex	*51.45%*
EMallclass-lex	*51.38%*
EMclass-corpus-lex	**52.20%**

References

Richa Bhayani Alec Go and Lei Huang. 2009. Twitter sentiment classification using distant supervision. *Processing*.

Cecilia Ovesdotter Alm, Dan Roth, and Richard Sproat. 2005. Emotions from text: machine learning for text-based emotion prediction. In *Proceed-*

ings of the conference on Human Language Technology and Empirical Methods in Natural Language Processing, HLT '05, pages 579–586, Stroudsburg, PA, USA. Association for Computational Linguistics.

S. Aman and S. Szpakowicz. 2008. Using roget's thesaurus for fine-grained emotion recognition. In *International Joint Conference on Natural Language Processing*.

Vipin Balachandran, Deepak P, and Deepak Khemani. 2012. Interpretable and reconfigurable clustering of document datasets by deriving word-based rules. *Knowl. Inf. Syst.*, 32(3):475–503.

Johan Bollen, Alberto Pepe, and Huina Mao. 2009. Modelling public mood and emotion : Twitter sentiment and socio-economic phenomena. In *CoRR*.

Danah Boyd, Scott Golder, and Gilad Lotan. 2010. Tweet, tweet, retweet: Conversational aspects of retweeting on twitter. In *Proceedings of the 2010 43rd Hawaii International Conference on System Sciences, Washington, DC, USA*.

P. Deepak and Sutanu Chakraborti. 2012. Finding relevant tweets. In *WAIM*, pages 228–240.

P. Deepak and Karthik Visweswariah. 2014. Unsupervised solution post identification from discussion forums. In *ACL*.

P. Deepak, Karthik Visweswariah, Nirmalie Wiratunga, and Sadiq Sani. 2012. Two-part segmentation of text documents. In *CIKM*, pages 793–802.

Lars E.Holzman and Pottenger William M. 2003. Classification of emotions in internet chat : An application of machine learning using speech phonemes. Technical report, Technical report, Leigh University.

Paul Ekman. 1992. An argument for basic emotions. *Cognition and Emotion*, 6(3):169–200.

Virginia Francisco and Pablo Gervas. 2006. Automated mark up of affective information in english text. *Text, Speech and Dialouge*, volume 4188 of Lecture Notes in Computer Science:375–382.

David John, Anthony C. Boucouvalas, and Zhe Xu. 2006. Representing emotinal momentum within expressive internet communication. In *In Proceedings of the 24th IASTED international conference on Internet and multimedia systems and applications, pages 183-188, Anaheim, CA, ACTA Press*.

J. Johnson J. Guthrie K. Roberts, M.A. Roach and S.M. Harabagiu. 2012. "empatweet: Annotating and detecting emotions on twitter",. In *in Proc. LREC, 2012, pp.3806-3813*.

Elsa Kim, Sam Gilbert, J.Edwards, and Erhardt Graeff. 2009. Detecting sadness in 140 characters: Sentiment analysis of mourning of michael jackson on twitter.

Xiaoyong Liu and W Bruce Croft. 2005. Statistical language modeling for information retrieval. Technical report, DTIC Document.

Chunling Ma, Helmut Prendinger, and Mitsuru Ishizuka. 2005. Emotion estimation and reasoning based on affective textual interaction. In *First International Conference on Affective Computing and Intelligent Interaction (ACII-2005), pages 622-628, Beijing, China*.

Rada Mihalcea and Hugo Liu. 2006. A corpus-based approach for finding happiness. In *In AAAI-2006 Spring Symposium on Computational Approaches to Analysing Weblogs, pages 139-144. AAAI press*.

Saif M. Mohammad and Tony Yang. 2011. Tracking seniment in mail : How genders differ on emotional axes. In *In Proceedings of the 2nd Workshop on Computational Approaches to Subjectivity and Sentiment Analysis(WASSA 2011), pages 70- 79, Portland, Oregon. Association for Computational Linguistics*.

Saif Mohammad. 2012a. #emotional tweets. In *The First Joint Conference on Lexical and Computational Semantics – Volume 1: Proceedings of the main conference and the shared task, and Volume 2: Proceedings of the Sixth International Workshop on Semantic Evaluation (SemEval 2012)*.

Saif M. Mohammad. 2012b. Portable features for classifying emotional text. In *Conference of the North American Chapter of the Association for Computational Linguistics: Human Language Technologies, pages 587-591, Montreal , Canada*.

Alena Neviarouskaya, Helmut Prendinger, and Mitsuru Ishizuka. 2010. Recognition of affect, judgment, and appreciation in text. In *Proceedings of the 23rd International Conference on Computational Linguistics*, COLING '10, pages 806–814, Stroudsburg, PA, USA. Association for Computational Linguistics.

D. Kirson P. Shaver, J. Schwartz. 1987. Emotion knowledge: Further exploration of a prototype approach. *Journal of Personality and Social Psychology*, Vol 52 no 6:1061 – 1086.

W Parrott. 2001. Emotions in social psychology. *Psychology Press, Philadelphia*.

Lisa Pearl and Mark Steyvers. 2010. Identifying emotions, intentions and attitudes in text using a game with a purpose. In *In Proceedings of the NAACL-HLT 2010 Workshop on Computational Approaches to Analysis and Generation of Emotion in Text, Los Abgeles, California*.

R. Plutchik. 1980. A general psychoevolutionary theory of emotion. *In R. Plutchik & H. Kellerman (Eds.), Emotion: Theory, research, and experience:*, Vol. 1. Theories of emotion (pp. 3-33). New York: Academic:(pp. 3–33).

Ashequl Qadir and Ellen Riloff. 2013. Bootstrapped learning of emotion hashtahs #hashtags4you. In *In the 4th Workshop on Computational Approaches to Subjectivity, Sentiment & Social Media Analysis (WASSA 2013).*

Tapas Ray. 2011. The 'story' of digital excess in revolutions of the arab spring. *Journal of Media Practice*, 12(2):189–196.

Peter D. Turney Saif M. Mohammad. 2013. Crowdsourcing a word-emotion association lexicon. *Computational Intelligence, 29 (3), 436-465, Wiley Blackwell Publishing Ltd, 2013*, 29(3):436–465.

Prendinger H. Ishizuka M. Shaikh, M.A.M., 2009. *A Linguistic Interpretation of the OCC Emotion Model for Affect Sensing from Text*, chapter 4, pages 45–73.

Julia Skinner. 2011. Social media and revolution: The arab spring and the occupy movement as seen though three information studies paradigms. *Sprouts: Working papers on Information Systems*, 11(169).

Carlo Strapparava and Alessandro Valitutti. 2004. Wordnet-affect: an affective extension of wordnet. Technical report, ITC-irst, Istituto per la Ricerca Scienti?ca e Tecnologica I-38050 Povo Trento Italy.

Wenbo Wang, Lu Chen, Krishnaprasad Thirunarayan, and Amit P. Sheth. 2012. Harnessing twitter "big data" for automatic emotion identification. In *Proceedings of the 2012 ASE/IEEE International Conference on Social Computing and 2012 ASE/IEEE.*

C. Yang, K. H. Y. Lin, and H. H. Chen. 2007. Emotion classification using web blog corpora. In *Proceedings of the IEEE/WIC/ACM International Conference on Web Intelligence*, WI '07, pages 275–278, Washington, DC, USA. IEEE Computer Society.

Liu Wenyin Qing Li Yanghui Rao, Xiaojun Quan and Mingliang Chen. 2013. Building word-emotion mapping dictionary for online news. In *In Proceedings of the 4th Workshop on Computational Approaches to Subjectivity, Sentiment and Social Media Analysis, WASSA 2013.*

Improvement of a Naive Bayes Sentiment Classifier Using MRS-Based Features

Jared Kramer
University of Washington
Seattle, WA
jaredkk@uw.edu

Clara Gordon
University of Washington
Seattle, WA
cgordon1@uw.edu

Abstract

This study explores the potential of using deep semantic features to improve binary sentiment classification of paragraph-length movie reviews from the IMBD website. Using a Naive Bayes classifier as a baseline, we show that features extracted from Minimal Recursion Semantics representations in conjunction with back-off replacement of sentiment terms is effective in obtaining moderate increases in accuracy over the baseline's n-gram features. Although our results are mixed, our most successful feature combination achieves an accuracy of 89.09%, which represents an increase of 0.76% over the baseline performance and a 6.48% reduction in error.

1 Introduction

Text-based sentiment analysis offers valuable insight into the opinions of large communities of reviewers, commenters and customers. In their survey of the field, Pang and Lee (2008) highlight the importance of sentiment analysis across a range of industries, including review aggregation websites, business intelligence, and reputation management. Detection and classification of sentiment can improve downstream performance in applications sensitive to user opinions, such as question-answering, automatic product recommendations, and social network analysis (ibid., p. 12).

While previous research in sentiment analysis has investigated the extraction of features from syntactic dependency trees, semantic representations appear to be underused as a resource for modeling opinion in text. Indeed, to our knowledge, there has been no research using semantic dependencies created by a precision grammar for sentiment analysis. The goal of the present research is to address this gap by augmenting a baseline classifier with features based on Minimal Resursion Semantics (MRS; Copestake et al., 2005), a formal semantic representation provided by the English Resource Grammar (ERG; Flickinger, 2000). An MRS is a connected graph in which semantic entities may be linked directly through shared arguments or indirectly through handle or qeq constraints, which denote equality modulo quantifier insertion (Copestake et al., 2005). This schema allows for underspecification of quantifier scope.

Using Narayanan et al.'s (2013) Naive Bayes sentiment classifier as a baseline, we test the effectiveness of eight feature types derived from MRS. Our feature pipeline crawls various links in the MRS representations of sentences in our corpus of paragraph-length movie reviews and outputs simple, human-readable features based on various types of semantic relationships. This improved system achieves modest increases in binary sentiment classification accuracy for several of the feature combinations tested.[1]

In the following sections, we summarize previous research in MRS feature extraction and sentiment classification, describe the baseline system and our modifications to it, and outline our approach to parsing our data, constructing features, and integrating them into the existing system. Finally, we report our findings, examine in more detail where our improved system succeeded and failed in relation to the baseline, and suggest avenues for further research in sentiment analysis with MRS-based features.

2 Context and Related Work

Current approaches to sentiment analysis tasks typically use supervised machine learning meth-

[1]Because this task consists of binary classification on an evenly split dataset and every test document is assigned a class, simple accuracy is the most appropriate measure of performance.

*Proceedings of the Third Joint Conference on Lexical and Computational Semantics (*SEM 2014)*, pages 22–29,
Dublin, Ireland, August 23-24 2014.

ods with bag-of-words features as a baseline, and for classification of longer documents like the ones in our dataset, such features remain a powerful tool of analysis. Wang and Manning (2012) compare the performance of several machine learning algorithms using uni- and bigram features from a variety of common sentiment datasets, including the IMDB set used in this project. They report that that SVM classifiers generally perform better sentiment classification on paragraph-length reviews, while Native Bayes classifiers produce better results for "snippets," or short phrases (ibid., p. 91). For our dataset, they obtain the highest accuracies using a hybrid approach, SVM with Naive Bayes features, which results in 91.22% accuracy (ibid., p. 93). This appears to be the best test result to date on this dataset. Although we use a Naive Bayes classifier in our project, alternative machine learning algorithms are a promising topic of further future investigation (see §6).

Two existing areas of research have direct relevance to this project: MRS feature extraction, and sentiment analysis using features based on deep linguistic representations of data. In their work on machine translation, Oepen et al. (2007) define a type of MRS triple based on elementary dependencies, a simplified "variable-free" representation of predicate-argument relations in MRS (p. 5). Fujita et al. (2007) and Pozen (2013) develop similar features for HPSG parse selection, and Pozen experiments with replacing segments of predicate values in triple features with WordNet sense, POS, and lemma information (2013, p. 32).

While there has not yet been any research on using MRS features in sentiment analysis, there has been work on extracting features from deep representations of data for sentiment analysis. In working with deep representations such as MRSes or dependency parses, there are myriad sub-graphs that can be used as features. However these features are often quite sparse and do not generalize well. Joshi & Rose (2009) improve performance of a sentiment classifier by incorporating triples consisting of words and grammatical relations extracted from dependency parses. To increase the generalizability of these triples, they perform back-off by replacing words with part-of-speech tags. Similarly, Arora et al. (2010) extract features from dependency parses by using sentiment back-off to identify potentially meaningful portions of the dependency graph. Given this success combining back-off with sub-graph features, we design several feature types following a similar methodology.

2.1 The IMBD Dataset

We use a dataset of 50,000 movie reviews crawled from the IMDB website, originally developed by Maas et al. (2011). The dataset is split equally between training and test sets. Both training and test sets contain equal numbers of positive and negative reviews, which are defined according to the number of stars assigned by the author on the IMBD website: one to four stars for negative reviews, and seven to ten stars for positive reivews. The reviews vary in length but generally contain between five and fifteen sentences. The Natural Language ToolKit's (NLTK; Loper and Bird, 2002) sentence tokenizer distinguishes 616,995 sentences in the dataset.

Unlike previous research over this dataset, we divide the 25,000 reviews of the test set into two development sets and a final test set. As such, our results are not directly comparable to those of Wang & Manning (2012).

2.2 The Baseline System

The system we use as a baseline, created by Narayanan et al. (2013), implements several small but innovative improvements to a simple Naive Bayes classifier. In the training phase, the baseline performs simple scope of negation annotation on the surface string tokens. Any word containing the characters `not`, `n't` or `no` triggers a "negated" state, in which all following n-grams are prepended with `not_`. This continues until either a punctuation delimiter (?.,!:;) or another negation trigger is encountered.

During training, when an n-gram feature is read into the classifier, it is counted toward $P(f|c)$, and the same feature with `not_` prepended is counted toward $P(f|\hat{c})$, where c is the document class and $\hat{c}$ is the opposite class. Singleton features are then pruned away. Finally, the system runs a set of feature-filtering trials, in which the pruned features are ranked by mutual information score. These trials start at a base threshold of 100,000 features, and the number of features is increased stepwise in increments of 50,000. The feature set that produces the highest accuracy in trials over a development data set is then retained and used to classify the test data. Table 1 shows the ten most informative features, ranked by mutual informa-

Top N-Grams	
1. worst	6. awful
2. bad	7. great
3. not_the worst	8. waste
4. the worst	9. excellent
5. not_worst	10. not_not_even

Table 1: Top MI-ranked baseline n-gram Features.

tion score, out of the 12.1 million n-gram features generated by our baseline.

Before modifying the baseline system's code, we reproduced their reported accuracy figure of 88.80% over the entire 25,000 review test set. However, it appears the baseline system used the test data as development data. In order to address this, we split the data as into development sets as described above. When we ran the baseline system over our final test set, we obtained accuracies of 88.34% pre-feature filtering and 88.29% post-feature filtering; our division of the original test set into development and test sets accounts for this discrepancy.

3 Methodology

Our approach to this task consisted of three general stages: obtaining MRSes for the dataset, implementing a feature pipeline to process the MRSes, and integrating the new features into the classifier. In this section we will describe each of these processes in turn.

3.1 Parsing with the ERG

Because most of the reviews in our data set appear to be written in Standard English, we perform minimal pre-processing before parsing the dataset with the ERG. We use NLTK's sentence tokenization function in our pipeline, along with their HTML-cleaning function to remove some stray HTML-style tags we encountered in the data.

To obtain MRS parses of the data, we use ACE version 0.9.17, an "efficient processor for DELPH-IN HPSG grammars."[2] ACE's simple command line interface allows the parsing pipeline to output MRS data in a single line to a separate directory of MRS data files. We used the 1212 ERG grammar image[3] and specified root conditions that would allow for parses of the informal and fragmented sentences sometimes found in our dataset: namely, the `root_informal`, `root_frag` and `root_inffrag` ERG root nodes.

Parsing with these conditions resulted in 81.11% coverage over the entire dataset. After manual inspection of sentences that failed to parse, we found that irregularities in spelling and punctuation accounted for the majority of these failures and further cleaning of the data would yield higher coverage.

3.2 Feature Design

Our main focus in feature design is capturing relevant semantic relationships between sentiment terms that extend beyond the trigram boundary. Our entry point into the MRS is the elementary predication (EP), and our pipeline algorithm explores the three main EP components: arguments and associated variables, label, and predicate symbol. We also use the set of handle constraints in crawling the links between EPs.

We use two main categories of crawled MRS features: Predicate-Relation-Predicate (PRP) triples, a term borrowed from (Pozen, 2013), and Shared-Label (SL) features. Our feature template consists of eight feature subtypes, including plain EP symbols (type 1), five PRP features (types 2 through 6) and two SL features (types 7 and 8). Table 2 gives examples of each type, along with the unpruned counts of distinct features gathered from our training data. The examples for types 1 through 6 are taken from the abridged MRS example in Figure 1. Note that an *&* character separates predicate and argument components in the feature strings. The type 7 and 8 examples are taken from MRS of sentences featuring the phrases *successfully explores* and *didn't flow well*, respectively.

In our feature extraction pipeline, we use Goodman's pyDelphin[4] tool, a Python module that allows for easy manipulation and querying of MRS constituents. This tool allows our pipeline to quickly process the ERG output files, obtain argument and handle constraint information, and output the features for each MRS into a feature file to be read by our classifier. If the grammar has not returned an analysis for a particular sentence, the

[2]Available at http://sweaglesw.org/linguistics/ace/. Accessed January 15, 2014.

[3]Available at http://www.delph-in.net/erg/. Accessed January 15, 2014.

[4]Available at https://github.com/goodmami/pydelphin. Accessed January 20, 2014.

There is nothing redeeming about this trash.

```
[LTOP: h0
INDEX:e2 [e SF:prop TENSE:pres MOOD:indicative PROG:- PERF:-]
<[_be_v_there_rel<6:8> LBL:h1 ARG0:e2 ARG1:x4] [thing_rel<9:16> LBL:h5 ARG0:x4] [_no_q_rel<9:16>
LBL:h6 ARG0:x4 RSTR:h7 BODY:h8] ["_redeem_v_for_rel"<17:26> LBL:h5 ARG0:e9 ARG1:x4 ARG2:x10]
["_about_x_deg_rel"<27:32> LBL:h11 ARG0:e12 ARG1:u13] [_this_q_dem_rel<33:37> LBL:h11 ARG0:x10 RSTR:h14
BODY:h15] ["_trash_n_1_rel"<38:44> LBL:h16 ARG0:x10]>
HCONS: <h0 qeq h1 h7 qeq h5 h14 qeq h16>]
```

Figure 1: Sample abridged MRS, with mood, tense, and other morphosemantic features removed. Each EP is enclosed in square brackets, bold type denotes predicate values.

Type	Description	Example	Count
1	Pred value	`_no_q_rel`	4,505,389
2	PRP: all	`_no_q_rel&RSTR&"_redeem_v_for_rel"`	10,255,021
3	PRP: string preds only	`"_redeem_v_for_rel"&ARG2&"_trash_n_1_rel"`	941,831
4	PRP: first pred back-off	`"_POS_v__rel"&ARG2&"_trash_n_1_rel"`	635,047
5	PRP: seond pred back-off	`"_redeem_v_for_rel"&ARG2&"_NEG_n__rel"`	621,929
6	PRP: double back-off	`"_POS_v__rel"&ARG2&"_NEG_n__rel"`	20,962
7	SL: handle not a `neg_rel` arg	`"_successful_a_1_rel"&"_explore_v_1_rel"`	589,887
8	SL: handle a `neg_rel` arg	`neg_rel&"_flow_v_1_rel"&"_well_a_1_rel"`	43,427

Table 2: Sample features (Note: Types 1 - 6 are taken from the MRS in Figure 1)

pipeline simply does not output any features for that sentence.

3.2.1 MRS Crawling

In their revisiting of the 2012 SEM scope of negation shared task, Packard et al. (2014) improve on the previous best performance using a relatively simple set of MRS crawling techniques. We make use of two of these techniques, "argument crawling" and "label crawling" in extracting our PRP and SL features (ibid., p. 3). Both include selecting an "active EP" and adding to its scope all EPs that conform to certain specifications. Argument crawling selects all EPs whose distinguished variable or label is an argument of the active EP, while label crawling adds EPs that share a label with the active EP (ibid., p. 3).

Our features are constructed in a similar fashion; for every EP in an MRS, the pipeline selects all EPs linked to the current EP and constructs features from this group of "in-scope" EPs. PRP and SL features are obtained through one "layer" of argument and label crawling, respectively. After observing a number of noisy and uninformative features in our preliminary feature vectors, we excluded a small number of EPs from being considered as the "active EP" in our pipeline algorithm: `udef_q_rel`, `proper_q_rel`, `named_rel`, `pron_rel`, and `pronoun_q_rel`. More information about what exactly these EPs represent can be found in Copestake et al. (2005).

3.2.2 PRP Features

These feature types are a version of the dependency triple features used in Oepen et al. (2007) and Fujita et al. (2007). We define the linking relation as one in which the value of any argument of the first EP matches the distinguished variable or label of the second EP. For handle variables, we count any targets of a qeq constraint headed by that variable as equivalent. We use the same set of EP arguments as Pozen (2013) to link predicates in our PRP features: `ARG`, `ARG1-N`, `L-INDEX`, `R-INDEX`, `L-HANDL`, `R-HANDL`, and `RESTR` (p. 31).

We also use a set of negative and positive word lists from the social media domain, developed by Hu and Liu (2004), for back-off replacement in PRP features. Our pipeline algorithm attempts back-off replacement for all EPs in all PRP triples. If the surface string portion of the predicate value

Feature Types	Pre-Feature Filtering	Post-Feature Filtering
baseline (n-grams only)	88.337	88.289
1	88.289	88.517
2	87.857	87.809
3	88.589	88.757
4	88.673	88.757
5	**88.709**	**88.817**
6	88.337	88.301
7	88.193	88.205
8	88.361	88.265

Table 3: Individual MRS feature trial results

Feature Types	Pre-Feature Filtering	Post-Feature Filtering
baseline (n-grams only)	88.337	88.289
n-grams with back-off	87.293	87.503
MRS only (all types)	88.253	87.977
n-grams, **4**, **5**	88.709	88.781
n-grams, **3**, **4**, **5**, 7, 8	**88.961**	88.853
n-grams, 1, **4**, **5**	88.637	88.865
n-grams, **3**, **4**, **5** 8	88.853	88.961
n-grams, **3**, **4**, **5**, 7	88.889	88.973
n-grams, 1, **3**, **4**, **5**	88.793	89.021
n-grams, **3**, **4**, **5**	88.865	**89.093**

Table 4: Combination feature results

matches any of the entries in the lexicon, the pipeline produces a back-off predicate value by replacing that portion with NEG or POS and stripping the sense category marker. These replacements appear in various positions in feature types 4, 5, and 6 (see Table 2).

3.2.3 SL Features

To further explore the relationships in the MRS, we include this second feature category in our feature template, which links together EPs that share a handle variable. We limit SL features to groups of EPs linked by a handle variable that is also an argument of another EP, or the target of a qeq constraint of such a variable. Our pipeline is therefore able to extract both PRP and SL features in a single pass through the arguments of each EP. Feature type 7 consists of shared-label groupings of two or more EPs, where the handle is not the ARG1 of a neg_rel EP. Type 8 includes groups of one or more EPs where the handle is a neg_rel argument, with neg_rel prepended to the feature string.

Features of type 7 tend to capture relationships between modifiers, such as adverbs and adjectives, and modified entities. Features of type 8 were intended to provide some negation information, though our goals of more fully analyzing scope of negation in our dataset remain unrealized at this point. We reasoned that the lemmatization of string predicate values might provide some useful back-off for the semantic entities involved in negation and modification.

4 Evaluation

To test our MRS features, we adapted our baseline to treat them much like the n-gram features. As with n-grams, each MRS feature is counted toward the probability of the class of its source document, and a negated version of that feature, with not_ prepended, is counted toward the opposite class. We ran our feature filtering trials using the first development set, then obtained preliminary accuracy figures from our second development set. We began with each feature type in isolation and used these results to inform later experiments using combinations of feature types. The numbers reported here are the results over the final, held-out test set.

Our final test accuracies indicate that three feature types produce the best gains in accuracy: back-off PRPs with first- and second-predicate replacement (types 4 and 5), and PRPs with string predicates only (type 3). Table 3 displays isolated feature test results, while Table 4 ranks the top seven feature combinations in ascending order by post-feature filtering accuracies. The bolded feature types show that all of the best combination runs include one or more of the top three features mentioned above. Notable also are the accuracies for MRS-based features alone, which fall very close to the baseline. The best accuracies for pre- and post-feature filtering tests appear in bold.

The highest accuracy, achieved by running a feature-filtered combination of the baseline's n-gram features and feature types 3, 4, and 5, resulted in a 0.80% increase over the baseline performance with feature filtering, and a 0.76% increase in the best baseline accuracy overall (obtained without feature filtering). The experimental best run successfully categorizes 63 more of the 8333 test documents than the baseline best run. Although these gains are small, they account for a 6.48% reduction in error.

Most Informative MRS Features
`not_"_NEG_a__rel"&ARG1&_the_q_rel`
`"_NEG_a__rel"&ARG1&_the_q_rel`
`"_POS_a__rel"&ARG1&_the_q_rel`
`not_"_POS_a__rel"&ARG1&_the_q_rel`
`"_POS_a__rel"&ARG1&_a_q_rel`
`not_"_POS_a__rel"&ARG1&_a_q_rel`
`not_"_NEG_a__rel"&ARG1&"_movie_n_of_rel"`
`"_NEG_a__rel"&ARG1&"_movie_n_of_rel"`
`_a_q_rel&RSTR&"_POS_a__rel"`
`not__a_q_rel&RSTR&"_POS_a__rel"`
`not_"_NEG_a__rel"&ARG1&udef_q_rel`
`"_NEG_a__rel"&ARG1&udef_q_rel`
`superl_rel&ARG1&"_POS_a__rel"`
`not_superl_rel&ARG1&"_POS_a__rel"`
`_and_c_rel&LHNDL&"_POS_a__rel"`

Table 5: Most informative MRS features

5 Discussion

5.1 The Most Successful Experiments

The test accuracies indicate that our back-off replacement method, in combination with the simple predicate-argument relationships captured in PRP triples, is the most successful aspect of feature design in this project. However, as our error analysis indicates, back-off is the likely source of many of our system's errors (see §5.2). Table 5 lists the 15 most informative MRS features from our best run based on mutual information score, all of which are of feature type 4 or 5. Note that the `not_` prepended to some features is a function of way our classifier reads in binary features (as described in §2.2), not an indication of grammatical negation. The success of these partial back-off features confirms our intuition that the semantic relationships between sentiment-laden terms and other entities in the sentence offer a reliable indicator of author sentiment. When we performed back-off replacement directly on the surface strings and ran our classifier with n-grams only, we obtained accuracies of 87.29% pre-feature filtering and 87.50% post-feature filtering, a small decrease from the baseline performance (see Table 4). This lends additional support to the idea that the *combination* of sentiment back-off and semantic dependencies is significant. These results also fit with the findings of of Joshi and Rose (2009), who determined that back-off triple features provide "more generalizable and useful patterns" in sentiment data than lexical dependency features alone (p. 316).

Despite these promising results, we found that the separate EP values (type 1), PRP triples without replacement (type 2), PRPs with double replacement (type 6) and SL features (types 7 and 8) have very little effect on accuracy by themselves. For type 1, we suspect that EP values alone don't contribute enough information beyond basic n-gram features. We had hypothesized that the lemmatization in these values might provide some helpful back-off. However, this effect is likely drowned out by the lack of any scope of negation handling in the MRS features.

We attribute the failure of the SL features to the fact that they often capture EPs originating in adjacent tokens in the surface string, which does not improve on the n-gram features. Lastly, we believe the relative sparsity of double back-off features was the primary reason they did not produce meaningful results.

These results also call into question the usefulness of the feature filtering trials in our baseline. By design, these trials produce performance increases on the dataset on which they are run. However, filtering produces small and inconsistent gains for the final held-out test set.

Error Types	
Misleading back-off	31
Plot summary / Noise	20
Obscure Words / Data Sparsity	7
Data Error	3
Nonsensical Review	3
Reason Unsure	40

Table 6: Error types from top MRS experiment

5.2 Error Analysis

We manually inspected the 104 reviews from the final test set that were correctly classified by the best run of the baseline system but incorrectly classified by the best run of our improved system. This set contains 50 false negatives, and 54 false positives. We classified them according to five subjective categories: misleading back-off, in which many of the sentiment terms have a polarity opposite to the overall review; excess plot sum-

	Incorrectly classified	Correctly classified
Negative docs	"_POS_a__rel"&ARG1&_the_q_rel	"_NEG_n__rel"&ARG0&udef_q_rel
	"_POS_a__rel"&ARG1&_a_q_rel	"_NEG_a__rel"&ARG1&_the_q_rel
	"_POS_a__rel"&ARG1&udef_q_rel	"_NEG_a__rel"&ARG1&udef_q_rel
	"_NEG_n__rel"&ARG0&udef_q_rel	"_POS_a__rel"&ARG1&_a_q_rel
	_a_q_rel&RSTR&"_POS_a__rel"	_the_q_rel&RSTR&"_NEG_n__rel"
Positive docs	"_NEG_n__rel"&ARG0&udef_q_rel	"_POS_a__rel"&ARG1&_a_q_rel
	"_NEG_v__rel"&ARG1&pronoun_q_rel	"_POS_a__rel"&ARG1&_the_q_rel
	"_NEG_v__rel"&ARG1&pron_rel	_a_q_rel&RSTR&"_POS_a__rel"
	"_NEG_a__rel"&ARG1&udef_q_rel	"_NEG_n__rel"&ARG0&udef_q_rel
	"_NEG_a__rel"&ARG1&_the_q_rel	"_POS_a__rel"&ARG1&udef_q_rel

Table 7: Most frequent features in test data by polarity and classification result

mary or off-topic language; use of obscure words not likely to occur frequently in the data; miscategorization in the dataset; and confusing or nonsensical language. The counts for these categories appear in Table 6.

The prevalence of errors in the first category is revealing, and relates to certain subcategories of review that confound our sentiment back-off features. For horror films in particular, words that would generally convey negative sentiment (*creepy*, *horrible*, *gruesome*) are instead used positively. This presents an obvious problem for sentiment back-off, which relies on the assumption that words are generally used with the same intent.

To explore this further, we collected counts of the most frequent features in these 104 reviews, and compared them to feature counts for correctly classified documents of the same class. The stark contrast between the back-off polarities of the features extracted and the polarity of the documents suggests that these feature types are overgeneralizing and misleading the classifier (see Table 7). While the course-grained polarity of sentiment terms is often a good indicator of overall review polarity, our system has difficulty with cases in which many sentiment terms do not align with the review sentiment. Our back-off PRP features do not include scope of negation handling, so even if these terms are negated, our classifier in its current form is unable to take advantage of that information.

Further manual observation of the feature vectors from these documents suggests that the sentiment lexicon contains elements that are not suited to the movie review domain; *plot*, for example is classified as a negative term. These results point to the need for a more domain-specific sentiment lexicon, and perhaps additional features that look at the combination of sentiment terms present in a review. LDA models could provide some guidance in capturing and analyzing co-occurring groups of sentiment terms.

6 Conclusions and Future Work

Our attempt to improve binary sentiment classification with MRS-based features is motivated by a desire to move beyond shallow approaches and explore the potential for features based on semantic dependencies. Our preliminary results are promising, if modest, and point to back-off replacement as a useful tool in combination with the relationships captured by predicate triples.

There are a number of potential areas for improvement and further development of our approach. In light of Wang and Manning's (2012) results using an SVM classifier on the same dataset, one obvious direction would be to experiment with this and other machine learning algorithms. Additionally, the ability to account for negation in the MRS features types as in Packard et al. (2014) would likely mitigate some of the errors caused by the back-off PRP features

Another possibility for expansion would be the development of features using larger feature subgraphs. Because of concerns about runtime and data sparsity, we crawl only one level of the MRS and examine a limited set of relationships. The success of Socher et al.'s (2013) Recursive Neural Tensor Network suggest that with enough data, it is possible to capture the complex compositional effects of various sub-components. Given their success with syntactic dependencies, and the research presented here, we believe semantic dependencies will be a fruitful avenue for future research in sentiment analysis. This project has been an exciting first step into uncharted territory, and suggests the potential to further exploit the MRS in sentiment analysis applications. Nonetheless, the performance gains we were able to observe demonstrate the power of using semantic representations produced by a linguistically motivated, broad-coverage parser as an information source in a semantically sensitive task such as sentiment analysis.

Acknowledgments

Thanks to our professor, Emily Bender, for providing her expertise and guidance at all stages of this project.

We're grateful to Michael Goodman for making his pyDelphin module freely available, guiding us in using it, and providing timely troubleshooting and support via email for the duration of this project. Thanks to Woodley Packard, who provided helpful advice on getting the best use out of ACE.

References

S. Arora, E. Mayfield, C Penstein-Rosé, and E Nyberg. 2010. Sentiment Classification using Automatically Extracted Subgraph Features. In *Proceedings of the NAACL HLT 2010 Workshop on Computational Approaches to Analysis and Generation of Emotion in Text*, pp. 131 - 139. Los Angeles, CA.

A. Copestake, D. Flickinger, C. Pollard, and I. A. Sag. 2005. Minimal Recursion Semantics: An Introduction. *Research on Natural Language and Computation*, 3(4), pp. 281 - 332.

D. Flickinger. 2000. On building a more efficient grammar by exploiting types. *Natural Language Engineering*,, 6(1), pp. 15 - 28.

S. Fujita, F. Bond, S. Oepen, T. Tanaka. 2010. Exploiting semantic information for HPSG parse selection. *Research on Language and Computation*. 8(1): 1-22

M. Hu and B. Liu. 2004. Mining and Summarizing Customer Reviews. In *Proceedings of the ACM SIGKDD International Conference on Knowledge Discovery and Data Mining (KDD-2004)*. Seattle, WA.

M. Joshi and C Penstein Rosé. 2009. Generalizing Dependency Features for Opinion Mining. In *Proceedings of the ACL-IJCNLP 2009 Conference Short Papers*, pp. 313 - 316. Suntec, Singapore.

E. Loper, and S., Bird. 2002. NLTK: The Natural Language Toolkit. In Proceedings of the ACL Workshop on Effective Tools and Methodologies for Teaching Natural Language Processing and Computational Linguistics. Philadelphia: Association for Computational Linguistics

L. Jia, C. Yu, and W. Meng. 2009. The effect of negation on sentiment analysis and retrieval effectiveness. In *Proceedings of the 18th ACM conference on Information and knowledge management (CIKM '09)*, pp. 1827 - 1830. Hong Kong, China.

A. L. Maas, R. E. Daly, Peter T. Pham, Dan Huang, Andrew Y. Ng, and C. Potts. 2011. Learning word vectors for sentiment analysis. In *Proceedings of the 49th Annual Meeting of the Association for Computational Linguistics: Human Language Technologies*, pp. 142 - 150. Portland, Oregon.

V. Narayanan, I. Arora, and A. Bhatia. 2013. Fast and accurate sentiment classification using an enhanced Naive Bayes'model. *Intelligent Data Engineering and Automated Learning IDEAL function Lecture Notes in Computer Science*, 8206:194 - 201.

S. Oepen, E. Velldal, J. Lonning, P. Meurer, V. Rosn, and D. Flickinger. 2007. Towards Hybrid Quality Oriented Machine Translation. In *Proceedings of the 11th International Conference on Theoretical and Methodological Issues in Machine Translation.*

W. Packard, E. M. Bender, J. Read, S. Oepen and R. Dridan. 2014. Simple Negation Scope Resolution Through Deep Parsing: A Semantic Solution to a Semantic Problem. In *Proceedings of the 52nd Annual Meeting of the Association for Computational Linguistics*. Baltimore, MD.

B. Pang and L. Lee. 2008. Opinion Mining and Sentiment Analysis. *Foundations and Trends in Information Retrieval*, 2(1-2):1 - 135.

Z. Pozen. 2013. Using Lexical and Compositional Semantics to Improve HPSG Parse Selection. *Master's Thesis, University of Washington.*

R. Socher, A. Perelygin, J. Wu, J. Chuang. C. Manning, A. Ng, and C. Potts 2013. Recursive Deep Models for Semantic Compositionality Over a Sentiment Treebank In *Proceedings of the 2013 Conference on Empirical Methods in Natural Language Processing*, pp. 1631-1642. Seattle, WA.

S. Wang and C. D. Manning. 2012. Baselines and Bigrams: Simple, Good Sentiment and Topic Classication. In *Proceedings of the 50th Annual Meeting of the Association for Computational Linguistics*, pp. 90 94. Jeju, Republic of Korea.

A Yeh. 2000. More accurate tests for the statistical significance of result differences. In *Proceedings of the 18th Conference on Computational Linguistics (COLING)*, pp. 147 - 153.

Sense and Similarity: A Study of Sense-level Similarity Measures

Nicolai Erbs[†], **Iryna Gurevych**[†‡] **and Torsten Zesch**[§]

† UKP Lab, Technische Universität Darmstadt
‡ Information Center for Education, DIPF, Frankfurt
§ Language Technology Lab, University of Duisburg-Essen
http://www.ukp.tu-darmstadt.de

Abstract

In this paper, we investigate the difference between word and sense similarity measures and present means to convert a state-of-the-art word similarity measure into a sense similarity measure. In order to evaluate the new measure, we create a special sense similarity dataset and re-rate an existing word similarity dataset using two different sense inventories from WordNet and Wikipedia. We discover that word-level measures were not able to differentiate between different senses of one word, while sense-level measures actually increase correlation when shifting to sense similarities. Sense-level similarity measures improve when evaluated with a re-rated sense-aware gold standard, while correlation with word-level similarity measures decreases.

1 Introduction

Measuring similarity between words is a very important task within NLP with applications in tasks such as word sense disambiguation, information retrieval, and question answering. However, most of the existing approaches compute similarity on the word-level instead of the sense-level. Consequently, most evaluation datasets have so far been annotated on the word level, which is problematic as annotators might not know some infrequent senses and are influenced by the more probable senses. In this paper, we provide evidence that this process heavily influences the annotation process. For example, when people are presented the word pair *jaguar* - *gamepad* only few people know that

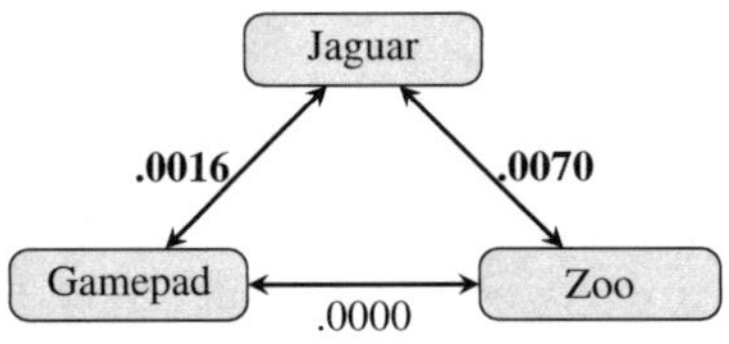

Figure 1: Similarity between words.

jaguar is also the name of an Atari game console.[1] People rather know the more common senses of *jaguar*, i.e. the car brand or the animal. Thus, the word pair receives a low similarity score, while computational measures are not so easily fooled by popular senses. It is thus likely that existing evaluation datasets give a wrong picture of the true performance of similarity measures.

Thus, in this paper we investigate whether similarity should be measured on the sense level. We analyze state-of-the-art methods and describe how the word-based Explicit Semantic Analysis (ESA) measure (Gabrilovich and Markovitch, 2007) can be transformed into a sense-level measure. We create a sense similarity dataset, where senses are clearly defined and evaluate similarity measures with this novel dataset. We also re-annotate an existing word-level dataset on the sense level in order to study the impact of sense-level computation of similarity.

2 Word-level vs. Sense-level Similarity

Existing measures either compute similarity (i) on the word level or (ii) on the sense level. Similarity on the word level may cover any possible sense of the word, where on the sense level only the actual sense is considered. We use Wikipedia Link Mea-

[1] If you knew that it is a certain sign that you are getting old.

*Proceedings of the Third Joint Conference on Lexical and Computational Semantics (*SEM 2014)*, pages 30–39,
Dublin, Ireland, August 23-24 2014.

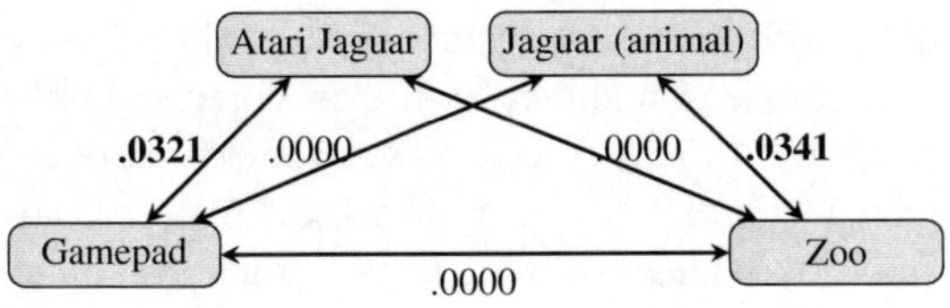

Figure 2: Similarity between senses.

sure (Milne, 2007) and Lin (Lin, 1998) as examples of sense-level similarity measures[2] and ESA as the prototypical word-level measure.[3]

The Lin measure is a widely used graph-based similarity measure from a family of similar approaches (Budanitsky and Hirst, 2006; Seco et al., 2004; Banerjee and Pedersen, 2002; Resnik, 1999; Jiang and Conrath, 1997; Grefenstette, 1992). It computes the similarity between two senses based on the information content (IC) of the lowest common subsumer (lcs) and both senses (see Formula 1).

$$\text{sim}_{\text{lin}} = \frac{2\,IC(lcs)}{IC(sense1) + IC(sense2)} \tag{1}$$

Another type of sense-level similarity measure is based on Wikipedia that can also be considered a sense inventory, similar to WordNet. Milne (2007) uses the link structure obtained from articles to count the number of shared incoming links of articles. Milne and Witten (2008) give a more efficient variation for computing similarity (see Formula 2) based on the number of links for each article, shared links $|A \cap B|$ and the total number of articles in Wikipedia $|W|$.

$$\text{sim}_{\text{LM}} = \frac{\log max(|A|, |B|) - \log|A \cap B|}{\log|W| - \log min(|A|, |B|)} \tag{2}$$

All sense-level similarity measures can be converted into a word similarity measure by computing the maximum similarity between all possible sense pairs. Formula 3 shows the heuristic, with S_n being the possible senses for word n, sim_w the word similarity, and sim_s the sense similarity.

$$\text{sim}_w(w_1, w_2) = \max_{s_1 \in S_1, s_2 \in S_2} \text{sim}_s(s1, s2) \tag{3}$$

Explicit Semantic Analysis (ESA) (Gabrilovich and Markovitch, 2007) is a widely used word-level similarity measure based on Wikipedia as a background document collection. ESA constructs a n-dimensional space, where n is the number of articles in Wikipedia. A word is transformed in a vector with the length n. Values of the vector are determined by the term frequency in the corresponding dimension, i.e. in a certain Wikipedia article. The similarity of two words is then computed as the inner product (usually the cosine) of the two word vectors.

We now show how ESA can be adapted successfully to work on the sense-level, too.

2.1 DESA: Disambiguated ESA

In the standard definintion, ESA computes the term frequency based on the number of times a term—usually a word—appears in a document. In order to make it work on the sense level, we will need a large sense-disambiguated corpus. Such a corpus could be obtained by performing word sense disambiguating (Agirre and Edmonds, 2006; Navigli, 2009) on all words. However, as this is an error-prone task and we are more interested to showcase the overall principle, we rely on Wikipedia as an already manually disambiguated corpus. Wikipedia is a highly linked resource and articles can be considered as senses.[4] We extract all links from all articles, with the link target as the term. This approach is not restricted to Wikipedia, but can be applied to any resource containing connections between articles, such as Wiktionary (Meyer and Gurevych, 2012b). Another reason to select Wikipedia as a corpus is that it will allow us to directly compare similarity values with the Wikipedia Link Measure as described above.

After this more high-level introduction, we now focus on the mathematical foundation of ESA and disambiguated ESA (called ESA on senses). ESA and ESA on senses count the frequency of each term (or sense) in each document. Table 1 shows the corresponding term-document matrix for the example in Figure 1. The term *Jaguar* appears in all shown documents, but the term *Zoo* appears in the articles *Dublin Zoo* and *Wildlife Park*.[5] A manual analysis shows that *Jaguar* appears with different senses in the articles *D-pad*[6] and *Dublin Zoo*.

[2]We selected these measures because they are intuitive but still among the best performing measures.

[3]Hassan and Mihalcea (2011) classify these measures as corpus-based and knowledge-based.

[4]Wikipedia also contains pages with a list of possible senses called *disambiguation pages*, which we filter.

[5]In total it appears in 30 articles but we shown only few example articles.

[6]A D-pad is a directional pad for playing computer games.

Articles	Terms		
	Jaguar	*Gamepad*	*Zoo*
# articles	3,496	30	7,553
Dublin Zoo	1	0	25
Wildlife Park	1	0	3
D-pad	1	0	0
Gamepad	4	1	0
...	...	...	...

Table 1: Term-document-matrix for frequencies in a corpus if words are used as terms

Articles	Terms			
	Atari Jaguar	Gamepad	Jaguar (animal)	Zoo
# articles	156	86	578	925
Dublin Zoo	0	0	2	1
Wildlife Park	0	0	1	1
D-pad	1	1	0	0
Gamepad	1	0	0	0
...	...	...	...	...

Table 2: Term-document-matrix for frequencies in a corpus if senses are used as terms

By comparing the vectors without any modification, we see that the word pairs *Jaguar—Zoo* and *Jaguar—Gamepad* have vector entries for the same document, thus leading to a non-zero similarity. Vectors for the terms *Gamepad* and *Zoo* do not share any documents, thus leading to a similarity of zero.

Shifting from words to senses changes term frequencies in the term-document-matrix in Table 2. The word *Jaguar* is split in the senses *Atari Jaguar* and *Jaguar (animal)*. Overall, the term-document-matrix for the sense-based similarity shows lower frequencies, usually zero or one because in most cases one article does not link to another article or exactly once. Both senses of *Jaguar* do not appear in the same document, hence, their vectors are orthogonal. The vector for the term *Gamepad* differs from the vector for the same term in Table 1. This is due to two effects: (i) There is no link from the article *Gamepad* to itself, but the term is mentioned in the article and (ii) there exists a link from the article *D-pad* to *Gamepad*, but using another term.

The term-document-matrices in Table 1 and 2 show unmodified frequencies of the terms. When comparing two vectors, both are normalized in a prior step. Values can be normalized by the inverse logarithm of their document frequency. Term frequencies can also be normalized by weighting them with the inverse frequency of links pointing to an article (document or articles with many links pointing to them receive lower weights as documents with only few incoming links.) We normalize vector values with the inverse logarithm of article frequencies.

Besides comparing two vectors by measuring the angle between them (cosine), we also experiment with a language model variant. In the language model variant we calculate for both vectors the ratio of links they both share. The final similarity value is the average for both vectors. This is somewhat similar to the approach of Wikipedia Link Measure by Milne (2007). Both rely on Wikipedia links and are based on frequencies of these links. We show that—although, ESA and Link Measure seem to be very different—they both share a general idea and are identical with a certain configuration.

2.2 Relation to the Wikipedia Link Measure

Link Measure counts the number of incoming links to both articles and the number of shared links. In the originally presented formula by Milne (2007) the similarity is the cosine of vectors for incoming or outgoing links from both articles. Incoming links are also shown in term-document-matrices in Table 1 and 2, thus providing the same vector information. In Milne (2007), vector values are weighted by the frequency of each link normalized by the logarithmic inverse frequency of links pointing to the target. This is one of the earlier described normalization approaches. Thus, we argue that the Wikipedia Link Measure is a special case of our more general ESA on senses approach.

3 Annotation Study I: Rating Sense Similarity

We argue that human judgment of similarity between words is influenced by the most probable sense. We create a dataset with ambiguous terms and ask annotators to rank the similarity of senses and evaluate similarity measures with the novel dataset.

3.1 Constructing an Ambiguous Dataset

In this section, we discuss how an evaluation dataset should be constructed in order to correctly asses the similarity of two senses. Typically, evaluation datasets for word similarity are constructed by letting annotators rate the similarity between both words without specifying any senses for these words. It is common understanding that annotators judge the similarity of the combination of senses with the highest similarity.

We investigate this hypothesis by constructing a new dataset consisting of 105 ambiguous word pairs. Word pairs are constructed by adding one word with two clearly distinct senses and a second word, which has a high similarity to only one of the senses. We first ask two annotators[7] to rate the word pairs on a scale from 0 (not similar at all) to 4 (almost identical). In the second round, we ask the same annotators to rate 277 sense[8] pairs for these word pairs using the same scale.

The final dataset thus consists of two levels: (i) word similarity ratings and (ii) sense similarity ratings. The gold ratings are the averaged ratings of both annotators, resulting in an agreement[9] of .510 (Spearman: .598) for word ratings and .792 (Spearman: .806) for sense ratings.

Table 3 shows ratings of both annotators for two word pairs and ratings for all sense combinations. In the given example, the word *bass* has the senses of the fish, the instrument, and the sound. Annotators compare the words and senses to the words *Fish* and *Horn*, which appear only in one sense (most frequent sense) in the dataset.

The annotators' rankings contradict the assumption that the word similarity equals the similarity of the highest sense. Instead, the highest sense similarity rating is higher than the word similarity rating. This may be caused—among others—by two effects: (i) the correct sense is not known or not recalled, or (ii) the annotators (unconsciously) adjust their ratings to the probability of the sense. Although, the annotation manual stated that Wikipedia (the source of the senses) could be used to get informed about senses and that any sense for the words can be selected, we see both effects in the annotators' ratings. Both annotators rated the similarity between *Bass* and *Fish* as very low (1 and 2). However, when asked to rate the similarity between the sense *Bass (Fish)* and *Fish*, both annotators rated the similarity as high (4). Accordingly, for the word pair *Bass* and *Horn*, word similarity is low (1) while the highest sense frequency is medium to high (3 and 4).

3.2 Results & Discussion

We evaluated similarity measures with the previously created new dataset. Table 4 shows correlations of similarity measures with human ratings. We divide the table into measures computing similarity on word level and on sense level. ESA works entirely on a word level, Lin (WordNet) uses WordNet as a sense inventory, which means that senses differ across sense inventories.[10] ESA on senses and Wikipedia Link Measure (WLM) compute similarity on a sense-level, however, similarity on a word-level is computed by taking the maximum similarity of all possible sense pairs.

Results in Table 4 show that word-level measures return the same rating independent from the sense being used, thus, they perform good when evaluated on a word-level, but perform poorly on a sense-level. For the word pair *Jaguar—Zoo*, there exist two sense pairs *Atari Jaguar—Zoo* and *Jaguar (animal)—Zoo*. Word-level measures return the same similarity, thus leading to a very low correlation. This was expected, as only sense-based similarity measures can discriminate between different senses of the same word. Somewhat surprisingly, sense-level measures perform also well on a word-level, but their performance increases strongly on sense-level. Our novel measure ESA on senses provides the best results. This is expected as the ambiguous dataset contains many infrequently used senses, which annotators are not aware of.

Our analysis shows that the algorithm for comparing two vectors (i.e. cosine and language model) only influences results for ESA on senses when computed on a word-level. Correlation for Wikipedia Link Measure (WLM) differs depending on whether the overlap of incoming or outgoing links are computed. WLM on word-level using incoming links performs better, while the difference on sense-level evaluation is only marginal. Results show that an evaluation on the level of words and senses may influence performance of measures strongly.

3.3 Pair-wise Evaluation

In a second experiment, we evaluate how well sense-based measures can decide, which one of

[7] Annotators are near-native speakers of English and have university degrees in cultural anthropology and computer science.

[8] The sense of a word is given in parentheses but annotators have access to Wikipedia to get information about those senses.

[9] We report agreement as Krippendorf α with a quadratic weight function.

[10] Although, there exists sense alignment resources, we did not use any alignment.

Word 1	Word 2	Sense 1	Sense 2	Annotator 1 Words	Annotator 1 Senses	Annotator 2 Words	Annotator 2 Senses
		Bass (Fish)			**4**		**4**
Bass	**Fish**	Bass (Instrument)	Fish (Animal)	**1**	1	**1**	1
		Bass (Sound)			1		1
		Bass (Fish)			1		1
Bass	**Horn**	Bass (Instrument)	Horn (Instrument)	**2**	**3**	**1**	**4**
		Bass (Sound)			**3**		3

Table 3: Examples of ratings for two word pairs and all sense combinations with the highest ratings marked bold

	measure	Word-level Spearman	Word-level Pearson	Sense-level Spearman	Sense-level Pearson
Word measures	ESA	**.456**	.239	-.001	.017
	Lin (WordNet)	.298	.275	.038	.016
Sense measures	ESA on senses (Cosine)	.292	.272	**.642**	.348
	ESA on senses (Lang. Mod.)	.185	.256	**.642**	**.482**
	WLM (out)	.190	.193	.537	.372
	WLM (in)	.287	**.279**	.535	.395

Table 4: Correlation of similarity measures with a human gold standard of ambiguous word pairs.

two sense pairs for one word pair have a higher similarity. We thus create for every word pair all possible sense pairs[11] and count cases where one measure correctly decides, which is the sense pair with a higher similarity.

Table 5 shows evaluation results based on a minimal difference between two sense pairs. We removed all sense pairs with a lower difference of their gold similarity. Column *#pairs* gives the number of remaining sense pairs. If a measure classifies two sense pairs wrongly, it may either be because it rated the sense pairs with an equal similarity or because it reversed the order.

Results show that accuracy increases with increasing minimum difference between sense pairs. Figure 3 emphasizes this finding. Overall, accuracy for this task is high (between .70 and .83), which shows that all the measures can discriminate sense pairs. WLM (out) performs best for most cases with a difference in accuracy of up to .06.

When comparing these results to results from Table 4, we see that correlation does not imply accurate discrimination of sense pairs. Although, ESA on senses has the highest correlation to human ratings, it is outperformed by WLM (out) on the task of discriminating two sense pairs. We see that results are not stable across both evaluation scenarios, however, ESA on senses achieves the highest correlation and performs similar to WLM (out) when comparing sense pairs pair-wise.

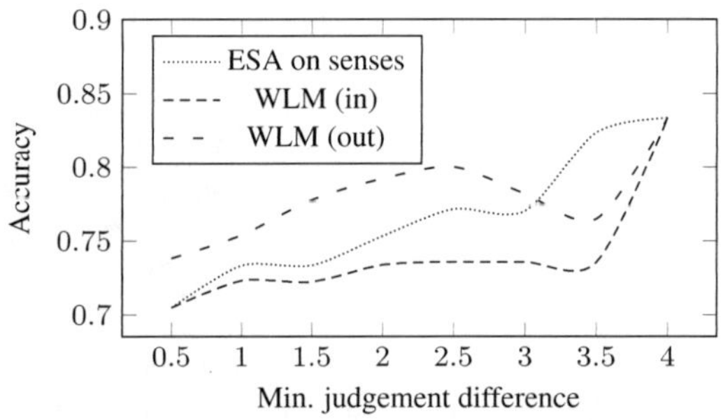

Figure 3: Accuracy distribution depending on minimum difference of similarity ratings

4 Annotation Study II: Re-rating of RG65

We performed a second evaluation study where we asked three human annotators[12] to rate the similarity of word-level pairs in the dataset by Rubenstein and Goodenough (1965). We hypothesize that measures working on the sense-level should have a disadvantage on word-level annotated datasets due to the effects described above that influence annotators towards frequent senses. In our annotation

[11]For one word pair with two senses for one word, there are two possible sense pairs. Three senses result in three sense pairs.

[12]As before, all three annotators are near-native speakers of English and have a university degree in physics, engineering, and computer science.

Min. diff.	#pairs	measure	Correct	Wrong: Reverse	Wrong: Values equal	Accuracy
0.5	420	ESA on senses	296	44	80	.70
		WLM (in)	296	62	62	.70
		WLM (out)	310	76	34	**.74**
1.0	390	ESA on senses	286	38	66	.73
		WLM (in)	282	52	56	.72
		WLM (out)	294	64	32	**.75**
1.5	360	ESA on senses	264	34	62	.73
		WLM (in)	260	48	52	.72
		WLM (out)	280	54	26	**.78**
2.0	308	ESA on senses	232	28	48	.75
		WLM (in)	226	36	46	.73
		WLM (out)	244	46	18	**.79**
2.5	280	ESA on senses	216	22	42	.77
		WLM (in)	206	32	42	.74
		WLM (out)	224	38	18	**.80**
3.0	174	ESA on senses	134	10	30	.77
		WLM (in)	128	20	26	.74
		WLM (out)	136	22	16	**.78**
3.50	68	ESA on senses	56	4	8	**.82**
		WLM (in)	50	6	12	.74
		WLM (out)	52	6	10	.76
4.0	12	ESA on senses	10	2	0	**.83**
		WLM (in)	10	2	0	**.83**
		WLM (out)	10	2	0	**.83**

Table 5: Pair-wise comparison of measures: Results for ESA on senses (language model) and ESA on senses (cosine) do not differ

studies, our aim is to minimize the effect of sense weights.

In previous annotation studies, human annotators could take sense weights into account when judging the similarity of word pairs. Additionally, some senses might not be known by annotators and, thus receive a lower rating. We minimize these effects by asking annotators to select the best sense for a word based on a short summary of the corresponding sense. To mimic this process, we created an annotation tool (see Figure 4), for which an annotator first selects senses for both words, which have the highest similarity. Then the annotator ranks the similarity of these sense pairs based on the complete sense definition.

A single word without any context cannot be disambiguated properly. However, when word pairs are given, annotators first select senses based on the second word, e.g. if the word pair is *Jaguar* and *Zoo*, an annotator will select the wild animal for *Jaguar*. After disambiguating, an annotator assigns a similarity score based on both selected senses. To facilitate this process, a definition of each possible sense is shown.

As in the previous experiment, similarity is annotated on a five-point-scale from 0 to 4. Although, we ask annotators to select senses for word pairs, we retrieve only one similarity rating for each word pair, which is the sense combination with the highest similarity.

No sense inventory To compare our results with the original dataset from Rubenstein and Goodenough (1965), we asked annotators to rate similarity of word pairs without any given sense repository, i.e. comparing words directly. The annotators reached an agreement of .73. The resulting gold standard has a high correlation with the original dataset (.923 Spearman and .938 Pearson). This is in line with our expectations and previous work that similarity ratings are stable across time (Bär et al., 2011).

Wikipedia sense inventory We now use the full functionality of our annotation tool and ask annotators to first, select senses for each word and second, rate the similarity. Possible senses and definitions for these senses are extracted from Wikipedia.[13] The same three annotators reached

[13] We use the English Wikipedia version from June 15th, 2010.

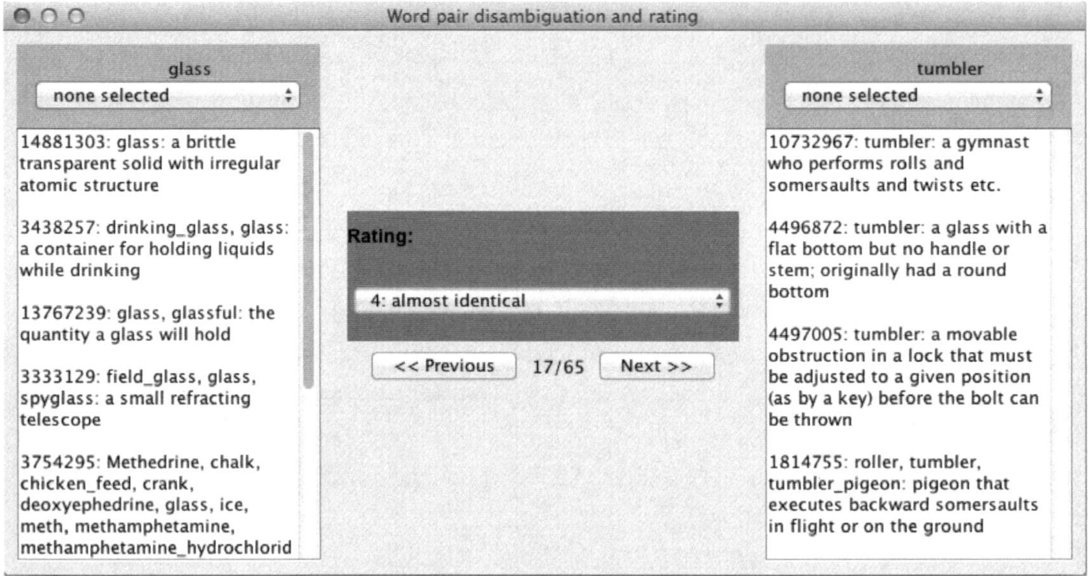

Figure 4: User interface for annotation studies: The example shows the word pair *glass—tumbler* with no senses selected. The interface shows WordNet definitons of possible senses in the text field below the sense selection. The highest similarity is selected as sense 4496872 for tumbler is a drinking glass.

an agreement of .66. The correlation to the original dataset is lower than for the re-rating (.881 Spearman, .896 Pearson). This effect is due to many entities in Wikipedia, which annotators would typically not know. Two annotators rated the word pair *graveyard—madhouse* with a rather high similarity because both are names of music bands (still no very high similarity because one is a rock and the other a jazz band).

WordNet sense inventory Similar to the previous experiment, we list possible senses for each word from a sense inventory. In this experiment, we use WordNet senses, thus, not using any named entity. The annotators reached an agreement of .73 and the resulting gold standard has a high correlation with the original dataset (.917 Spearman and .928 Pearson).

Figure 5 shows average annotator ratings in comparison to similarity judgments in the original dataset. All re-rating studies follow the general tendency of having higher annotator judgments for similar pairs. However, there is a strong fluctuation in the mid-similarity area (1 to 3). This is due to fewer word pairs with such a similarity.

4.1 Results & Discussion

We evaluate the similarity measures using Spearman and Pearson correlation with human similarity judgments. We calculate correlations to four human judgments: (i) from the original dataset (Orig.), (ii) from our re-rating study (Rerat.), (iii) from our study with senses from Wikipedia (WP), and (iv) with senses from WordNet (WN). Table 6 shows results for all described similarity measures.

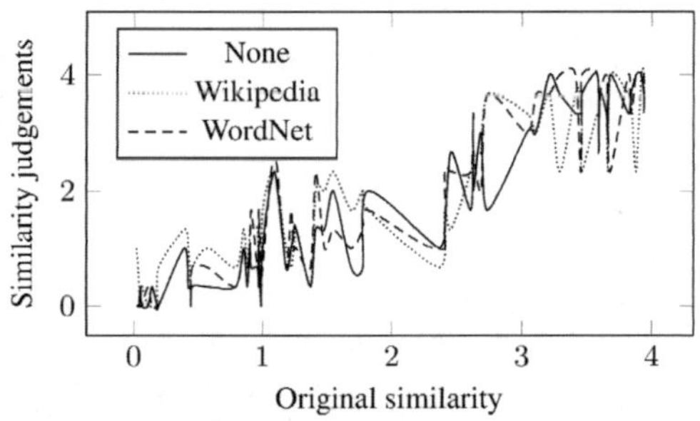

Figure 5: Correlation curve of rerating studies

ESA[14] achieves a Spearman correlation of .751 and a slightly higher correlation (.765) on our re-rating gold standard. Correlation then drops when compared to gold standards with senses from Wikipedia and WordNet. This is expected as the gold standard becomes more sense-aware.

Lin is based on senses in WordNet but still out-

[14]ESA is used with normalized text frequencies, a constant document frequency, and a cosine comparison of vectors.

measure	Spearman Orig.	Rerat.	WP	WN	Pearson Orig.	Rerat.	WP	WN
ESA	.751	.765	.704	.705	.647	.694	.678	.625
Lin	**.815**	.768	.705	.775	**.873**	**.840**	**.798**	**.846**
ESA on senses (lang. mod.)	.733	.765	.782	.751	.703	.739	.739	.695
ESA on senses (cosine)	.775	**.810**	**.826**	**.795**	.694	.712	.736	.699
WLM (in)	.716	.745	.754	.733	.708	.712	.740	.707
WLM (out)	.583	.607	.652	.599	.548	.583	.613	.568

Table 6: Correlation of similarity measures with a human gold standard on the word pairs by Rubenstein and Goodenough (1965). Best results for each gold standard are marked bold.

performs all other measures on the original gold standard. Correlation reaches a high value for the gold standard based on WordNet, as the same sense inventory for human annotations and measure is applied. Values for Pearson correlation emphasizes this effect: Lin reaches the maximum of .846 on the WordNet-based gold standard.

Correspondingly, the similarity measures ESA on senses and WLM reach their maximum on the Wikipedia-based gold standard. As for the ambiguous dataset in Section 3 ESA on senses outperforms both WLM variants. Cosine vector comparison again outperforms the language model variant for Spearman correlation but impairs it in terms of Pearson correlation. As before WLM (in) outperforms WLM (out) across all datasets and both correlation metrics.

Is word similarity sense-dependent? In general, sense-level similarity measures improve when evaluated with a sense-aware gold standard, while correlation with word-level similarity measures decreases. A further manual analysis shows that sense-level measures perform good when rating very similar word pairs. This is very useful for applications such as information retrieval where a user is only interested in very similar documents.

Our evaluation thus shows that word similarity should not be considered without considering the effect of the used sense inventory. The same annotators rate word pairs differently if they can specify senses explicitly (as seen in Table 3). Correspondingly, results for similarity measures depend on which senses can be selected. Wikipedia contains many entities, e.g. music bands or actors, while WordNet contains fine-grained senses for things (e.g. narrow senses of glass as shown in Figure 4). Using the same sense inventory as the one, which has been used in the annotation process, leads to a higher correlation.

5 Related Work

The work by Schwartz and Gomez (2011) is the closest to our approach in terms of sense annotated datasets. They compare several sense-level similarity measures based on the WordNet taxonomy on sense-annotated datasets. For their experiments, annotators were asked to select senses for every word pair in three similarity datasets. Annotators were not asked to re-rate the similarity of the word pairs, or the sense pairs, respectively. Instead, similarity judgments from the original datasets are used. Possible senses are given by WordNet and the authors report an inter-annotator agreement of .93 for the RG dataset.

The authors then compare Spearman correlation between human judgments and judgments from WordNet-based similarity measures. They focus on differences between similarity measures using the sense annotations and the maximum value for all possible senses. The authors do not report improvements across all measures and datasets. Of ten measures and three datasets, using sense annotations, improved results in nine cases. In 16 cases, results are higher when using the maximum similarity across all possible senses. In five cases, both measures yielded an equal correlation. The authors do not report any overall tendency of results. However, these experiments show that switching from words to senses has an effect on the performance of similarity measures.

The work by Hassan and Mihalcea (2011) is the closest to our approach in terms of similarity measures. They introduce Salient Semantic Analysis (SAS), which is a sense-level measure based on links and disambiguated senses in Wikipedia articles. They create a word-sense-matrix and compute similarity with a modified cosine metric. However, they apply additional normalization factors to optimize for the evaluation metrics which makes a direct comparison of word-level and sense-level variants difficult.

Meyer and Gurevych (2012a) analyze verb similarity with a corpus from Yang and Powers (2006) based on the work by Zesch et al. (2008). They apply variations of the similarity measure ESA by Gabrilovich and Markovitch (2007) using Wikipedia, Wiktionary, and WordNet. Meyer and Gurevych (2012a) report improvements using a disambiguated version of Wiktionary. Links in Wiktionary articles are disambiguated and thus transform the resource to a sense-based resource. In contrast to our work, they focus on the similarity of verbs (in comparison to nouns in this paper) and it applies disambiguation to improve the underlying resource, while we switch the level, which is processed by the measure to senses.

Shirakawa et al. (2013) apply ESA for computation of similarities between short texts. Texts are extended with Wikipedia articles, which is one step to a disambiguation of the input text. They report an improvement of the sense-extended ESA approach over the original version of ESA. In contrast to our work, the text itself is not changed and similarity is computed on the level of texts.

6 Summary and Future Work

In this work, we investigated word-level and sense-level similarity measures and investigated their strengths and shortcomings. We evaluated how correlations of similarity measures with a gold standard depend on the sense inventory used by the annotators.

We compared the similarity measures ESA (corpus-based), Lin (WordNet), and Wikipedia Link Measure (Wikipedia), and a sense-enabled version of ESA and evaluated them with a dataset containing ambiguous terms. Word-level measures were not able to differentiate between different senses of one word, while sense-level measures could even increase correlation when shifting to sense similarities. Sense-level measures obtained accuracies between .70 and .83 when deciding which of two sense pairs has a higher similarity.

We performed re-rating studies with three annotators based on the dataset by Rubenstein and Goodenough (1965). Annotators were asked to first annotate senses from Wikipedia and WordNet for word pairs and then judge their similarity based on the selected senses. We evaluated with these new human gold standards and found that correlation heavily depends on the resource used by the similarity measure and sense repository a human annotator selected. Sense-level similarity measures improve when evaluated with a sense-aware gold standard, while correlation with word-level similarity measures decreases. Using the same sense inventory as the one, which has been used in the annotation process, leads to a higher correlation. This has implications for creating word similarity datasets and evaluating similarity measures using different sense inventories.

In future work we would like to analyze how we can improve sense-level similarity measures by disambiguating a large document collection and thus retrieving more accurate frequency values. This might reduce the sparsity of term-document-matrices for ESA on senses. We plan to use word sense disambiguation components as a preprocessing step to evaluate whether sense similarity measures improve results for text similarity. Additionally, we plan to use sense alignments between WordNet and Wikipedia to enrich the term-document matrix with additional links based on semantic relations.

The datasets, annotation guidelines, and our experimental framework are publicly available in order to foster future research for computing sense similarity.[15]

Acknowledgments

This work has been supported by the Volkswagen Foundation as part of the Lichtenberg-Professorship Program under grant No. I/82806, by the Klaus Tschira Foundation under project No. 00.133.2008, and by the German Federal Ministry of Education and Research (BMBF) within the context of the Software Campus project *open window* under grant No. 01IS12054. The authors assume responsibility for the content. We thank Pedro Santos, Michèle Spankus and Markus Bücker for their valuable contribution. We thank the anonymous reviewers for their helpful comments.

[15] `www.ukp.tu-darmstadt.de/data/text-similarity/sense-similarity/`

References

Eneko Agirre and Philip Edmonds. 2006. *Word Sense Disambiguation: Algorithms and Applications*. Springer.

Satanjeev Banerjee and Ted Pedersen. 2002. An Adapted Lesk Algorithm for Word Sense Disambiguation using WordNet. In *Computational Linguistics and Intelligent Text*, pages 136—-145.

Daniel Bär, Torsten Zesch, and Iryna Gurevych. 2011. A Reflective View on Text Similarity. In *Proceedings of the International Conference on Recent Advances in Natural Language Processing*, pages 515–520, Hissar, Bulgaria.

Alexander Budanitsky and Graeme Hirst. 2006. Evaluating WordNet-based Measures of Lexical Semantic Relatedness. *Computational Linguistics*, 32(1):13–47.

Evgeniy Gabrilovich and Shaul Markovitch. 2007. Computing Semantic Relatedness using Wikipedia-based Explicit Semantic Analysis. In *Proceedings of the 20th International Joint Conference on Artifical Intelligence*, pages 1606–1611.

Gregory Grefenstette. 1992. Sextant: Exploring Unexplored Contexts for Semantic Extraction from Syntactic Analysis. In *Proceedings of the 30th Annual Meeting of the Association for Computational Linguistics*, pages 324—-326, Newark, Delaware, USA. Association for Computational Linguistics.

Samer Hassan and Rada Mihalcea. 2011. Semantic Relatedness Using Salient Semantic Analysis. In *Proceedings of the 25th AAAI Conference on Artificial Intelligence, (AAAI 2011)*, pages 884–889, San Francisco, CA, USA.

Jay J Jiang and David W Conrath. 1997. Semantic Similarity based on Corpus Statistics and Lexical Taxonomy. In *Proceedings of 10th International Conference Research on Computational Linguistics*, pages 1–15.

Dekang Lin. 1998. An Information-theoretic Definition of Similarity. In *In Proceedings of the International Conference on Machine Learning*, volume 98, pages 296—-304.

Christian M. Meyer and Iryna Gurevych. 2012a. To Exhibit is not to Loiter: A Multilingual, Sense-Disambiguated Wiktionary for Measuring Verb Similarity. In *Proceedings of the 24th International Conference on Computational Linguistics*, pages 1763–1780, Mumbai, India.

Christian M. Meyer and Iryna Gurevych. 2012b. Wiktionary: A new rival for expert-built lexicons? Exploring the possibilities of collaborative lexicography. In Sylviane Granger and Magali Paquot, editors, *Electronic Lexicography*, chapter 13, pages 259–291. Oxford University Press, Oxford, UK, November.

David Milne and Ian H Witten. 2008. Learning to Link with Wikipedia. In *Proceedings of the 17th ACM Conference on Information and Knowledge Management*, pages 509—-518.

David Milne. 2007. Computing Semantic Relatedness using Wikipedia Link Structure. In *Proceedings of the New Zealand Computer Science Research Student Conference*.

Roberto Navigli. 2009. Word Sense Disambiguation: A Survey. *ACM Computing Surveys*, 41(2):1–69.

Philip Resnik. 1999. Semantic Similarity in a Taxonomy: An Information-based Measure and its Application to Problems of Ambiguity in Natural Language. *Journal of Artificial Intelligence Research*, 11:95–130.

Herbert Rubenstein and John B Goodenough. 1965. Contextual Correlates of Synonymy. *Communications of the ACM*, 8(10):627—-633.

Hansen A Schwartz and Fernando Gomez. 2011. Evaluating Semantic Metrics on Tasks of Concept Similarity. In *FLAIRS Conference*.

Nuno Seco, Tony Veale, and Jer Hayes. 2004. An Intrinsic Information Content Metric for Semantic Similarity in WordNet. In *Proceedings of European Conference for Artificial Intelligence*, number Ic, pages 1089–1093.

Masumi Shirakawa, Kotaro Nakayama, Takahiro Hara, and Shojiro Nishio. 2013. Probabilistic Semantic Similarity Measurements for Noisy Short Texts using Wikipedia Entities. In *Proceedings of the 22nd ACM International Conference on Information & Knowledge Management*, pages 903–908, New York, New York, USA. ACM Press.

Dongqiang Yang and David MW Powers. 2006. Verb Similarity on the Taxonomy of WordNet. In *Proceedings of GWC-06*, pages 121—-128.

Torsten Zesch, Christof Müller, and Iryna Gurevych. 2008. Using Wiktionary for Computing Semantic Relatedness. In *Proceedings of the Twenty-Third AAAI Conference on Artificial Intelligence*, pages 861–867, Chicago, IL, USA.

An Iterative 'Sudoku Style' Approach to Subgraph-based Word Sense Disambiguation

Steve L. Manion
University of Canterbury
Christchurch, New Zealand
steve.manion
@pg.canterbury.ac.nz

Raazesh Sainudiin
University of Canterbury
Christchurch, New Zealand
r.sainudiin
@math.canterbury.ac.nz

Abstract

We introduce an *iterative* approach to subgraph-based Word Sense Disambiguation (WSD). Inspired by the Sudoku puzzle, it significantly improves the *precision* and *recall* of disambiguation. We describe how *conventional* subgraph-based WSD treats the two steps of (1) subgraph construction and (2) disambiguation via graph centrality measures as ordered and atomic. Consequently, researchers tend to focus on improving either of these two steps individually, overlooking the fact that these steps can complement each other if they are allowed to interact in an iterative manner. We tested our iterative approach against the conventional approach for a range of well-known graph centrality measures and subgraph types, at the sentence and document level. The results demonstrated that an average performing WSD system which embraces the iterative approach, can easily compete with state-of-the-art. This alone warrants further investigation.

1 Introduction

Explicit WSD is a two-step process of analysing a word's contextual use then deducing its intended sense. When Kilgarriff (1998) established SENSEVAL, the collaborative framework and forum to evaluate WSD, unsupervised systems performed poorly in comparison to their supervised counterparts (Palmer et al., 2001; Snyder and Palmer, 2004). A review of the literature shows there has been a healthy *rivalry* between the two, in which proponents of unsupervised WSD have long sought to vindicate its potential since two decades ago (Yarowsky, 1995) to even more recent times (Ponzetto and Navigli, 2010).

As Pedersen (2007) rightly states, supervised systems are bound by their training data, and therefore are limited in portability and flexibility in the face of new domains, changing applications, or different languages. This *knowledge acquisition bottleneck*, coined by Gale et al. (1992), can be alleviated by unsupervised systems that exploit the portability and flexibility of Lexical Knowledge Bases (LKBs). As of 2007, SENSEVAL became SEMEVAL, offering a more diverse range of semantic tasks. Unsupervised knowledge-based WSD has since had its performance evaluated in terms of *granularity* (Navigli et al., 2007), *domain* (Agirre et al., 2010), and *cross/multi-linguality* (Lefever and Hoste, 2010; Lefever and Hoste, 2013; Navigli et al., 2013). Results from these tasks have demonstrated unsupervised systems are now a competitive and robust alternative to supervised systems, especially given the ever changing task-orientated settings WSD is evaluated in.

One such class of unsupervised knowledge-based WSD systems that we seek to improve in this paper constructs semantic subgraphs from LKBs, and then runs graph-based centrality measures such as PageRank (Brin and Page, 1998) over them to finally select the senses (as nodes) ranked as the most relevant. This class is known as *subgraph-based* WSD, characterised over the last decade by performing the two key steps of (1) subgraph construction and (2) disambiguation via graph centrality measures, in an ordered atomic sequence. We refer to this characteristic as the *conventional* approach to subgraph-based WSD. We propose an *iterative* approach to subgraph-based WSD that allows for interaction between the two major steps in an incremental manner

*Proceedings of the Third Joint Conference on Lexical and Computational Semantics (*SEM 2014)*, pages 40–50,
Dublin, Ireland, August 23-24 2014.

and demonstrate its effectiveness across a range of graph-based centrality measures and subgraph construction methods at the sentence and document levels of disambiguation.

2 The Conventional Subgraph Approach

The *conventional* approach to subgraph WSD firstly benefits from some preprocessing, in which words in a sequence $\mathcal{W}$, are mapped to their lemmatisations[1] in a set $\mathcal{L}$, such that $(w_1, ..., w_m) \mapsto \{\ell_1, ..., \ell_m\}$. This facilitates better lexical alignment with the LKB to be exploited. Let this LKB be a large semantic graph $\mathcal{G} = (\mathcal{S}, \mathcal{E})$, such that $\mathcal{S}$ is a set of vertices representing all known word senses, and $\mathcal{E}$ be a set of edges defining semantic relationships that exist between senses. Now given we wish to disambiguate $\ell_i \in \mathcal{L}$, let $R(\ell_i)$ be a function that *Retrieves* from $\mathcal{G}$, all the senses, $\{s_{i,1}, s_{i,2}, ..., s_{i,k}\}$, that ℓ_i could refer to, noting that i is an anchor to the original word w_i.

2.1 Step 1: Subgraph Construction

For unsupervised subgraph-based WSD, the key publications that have advanced the field broadly construct subgraph, $\mathcal{G}_\mathcal{L}$, as either a union of *subtree paths*, *shortest paths*, or *local edges*[2]. First we initialise $\mathcal{G}_\mathcal{L}$, by setting $\mathcal{S}_\mathcal{L} := \bigcup_{i=1}^{n} R(\ell_i)$ and $\mathcal{E}_\mathcal{L} := \emptyset$. Next we add edges to $\mathcal{E}_\mathcal{L}$, depending on the desired subgraph type, by adding either the:

(a) *Subtree paths* of up to length L, via a Depth-First Search (DFS) of $\mathcal{G}$. In brief, **for each** sense $s_a \in \mathcal{S}_\mathcal{L}$, **if** a new sense $s_b \in \mathcal{S}_\mathcal{L}$, i.e. $s_b \neq s_a$, is encountered along a path $P_{a \to b} = \{\{s_a, s\}, ..., \{s', s_b\}\}$ with path-length $|P_{a \to b}| \leq L$, **then** add $P_{a \to b}$ to $\mathcal{G}_\mathcal{L}$. [cf. Navigli and Velardi (2005), Navigli and Lapata (2007), or Navigli and Lapata (2010)]

(b) *Shortest paths*, via a Breadth-First Search (BFS) of $\mathcal{G}$. In brief, **for each** sense pair $s_a, s_b \in \mathcal{S}_\mathcal{L}$, find the shortest path $P_{a \to b} = \{\{s_a, s\}, ..., \{s', s_b\}\}$; **if** such a path $P_{a \to b}$ exists and (optionally) $|P_{a \to b}| \leq L$, **then** add $P_{a \to b}$ to $\mathcal{G}_\mathcal{L}$ [cf. Agirre and Soroa (2008), Agirre and Soroa (2009), or Gutiérrez et al. (2013)]

(c) *Local edges* up to a local distance D. In brief, **for each** sense pair $s_a, s_b \in \mathcal{S}_\mathcal{L}$, **if** the distance in the text $|b - a|$ between the corresponding words w_a and w_b satisfies $|b - a| \leq D$, **then** add edge $\{s_a, s_b\}$ to $\mathcal{G}_\mathcal{L}$ (preferably with edge-weights). [cf. Mihalcea (2005) or Sinha and Mihalcea (2007)] (Note that this subgraph is a hybrid, because only its vertices belong to $\mathcal{G}$)

In practice, subgraph edges may be *directed*, *weighted*, *collapsed*, or *filtered*. However to keep the distinctions between subgraph types simple, we do not include this in our formalisation.

2.2 Step 2: Disambiguation

To disambiguate each lemma $\ell_i \in \mathcal{L}$, its corresponding senses, $R(\ell_i) = \{s_{i,1}, s_{i,2}, ..., s_{i,k}\}$, are scored by a graph-based centrality measure ϕ, over subgraph $\mathcal{G}_\mathcal{L}$, to estimate the most appropriate sense, $\hat{s}_{i,*} = \arg\max_{s_{i,j} \in R(\ell_i)} \phi(s_{i,j})$. The estimated sense $\hat{s}_{i,*}$ is then assigned to word w_i.

2.3 Algorithm for Conventional Approach

With both steps formalised, we can now illustrate the conventional subgraph approach in Algorithm 1. Let $\mathcal{L}$ be taken as *input*, and let the disambiguation results $\mathcal{D} = \{\hat{s}_{1,*}, ..., \hat{s}_{m,*}\}$ be produced as *output* to assign to $\mathcal{W} = (w_1, ..., w_m)$.

Algorithm 1: Conventional Approach

```
Input: L
Output: D
D ← ∅;
G_L ← ConstructSubGraph(L);
foreach ℓ_i ∈ L do
    ŝ_{i,*} ← argmax_{s_{i,j} ∈ R(ℓ_i)} φ(s_{i,j});
    put ŝ_{i,*} in D;
```

To begin with, $\mathcal{D}$ is initialised as an empty set and ConstructSubGraph($\mathcal{L}$) constructs one of the three subgraphs described in section 2.1. Next for each $\ell_i \in \mathcal{L}$, by running a graph based centrality measure ϕ over $\mathcal{G}_\mathcal{L}$, the most appropriate sense $\hat{s}_{i,*}$ is estimated, and placed in set $\mathcal{D}$. Effectively, $\mathcal{L}$ is a context window based on document or sentence size, therefore this algorithm is run for each context window division. Note that Algorithm 1 would require a little extra complexity to handle local edge subgraphs, due to its context window needing to satisfy $\mathcal{L} = \{\ell_{i-D}, ..., \ell_{i+D}\}$.

[1] For a detailed explanation of the processes leading up to lemmatisation (and beyond), *see* Navigli (2009, p12)

[2] 'Local' describes the *local context*, typically this is the 2 or 3 words either side of a word, *see* Yarowsky (1993)

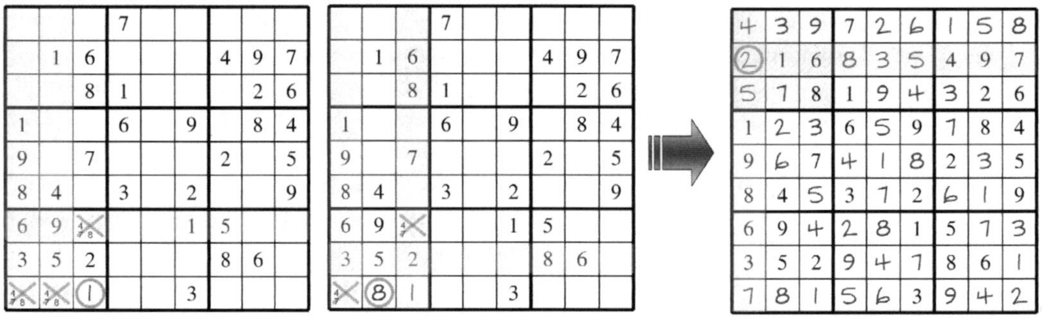

(a) 1st Row/Column Elimination (b) 2nd Row/Column Elimination (c) Row/Column/Box Completion

Figure 1: Iterative Solving of Sudoku Grids

3 The Iterative Subgraph Approach

3.1 What is Iterative WSD?

The key observation to make about the conventional approach in Algorithm 1, is for input $\mathcal{L}$, constructing subgraph $\mathcal{G}_{\mathcal{L}}$ and performing disambiguation are two ordered atomic steps. Notice that there is no iteration between them, because the first step of subgraph construction is never revisited for each $\mathcal{L}$. For the conventional process to be iterative, then for $\ell_a, \ell_b \in \mathcal{L}$ a previous disambiguation of ℓ_a, would need to influence a consecutive disambiguation of ℓ_b, through an iterative re-construction of $\mathcal{G}_{\mathcal{L}}$ between each disambiguation. This key difference illustrated by Figure 2, is the level of iterative WSD we aspire to.

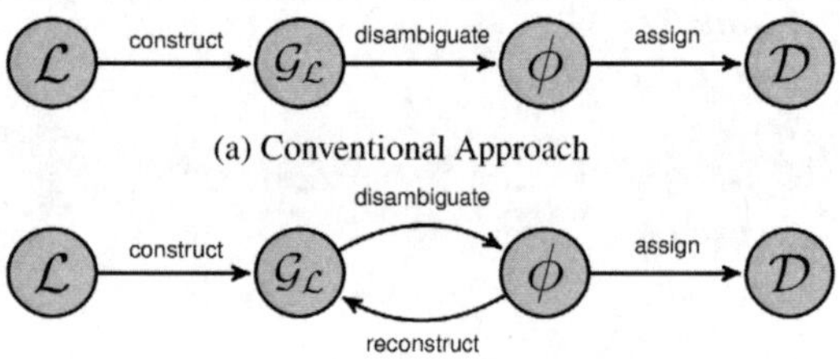

(a) Conventional Approach

(b) Interactively Iterative Approach

Figure 2: The Key Difference In Approach

It is important to note, the term *iterative* can already be found in WSD literature, therefore we take the opportunity here to make a distinction. Firstly, a graph based centrality measure ϕ may be iterative, such as PageRank (Brin and Page, 1998) or Hyperlink-Induced Topic Search (HITS) (Kleinberg, 1999). In the experiments by Mihalcea (2005) in which PageRank was run over *local edge* subgraphs (as described in 2.1 (c)), it is easy to perceive the WSD process itself as iterative.

Iteration can again be taken further, as observed with Personalised PageRank in which Agirre and Soroa (2009) apply the idea of biasing values in the random surfing vector, v, (*see* (Haveliwala, 2003)). For their run labelled "Ppr_w2w", in order to avoid senses anchored to the same lemma assisting each other's ϕ score, the random surfing vector v is iteratively updated as ℓ_i changes, to ensure context senses $s_{a,j} \in v$ such that $a \neq i$ are the only senses that receive probability mass.

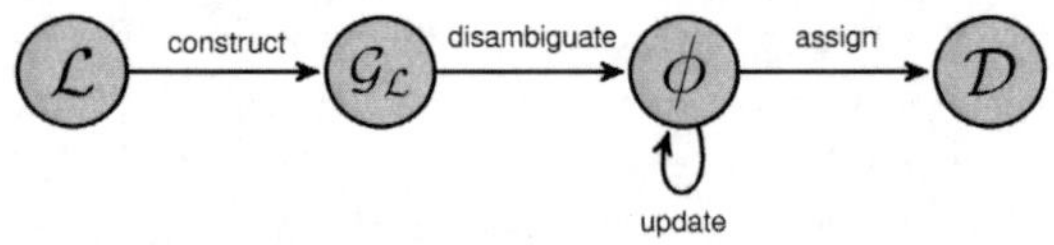

Figure 3: Atomically Iterative Approach

In summary, iteration in the literature either describes ϕ as being iterative or being iteratively adjusted, both of which are contained in the disambiguation step alone as shown in Figure 3. This is iteration at the atomic level and should not be conflated with the interactive level of iteration that we propose as seen in Figure 2 (b).

3.2 Iteratively Solving a Sudoku Grid

In Figures 1 (a), (b), and (c), we observe the solving of a Sudoku puzzle, in which the numbers from 1 to 9 must be assigned only once to each *column*, *row*, and 3x3 *square*. Each time a number is assigned and the Sudoku grid is updated, this is an *iteration*. For example, in the south west square of grid (a) (i.e. Figure 1 (a)) unknown cells can be assigned $\{1, 4, 7, 8\}$. Given that 1 has already been assigned to the 7th row and the 1st and 2nd columns, this singles it down to one cell it can be assigned to. The iteration of grid

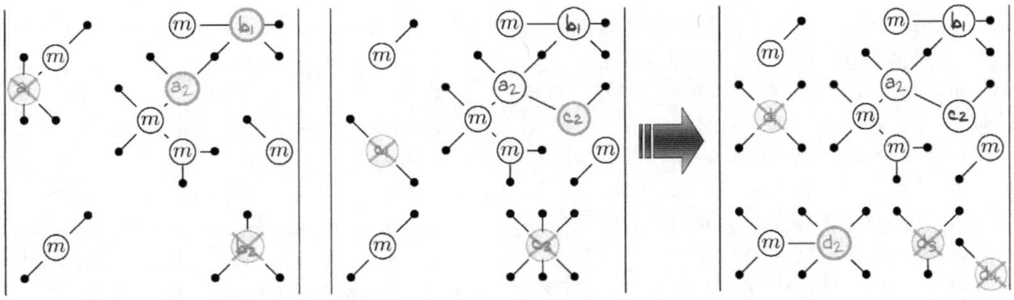

(a) x2 Bi-semous Eliminations (b) x1 Tri-semous Elimination (c) (ρ_{max})-semous Completion

Figure 4: Iterative Disambiguating of Subgraphs

(a), now makes possible the iteration of grid (b) to eliminate the number 8 as the only possibility for its assigned cell. This iterative process continues until we reach the completed puzzle in grid (c). Therefore in WSD terminology, with each cell we *disambiguate*, a new grid is *constructed*, in which knowledge is passed on to each consecutive iteration.

Continuing with this line of thought, each unsolved cell is *ambiguous*, with a degree of *polysemy* ρ, such that $\rho_{max} \leq 9$. Again, the initial Sudoku grid has pre-solved cells, of which are *monosemous*. This brings us to another key observation. Typically in Sudoku, it is necessary to solve the least polysemous cells first, before you can solve the more polysemous cells with a certainty. As the conventional approach exhibits no Sudoku-like iteration, cells are solved without regard to the ρ value of the cell, or any interactive exploitation of previously solved cells.

3.3 Iteratively Constructing a Subgraph

In our 'Sudoku style' approach, we propose disambiguating each ℓ_i in order of increasing polysemy ρ, iteratively reconstructing subgraph $\mathcal{G}_\mathcal{L}$ to reflect 1) previous disambiguations and 2) the ρ value of lemmas being disambiguated in the current iteration. This is illustrated in Figures 4 (a), (b), and (c) above.

Let m-labelled vertices describe monosemous lemmas. In graph (a) (i.e. Figure 4) we observe two bi-semous lemmas, a and b, in which our arbitrary graph-based centrality measure ϕ has selected the second sense of a (i.e. a_2) and the first sense of b (i.e. b_1) to be placed in $\mathcal{D}$. For the next iteration, you will notice the alternative senses for a and b are removed from $\mathcal{G}_\mathcal{L}$ for the disambiguation of tri-semous lemma c. The second sense of lemma c manages to be selected by ϕ with the help of the previous disambiguation of lemma a. This interactive and iterative process continues until we reach the most polysemous lemma, which in our example is d with $\rho_{max} = 4$ in graph (c).

3.4 Algorithm for Iterative Approach

We can formally describe what is happening in Figure 4 with Algorithm 2. Effectively, this is a recreation of Algorithm 1, which highlights the differences in the conventional and iterative approach.

Algorithm 2: Iterative Approach

Input: $\mathcal{L}$
Output: $\mathcal{D}$
$\mathcal{D} \leftarrow$ `GetMonosemous` ($\mathcal{L}$);
$\mathcal{A} \leftarrow \emptyset$;
for $\rho \leftarrow 2$ **to** ρ_{max} **do**
  $\mathcal{A} \leftarrow$ `AddPolysemous` ($\mathcal{L}, \rho$);
  $\mathcal{G}_\mathcal{L} \leftarrow$ `ConstructSubGraph` ($\mathcal{A},\mathcal{D}$);
  foreach $\ell_i \in \mathcal{A}$ **do**
    $\hat{s}_{i,*} \leftarrow \arg\max_{s_{i,j} \in S(\ell_i)} \phi(s_{i,j})$;
    if $\hat{s}_{i,*}$ *exists* **then**
      remove ℓ_i from $\mathcal{A}$;
      put $\hat{s}_{i,*}$ in $\mathcal{D}$;

Firstly, as it reads `GetMonosemous`($\mathcal{L}$) places all the senses of the monosemous lemmas into the set of *disambiguated* lemmas $\mathcal{D}$. This is the equivalent of copying out an unsolved Sudoku grid onto a piece of paper and adding in all the initial hint numbers. Next the set $\mathcal{A}$ which holds all *ambiguous* lemmas of polysemy $\leq \rho$ is initialised as an empty set. Now we are ready to iterate through values of ρ, beginning from the first iteration, by adding all bi-semous lemmas to

$\mathcal{A}$ with the function AddPolysemous($\mathcal{L}, \rho$), notice ρ places a restriction on the degree of polysemy a lemma $\ell_i \in \mathcal{L}$ can have before being added to $\mathcal{A}$.

We are now ready to create the first subgraph $\mathcal{G}_\mathcal{L}$ with function ConstructSubGraph($\mathcal{A}, \mathcal{D}$). This previously used function in Algorithm 1, is now modified to take the ambiguous lemmas of polysemy $\leq \rho$ in set $\mathcal{A}$ and previously disambiguated lemma senses in set $\mathcal{D}$. The resulting graph has a limited degree of polysemy and is constructed based on previous disambiguations.

From this point on the given graph centrality measure ϕ is run over $\mathcal{G}_\mathcal{L}$. For the lemmas that are disambiguated, they are removed from $\mathcal{A}$ and the selected sense is added to $\mathcal{D}$. For those lemmas that are not (i.e. $\hat{s}_{i,*}$ does not exist[3]) they remain in $\mathcal{A}$ to be involved in reattempted disambiguations in consecutive iterations. As more lemmas are disambiguated, it is more likely that previously difficult to disambiguate lemmas become much easier to solve, just like at the end of a Sudoku puzzle it gets easier as you get closer to completing it.

4 Evaluations

In our evaluations we set out to understand a number of aspects. The first evaluation is a *proof of concept*, to understand whether an iterative approach to subgraph WSD can in fact achieve better performance than the conventional approach. The second set of experiments seeks to understand how the iterative approach works and the performance *benefits* and *penalties* of implementing the iterative approach. Finally the third experiment is an *elementary attempt* at optimising the iterative approach to defeat the MFS baseline.

4.1 LKB & Dataset

For an evaluation, we have chosen the multilingual LKB known as BabelNet (Navigli and Ponzetto, 2012a). It weaves together several other LKBs, most notably WordNet (Fellbaum, 1998) and Wikipedia. It also can be easily accessed with the BabelNet API, of which we have built our code base around. All experiments are conducted on the most recent SemEval WSD dataset, of which is the SemEval 2013 Task 12 Multilingual WSD (English) data set.

[3]This can happen if ℓ_i does not map to any senses, or alternatively all the senses that are mapped to are filtered out of the subgraph before disambiguation (explained later).

4.2 Graph Centrality Measures Evaluated

To demonstrate the effectiveness of our iterative approach, we selected a range of WSD graph-based centrality measures often experimented with in the literature. Firstly ϕ does not need to be a complicated measure, this is demonstrated by the success of ranking senses by their number of incoming and outgoing edges. Even though it is very simple, it performs surprisingly well against others for both In-Degree (Navigli and Lapata, 2007) and Out-Degree (Navigli and Ponzetto, 2012a)

Next we employ graph centrality measures that are primarily used to disambiguate the *semantic web*, such as PageRank (Brin and Page, 1998), HITS Kleinberg (1999), and a *personalised* PageRank (Haveliwala, 2003); which have since been applied to WSD by Mihalcea (2005), Navigli and Lapata (2007), and Agirre and Soroa (2009) respectively. We also include Betweeness Centrality (Freeman, 1979) which is taken from the analysis of social networks.

These methods are well known and applied across many disciplines, therefore we will leave it to the reader to follow up on the specifics of these graph centrality measures. However we do explicitly define our last measure, Sum Inverse Path Length (Navigli and Ponzetto, 2012a; Navigli and Ponzetto, 2012b) in Equation (1) which was designed with WSD in mind, thus is less well known.

$$\phi(s) = \sum_{p \in P_{s \rightarrow c}} \frac{1}{e^{|p|-1}} \qquad (1)$$

This measure scores a sense by summing up the scores of all paths that connect to other senses in $\mathcal{G}_\mathcal{L}$ (i.e. senses that are not intermediate nodes, but have a mapping back to a lemma in the context window $\mathcal{L}$). In the words of Navigli and Ponzetto (2012a), $P_{s \rightarrow c}$ is the set of paths connecting s to other senses of context words, with $|p|$ as the number of edges in the path p and each path is scored with the exponential inverse decay of the path length.

4.3 Experiment 1: Proof of Concept

4.3.1 Experiment 1: Setup

For this experiment we simply set out to see how the iterative approach performed compared to the conventional approach in a range of experimental conditions. Directed and unweighted subgraphs were used, namely subtree paths and shortest paths subgraphs with $L = 2$. To address the issue of

$\mathcal{G}_{\mathcal{L}}$	ϕ	Conventional Doc			Iterative Doc			Improvement		
		P	R	F	P	R	F	ΔP	ΔR	ΔF
SubTree Paths	In-Degree	**61.70**	**55.51**	**58.44**	**65.39**	**63.74**	**64.55**	+3.69	+8.23	+6.11
	Out-Degree	54.23	48.78	51.36	57.70	56.23	56.96	+3.47	+7.45	+5.60
	Betweenness Centrality	59.29	53.34	56.15	63.43	61.82	62.61	+4.14	+8.48	+6.46
	Sum Inverse Path Length	56.58	50.90	53.59	58.86	57.37	58.11	+2.28	+6.47	+4.52
	HITS(hub)	54.69	49.20	51.80	59.71	58.20	58.95	**+5.02**	**+9.00**	**+7.15**
	HITS(authority)	57.45	51.68	54.41	61.62	60.06	60.83	+4.17	+8.38	+6.42
	PageRank	60.09	54.06	56.91	64.07	62.44	63.24	+3.98	+8.38	+6.33
Shortest Paths	In-Degree	**63.06**	**56.08**	**59.36**	65.36	63.06	64.19	+2.30	+6.98	+4.83
	Out-Degree	57.07	50.75	53.72	61.14	58.90	60.01	+4.07	+8.15	+6.29
	Betweenness Centrality	60.33	53.65	56.79	**65.52**	**63.22**	**64.35**	**+5.19**	**+9.57**	**+7.56**
	Sum Inverse Path Length	57.53	51.16	54.16	61.19	58.98	60.06	+3.66	+7.82	+5.90
	HITS(hub)	57.48	51.11	54.11	62.14	59.96	61.03	+4.66	+8.85	+6.92
	HITS(authority)	60.91	54.16	57.34	63.54	61.30	62.40	+2.63	+7.14	+5.06
	PageRank	61.14	54.37	57.55	65.25	62.96	64.09	+4.11	+8.59	+6.54

Table 1: Improvements of using the Iterative Approach at the Document Level

$\mathcal{G}_{\mathcal{L}}$	ϕ	Conventional Sent			Iterative Sent			Improvement		
		P	R	F	P	R	F	ΔP	ΔR	ΔF
SubTree Paths	In-Degree	**60.83**	**50.70**	**55.30**	**61.80**	**56.23**	**58.88**	+0.97	+5.53	+3.58
	Out-Degree	56.18	46.82	51.07	59.64	54.11	56.74	+3.46	+7.29	+5.67
	Betweenness Centrality	59.40	49.51	54.01	61.66	56.08	58.74	+2.26	+6.57	+4.73
	Sum Inverse Path Length	56.68	47.23	51.52	59.45	54.00	56.60	+2.77	+6.77	+5.08
	HITS(hub)	55.49	46.25	50.45	59.51	54.06	56.65	**+4.02**	**+7.81**	**+6.20**
	HITS(authority)	56.80	47.34	51.64	60.30	54.84	57.44	+3.50	+7.50	+5.80
	PageRank	59.71	49.77	54.29	60.56	55.04	57.67	+0.85	+5.27	+3.38
Shortest Paths	In-Degree	**58.13**	**32.75**	**41.89**	63.79	42.11	50.73	+5.66	+9.36	+8.84
	Out-Degree	54.64	30.78	39.38	61.79	40.66	49.05	**+7.15**	**+9.88**	**+9.67**
	Betweenness Centrality	57.94	32.64	41.76	**64.11**	**42.32**	**50.98**	+6.17	+9.68	+9.22
	Sum Inverse Path Length	55.65	31.35	40.11	62.39	41.02	49.50	+6.74	+9.67	+9.39
	HITS(hub)	56.11	31.61	40.44	62.74	41.28	49.80	+6.63	+9.67	+9.36
	HITS(authority)	55.74	31.40	40.17	62.74	41.28	49.80	+7.00	+9.88	+9.36
	PageRank	57.58	32.44	41.50	63.82	42.16	50.78	+6.24	+9.72	+9.28

Table 2: Improvements of using the Iterative Approach at the Sentence Level

senses anchored to the same lemma assisting each other's ϕ score (as discussed in Section 3.1), the `SENSE_SHIFTS` filter that is provided by the BabelNet API was also applied. This filter removes any path $P_{a \to b}$ such that $s_a, s_b \in R(\ell_i)$. Disambiguation was attempted at the document and sentence level, making use of the eight well-known graph centrality measures listed in section 4.2. For this experiment no means of optimisation were applied. Therefore Personalised PageRank was not used, and traditional PageRank took on a uniform random surfing vector. Default values of 0.85 and 30 for damping factor and maximum iterations were set respectively.

4.3.2 Experiment 1: Observations

First and foremost, it is clear from Table 1 and 2 that the iterative approach outperforms the conventional approach, regardless of the subgraph used, level of disambiguation, or the graph centrality measure employed. Since no graph centrality measure or subgraph were optimised, let this experiment prove that the iterative approach has the potential to improve any WSD system that implements it.

At the document level for both subgraphs the F-Scores were very close to the Most Frequent Sense (MFS) baseline for this task of 66.50. It is notoriously hard to beat and only one team (Gutiérrez et al., 2013) managed to beat it for this task. For all subtree subgraphs, we observe that In-Degree is clearly the best choice of centrality measure, while HITS (hub) enjoys the most improvement. We also observe that applying the iterative approach to Betweenness Centrality on shortest paths is a great combination at both the document and sentence level, most probably due to the measure being based on shortest paths. Furthermore it is worth noting, the results at the sentence level for all graph centrality measures on shortest path subgraphs are quite poor, but highly improved, this is likely to our restriction of $L = 2$ causing the subgraphs to be much sparser and broken up into many components.

We also provide here an example from the data set in which the incorrect disambiguation of the lemma *cup* via the conventional approach was corrected by the iterative approach. This example is the seventh sentence in the eleventh document (`d011.s007`). Each word's degree of polysemy is denoted in square brackets.

"Spanish **[1]football players** playing in the All-Star **[4]League** and in powerful **[12]clubs** of the **[2]Premier League** of **[9]England** are during the **[5]year** very active in **[4]league** and local **[8]cup [7]competitions** and there are high-level **[25]shocks** in the **[10]European Cups** and **[2]European Champions League**."

The potential graph constructed from this sentence is illustrated in Figure 5 as a shortest paths subgraph. The darker edges portray the subgraph iteratively constructed up to a polysemy $\rho \leq 8$ (in order to disambiguate *cup*), whereas the lighter edges portray the greater subgraph constructed if the conventional approach is employed. Note that although the lemma *cup* has eight senses, only three are shown due to the application of the previously mentioned SENSE_SHIFTS filter. The remaining five senses of *cup* were filtered out since they were not able to link to a sense up to $L = 2$ hops away that is anchored to an alterative lemma.

- **cup#1** - A small open container usually used for drinking; usually has a handle.
- **cup#7** - The hole (or metal container in the hole) on a golf green.
- **cup#8** - A large metal vessel with two handles that is awarded as a trophy to the winner of a competition.

Given the context, the eighth sense of cup is the correct sense, the type we know as a trophy. For the conventional approach, if ϕ is a centrality measure of Out-Degree then the eighth sense of cup is easily chosen by having one extra outgoing edge than the other two senses for *cup*. Yet if ϕ is a centrality measure of In-Degree or Betweenness Centrality, all three senses of cup now have the same score, zero. Therefore in our results the first sense is chosen which is incorrect. On the other hand, if

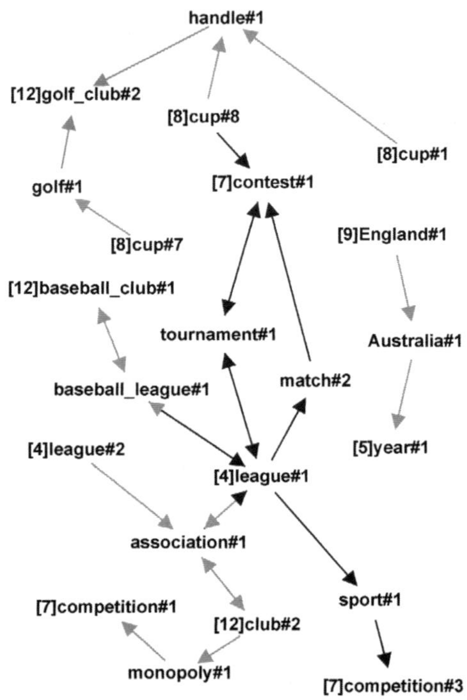

Figure 5: Conventional vs Iterative Subgraph

the subgraph was constructed iteratively with disambiguation results providing feedback to consecutive constructions, this could have been avoided. The shortest paths cup#1→handle#1→golf_club#2 and cup#7→golf#1→golf_club#2 only exist because the sense golf_club#2 (anchored to the more polysemous lemma *club*) is present, if it was not then the SENSE_SHIFTS filter would have removed these alternative senses. This demonstrates that if the senses of more polysemous lemmas are introduced into the subgraph too soon, they can interfere rather than help with disambiguation.

Secondly with each disambiguation at lower levels of polysemy, a more stable context is constructed to perform the disambiguation of much more polysemous lemmas later. Therefore in Figure 5 an iteratively constructed subgraph with *cup* already disambiguated, would mean the other two senses of *cup* would no longer be present. This ensures that club#2 (the correct answer) would have a much stronger chance of being selected than golf_club#2, which would have only one incoming edge from handle#1. Note the conventional approach would lend golf_club#2 one extra incoming edge than club#2 has, which could be problematic if ϕ is a centrality measure of In-Degree.

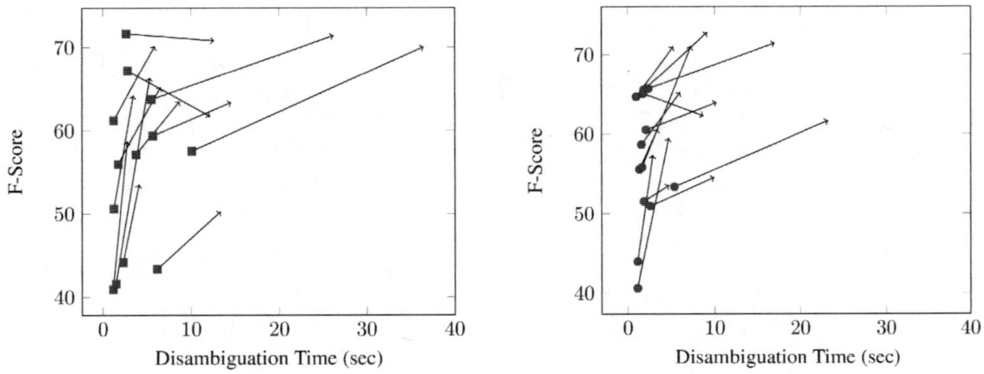

(a) ϕ = Betweenness Centrality

(b) ϕ = PageRank

Figure 6: For each of the 13 documents, performance (F-Score) is plotted against time to disambiguate, for $\mathcal{G}_{\mathcal{L}}$ = Shortest Paths. The squares (PageRank) and circles (Betweenness Centrality) plot the conventional approach. The arrows show the effect caused by applying the iterative approach, with the arrow head marking its F-Score and time to disambiguate.

4.4 Experiment 2: Performance

4.4.1 Experiment 2: Setup

An obvious caveat of the iterative approach is that it requires the construction of several subgraphs as ρ increases, which of course will require extra computation and time which is a penalty for the improved precision and recall. We decided to investigate the extent to which this happens. We selected Betweenness Centrality and PageRank from Experiment 1, in which both use shortest path subgraphs at the document level. This is because a) they acquired good results at the document level and b) with only 13 documents there are less data points on the plots making it easier to read as opposed to the hundreds of sentences.

4.4.2 Experiment 2: Observations

Firstly from Figures 6(a) and (b) we see that there is a substantial improvement in F-Score for almost all documents, except for two for ϕ = Betweenness Centrality and one for ϕ = PageRank. With some exceptions, for most documents the increased amount of time to disambiguate is not unreasonable. For this experiment, applying the iterative approach to Betweenness Centrality resulted in a mean 231% increase in processing time, from 3.54 to 11.73 seconds to acquire a mean F-Score improvement of +8.85. Again for PageRank, a mean increase of 343% in processing time, from 1.95 to 8.64 seconds to acquire a F-Score improvement of +7.16 was observed.

We wanted to investigate why in some cases, the iterative approach can produce poorer results than the conventional approach. We looked at aspects of the subgraphs such as order, size, density, and number of components. Eventually we came to the conclusion that, just like in a Sudoku puzzle, if there are not enough hints to start with, the possibility of finishing the puzzle becomes slim.

Therefore we suspected that if there were not enough monosemous lemmas, to construct the initial $\mathcal{G}_{\mathcal{L}}$, then the effectiveness of the iterative approach could be negated. It turns out, as observed in Figures 7(a) and (b) on the following page that this does effect the outcome. On the horizontal axis, document monosemy represents the percentage of lemmas in a document, not counting duplicates, that are monosemous. The vertical axis on the other hand represents the difference in F-Score between the conventional and iterative approach. Through a simple linear regression of the scatter plot, we observe an increased effectiveness of the iterative approach. This observation is important, because a WSD system may decide on which approach to use based on a document's monosemy.

With m representing document monosemy, and ΔF representing the change in F-Score induced by the iterative approach, the slopes observed in Figures 7(a) and (b) are denoted by Equations (2) and (3) respectively.

$$\Delta F = 0.53m - 0.11 \quad (2)$$

$$\Delta F = 0.60m - 3.07 \quad (3)$$

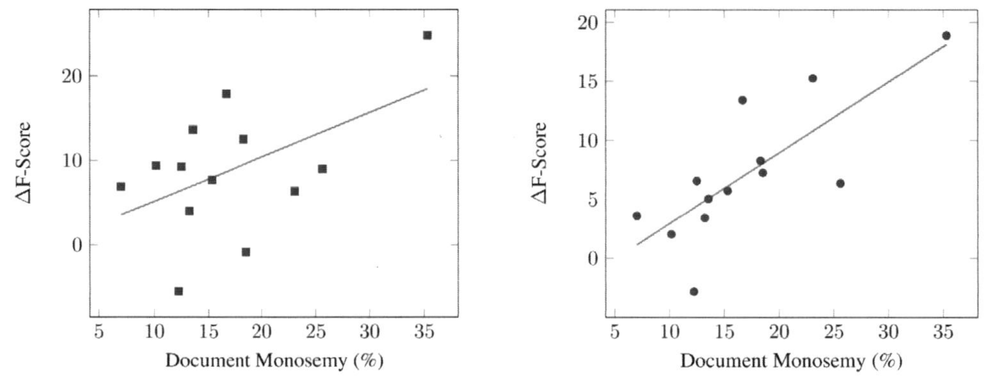

(a) ϕ = Betweenness Centrality

(b) ϕ = PageRank

Figure 7: Both PageRank (squares) and Betweenness Centrality (circles) are plotted. Each data plot represents the change in F-Score when the iterative approach replaces the conventional approach with respect to the monosemy of the document.

4.5 Experiment 3: A Little Optimisation

Briefly, we made an effort into optimising the iterative approach with subtree subgraphs, and compared these results with systems from SemEval 2013 Task 12 (Navigli et al., 2013) in Table 3.

Team	System	P	R	F
UMCC-DLSI	Run-2^{+}	68.50	68.50	68.50
UMCC-DLSI	Run-3^{+}	68.00	68.00	68.00
UMCC-DLSI	Run-1^{+}	67.70	67.70	67.70
SUDOKU	It-PPR[M]$^{+}$	67.41	67.30	67.36
MACHINE	**MFS**	66.50	66.50	66.50
SUDOKU	It-PPR[M]	67.20	65.49	66.33
SUDOKU	It-PR[U]	64.07	62.44	63.24
SUDOKU	It-PD	63.58	61.47	62.51
DAEBAK!	PD^{+}	60.50	60.40	60.40
GETALP	BN-1^{+}	58.30	58.30	58.30
SUDOKU	PR[U]	60.09	54.06	56.91
GETALP	BN-2^{+}	56.80	56.80	56.80

Table 3: Comparison to SemEval 2013 Task 12

Firstly, we were able to marginally improve our original result as team DAEBAK! (Manion and Sainudiin, 2013), by applying the iterative approach to our Peripheral Diversity centrality measure (It-PD). Next we tried Personalised PageRank (It-PPR[M]) with a surfing vector biased towards only *M*onosemous senses. We also included regular PageRank (It-/PR[U]) with a *U*niform surfing vector as a reference point. It-PPR[M] almost defeated the MFS baseline of 66.50, but lacked recall. To rectify this, the MFS baseline was used as a back-off strategy (It-PPR[M]$^{+}$)[4], which then led to us beating the MFS baseline. As for the other teams, GETALP (Schwab et al., 2013) made use of an Ant Colony algorithm, while UMCC-DLSI (Gutiérrez et al., 2013) also made use of PPR, except they based the surfing vector on SemCor (Miller et al., 1993) sense frequencies, set $L = 5$ for shortest paths subgraphs, and disambiguated using resources external to BabelNet. Since their implementation of PPR beats ours, it would be interesting to see how effective the iterative approach could be on their results.

[4]Note that plus^{+} implies the use of a back-off strategy.

5 Conclusion & Future Work

In this paper we have shown that the iterative approach can substantially improve the results of regular subgraph-based WSD, even to the point of defeating the MFS baseline without doing anything complicated. This is regardless of the subgraph, graph centrality measure, or level of disambiguation. This research can still be extended further, and we encourage other researchers to rethink their own approaches to unsupervised knowledge-based WSD, particularly in regards to the interaction of subgraphs and centrality measures.

Resources

Codebase and resources are at first author's homepage: `http://www.stevemanion.com`.

Acknowledgments

This research was completed with the help of the Korean Foundation Graduate Studies Fellowship: `http://en.kf.or.kr/`

References

Eneko Agirre and Aitor Soroa. 2008. Using the Multilingual Central Repository for Graph-Based Word Sense Disambiguation. In *Proceedings of LREC*, pages 1388–1392, Marrakech, Morocco. European Language Resources Association.

Eneko Agirre and Aitor Soroa. 2009. Personalizing PageRank for Word Sense Disambiguation. In *Proceedings of the 12th Conference of the European Chapter of the ACL*, pages 33–41, Athens, Greece. Association for Computational Linguistics.

Eneko Agirre, Oier Lopez De Lacalle, Christiane Fellbaum, Maurizio Tesconi, Monica Monachini, Piek Vossen, and Roxanne Segers. 2010. SemEval-2010 Task 17: All-words Word Sense Disambiguation on a Specific Domain. In *Proceedings of the 5th International Workshop on Semantic Evaluation*, pages 75–80, Uppsala, Sweden. Association for Computational Linguistics.

Sergey Brin and Lawrence Page. 1998. The Anatomy of a Large-scale Hypertextual Web Search Engine. *Computer Networks and ISDN Systems*, 30:107 – 117.

Christiane Fellbaum. 1998. *WordNet: An Electronic Lexical Database*. MIT Press, Cambridge, MA.

Linton C. Freeman. 1979. Centrality in Social Networks Conceptual Clarification. *Social Networks*, 1(3):215–239.

William A Gale, Kenneth W Church, and David Yarowsky. 1992. A Method for Disambiguating Word Senses in a Large Corpus. *Computers and the Humanities*, 26:415 – 439.

Yoan Gutiérrez, Antonio Fernández Orquín, Andy González, Andrés Montoyo, Rafael Muñoz, Rainel Estrada, Dennys D Piug, Jose I Abreu, and Roger Pérez. 2013. UMCC_DLSI: Reinforcing a Ranking Algorithm with Sense Frequencies and Multidimensional Semantic Resources to solve Multilingual Word Sense Disambiguation. In *Proceedings of the 7th International Workshop on Semantic Evaluation (SemEval 2013), in conjunction with the Second Joint Conference on Lexical and Computational Semantics (*SEM 2013)*, pages 241–249, Atlanta, Georgia. Association for Computational Linguistics.

T.H. Haveliwala. 2003. Topic-Sensitive Pagerank: A Context-Sensitive Ranking Algorithm for Web Search. *IEEE Transactions on Knowledge and Data Engineering*, 15(4):784–796.

Adam Kilgarriff. 1998. SENSEVAL: An Exercise in Evaluating Word Sense Disambiguation Programs. In *Conference Proceedings of LREC*, pages 581–585, Granada, Spain.

Jon M. Kleinberg. 1999. Authoritative Sources in a Hyperlinked Environment. *Journal of the ACM*, 46(5):604–632.

Els Lefever and Veronique Hoste. 2010. SemEval-2010 Task 3: Cross-lingual Word Sense Disambiguation. In *Proceedings of the 5th International Workshop on Semantic Evaluation*, pages 82–87, Boulder, Colorado. Association for Computational Linguistics.

Els Lefever and Veronique Hoste. 2013. SemEval-2013 Task 10: Cross-lingual Word Sense Disambiguation. In *Proceedings of the 7th International Workshop on Semantic Evaluation (SemEval 2013), in conjunction with the Second Joint Conference on Lexical and Computational Semantics (*SEM 2013)*, Atlanta, Georgia. Association for Computational Linguistics.

Steve L. Manion and Raazesh Sainudiin. 2013. DAEBAK!: Peripheral Diversity for Multilingual Word Sense Disambiguation. In *Proceedings of the 7th International Workshop on Semantic Evaluation (SemEval 2013), in conjunction with the Second Joint Conference on Lexical and Computational Semantics (*SEM 2013)*, pages 250–254, Atlanta, Georgia. Association for Computational Linguistics.

Rada Mihalcea. 2005. Unsupervised Large-Vocabulary Word Sense Disambiguation with Graph-based Algorithms for Sequence Data Labeling. In *Proceedings of the conference on Human Language Technology and Empirical Methods in Natural Language Processing*, pages 411–418, Vancouver, Canada. Association for Computational Linguistics.

George A. Miller, Claudia Leacock, Randee Tengi, and Ross T. Bunker. 1993. A Semantic Concordance. In *Proceedings of the Workshop on Human Language Technology - HLT '93*, pages 303–308, Morristown, NJ, USA. Association for Computational Linguistics.

Roberto Navigli and Mirella Lapata. 2007. Graph Connectivity Measures for Unsupervised Word Sense Disambiguation. In *Proceedings of the 20th International Joint Conference on Artificial Intelligence (IJCAI)*, pages 1683–1688.

Roberto Navigli and Mirella Lapata. 2010. An Experimental Study of Graph Connectivity for Unsupervised Word Sense Disambiguation. *IEEE Transactions on Pattern Analysis and Machine Intelligence*, 32(4):678 – 692.

Roberto Navigli and Simone Paolo Ponzetto. 2012a. BabelNet: The Automatic Construction, Evaluation and Application of a Wide-Coverage Multilingual Semantic Network. *Artificial Intelligence*, 193:217–250.

Roberto Navigli and Simone Paolo Ponzetto. 2012b. Joining Forces Pays Off: Multilingual Joint Word Sense Disambiguation. In *Proceedings of the 2012 Joint Conference on Empirical Methods in Natural Language Processing and Computational Natural Language Learning*, pages 1399–1410, Jeju Island, Korea. Association for Computational Linguistics.

Roberto Navigli and Paola Velardi. 2005. Structural Semantic Interconnections: A Knowledge-based Approach to Word Sense Disambiguation. *IEEE Transactions on Pattern Analysis and Machine Intelligence*, 27(7):1075–1086.

Roberto Navigli, Kenneth C Litkowski, and Orin Hargraves. 2007. SemEval-2007 Task 07: Coarse-Grained English All-Words Task. In *Proceedings of the 4th International Workshop on Semantic Evaluations*, pages 30–35, Prague, Czech Republic. Association for Computational Linguistics.

Roberto Navigli, David Jurgens, and Daniele Vannella. 2013. SemEval-2013 Task 12: Multilingual Word Sense Disambiguation. In *Proceedings of the 7th International Workshop on Semantic Evaluation (SemEval 2013), in conjunction with the Second Joint Conference on Lexical and Computational Semantics (*SEM 2013)*. Association for Computational Linguistics.

Roberto Navigli. 2009. Word Sense Disambiguation: A Survey. *ACM Computing Surveys*, 41(2):10:1 – 10:69.

Martha Palmer, Christiane Fellbaum, Scott Cotton, Lauren Delfs, and Hoa Trang Dang. 2001. English Tasks: All-Words and Verb Lexical Sample. In *Proceedings of SENSEVAL-2 Second International Workshop on Evaluating Word Sense Disambiguation Systems*, pages 21–24, Toulouse, France. Association for Computational Linguistics.

Ted Pedersen. 2007. Unsupervised Corpus-Based Methods for WSD. In Eneko Agirre and Philip Edmonds, editors, *Word Sense Disambiguation: Algorithms and Applications*, chapter 6, pages 133–166. Springer, New York.

Simone Paolo Ponzetto and Roberto Navigli. 2010. Knowledge-rich Word Sense Disambiguation Rivaling Supervised Systems. *Proceedings of the 48th Annual Meeting of the ACL*, pages 1522–1531.

Didier Schwab, Andon Tchechmedjiev, Jérôme Goulian, Mohammad Nasiruddin, Gilles Sérasset, and Hervé Blanchon. 2013. GETALP: Propagation of a Lesk Measure through an Ant Colony Algorithm. In *Proceedings of the 7th International Workshop on Semantic Evaluation (SemEval 2013), in conjunction with the Second Joint Conference on Lexical and Computational Semantics (*SEM 2013)*, pages 232–240, Atlanta, Georgia. Association for Computational Linguistics.

Ravi Sinha and Rada Mihalcea. 2007. Unsupervised Graph-based Word Sense Disambiguation Using Measures of Word Semantic Similarity. In *Proceedings of the International Conference on Semantic Computing*, pages 363 – 369. IEEE.

Benjamin Snyder and Martha Palmer. 2004. The English All-Words Task. In *Proceedings of the Third International Workshop on the Evaluation of Systems for the Semantic Analysis of Text*, pages 41–43, Barcelona, Spain. Association for Computational Linguistics.

David Yarowsky. 1993. One Sense Per Collocation. In *Proceedings of the workshop on Human Language Technology - HLT '93*, pages 266–271, Morristown, NJ, USA. Association for Computational Linguistics.

David Yarowsky. 1995. Unsupervised Word Sense Disambiguation Rivaling Supervised Methods. In *Proceedings of the 33rd Annual Meeting of the ACL*, pages 189–196, Cambridge, MA. Association for Computational Linguistics.

Exploring ESA to Improve Word Relatedness

Nitish Aggarwal **Kartik Asooja** **Paul Buitelaar**
Insight Centre for Data Analytics
National University of Ireland
Galway, Ireland
firstname.lastname@deri.org

Abstract

Explicit Semantic Analysis (ESA) is an approach to calculate the semantic relatedness between two words or natural language texts with the help of concepts grounded in human cognition. ESA usage has received much attention in the field of natural language processing, information retrieval and text analysis, however, performance of the approach depends on several parameters that are included in the model, and also on the text data type used for evaluation. In this paper, we investigate the behavior of using different number of Wikipedia articles in building ESA model, for calculating the semantic relatedness for different types of text pairs: word-word, phrase-phrase and document-document. With our findings, we further propose an approach to improve the ESA semantic relatedness scores for words by enriching the words with their explicit context such as synonyms, glosses and Wikipedia definitions.

1 Introduction

Explicit Semantic Analysis (ESA) is a distributional semantic model (Harris, 1954) that computes the relatedness scores between natural language texts by using high dimensional vectors. ESA builds the high dimensional vectors by using the explicit concepts defined in human cognition. Gabrilovich and Markovitch (2007) introduced the ESA model in which Wikipedia and Open Directory Project[1] was used to obtain the explicit concepts. ESA considers every Wikipedia article as a unique explicit topic. It also assumes that the articles are topically orthogonal. However, recent work (Gottron et al., 2011) has shown that by using the documents from Reuters corpus instead of Wikipedia articles can also achieve comparable results. ESA model includes various parameters (Sorg and Cimiano, 2010) that play important roles on its performance. Therefore, the model requires further investigation in order to better tune the parameters.

ESA model has been adapted very quickly in different fields related to text analysis, due to the simplicity of its implementation and the availability of Wikipedia corpus. Gabrilovich and Markovitch (2007) evaluated the ESA against word relatedness dataset WN353 (Finkelstein et al., 2001) and document relatedness dataset Lee50 (Lee et al., 2005) by using all the articles from Wikipedia snapshot of 11 Nov, 2005. However, the results reported using different implementations (Polajnar et al., 2013) (Hassan and Mihalcea, 2011) of ESA on same datasets (WN353 and Lee50) vary a lot, due the specificity of ESA implementation. For instance, Hassan and Mihalcea (2011) found a significant difference between the scores obtained from their own implementation and the scores reported in the original article (Gabrilovich and Markovitch, 2007).

In this paper, first, we investigate the behavior of ESA model in calculating the semantic relatedness for different types of text pairs: word-word, phrase-phrase and document-document by using different number of Wikipedia articles for building the model. Second, we propose an approach

[1] http://www.dmoz.org

*Proceedings of the Third Joint Conference on Lexical and Computational Semantics (*SEM 2014)*, pages 51–56,
Dublin, Ireland, August 23-24 2014.

for context enrichment of words to improve the performance of ESA on word relatedness task.

2 Background

The ESA model can be described as a method of obtaining the relatedness score between two texts by quantifying the distance between two high dimensional vectors. Every explicit concept represents a dimension of the ESA vector, and the associativity weight of a given word with the explicit concept can be taken as magnitude of the corresponding dimension. For instance, there is a word *t*, ESA builds a vector *v*, where $v = \sum_{i=0}^{N} a_i * c_i$ and c_i is i^{th} concept from the explicit concept space, and a_i is the associativity weight of word t with the concept c_i. Here, *N* represents the total number of concepts. In our implementation, we build ESA model by using Wikipedia articles as explicit concepts, and take the TFIDF weights as associativity strength. Similarly, ESA builds the vector for natural language text by considering it as a bag of words. Let $T = \{t_1, t_2, t_3 ... t_n\}$, where *T* is a natural language text that has n words. ESA generates the vector *V*, where $V = \sum_{t_k \epsilon T} v_k$ and $v = \sum_{i=0}^{N} a_i * c_i$. v_k represents the ESA vector of a individual words as explained above. The relatedness score between two natural language texts is calculated by computing cosine product of their corresponding ESA vectors.

In recent years, some extensions (Polajnar et al., 2013) (Hassan and Mihalcea, 2011) (Scholl et al., 2010) have been proposed to improve the ESA performance, however, they have not discussed the consistency in the performance of ESA. Polajnar et al. (2013) used only 10,000 Wikipedia articles as the concept space, and got significantly different results on the previously evaluated datasets. Hassan and Mihalcea (2011) have not discussed the ESA implementation in detail but obtained significantly different scores. Although, these proposed extensions got different baseline ESA scores but they improve the relatedness scores with their additions. Polajnar et al. (2013) used the concept-concept correlation to improve the ESA model. Hassan and Mihalcea (2011) proposed a model similar to ESA, which builds the high dimensional vector of salient concepts rather than explicit concepts. Gortton et al. (2011) investigated the ESA performance for document relatedness and showed that ESA scores are not tightly dependent on the explicit concept spaces.

Minimum unique words (K)	**Total number of articles (N)**
100	438379
300	110900
500	46035
700	23608
900	13718
1100	8322
1300	5241
1500	3329
1700	2126
1900	1368

Table 1: The total number of retrieved articles for different values of K

3 Investigation of ESA model

Although Gortton et al. (2011) has shown that ESA performance on document pairs does not get affected by using different number of Wikipedia articles, we further examine it for word-word and phrase-phrase pairs. We use three different datasets WN353, SemEvalOnWN (Agirre et al., 2012) and Lee50. WN353 contains 353 word pairs, SemEvalOnWN consists of 750 short phrase/sentence pairs, and Lee50 is a collection of 50 document pairs. All these datasets contain relatedness scores given by human annotators. We evaluate ESA model on these three datasets against different number of Wikipedia articles. In order to select different number of Wikipedia articles, we sort them according to the total number of unique words appearing in each article. We select N articles, where N is total number of articles which have at least K unique words. Table 1 shows the total number of retrieved articles for different values of K. We build 20 different ESA models with the different values of N retrieved by varying K from 100 to 2000 with an interval of 100. Figure 1 illustrates Spearman's rank correlation of all the three types of text pairs on Y-axis while X-axis shows the different values of N which are taken to build the model. It shows that ESA model generates very consistent results for phrase pairs similar to the one reported in (Aggarwal et al., 2012), how-

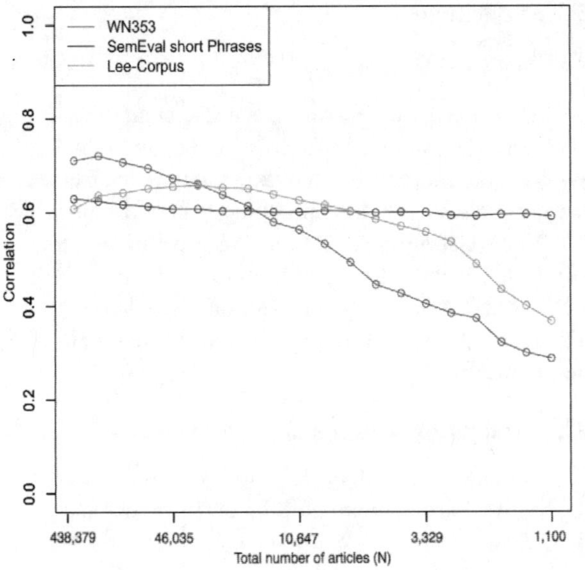

Figure 1: ESA performance on different types of text pairs by varying the total number of articles

ever, the correlation scores decreases monotonously in the case of word pairs as the number of articles goes down. In the case of document pairs, ESA produces similar results until the value of N is chosen according to K = 1000, but after that, it decreases quickly because the number of articles becomes too low for making a good enough ESA model. All this indicates that word-word relatedness scores have a strong impact of changing the N in comparison of document-document or phrase-phrase text pairs. An explanation to this is that the size of the ESA vector for a word solely depends upon the popularity of the given word, however, in the case of text, the vector size depends on the popularity summation of all the words appearing in the given text. It suggests that the word relatedness problem can be reduced to short text relatedness by adding some related context with the given word. Therefore, to improve the ESA performance for word relatedness, we propose an approach for context enrichment of words. We perform context enrichment by concatenating related context with the given word and use this context to build the ESA vector, which transforms the word relatedness problem to phrase relatedness.

4 Context Enrichment

Context enrichment is performed by concatenating the context defining text to the given word before building the ESA vector. Therefore, instead of building the ESA vector of a word, the vector is built for the short text that is obtained after concatenating the related context. This is similar to classical query expansion task (Aggarwal and Buitelaar, 2012; Pantel and Fuxman, 2011), where related concepts are concatenated with a query to improve the information retrieval performance. We propose three different methods to obtain related context: 1) WordNet-based Context Enrichment 2) Wikipedia-based Context Enrichment, and 3) WikiDefinition-based Context Enrichment.

4.1 WordNet-based Context Enrichment

WordNet-based context enrichment uses the WordNet synonyms to obtain the context, and concatenates them into the given word to build the ESA vector. However, WordNet may contain more than one synset for a word, where each synset represents a different semantic sense. Therefore, we obtain more than one contexts for a given word, by concatenating the different synsets. Further, we calculate ESA score of every context of a given word against all the contexts of the other word which is being compared, and consider the highest score as the final relatedness score. For instance, there is a given word pair "train and car", car has 8 different synsets that build 8 different contexts, and train has 6 different synsets that build 6 different contexts. We calculate the ESA score of these 8 contexts of car to the 6 contexts of train, and finally select the highest obtained score from all of the 24 calculated scores.

4.2 Wikipedia-based Context Enrichment

In this method, the context is defined by the word usage in Wikipedia articles. We retrieve top 5 Wikipedia articles by querying the articles' content, and concatenate the short abstracts of the retrieved articles to the given word to build the ESA vector. Short abstract is the first two sentences of Wikipedia article and has a maximum limit of 500 characters. In order to retrieve the top 5 articles from Wikipedia for a given word, we build an index of all Wikipedia articles and use TF-IDF scores. We further explain our implementation in Section 5.1.

4.3 WikiDefinition-based Context Enrichment

This method uses the definition of a given word from Wikipedia. To obtain a definition from Wikipedia, we first try to find a Wikipedia article on the given word by matching the Wikipedia title. As definition, we take the short abstract of the Wikipedia article. For instance, for a given word "train", we take the Wikipedia article with the title "Train"[2]. If there is no such Wikipedia article, then we use the previous method "Wikipedia-based Context Enrichment" to get the context defining text for the given word. In contrary to the previous method for defining context, here we first try to get a more precise context as it comes from the Wikipedia article on that word only. After obtaining the definition, we concatenate it to the given word to build the ESA vector. At the time of experimentation, we were able to find 339 words appearing as Wikipedia articles out of 437 unique words in the WN353 dataset.

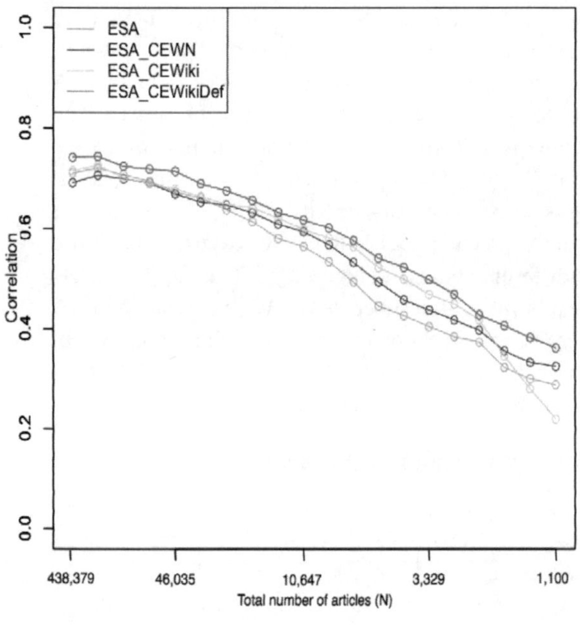

Figure 2: Effect of different types of context enrichments on WN353 gold standard

[2]http://en.wikipedia.org/wiki/Train

5 Experiment

5.1 ESA implementation

In this section, we describe the implementation of ESA and the parameters used to build the model. We build an index over all Wikipedia articles from the pre-processed Wikipedia dump from November 11, 2005 (Gabrilovich, 2006). We use Lucene[3] to build the index and retrieve the articles using TF-IDF scores. As described in section 3, we build 20 different indices with different values of total number of articles (N).

5.2 Results and Discussion

To evaluate the effect of the aforementioned approaches for context enrichment, we compare the results obtained by them against the results generated by ESA model as a baseline. We calculated the scores on WN353 word pairs dataset by using ESA, WordNet-based Context Enrichment (ESA_CEWN), Wikipedia-based Context Enrichment (ESA_CEWiki) and WikiDcfition-based Context Enrichment (ESA_CEWikiDef). Further, we examine the performance of context enrichment approaches by reducing the total number of articles taken to build the model. Figure 2 shows that the proposed methods of context enrichment significantly improve over the ESA scores for different values of N.

Table 2 reports the results obtained by using different context enrichments and ESA model. It shows Spearman's rank correlation on four different values of N. All the proposed context enrichment methods improve over the ESA baseline scores. Context enrichments based on Wikipedia outperforms the other methods, and ESA_CEWikiDef significantly improves over the ESA baseline. Moreover, given a very less number of Wikipedia articles used for building the model, ESA_CEWikiDef obtains a correlation score which is considerably higher than the one obtained by ESA baseline. ESA_CEWN and ESA_CEWiki can include some unrelated context as they do not care about the semantic sense of the given word, for instance, for a given word "car", ESA_CEWiki

[3]https://lucene.apache.org/

K	Total articles (N)	ESA	ESA_CEWN	ESA_CEWiki	ESA_CEWikiDef
100	438,379	0.711	0.692	0.724	**0.741**
200	221,572	0.721	0.707	0.726	**0.743**
500	46,035	0.673	0.670	0.679	**0.698**
1000	10,647	0.563	0.593	0.598	**0.614**

Table 2: Spearman rank correlation scores on WN353 gold standard

includes the context about the word "car" at surface level rather than at the semantic level. However, ESA_CEWikiDef only includes the definition if it does not refer to more than one semantic sense, therefore, ESA_CEWikiDef outperforms all other types of context enrichment.

We achieved best results in all the cases by taking all the articles which has a minimum of 200 unique words (K=200). This indicates that further increasing the value of K considerably decreases the value of N, consequently, it harms the overall distributional knowledge of the language, which is the core of ESA model. However, decreasing the value of K introduces very small Wikipedia articles or stubs, which do not provide enough content on a subject.

6 Conclusion

In this paper, we investigated the ESA performance for three different types of text pairs: word-word, phrase-phrase and document-document. We showed that ESA scores varies significantly for word relatedness measure with the change in the number (N) and length (≈K which is the number of unique words) of the Wikipedia articles used for building the model. Further, we proposed context enrichment approaches for improving word relatedness computation by ESA. To this end, we presented three different approaches: 1) WordNet-based, 2) Wikipedia-based, and 3) WikiDefinition-based, and we realized that concatenating the context defining text improves the ESA performance for word relatedness task.

Acknowledgments

This work has been funded in part by a research grant from Science Foundation Ireland (SFI) under Grant Number SFI/12/RC/2289 (INSIGHT) and by the EU FP7 program in the context of the project LIDER (610782).

References

Nitish Aggarwal and Paul Buitelaar. 2012. Query expansion using wikipedia and dbpedia. In *CLEF*.

Nitish Aggarwal, Kartik Asooja, and Paul Buitelaar. 2012. DERI&UPM: Pushing corpus based relatedness to similarity: Shared task system description. In *Proceedings of the First Joint Conference on Lexical and Computational Semantics - Volume 1: Proceedings of the Main Conference and the Shared Task, and Volume 2: Proceedings of the Sixth International Workshop on Semantic Evaluation*, SemEval '12, pages 643–647, Stroudsburg, PA, USA. Association for Computational Linguistics.

Eneko Agirre, Mona Diab, Daniel Cer, and Aitor Gonzalez-Agirre. 2012. Semeval-2012 task 6: A pilot on semantic textual similarity. In *Proceedings of the First Joint Conference on Lexical and Computational Semantics-Volume 1: Proceedings of the main conference and the shared task, and Volume 2: Proceedings of the Sixth International Workshop on Semantic Evaluation*, pages 385–393. Association for Computational Linguistics.

Lev Finkelstein, Evgeniy Gabrilovich, Yossi Matias, Ehud Rivlin, Zach Solan, Gadi Wolfman, and Eytan Ruppin. 2001. Placing search in context: The concept revisited. In *Proceedings of the 10th international conference on World Wide Web*, pages 406–414. ACM.

Evgeniy Gabrilovich and Shaul Markovitch. 2007. Computing semantic relatedness using wikipedia-based explicit semantic analysis. In *Proceedings of the 20th international joint conference on Artifical intelligence*, IJCAI'07, pages 1606–1611, San Francisco, CA, USA. Morgan Kaufmann Publishers Inc.

Evgeniy Gabrilovich. 2006. *Feature generation for textual information retrieval using world knowledge*. Ph.D. thesis, Technion - Israel Institute of Technology, Haifa, Israel, December.

Thomas Gottron, Maik Anderka, and Benno Stein. 2011. Insights into explicit semantic analysis. In *Proceedings of the 20th ACM international conference on Information and knowledge management*, pages 1961–1964. ACM.

Zellig Harris. 1954. Distributional structure. In *Word 10 (23)*, pages 146–162.

Samer Hassan and Rada Mihalcea. 2011. Semantic relatedness using salient semantic analysis. In *AAAI*.

Michael David Lee, BM Pincombe, and Matthew Brian Welsh. 2005. An empirical evaluation of models of text document similarity. *Cognitive Science*.

Patrick Pantel and Ariel Fuxman. 2011. Jigs and lures: Associating web queries with structured entities. In *ACL*, pages 83–92.

Tamara Polajnar, Nitish Aggarwal, Kartik Asooja, and Paul Buitelaar. 2013. Improving esa with document similarity. In *Advances in Information Retrieval*, pages 582–593. Springer.

Philipp Scholl, Doreen Böhnstedt, Renato Domínguez García, Christoph Rensing, and Ralf Steinmetz. 2010. Extended explicit semantic analysis for calculating semantic relatedness of web resources. In *Sustaining TEL: From Innovation to Learning and Practice*, pages 324–339. Springer.

Philipp Sorg and Philipp Cimiano. 2010. An experimental comparison of explicit semantic analysis implementations for cross-language retrieval. In *Natural Language Processing and Information Systems*, pages 36–48. Springer.

Identifying semantic relations in a specialized corpus through distributional analysis of a cooccurrence tensor

Gabriel Bernier-Colborne
OLST (Université de Montréal)
C.P. 6128, succ. Centre-Ville
Montréal (Québec) Canada H3C 3J7
gabriel.bernier-colborne@umontreal.ca

Abstract

We describe a method of encoding cooccurrence information in a three-way tensor from which HAL-style word space models can be derived. We use these models to identify semantic relations in a specialized corpus. Results suggest that the tensor-based methods we propose are more robust than the basic HAL model in some respects.

1 Introduction

Word space models such as LSA (Landauer and Dumais, 1997) and HAL (Lund et al., 1995) have been shown to identify semantic relations from corpus data quite effectively. However, the performance of such models depends on the parameters used to construct the word space. In the case of HAL, parameters such as the size of the context window can have a significant impact on the ability of the model to identify semantic relations and on the types of relations (e.g. paradigmatic or syntagmatic) captured.

In this paper, we describe a method of encoding cooccurrence information which employs a three-way tensor instead of a matrix. Because the tensor explicitly encodes the distance between a target word and the context words that co-occur with it, it allows us to extract matrices corresponding to HAL models with different context windows without repeatedly processing the whole corpus, but it also allows us to experiment with different kinds of word spaces. We describe one method whereby features are selected in different slices of the tensor corresponding to different distances between the target and context words, and another which uses SVD for dimensionality reduction. Models are evaluated and compared on reference data extracted from a specialized dictionary of the environment domain, as our target application is the identification of lexico-semantic relations in specialized corpora. Preliminary results suggest the tensor-based methods are more robust than the basic HAL model in some respects.

2 Related Work

The tensor encoding method we describe is based on the Hyperspace Analogue to Language, or HAL, model (Lund et al., 1995; Lund and Burgess, 1996), which has been shown to be particularly effective at modeling paradigmatic relations such as synonymy. In the HAL model, word order is taken into account insofar as the word vectors it produces contain information about both the cooccurrents that precede a word and those that follow it. In recent years, there have been several proposals that aim to add word order information to models that rely mainly on word context information (Jones and Mewhort, 2007; Sahlgren et al., 2008), including models based on multi-way tensors. Symonds et al. (2011) proposed an efficient tensor encoding method which builds on unstructured word space models (i.e. models based on simple cooccurrence rather than syntactic structure) by adding order information. The method we describe differs in that it explicitly encodes the distance between a target word and its cooccurrents.

Multi-way tensors have been used to construct different kinds of word space models in recent years. Turney (2007) used a word-word-pattern tensor to model semantic similarity, Van de Cruys (2009) used a tensor containing corpus-derived subject-verb-object triples to model selectional preferences, and Baroni and Lenci (2010) proposed a general, tensor-based framework for structured word space models. The tensor encoding method we describe differs in that it is based on an unstructured word space model, HAL.

*Proceedings of the Third Joint Conference on Lexical and Computational Semantics (*SEM 2014)*, pages 57–62,
Dublin, Ireland, August 23-24 2014.

3 HAL

The HAL model employs a sliding context window to compute a word-word cooccurrence matrix, which we will note $\mathbf{A}$, in which value a_{ij} is based on the number of times context word w_j appears within the context window of target word w_i. Thus, words that share cooccurrents will be closer in word space. If equal weight is given to all context words in the window, regardless of distance, we call the context window *rectangular*. In the original HAL model, the values added to $\mathbf{A}$ are inversely proportional to the distance between the target word and context word in a given context. In this case, the context window is *triangular*.

In the HAL model, the cooccurrence matrix is computed by considering only the context words that occur before the target word. Once the matrix has been computed, row vector $\mathbf{a}_{i:}$ contains cooccurrence information about words preceding w_i, and column vector $\mathbf{a}_{:i}$ contains information about those that follow it. The row vector and column vector of each target word are concatenated, such that the resulting word vectors contain information about both left-cooccurrents and right-cooccurrents. We call this type of context window *directional*, following (Sahlgren, 2006), as opposed to a *symetric* context window, in which cooccurrence counts in the left and right contexts are summed. In our experiment, we only use one type of context window (directional and rectangular), but models corresponding to different types of context windows can be derived from the cooccurrence tensor we describe in section 4.

Once the values in $\mathbf{A}$ have been computed, they can be weighted using schemes such as TF-ITF (Lavelli et al., 2004) and Positive Pointwise Mutual Information (PPMI), which we use here as it has been shown to be particularly effective by Bullinaria and Levy (2007). Finally, a distance or similarity measure is used to compare word vectors. Lund and Burgess (1996) use Minkowski distances. We will use the cosine similarity, as did Schütze (1992) in a model similar to HAL and which directly influenced its development.

4 The Cooccurrence Tensor

In the following description of the cooccurrence tensor, we follow the notational guidelines of (Kolda, 2006), as in (Turney, 2007; Baroni and Lenci, 2010). Let W be the vocabulary[1], which we index by i to refer to a target word and by j for context words. Furthermore, let P, indexed by k, be a set of positions, relative to a target word w_i, in which a context word w_j can co-occur with w_i. In other words, this is the signed distance between w_j and w_i, in number of words. For instance, in the sentence "a dog bit the mailman", we would say that "dog" co-occurs with "bit" in position -1. If we only consider the words directly adjacent to a target word, then $P = \{-1, +1\}$. If the tensor encoding method is used to generate HAL-style cooccurrence matrices corresponding to different context windows, then P would include all positions in the largest window under consideration.

In a cooccurrence matrix $\mathbf{A}$, a_{ij} contains the frequency at which word w_j co-occurs with word w_i in a fixed context window. Rather than computing matrices using fixed-size context windows, we can construct a cooccurrence tensor $\mathcal{X}$, a labeled three-way tensor in which values x_{ijk} indicate the frequency at which word w_j co-occurs with word w_i in position p_k. Table 1 illustrates a cooccurrence tensor for the sentence "dogs bite mailmen" using a context window of 1 ($P = \{-1, +1\}$), in the form of a nested table.

In tensor $\mathcal{X}$, $\mathbf{x}_{i:k}$ denotes the row vector of w_i at position p_k, $\mathbf{x}_{:jk}$ denotes the column vector of word w_j at position p_k and $\mathbf{x}_{ij:}$ denotes the tube vector indicating the frequency at which w_j co-occurs with w_i in each of the positions in P.

HAL-style cooccurrence matrices corresponding to different context windows can be extracted from the tensor by summing and concatenating various slices of the tensor. A frontal slice $\mathbf{X}_{::k}$ represents a $I \times J$ cooccurrence matrix for position p_k. A cooccurrence matrix corresponding to a symetric context window of size n can be extracted by summing the slices $\mathbf{X}_{::k}$ for $p_k \in \{-n, -n+1, \ldots, n\}$. For a directional window, we first sum the slices for $p_k \in \{-n, \ldots, -1\}$, then sum the slices for $p_k \in \{1, \ldots, n\}$, then concatenate the 2 resulting matrices horizontally.

Thus, summing and concatenating slices allows us to extract HAL-style cooccurrence matrices. A different kind of model can also be obtained by concatenating slices of the tensor. For instance, if we concatenate $\mathbf{X}_{::k}$ for $p_k \in \{-2, -1, +1, +2\}$ horizontally, we obtain a matrix containing a vec-

[1] We assume that the target and context words are the same set, but this need not be the case.

	j=1:dog		*j=2:bite*		*j=3:mailman*	
	k=1:−1	k=2:+1	k=1:−1	k=2:+1	k=1:−1	k=2:+1
i=1:dog	0	0	0	1	0	0
i=2:bite	1	0	0	0	0	1
i=3:mailman	0	0	1	0	0	0

Table 1: A $3 \times 3 \times 2$ cooccurrence tensor.

tor of length $4J$ (instead of the $2J$-length vectors of the HAL model) for each target word, which encodes cooccurrence information about 4 specific positions relative to that word. We will refer to this method as the tensor slicing method. Note that if $P = \{-1, 1\}$ the resulting matrix is identical to a HAL model with context size 1

As the size of the resulting vectors is KJ, this method can result in very high-dimensional word vectors. In the original HAL model, Lund et al. (1995) reduced the dimensionality of the vectors through feature selection, by keeping only the features that have the highest variance. Schütze (1992), on the other hand, used truncated SVD for this purpose. Both techniques can be used with the tensor slicing method. In our experiment, SVD was applied to the matrices obtained by concatenating tensor slices horizontally[2]. As for feature selection, a fixed number of features (those with the highest variance) were selected from each slice of the tensor, and these reduced slices were then concatenated.

It must be acknowledged that this tensor encoding method is not efficient in terms of memory. However, this was not a major issue in our experimental setting, as the size of the vocabulary was small (5K words), and we limited the number of positions in P to 10. Also, a sparse tensor was used to reduce memory consumption.

5 Experiment

5.1 Corpus and Preprocessing

In this experiment, we used the PANACEA Environment English monolingual corpus, which is freely distributed by ELDA for research purposes[3] (Catalog Reference ELRA-W0063). This corpus contains 28071 documents (~50 million tokens) dealing with different aspects of the environment domain, harvested from web sites using a focused crawler. The corpus was converted from XML to raw text, various string normalization operations were then applied, and the corpus was lemmatized using TreeTagger (Schmid, 1994). The vocabulary (W) was selected based on word frequency: we used the 5000 most frequent words in the corpus, excluding stop words and strings containing non-alphabetic characters. During computation of the cooccurrence tensor, OOV words were ignored (rather than deleted), and the context window was allowed to span sentence boundaries.

5.2 Evaluation Data

Models were evaluated using reference data extracted from DiCoEnviro[4], a specialized dictionary of the environment. This dictionary describes the meaning and behaviour of terms of the environment domain as well as the lexico-semantic relations between these terms. Of the various relations encoded in the dictionary, we focused on a subset of three paradigmatic relations: near-synonyms (terms that have similar meanings), antonyms (opposite meanings), and hyponyms (kinds of). 446 pairs containing a head-word and a related term were extracted from the dictionary. We then filtered out the pairs that contained at least one OOV term, and were left with 374 pairs containing two paradigmatically-related, single-word terms. About two thirds (246) of these examples were used for parameter selection, and the rest were set aside for a final comparison of the highest-scoring models.

[2]We also tried concatenating slices vertically (thus obtaining a matrix where rows correspond to <target word, position> tuples and columns correspond to context words) before applying SVD, then concatenating all row vectors corresponding to the same target word, but we will not report the results here for lack of space. Concatenating slices horizontally performed better and seems more intuitive, and the size of the resulting vectors is not dependent on the number of positions in P.

[3]http://catalog.elra.info/product_info.php?products_id=1184

[4]http://olst.ling.umontreal.ca/cgi-bin/dicoenviro/search_enviro.cgi (under construction).

5.3 Automatic Evaluation

Each model was automatically evaluated on the reference data as follows. For each <headword, related term> pair in the training set, we computed the cosine similarity between the headword and all other words in the vocabulary, then observed the rank of the related term in the sorted list of neighbours. The score used to compare models is recall at k (R@k), which is the percentage of cases where the related term is among the k nearest neighbours of the headword. It should be noted that a score of 100% is not always possible in this setting (depending on the value of k), as some headwords have more than 1 related term in the reference data. Nonetheless, since most (~70%) have 1 or 2 related terms, R@k for some small value of k (we use $k = 10$) should be a good indicator of accuracy. A measure that explicitly accounts for the fact that different terms have different numbers of related terms (e.g. R-precision) would be a good alternative.

5.4 Models Tested

We compared HAL and the tensor slicing method using either feature selection or SVD[5], as explained in section 4. We will refer to each of these models as HAL_{SEL}, TNSR_{SEL}, HAL_{SVD} and TNSR_{SVD}. Context sizes ranged from 1 to 5 words. For feature selection, the number of features could take values in $\{1000, 2000, \ldots, 10000\}$, 10000 being the maximum number of features in a HAL model using a vocabulary of 5000 words. In the case of TNSR_{SEL}, to determine the number of features selected per slice, we took each value in $\{1000, 2000, \ldots, 10000\}$, divided it by K (the number of positions in P), and rounded down. This way, once the slices are concatenated, the total number of features is equal to (or slightly less than) that of one of the HAL_{SEL} models, allowing for a straightforward comparison. When SVD was used instead of feature selection, the number of components could take values in $\{100, 200, ..., 1000\}$. In all cases, word vectors were weighted using PPMI and normalized[6].

[5]We used the SVD implementation (ARPACK solver) provided in the scikit-learn toolkit (Pedregosa et al., 2011).

[6]For HAL_{SEL} and TNSR_{SEL}, we apply PPMI weighting *after* feature selection. In the case of TNSR_{SEL}, we wanted to avoid weighting each slice of the tensor separately. We decided to apply weighting after feature selection in the case of HAL_{SEL} as well in order to enable a more straightforward comparison. We should also note that, in our experiments using HAL, PPMI weighting performed better when applied after feature selection, especially for low numbers of features.

absorb	**extreme**	**precipitation**
emit	severe	rainfall
sequester	intense	snowfall
convert	harsh	temperature
produce	catastrophic	rain
accumulate	unusual	evaporation
store	seasonal	runoff
radiate	mild	moisture
consume	cold	snow
remove	dramatic	weather
reflect	increase	deposition

Table 2: 10 nearest neighbours of 3 environmental terms using the HAL_{SEL} model.

6 Results

Table 2 illustrates the kinds of relations identified by the basic HAL_{SEL} model. It shows the 10 nearest neighbours of the verb *absorb*, the adjective *extreme* and the noun *precipitation*. If we compare these results with the paradigmatic relations encoded in DiCoEnviro, we see that, in the case of *absorb*, 3 of its neighbours are encoded in the dictionary, and all 3 are antonyms or terms having opposite meanings: *emit*, *radiate*, and *reflect*. As for *extreme*, the top 2 neighbours are both encoded in the dictionary as near-synonyms. Finally, *rain* and *snow* are both encoded as kinds of *precipitation*. Most of the other neighbours shown here are also paradigmatically related to the query terms. Thus, HAL seems quite capable of identifying the three types of paradigmatic relations we hoped to identify.

Table 3 shows the best R@10 achieved by each model on the training set, which was used to tune the context size and number of features or components, and their scores on the test set, which was only used to compare the best models. In the case of HAL_{SEL}, the best model has a context window size of 1 and uses 9K out of 10K available features. As for TNSR_{SEL}, the best model had a context size of 2 ($P = \{-2, -1, +1, +2\}$) and 10000 features (2500 per slice). It performed only slightly better on the training set, however it beat the HAL model with a wider margin on the test set.

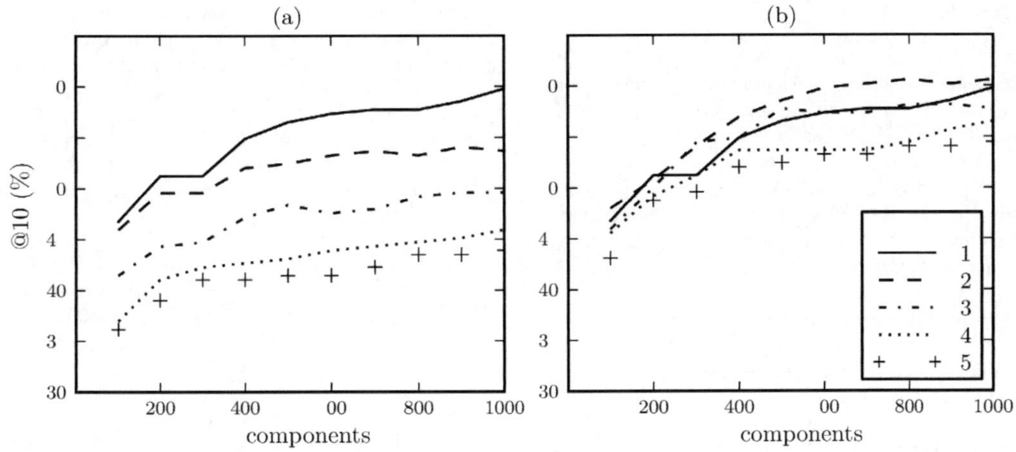

Figure 1: HAL vs. tensor slicing method using SVD for dimensionality reduction. R@10 is plotted against number of components. Models are identical when context size is 1. **(a)** HAL_{SVD} **(b)** $TNSR_{SVD}$

Model	Train	Test
HAL_{SEL}	60.57	57.03
$TNSR_{SEL}$	60.98	60.94
HAL_{SVD}	59.76	56.25
$TNSR_{SVD}$	60.57	60.16

Table 3: R@10 (%) of best models.

The best HAL_{SVD} model used a 1-word window and 1000 components, whereas the best $TNSR_{SVD}$ model had a context size of 2 and 800 components. Again, the tensor-based model slightly edged out the HAL model on the training set, but performed considerably better on the test set.

Further analysis of the results indeed suggests that the tensor slicing method is more robust in some respects than the basic HAL model. Figure 1 compares the performance of HAL_{SVD} and $TNSR_{SVD}$ on the training set, taking into account context size and number of components. It shows that the HAL model is quite sensitive to context size, narrower context performing better in this task. The tensor-based method reduces this gap in performance between context sizes, the gain being greater for larger context sizes. Furthermore, using the tensor-based method with a slightly wider context (2) raises R@10 for most values of the number of components. Results obtained with HAL_{SEL} and $TNSR_{SEL}$ follow the same trend, the tensor-based method being more robust with respect to context size. For lack of space, we only show the plot comparing HAL_{SVD} and $TNSR_{SVD}$.

7 Concluding Remarks

The work presented in this paper is still in its exploratory phase. The tensor slicing method we described has only been evaluated on one corpus and one set of reference data. Experiments would need to be carried out on common word space evaluation tasks in order to compare its performance to that of HAL and other word space models. However, our results suggest that the tensor-based methods are more robust than the basic HAL model to a certain extent, and can improve accuracy. This could prove especially useful in settings where no reference data are available for parameter tuning.

Various possibilities offered by the cooccurrence tensor remain to be explored, such as weighting the number of features selected per slice using some function of the distance between words, extracting matrices from the tensor by applying various functions to the tube vectors corresponding to each word pair, and applying weighting functions that have been generalized to higher-order tensors (Van de Cruys, 2011) or tensor decomposition methods such as those described in (Turney, 2007).

Acknowledgements

We would like to thank the anonymous reviewers for their helpful and thorough comments. Funding was provided by the Social Sciences and Humanities Research Council of Canada.

References

Marco Baroni and Alessandro Lenci. 2010. Distributional memory: A general framework for corpus-based semantics. *Computational Linguistics*, 36(4):673–721.

John A Bullinaria and Joseph P Levy. 2007. Extracting semantic representations from word co-occurrence statistics: A computational study. *Behavior Research Methods*, 39(3):510–526.

Michael N Jones and Douglas JK Mewhort. 2007. Representing word meaning and order information in a composite holographic lexicon. *Psychological Review*, 114(1):1–37.

Tamara Gibson Kolda. 2006. Multilinear operators for higher-order decompositions. Technical Report SAND2006-2081, Sandia National Laboratories.

Thomas K Landauer and Susan T Dumais. 1997. A solution to Plato's problem: The latent semantic analysis theory of acquisition, induction, and representation of knowledge. *Psychological Review*, 104(2):211.

Alberto Lavelli, Fabrizio Sebastiani, and Roberto Zanoli. 2004. Distributional term representations: An experimental comparison. In *Proceedings of the 13th ACM International Conference on Information and Knowledge Management*, pages 615–624. ACM.

Kevin Lund and Curt Burgess. 1996. Producing high-dimensional semantic spaces from lexical co-occurrence. *Behavior Research Methods, Instruments, & Computers*, 28(2):203–208.

Kevin Lund, Curt Burgess, and Ruth Ann Atchley. 1995. Semantic and associative priming in high-dimensional semantic space. In *Proceedings of the 17th Annual Conference of the Cognitive Science Society*, volume 17, pages 660–665.

F. Pedregosa, G. Varoquaux, A. Gramfort, V. Michel, B. Thirion, O. Grisel, M. Blondel, P. Prettenhofer, R. Weiss, V. Dubourg, J. Vanderplas, A. Passos, D. Cournapeau, M. Brucher, M. Perrot, and E. Duchesnay. 2011. Scikit-learn: Machine learning in Python. *Journal of Machine Learning Research*, 12:2825–2830.

Magnus Sahlgren, Anders Holst, and Pentti Kanerva. 2008. Permutations as a means to encode order in word space. In *Proceedings of the 30th Annual Conference of the Cognitive Science Society*, pages 1300–1305. Cognitive Science Society.

Magnus Sahlgren. 2006. *The Word-Space Model: Using distributional analysis to represent syntagmatic and paradigmatic relations between words in high-dimensional vector spaces*. Ph.D. thesis, Stockholm University.

Helmut Schmid. 1994. Probabilistic part-of-speech tagging using decision trees. In *Proceedings of the International Conference on New Methods in Language Processing*.

Hinrich Schütze. 1992. Dimensions of meaning. In *Proceedings of the 1992 ACM/IEEE Conference on Supercomputing (Supercomputing'92)*, pages 787–796. IEEE Computer Society Press.

Michael Symonds, Peter D Bruza, Laurianne Sitbon, and Ian Turner. 2011. Modelling word meaning using efficient tensor representations. In *Proceedings of 25th Pacific Asia Conference on Language, Information and Computation*.

Peter Turney. 2007. Empirical evaluation of four tensor decomposition algorithms. Technical Report ERB-1152, National Research Council of Canada, Ottawa.

Tim Van de Cruys. 2009. A non-negative tensor factorization model for selectional preference induction. In *Proceedings of the Workshop on Geometrical Models of Natural Language Semantics*, pages 83–90. ACL.

Tim Van de Cruys. 2011. Two multivariate generalizations of pointwise mutual information. In *Proceedings of the Workshop on Distributional Semantics and Compositionality*, pages 16–20. ACL.

Learning the Peculiar Value of Actions

Daniel Dahlmeier
Research & Innovation, SAP Asia, Singapore
d.dahlmeier@sap.com

Abstract

We consider the task of automatically estimating the value of human actions. We cast the problem as a supervised learning-to-rank problem between pairs of action descriptions. We present a large, novel data set for this task which consists of challenges from the I Will If You Will Earth Hour challenge. We show that an SVM ranking model with simple linguistic features can accurately predict the relative value of actions.

1 Introduction

The question on how humans conceptualize value is of great interest to researchers in various fields, including linguistics (Jackendoff, 2006). The link between value and language arises from the fact that we cannot directly observe value due to its abstract nature and instead often study language expressions that describe actions which have some value attached to them. This creates an interesting link between the semantics of the words that describe the actions and the underlying moral value of the actions.

Jackendoff (2006) describes value as an "internal accounting system" for ethical decision processes that exhibits both *valence* (good or bad) and *magnitude* (better or worse). Most interestingly, value is governed by a "peculiar logic" that provides constraints on which actions are deemed morally acceptable and which are not. In particular, the principal of *reciprocity* states that the valence and magnitude of reciprocal actions (actions that are done "in return" for something else) should match, i.e., positive valued actions should match with positive valued reciprocal actions (reactions) of similar magnitude, and conversely negatively valued actions should match with negative valued reciprocal actions (reactions) of similar magnitude.

In this paper, we consider the task of automatically estimating the value of actions. We present a simple and effective method for learning the value of actions from ranked pairs of textual action descriptions based on a statistical learning-to-rank approach. Our experiments are based on a novel data set that we create from challenges submitted to the I Will if You Will Earth Hour challenge where participants pledge to do something daring or challenging if other people commit to sustainable actions for the planet. Our method achieves a surprisingly high accuracy of up to 94.72% in a 10-fold cross-validation experiment. The results show that the value of actions can accurately be estimated by machine learning methods based on lexical descriptions of the actions.

The main contribution of this paper is that we show how the semantics of value in language can accurately be learned from empirical data using a learning-to-rank approach. Our work shows an interesting link between empirical research on semantics in natural language processing and the concept of value.

2 The Logic of Value

Our approach is based on the concept of value as presented by Jackendoff (2006) who describes value as an abstract property that is attributed to objects, persons, and actions. He further describes logical inference rules that humans use to determine which actions are deemed morally acceptable and which are not. The most important inference rule for our work is the principal of *reciprocation*, things that are done "in return" for some other action (Fiengo and Lasnik, 1973). In English, this relation is often expressed by the prepo-

*Proceedings of the Third Joint Conference on Lexical and Computational Semantics (*SEM 2014)*, pages 63–68,
Dublin, Ireland, August 23-24 2014.

sition *for*, as shown by the following example sentences (Jackendoff, 2006).

1. Susan praised Sam *for* behaving nicely.
2. Fred cooked Lois dinner *for* fixing his computer.
3. Susan insulted Sam *for* behaving badly.
4. Lois slashed Fred's tires *for* insulting her.

The first two examples describe actions with positive value, while the last two examples describe actions with negative value. We expect that the valence values of reciprocal actions match: positively valued actions demand a positively valued action in return, while negatively valued actions trigger negatively valued responses. If we switch the example sentences and match positive actions with negative actions, we get sentences that sound counter-intuitive or perhaps comical (we prefix counter-intuitive sentences with a hash character '#').

1. #Susan insulted Sam for behaving nicely.
2. #Lois slashed Fred's tires for fixing her computer.

Similarly, we expect that the magnitudes of value between reciprocal actions match. Sentences where the magnitude of the value of the response action does not match the magnitude of the initial action seem odd or socially inappropriate (overacting/underacting).

1. #Fred cooked Lois dinner for saying hello to him.
2. #Fred cooked Lois dinner for rescuing all his relatives from certain death.
3. #Fred slashed Lois's tires for eating too little at dinner.
4. #Fred slashed Lois's tires for murdering his entire family.

We observe that reciprocal actions typically match each other in valence and magnitude. Coming back to our initial goal of learning the value of actions, this gives us a method for comparing the value of actions that were done in return to the same initial action.

3 I Will If You Will challenge

The I Will If You Will (IWIYW) challenge[1] is part of the World Wildlife Fund's Earth Hour campaign which has the goal to increase awareness of sustainability issues. In this challenge, participants make a pledge to do something daring or challenging if a certain number of people commit to sustainable actions for the planet. The challenges are created by ordinary people on the Earth Hour campaign website. Each challenge takes the form of a simple school yard dare: *I will do X, if you will do Y*, where *X* is typically some daring or challenging task that the challenge creator commits to do if a sufficient number of people commit to do action *Y* which is some sustainable action for the planet. Together with the textual description, each challenge includes the number of people that need to commit to doing *Y* in order for the challenge creator to perform *X*. Examples of the challenges are shown in Table 1.

I will quit smoking if you will start recycling. (500 people)
I will adopt a panda if you will start recycling. (1000 people)
I will dance gangnam style if you will plant a tree. (100 people)
I will dye my hair red if you will upload an IWIYW challenge. (500 people)
I will learn Java if you will upload an IWIYW challenge. (10,000 people)

Table 1: Examples of I Will If You Will challenges.

It is important to note that during the challenge creation on the IWIYW website, the *X* challenge is a free text input field that allows the author to come up with creative and interesting challenges. The sustainable actions *Y* and the number of people that need to commit to it are usually chosen from a fixed list of choices. As a result, there is a large number of different *X* actions and a comparably smaller number of *Y* actions. The collected challenges provide a unique data set that allows us to quantitatively measure the value of each promised task by the number of people that need to fulfill the sustainable action.

4 Method

In this section, we present our approach for estimating the value of actions. Our approach casts the problem as a supervised learning-to-rank problem between pairs of actions. Given, a textual description of an action a, we want to estimate its

[1] www.earthhour.org/i-will-if-you-will

value magnitude v. We represent the action a via a set of features that are extracted from the description of the action. We use a linear model that combines the features into a single scalar value for the value v

$$v = w^T \mathbf{x}^{\mathbf{a}}, \tag{1}$$

where $\mathbf{x}^{\mathbf{a}}$ is the feature vector for action description a and w is a learned weight vector. The goal is to learn a suitable weight vector w that approximates the true relationship between textual expressions of actions and their magnitude of value.

Instead of estimating the value directly, we take an alternative approach and consider the task of learning the relative ranking of pairs of actions. We follow the pairwise approach to ranking (Herbrich et al., 1999; Cao et al., 2007) that reduces ranking to a binary classification problem. Ranking the values v_1 and v_2 of two actions a_1 and a_2 is equivalent to determining the sign of the dot product between the weight vector w and the difference between the feature vectors $\mathbf{x}^{\mathbf{a_1}}$ and $\mathbf{x}^{\mathbf{a_2}}$.

$$\begin{aligned} v_1 > v_2 &\Leftrightarrow w^T \mathbf{x}^{\mathbf{a_1}} > w^T \mathbf{x}^{\mathbf{a_2}} \\ &\Leftrightarrow w^T \mathbf{x}^{\mathbf{a_1}} - w^T \mathbf{x}^{\mathbf{a_2}} > 0 \\ &\Leftrightarrow w^T (\mathbf{x}^{\mathbf{a_1}} - \mathbf{x}^{\mathbf{a_2}}) > 0 \end{aligned} \tag{2}$$

For each ranking pair of actions, we create two complimentary classification instances: $(\mathbf{x}^{\mathbf{a_1}} - \mathbf{x}^{\mathbf{a_2}}, l_1)$ and $(\mathbf{x}^{\mathbf{a_2}} - \mathbf{x}^{\mathbf{a_1}}, l_2)$, where the labels are $l_1 = +1, l_2 = -1$ if the first challenge has higher value than the second challenge and $l_1 = -1, l_2 = +1$ otherwise. We can train a standard linear classifier on the generated training instances to learn the weight vector w.

In the case of the IWIYW data, there is no explicit ranking between actions. However, we are able to create ranking pairs for the IWIYW data in the following way. As we have seen, there is only a small set of different *You Will* challenges that are reciprocal actions for a diverse set of *I Will* challenges. Thus, many *I Will* challenges will end up having the same *You Will* challenge. We can use the *You Will* challenges as a pivot to effectively "join" the *I Will* challenges. The number of required people to perform *Y* induces a natural ordering between the values of the *I Will* actions where a higher number of required participants means that the *I Will* task has higher value.

For example, for the challenges displayed in Table 1, we can use the common *You Will* challenges to create the following ranked challenge pairs.

$$\begin{aligned} &\text{I will quit smoking} < \text{I will adopt a panda} \\ &\text{I will dye my hair red} < \text{I will learn Java} \end{aligned} \tag{3}$$

According to the examples, adopting a panda has higher value than quitting smoking and learning Java has higher value than dying ones hair red. The third challenge does not share a common *You Will* challenge with any other challenge and therefore no ranking pairs can be formed with it.

As the IWIYW challenges are created online in a non-controlled environment, we have to expect that there is some noise in the automatically created ranked challenges. However, a robust learning algorithm has to be able to handle a certain amount of noise. We note that our method is not limited to the IWIYW data set but can be applied to any data set of actions where relative rankings are provided or can be induced.

4.1 Features

The choice of appropriate feature representations is crucial to the success of any machine learning method. We start by parsing each *I Will If You Will* challenge with a constituency parser. Because each challenge has the same *I Will If You Will* structure, it is easy to identify the subtrees that correspond to the *I Will* and *You Will* parts of the challenge. An example parse tree of a challenge is shown in Figure 1. The yield of the *You Will* subtree serves as a pivot to join different *I Will* challenges. To represent the *I Will* action a as a feature vector $\mathbf{x}^{\mathbf{a}}$, we extract the following lexical and syntax features from the *I Will* subtree of the sentence.

- **Verb:** We extract the verb of the *I Will* clause as a feature. To identify the verb, we pick the left-most verb of the *I Will* subtree based on its part-of-speech (POS) tag. We extract the lowercased word token as a feature. For example, for the sentence in Figure 1, the verb feature is *verb=quit*. If the verb is negated (the left sibling of the *I Will* subtree spans exactly the word *not*), we add the postfix *NOT* to the verb feature, for example *verb=quit_NOT*.

- **Object:** We take the right sibling of the *I will* verb as the object of the action. If the right sibling is a particle with constituent label PRT, e.g., *travel **around** the UK on bike*,

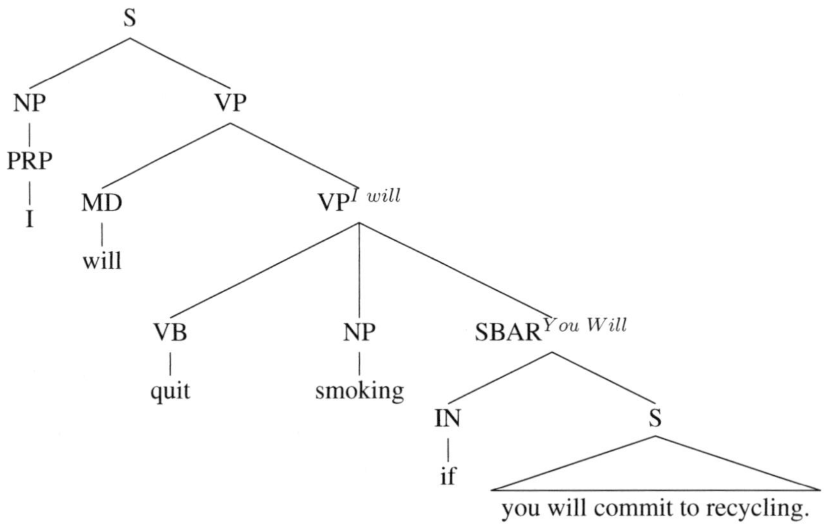

Figure 1: Parse tree of a *I Will If You Will* challenge. The subtrees governing the *I Will* and *You Will* part of the sentence are marked.

we skip the particle and take the next sibling as the object. If the object is a prepositional phrase with constituent tag PP, e.g., *go* ***without*** *electricity for a month*, we take the second child of the prepositional phrase as the object phrase. We then extract two features to represent the object. First, we extract the lowercased head word of the object as a feature. Second, we extract the concatenation of all the words in the yield of the object node as a single feature to capture the complete argument for longer objects. In our example sentence, the object head feature and the complete object feature are identical: *object_head=smoking* and *object=smoking*.

- **Unigram:** We take all lowercased words that are not stopwords in the *I Will* part of the sentence as binary features. In our example sentence, the unigram features *unigr_quit* and *unigr_smoking* would be active.

- **Bigram:** We take all lowercased bigrams in the *I Will* part of the sentence as binary features. We do not remove stopwords for bigram features. In our example sentence, the bigram features *bigr_quit_smoking* would be active.

We note that our method is not restricted to these feature templates. More sophisticated features, like tree kernels (Collins and Duffy, 2002) or semantic role labeling (Palmer et al., 2010), can be imagined.

5 Experiments

We evaluate our approach using standard 10-fold cross-validation and report macro-average accuracy scores for each of the feature sets. The classifier in all our experiments is a linear SVM implemented in SVM-light (Joachims, 2006).

5.1 Data

We obtained a snapshot of 18,290 challenges created during the 2013 IWIYW challenge. The snapshot was taken in mid May 2013, just 1.5 weeks before the 2013 Earth Hour event day. We perform the following pre-processing. We normalize the text to proper UTF-8 encoding and remove challenges where the complete sentence contained less than 7 tokens. These challenges were usually empty or incomplete. We filter the challenges using the `langid.py` tool (Lui and Baldwin, 2012) and only keep English challenges. We normalized the casing of the sentences by first lowercasing all texts and then re-casing each sentence with a simple re-casing model that replaces a word with its most frequent casing form. The re-casing model is trained on the Brown corpus (Ku and Francis, 1967). We tokenize the sentences with the Penn Treebank tokenizer. We parse the sentences with the Stanford parser (Klein and Manning, 2003a; Klein and Manning, 2003b) to ob-

Features	Accuracy
random	0.5000
verb	0.6241
unigrams	0.8481
unigrams + verb	0.8573
object	0.8904
verb + object	0.9115
bigrams	0.9251
unigrams + bigrams	0.9343
unigrams + bigrams + verb	0.9361
unigrams + bigrams + verb + object	**0.9472**

Table 2: Results of 10-fold cross-validation experiments.

tain a constituency parse tree for each challenge. After pre-processing, we are left with 5,499 challenges (4,982 unique), with 4,474 unique *I Will* challenges and 70 unique *You Will* challenges.

We create binary classifications examples between pairs of actions as described in Section 4. As we create all possible combinations between *I Will* challenges with common *You Will* challenges, the number of ranking pairs for training is large. In our case, we ended up with over 840,000 classification instances. We note that not every *I Will* action is guaranteed to be included in the final set of ranking pairs as challenges with a unique *You Will* part that is not found in any other challenge cannot be joined and are effectively ignored. However, this is not a problem for our experiments. The binary classification instances are used to train and test a ranking model for estimating the value of actions as described in the last section.

5.2 Results

The results of our cross-validation experiments are shown in Table 2.

The random baseline for all experiments is 50%. Just using the verb of the *I Will* action as a feature improves over the random baseline to 62.41%. Using a unigram bag-of-words representation of the actions achieves a very respectable score of 84.81%. When we combine unigrams with the verb feature, we achieve 85.73%. One of the most surprising results of our experiments is that the object of the action alone is a very effective feature, achieving 89.04%. When combined with the verb feature, the object feature achieves 91.15% which shows that the verb and object carry most of the relevant information that the model requires to gauge the value of actions. Using bigrams as features, seems to catch this information just as accurately, achieving 92.51% accuracy. The score is further improved by combining the different feature sets. The best result of 94.72% is obtained by combining all the features: unigrams, bigrams, verb, and object. In summary, these results show that our method is able to accurately predict the relative value of actions using simple linguistic features, which is the main contribution of this work.

6 Related Work

The concept of value and reciprocity has been extensively studied in the social sciences (Gergen and Greenberg, 1980), anthropology (Sahlins, 1972), economics (Fehr and Gächter, 2000), and philosophy (Becker, 1990). In linguistics, value has been studied by Jackendoff (2006). His work forms the starting point of our approach.

In natural language processing, there has been very little work on the concept of value. Paul *et al.* (2009) and Girju and Paul (2011) address the problem of semi-automatically mining patterns that encode reciprocal relationships using pronoun templates. Their work focuses on mining patterns of reciprocity while our work uses expressions of reciprocal actions to learn the value of actions.

None of the above works tries to estimate the value of actions, as we do in this work. In fact, we are not aware of any other work that tries to estimate the value of actions from lexical expressions of value.

7 Conclusion

We have presented a simple and effective method for learning the value of actions from reciprocal sentences. We show that our SVM-based ranking model with simple linguistic features is able to accurately rank pairs of actions from the I Will If You Will Earth Hour challenge, achieving an accuracy of up to 94.72%.

Acknowledgement

We thank Sid Das from Earth Hour for sharing the IWIYW data with us. We thank Marek Kowalkiewicz for helpful discussions. The research is partially funded by the Economic Development Board and the National Research Foundation of Singapore.

References

Lawrence C Becker, editor. 1990. *Reciprocity*. University of Chicago Press.

Zhe Cao, Tao Qin, Tie-Yan Liu, Ming-Feng Tsai, and Hang Li. 2007. Learning to rank: from pairwise approach to listwise approach. In *Proceedings of the 24th International Conference on Machine Learning (ICML)*, pages 129–136.

Michael Collins and Nigel Duffy. 2002. Convolution kernels for natural language. In *Advances in Neural Information Processing Systems 14 (NIPS 2001)*, pages 625–632.

Ernst Fehr and Simon Gächter. 2000. Cooperation and punishment in public goods experiments. pages 980–994.

Robert Fiengo and Howard Lasnik. 1973. The logical structure of reciprocal sentences in English. *Foundations of language*, pages 447–468.

Kenneth J. Gergen and Willis Richard H. Greenberg, Martin S., editors. 1980. *Social exchange: Advances in theory and research*. Plenum Press.

Roxana Girju and Michael J Paul. 2011. Modeling reciprocity in social interactions with probabilistic latent space models. *Natural Language Engineering*, 17(1):1–36.

Ralf Herbrich, Thore Graepel, and Klaus Obermayer. 1999. Support vector learning for ordinal regression. In *In Proceedings of the 1999 International Conference on Articial Neural Networks*, pages 97–102.

Ray Jackendoff. 2006. The peculiar logic of value. *Journal of Cognition and Culture*, 6(3-4):375–407.

Thorsten Joachims. 2006. Training linear SVMs in linear time. In *Proceedings of the 12th ACM SIGKDD international conference on Knowledge discovery and data mining*, pages 217–226.

Dan Klein and Christopher D. Manning. 2003a. Accurate unlexicalized parsing. In *Proceedings of the 41st Annual Meeting of the Association for Computational Linguistics (ACL 2003)*, pages 423–430.

Dan Klein and Christopher D. Manning. 2003b. Fast exact inference with a factored model for natural language parsing. *Advances in Neural Information Processing Systems 15 (NIPS 2002)*, pages 423–430.

Henry Ku and W. Nelson Francis. 1967. *Computational Analysis of Present-Day American English*. Brown University Press.

Marco Lui and Timothy Baldwin. 2012. An off-the-shelf language identification tool. In *Proceedings of the 50th Annual Meeting of the Association for Computational Linguistics (ACL 2012)*, pages 25–30.

Martha Palmer, Daniel Gildea, and Nianwen Xue. 2010. Semantic role labeling. *Synthesis Lectures on Human Language Technologies*, 3(1):1–103.

Michael Paul, Roxana Girju, and Chen Li. 2009. Mining the web for reciprocal relationships. In *Proceedings of the 13th Conference on Computational Natural Language Learning (CoNLL)*, pages 75–83.

Marshall D. Sahlins. 1972. *Stone age economics*. Transaction Publishers.

An analysis of textual inference in German customer emails

Kathrin Eichler*, **Aleksandra Gabryszak***, **Günter Neumann**†

*German Research Center for Artificial Intelligence (DFKI), Berlin
(kathrin.eichler|aleksandra.gabryszak@dfki.de)

†German Research Center for Artificial Intelligence (DFKI), Saarbrücken
(neumann@dfki.de)

Abstract

Human language allows us to express the same meaning in various ways. Recognizing that the meaning of one text can be inferred from the meaning of another can be of help in many natural language processing applications. One such application is the categorization of emails. In this paper, we describe the analysis of a real-world dataset of manually categorized customer emails written in the German language. We investigate the nature of textual inference in this data, laying the ground for developing an inference-based email categorization system. This is the first analysis of this kind on German data. We compare our results to previous analyses on English data and present major differences.

1 Introduction

A typical situation in customer support is that many customers send requests describing the same issue. Recognizing that two different customer emails refer to the same problem can help save resources, but can turn out to be a difficult task. Customer requests are usually written in the form of unstructured natural language text, i.e., when automatically processing them, we are faced with the issue of variability: Different speakers of a language express the same meanings using different linguistic forms. There are, in fact, cases where two sentences expressing the same meaning do not share a single word:

1. "Bild und Ton sind asynchron." [*Picture and sound are asynchronous.*]

2. "Die Tonspur stimmt nicht mit dem Film überein." [*The audio track does not match the video.*]

Detecting the semantic equivalence of sentences 1 and 2 requires several textual inference steps: At the lexical level, it requires mapping the word *picture* to *video* and *sound* to *audio track*. At the level of compositional semantics, it requires detecting the equivalence of the expressions *A and B are asynchronous* and *A does not match B*.

In this paper, we describe our analysis of a large set of manually categorized customer emails, laying the ground for developing an email categorization system based on textual inference. In our analysis, we compared each email text to the description of its associated category in order to investigate the nature of the inference steps involved. In particular, our analysis aims to give answers to the following questions: What text representation is appropriate for the email categorization task? What kind of inference steps are involved and how are they distributed in real-world data? Answering these questions will not only help us decide, which existing tools and resources to integrate in an inference-based email categorization system, but also, which non-existing tools may be needed in addition.

2 Related Work

The task of email categorization has been addressed by numerous people in the last decade. In the customer support domain, work to be mentioned includes Eichler (2005), Wicke (2010), and Eichler et al. (2012).

Approaching the task using textual inference relates to two tasks, for which active research is going on: Semantic Textual Similarity, which measures the degree of semantic equivalence (Agirre et al., 2012) of two texts, and Recognizing Textual Entailment (RTE), which is defined as recognizing, given a hypothesis H and a text T, whether the meaning of H can be inferred from (is *entailed* in) T (Dagan et al., 2005). The task of email categorization can be viewed as an RTE task, where T

*Proceedings of the Third Joint Conference on Lexical and Computational Semantics (*SEM 2014)*, pages 69–74,
Dublin, Ireland, August 23-24 2014.

refers to the email text and H refers to the category description. The goal then is to find out if the email text entails the category description, and if so, assign it to the respective category.

In connection with RTE, several groups have analyzed existing datasets in order to investigate the nature of textual inference. Bar-Haim (2010) introduces two levels of entailment, lexical and lexical-syntactic, and analyzes the contribution of each level and of individual inference mechanisms within each level over a sample from the first RTE Challenge test set (Dagan et al., 2005). He concludes that the main contributors are paraphrases and syntactic transformations.

Volokh and Neumann (2011) analyzed a subset of the RTE-7 (Bentivogli et al., 2011) development data to measure the complexity of the task. They divide the T/H pairs into three different classes, depending on the type of knowledge required to solve the problem: In class A, the relevant information is expressed with the same words in both T and H. In class B, the words used in T are synonyms to those used in H. In class C, recognizing entailment between H and T requires the use of logical inference and/or world knowledge. They conclude that for two thirds of the data a good word-level analysis is enough, whereas the remainder of the data contains diverse phenomena calling for a more sophisticated approach.

A detailed analysis of the linguistic phenomena involved in semantic inferences in the T-H pairs of the RTE-5 dataset was presented by (Cabrio and Magnini, 2013).

As the approaches described above, our analysis aims at measuring the contribution of inference mechanisms at different representation levels. However, we focus on a different type of text (customer request as compared to news) and a different language (German as compared to English). We thus expect our results to differ from the ones obtained in previous work.

3 Setup

3.1 Dataset

We analyzed a dataset consisting of a set of emails and a set of categories associated to these emails. The emails contain customer requests sent to the support center of a multimedia software company, and mainly concern the products offered by this company. Each email was manually assigned to one or more matching categories by a customer support agent (a domain expert). These categories, predefined by the data provider, represent previously identified problems reported by customers. All emails and category descriptions are written in German. As is common for this type of data, many emails contain spelling mistakes, grammatical errors or abbreviations, which make automatic text processing difficult. An anonymized[1] version of the dataset is available online[2]. Our data analysis was done on the original dataset. The data examples we use in the following, however, are taken from the anonymized dataset.

In our analysis, we manually compared the email texts to the descriptions of their associated categories in order to investigate the nature of the inference steps involved. In order to reduce the complexity of the task, we based our analysis on the subset of categories, for which the category text described a single problem (a single H, speaking in RTE terms). We also removed emails for which we were not able to relate the category description to the email text. However, we kept emails associated to several categories and analyzed all of the assignments. The reduced dataset we used for our analysis consists of 369 emails associated to 25 categories. The email lengths vary between 2 and 1246 tokens. Category descriptions usually consist of a single sentence or a phrase.

3.2 Task definition

The task of automatically assigning emails to matching categories can be viewed as an RTE task, where T refers to the email text and H refers to the category description. The goal then is to find out if the email text entails the category description, and if so, assign it to the respective category.

For the analysis of inference steps involved, we distinguish between two levels of inference: lexical semantics and compositional semantics. At the lexical level, we distinguish two different types of text representation: First, the bag-of-tokens representation, where both the email text and the category description are represented as the set of content word tokens contained in the respective text.

[1] The anonymization step was performed to eliminate references to the data provider and anonymize personal data about the customers. During this step, the data was transferred into a different product domain (online auction sales). However, the anonymized version is very similar to the original one in terms of language style (including spelling errors, anglicisms, abbreviations, and special characters).

[2] `http://www.excitement-project.eu/attachments/article/97/omq_public_email_data.zip`

Second, the bag-of-terms representation, where a "term" can consist of one or more content tokens occurring consecutively. At this level, following Bar Haim (2010), we assume that entailment holds between T (the email) and H (the category description) if every token (term) in H can be matched by a corresponding entailing token (term) in T.

At the level of compositional semantics, we represent each text as the set of complex expressions (combinations of terms linked syntactically and semantically) contained in it. At this level, we assume that entailment holds between T and H if every term in H is part of at least one complex expression that can be matched by a corresponding entailing expression in T.

The data analysis was carried out by two people separately (one of them an author of this paper), who analyzed each assignment of an email E to a category C based on predefined analysis guidelines. For each of the text representation types described above, the task of the annotators was to find, for each expression in the description of C, a semantically equivalent or entailing expression in E.[3] If such an expression was found, all involved inference steps were to be noted down in an annotation table. The predefined list of possible inference steps is explained in detail in the following.

4 Inference steps

4.1 Lexical semantics level

For each of the three different types of representation (token, term, complex expression), we distinguish various inference steps. At the lexical level, we distinguish among spelling, inflection, derivation, composition, lexical semantics at the token level and lexical semantics at the term level. This distinction was made based on the assumption that for each of these steps a different NLP tool or resource is required (e.g., a lemmatizer for inflection, a compound splitter for composition, a lexical-semantic net for lexical semantics). We also distinguish between token and term level lexical semantics, as, for term-level lexical semantics, we assume that a tool for detecting multi-token terms would be required.

[3]A preanalysis of the data revealed that in some cases, the entailment direction seemed to be flipped: Expressions in the category description entailed expressions in the email text, e.g. "Video" (*video*) → "Film" (*film*). In our analysis, we counted these as positive cases if the context suggested that both expressions were used to express the same idea. We consider this an interesting issue to be further investigated.

4.2 Compositional semantics level

At the level of compositional semantics, we consider inference steps involving complex expressions.[4] These steps go beyond the lexical level and would require the usage of at least a syntactic parser for detecting word dependencies and a tool for recognizing entailment between two complex expressions. At this level, we also record the frequency of three particular phenomena: particle verbs, negation, and light verb constructions, which we considered worth addressing separately.

Particle verbs are important when processing German because, unlike in English, they can occur both as one token or two, dependending on the syntactic construction, in which they are embedded (e.g., "aufnehmen" and "nehme [...] auf" [*(to) record*]. Recognizing the scope of negation can be required in cases where negation is expressed implicitly in one of the sentences, e.g., "A und B sind nicht synchron" [*A and B are not synchronous*] vs. "Es kommt zu Versetzung zwischen A und B" [*There is a misaligment between A and B*]. By *light verbs* we refer to verbs with little semantic content of their own, forming a linguistic unit with a noun or prepositional phrase, for which a single verb with a similar meaning exists, e.g., "Meldung kommt" [*message appears*] vs. "melden" [*notify*].

For example, for the text pair "Das Brennen bricht ab mit der Meldung X" [*Burning breaks with message X*] and "Beim Brennen kommt die Fehlermeldung X" [*When burning, error message X appears*], the word "Meldung" [*message*] was recorded as inference at the token level because it can be derived from "Fehlermeldung" [*error message*] using decomposition. The verb "bricht ab" [*break*] was considered inference at the level of compositional semantics because there is no lexical-semantic relation to the verb "kommt" [*appears*]. The verb can thus only be matched by considering the complete expression.

4.3 Possible effects on precision

The focus of the analysis described so far was on ways to improve recall in an email categorization system: We count the inference steps required to increase the amount of mappable information (similar to query expansion in information retrieval). However, the figures do not show the impact of these mappings on precision, i.e.,

[4]Additional lexical inference steps required at this level are not recorded.

whether an inference step we take would negatively affect the precision of the system. Taking a more precision-oriented view at the problem, we also counted the number of cases for which a more complex representation could be "helpful" (albeit not necessary). For example, inferring the negated expression "Programm kann die DVD nicht abspielen" [*Program cannot play the DVD*] from "Programm kann die DVD nicht laden"' [*Program does not load the DVD*] is possible at the lexical level, assuming that "abspielen" [*(to) play*] entails "laden" [*(to) load*]. However, knowing that both verbal expressions are negated is expected to be beneficial to precision, in order to avoid wrongly inferring a negated from a non-negated expression.

5 Results

5.1 Interannotator agreement

Our analysis was done by two people separately, which allowed us to measure the reliability of the annotation for the different inference steps. The kappa coefficient (Cohen, 1960) for spelling, inflection, derivation and composition ranged between 0.46 and 0.67, i.e., moderate to substantial agreement according to the scale proposed by Landis and Koch (1977). For lexical semantics, the value is only fair (0.38). An analysis showed that the identification of a lexical semantic relation is often not straightforward, and may require a good knowledge of the domain. For example, the verbs "aufrufen" [*call*] and "importieren" [*import*], which would usually not be considered to be semantically related, may in fact be used to describe the same action in the computer domain, referring to files. Also for the more complex inference steps, we measured only fair agreement, due to the number of positive and negative cases being very skewed. For the "helpful" cases, the values ranged between 0.73 and 0.79 (substantial agreement).

5.2 Distribution of inference steps

Table 1 summarizes the distribution of inference steps identified in our data for each text representation type, ordered by their frequency of occurrence.[5] For multi-token terms, particle verbs, and negation, the number of "helpful" cases is given in brackets.

Our results show that the most important inference step at the lexical level is lexical semantics. At the lexical level, we found 157 different word mappings. Only 26 of them correspond to a relation in GermaNet (Hamp and Feldweg, 1997), version 7.0. 48 of the involved words had no GermaNet entry at all, due to the word being an anglicism (e.g., "Error" instead of "Fehler"), a non-lexicalized compound (e.g., "Bildschirmbereich" [*screen area*]) or a highly domain- or application-specific word (for only 37.5% of the words missing in GermaNet, we found an entry in Wikipedia). In 72 cases, both words had a GermaNet entry, but no relation existed, usually because the relation was too domain-specific.

For more than 30% of the words (as compared to 10.1% in Bar-Haim's (2010) analysis on English), a morphological transformation is required, which can be explained by the high complexity of German morphology as compared to the morphology of English. Spelling mistakes or differences, which are not considered in other analyses, are also found in a considerable number of words, the reason being that customer emails are less well-formed than, for example, news texts.

The significance of multi-token terms was surprisingly high for German, where word combinations are usually expressed in the form of compounds (i.e., a single token). In our data, multi-token terms were usually compounds consisting of at least one anglicism (e.g., "USB Anschluss" [*USB port*]). This suggests that texts written in a domain language with a high proportion of English loan words may be more difficult to process than general language texts, as multi-token terms have to be recognized.

At the level of compositional semantics, it should be noted that, in many cases, recognizing the entailment relation between two expressions requires world or domain knowledge. Several of the mappings involved particle verbs or light verbs. Detecting negation scope is expected to be important in a precision-oriented system.

5.3 Comparing text representations

We also had a look at the amount of information left unmapped at each level. For the lexical level, we determined for how many of the content tokens (terms) occurring in the category descriptions, no matching expression was found in the associated emails. For the level of compositional semantics, we looked at each term left unmapped at the lexical level and tried to map a complex expression in

[5]Based on the steps agreed on after a consolidation phase.

Type of inference	Data example	Total (Share)
Lexical semantics (Token)	"Anfang" [*start*] → "Beginn" [*beginning*]	310 (20.2%)
Inflection	"startet" [*starts*] → "starten" [*start*]	206 (13.4%)
Derivation	"Import" [*import*] → "importieren" [*(to) import*]	164 (10.7%)
Composition	"Fehlermeldung" [*error message*] → "Meldung" [*message*]	158 (10.3%)
Spelling	"Dateine" → "Dateien" [*files*]	47 (3.1%)
Lexical semantics (Term)	"MPEG Datei" [*MPEG file*] → "Video" [*video*]	60 (4.1%) [+124 (8.6%)]
Particle verbs	"spielt [...] ab" [*play*] → "abspielen" [*play*]	26 (1.8%) [+34 (2.4%)]
Light verbs	"Meldung kommt" [*message appears*] → "melden" [*notify*]	17 (1.2%)
Negation	"Brennergerät kann nicht gefunden werden" [*Burning device cannot be found*] → "Es wird kein Brenner gefunden" [*No burner is found*]	8 (0.6%) [+121 (8.4%)]
Other complex expressions	"Das Brennen bricht ab mit der Meldung X" [*Burning breaks with message X*] → "Beim Brennen kommt die Fehlermeldung X" [*Burning yields error message X*]	83 (5.7%)

Table 1: Distribution of inference steps in the dataset.

which the term occurred. If for none of these expressions a matching expression was found in the email, the term was counted as non-mappable at this level.

Representation	Non-mappable	Share
Tokens	428 / 1538	27.8%
Terms	365 /1446	25.2%
Complex expressions	229 / 1446	15.8%

The above table shows that the majority of the required inference relates to the lexical level. Choosing a representation that allows us to map more complex expressions, increases the amount of mappable terms by almost 10%. However, even with this more complex representation, a considerable amount of terms (15.8%) cannot be mapped at all because the email text does not contain all information specified in the category description.

6 Conclusions

In our analysis, we examined the inference steps required to determine that the text of a category description can be inferred from the text of a particular email associated to this category. We identified major inference phenomena and determined their distribution in a German real-world dataset. Our analysis supports previous results for English data in that a large portion of the required inference relates to the lexical level. Choosing a representation that allows us to map more complex expressions significantly increases the amount of mappable expressions, but some expressions simply cannot be mapped because the categorization was done relying on partial information in the email.

Our results extend previous results by investigating inference steps specific to the German language (such as morphology, composition, and particle verbs). Some outcomes are unexpected for the German language, such as the high share of multi-token terms. Our analysis also stresses the importance of inference steps relying on domain-specific resources, i.e., for this type of data, the development of tools and resources to support inference in highly specialized domains is crucial.

We are currently using the results of our analysis to build an email categorization system that integrates linguistic resources and tools to expand the linguistic expressions in an incoming email with entailed expressions. This will allow us to measure the performance of such a system, in particular with respect to the effect on precision.

Acknowledgements

This work was partially supported by the EXCITEMENT project (EU grant FP7 ICT-287923) and the German Federal Ministry of Education and Research (Software Campus grant 01—S12050). We would like to thank OMQ GmbH for providing the dataset, Britta Zeller and Jonas Placzek for the data anonymization, and Stefania Racioppa for her help in the annotation phase.

References

Eneko Agirre, Daniel Cer, Mona Diab, and Aitor Gonzalez-Agirre. 2012. SemEval-2012 Task 6: A Pilot on Semantic Textual Similarity. In **SEM 2012: The First Joint Conference on Lexical and Computational Semantics (SemEval 2012)*, pages 385–393, Montréal, Canada, 7-8 June. Association for Computational Linguistics.

Roy Bar-Haim. 2010. *Semantic Inference at the Lexical-Syntactic Level*. Ph.D. thesis, Department of Computer Science, Bar Ilan University, Ramat Gan, Israel.

Luisa Bentivogli, Peter Clark, Ido Dagan, Hoa T. Dang, and Danilo Giampiccolo. 2011. The Seventh PASCAL Recognizing Textual Entailment Challenge. In *Proceedings of TAC*.

Elena Cabrio and Bernardo Magnini. 2013. Decomposing Semantic Inferences. *Linguistics Issues in Language Technology - LiLT. Special Issues on the Semantics of Entailment*, 9(1), August.

Jacob Cohen. 1960. A coefficient of agreement for nominal scales. *Educational and Psychological Measurement*, 20(1):37.

Ido Dagan, Oren Glickman, and Bernardo Magnini. 2005. The PASCAL Recognising Textual Entailment Challenge. In *Proceedings of the PASCAL Challenges Workshop on Recognising Textual Entailment*.

Kathrin Eichler, Matthias Meisdrock, and Sven Schmeier. 2012. Search and Topic Detection in Customer Requests - Optimizing a Customer Support System. *KI*, 26(4):419–422.

Kathrin Eichler. 2005. *Automatic classification of Swedish email messages*. Bachelor thesis, Eberhard-Karls-Universität, Tübingen, Germany.

Birgit Hamp and Helmut Feldweg. 1997. GermaNet - a Lexical-Semantic Net for German. In *In Proceedings of ACL workshop Automatic Information Extraction and Building of Lexical Semantic Resources for NLP Applications*, pages 9–15.

J. R. Landis and G. G. Koch. 1977. The Measurement of Observer Agreement for Categorical Data. *Biometrics*, 33(1):159–174, March.

Alexander Volokh and Günter Neumann. 2011. Using MT-Based Metrics for RTE. In *Proceedings of the 4th Text Analysis Conference (TAC 2011)*, Gaithersburg, Maryland, USA, November. National Institute of Standards and Technology.

Janine Wicke. 2010. *Automated Email Classification using Semantic Relationships*. Master thesis, KTH Royal Institute of Technology, Stockholm, Sweden.

Text Summarization through Entailment-based Minimum Vertex Cover

Anand Gupta[1], **Manpreet Kaur**[2], **Adarsh Singh**[2], **Aseem Goel**[2], **Shachar Mirkin**[3]
[1]Dept. of Information Technology, NSIT, New Delhi, India
[2]Dept. of Computer Engineering, NSIT, New Delhi, India
[3]Xerox Research Centre Europe, Meylan, France

Abstract

Sentence Connectivity is a textual characteristic that may be incorporated intelligently for the selection of sentences of a well meaning summary. However, the existing summarization methods do not utilize its potential fully. The present paper introduces a novel method for single-document text summarization. It poses the text summarization task as an optimization problem, and attempts to solve it using *Weighted Minimum Vertex Cover* (WMVC), a graph-based algorithm. Textual entailment, an established indicator of semantic relationships between text units, is used to measure sentence connectivity and construct the graph on which WMVC operates. Experiments on a standard summarization dataset show that the suggested algorithm outperforms related methods.

1 Introduction

In the present age of digital revolution with proliferating numbers of internet-connected devices, we are facing an exponential rise in the volume of available information. Users are constantly facing the problem of deciding what to read and what to skip. Text summarization provides a practical solution to this problem, causing a resurgence in research in this field.

Given a topic of interest, a standard search often yields a large number of documents. Many of them are not of the user's interest. Rather than going through the entire result-set, the reader may read a gist of a document, produced via summarization tools, and then decide whether to fully read the document or not, thus saving a substantial amount of time. According to Jones (2007), a summary can be defined as "a reductive transformation of source text to summary text through content reduction by selection and/or generalization on what is important in the source". Summarization based on content reduction by selection is referred to as *extraction* (identifying and including the important sentences in the final summary), whereas a summary involving content reduction by generalization is called *abstraction* (reproducing the most informative content in a new way).

The present paper focuses on extraction-based single-document summarization. We formulate the task as a graph-based optimization problem, where vertices represent the sentences and edges the connections between sentences. Textual entailment (Giampiccolo et al., 2007) is employed to estimate the degree of connectivity between sentences, and subsequently to assign a weight to each vertex of the graph. Then, the Weighted Minimum Vertex Cover, a classical graph algorithm, is used to find the minimal set of vertices (that is – sentences) that forms a cover. The idea is that such cover of well-connected vertices would correspond to a cover of the salient content of the document.

The rest of the paper is organized as follows: In Section 2, we discuss related work and describe the WMVC algorithm. In Section 3, we propose a novel summarization method, and in Section 4, experiments and results are presented. Finally, in Section 5, we conclude and outline future research directions.

2 Background

Extractive text summarization is the task of identifying those text segments which provide important information about the gist of the document – the salient units of the text. In (Marcu, 2008), salient units are determined as the ones that contain frequently-used words, contain words that are within titles and headings, are located at the beginning or at the end of sections, contain key phrases and are *the most highly connected to other parts*

*Proceedings of the Third Joint Conference on Lexical and Computational Semantics (*SEM 2014)*, pages 75–80,
Dublin, Ireland, August 23-24 2014.

of the text. In this work we focus on the last of the above criteria, connectivity, to find highly connected sentences in a document. Such sentences often contain information that is found in other sentences, and are therefore natural candidates to be included in the summary.

2.1 Related Work

The connectivity between sentences has been previously exploited for extraction-based summarization. Salton et al. (1997) generate intra-document links between passages of a document using automatic hypertext link generation algorithms. Mani and Bloedorn (1997) use the number of shared words, phrases and co-references to measure connectedness among sentences. In (Barzilay and Elhadad, 1999), lexical chains are constructed based on words relatedness.

Textual entailment (TE) was exploited recently for text summarization in order to find the highly connected sentences in the document. Textual entailment is an asymmetric relation between two text fragments specifying whether one fragment can be inferred from the other. Tatar et al. (2008) have proposed a method called Logic Text Tiling (LTT), which uses TE for sentence scoring that is equal to the number of entailed sentences and to form text segments comprising of highly connected sentences. Another method called Analog Textual Entailment and Spectral Clustering (ATESC), suggested in (Gupta et al., 2012), also uses TE for sentence scoring, using analog scores.

We use a graph-based algorithm to produce the summary. Graph-based ranking algorithms have been employed for text summarization in the past, with similar representation to ours. Vertices represent text units (words, phrases or sentences) and an edge between two vertices represent any kind of relationship between two text units. Scores are assigned to the vertices using some relevant criteria to select the vertices with the highest scores. In (Mihalcea and Tarau, 2004), content overlap between sentences is used to add edges between two vertices and Page Rank (Page et al., 1999) is used for scoring the vertices. Erkan and Radev (2004) use inter-sentence cosine similarity based on word overlap and *tf-idf* weighting to identify relations between sentences. In our paper, we use TE to compute connectivity between nodes of the graph and apply the weighted minimum vertex cover (wMVC) algorithm on the graph to select the sentences for the summary.

2.2 Weighted MVC

wMVC is a combinatorial optimization problem listed within the classical NP-complete problems (Garey and Johnson, 1979; Cormen et al., 2001). Over the years, it has caught the attention of many researchers, due to its NP-completeness, and also because its formulation complies with many real world problems.

Weighted Minimum Vertex Cover Given a weighted graph $G = (V, E, w)$, such that w is a positive weight (cost) function on the vertices, $w : V \rightarrow \mathbb{R}$, a weighted minimum vertex cover of G is a subset of the vertices, $C \subseteq V$ such that for every edge $(u, v) \in E$ either $u \in C$ or $v \in C$ (or both), and the total sum of the weights is minimized.

$$C = argmin_{C'} \sum_{v \in C'} w(v) \tag{1}$$

3 Weighted MVC for text summarization

We formulate the text summarization task as a wMVC problem. The input document to be summarized is represented as a weighted graph $G = (V, E, w)$, where each of $v \in V$ corresponds to a sentence in the document; an edge $(u, v) \in E$ exists if either u entails v or v entails u with a value at least as high as an empirically-set threshold. A weight w is then assigned to each sentence based on (negated) TE values (see Section 3.2 for further details). wMVC returns a cover C which is a subset of the sentences with a minimum total weight, corresponding to the best connected sentences in the document. The cover is our output – the summary of the input document.

Our proposed method, shown in Figure 1, consists of the following main steps.

1. Intra-sentence textual entailment score computation
2. Entailment-based connectivity scoring
3. Entailment connectivity graph construction
4. Application of wMVC to the graph

We elaborate on each of these steps in the following sections.

3.1 Computing entailment scores

Given a document d for which summary is to be generated, we represent d as an array of sentences

Id	Sentence
S_1	A representative of the African National Congress said Saturday the South African government may release black nationalist leader Nelson Mandela as early as Tuesday.
S_2	"There are very strong rumors in South Africa today that on Nov. 15 Nelson Mandela will be released," said Yusef Saloojee, chief representative in Canada for the ANC, which is fighting to end white-minority rule in South Africa.
S_3	Mandela the 70-year-old leader of the ANC jailed 27 years ago, was sentenced to life in prison for conspiring to overthrow the South African government.
S_4	He was transferred from prison to a hospital in August for treatment of tuberculosis.
S_5	Since then, it has been widely rumoured Mandela will be released by Christmas in a move to win strong international support for the South African government.
S_6	"It will be a victory for the people of South Africa and indeed a victory for the whole of Africa," Saloojee told an audience at the University of Toronto.
S_7	A South African government source last week indicated recent rumours of Mandela's impending release were orchestrated by members of the anti-apartheid movement to pressure the government into taking some action.
S_8	And a prominent anti-apartheid activist in South Africa said there has been "no indication (Mandela) would pe released today or in the near future."
S_9	Apartheid is South Africa's policy of racial separation.
Summary	"There are very strong rumors in South Africa today that on Nov.15 Nelson Mandela will pe released," said Yusef Saloojee, chief representative in Canada for the ANC, which is fighting to end white-minority rule in South Africa. He was transferred from prison to a hospital in August for treatment of tuberculosis. A South African government source last week indicated recent rumours of Mandela's impending release were orchestrated by members of the anti-apartheid movement to pressure the government into taking some action. Apartheid is South Africa's policy of racial separation.

Table 1: The sentence array of article *AP881113-0007* of cluster *do106* in the DUC'02 dataset.

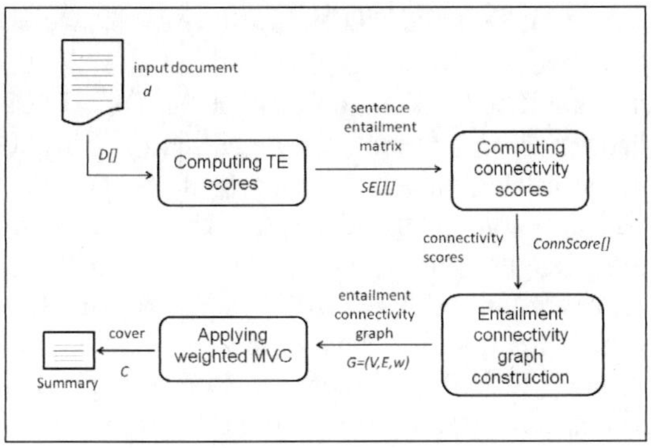

Figure 1: Outline of the proposed method.

$D_{1\times N}$. An example article is shown in Table 1. We use this article to demonstrate the steps of our algorithm.

Then, we compute a TE score between every possible pair of sentences in D using a textual entailment tool. TE scores for all the pairs are stored in a *sentence entailment matrix*, $SE_{N\times N}$. An entry $SE[i,j]$ in the matrix represents the extent by which sentence i entails sentence j. The sentence entailment matrix produced for our example document is shown in Table 2.

	S_1	S_2	S_3	S_4	S_5	S_6	S_7	S_8	S_9
S_1	-	0	0	0.04	0	0	0.001	0.02	0.02
S_2	0.02	-	0.01	0.04	0.06	0.01	0	0.01	0.04
S_3	0	0	-	0.09	0	0	0	0	0.04
S_4	0	0	0	-	0	0	0	0	0.01
S_5	0	0	0	0.04	-	0	0.01	0.01	0.04
S_6	0	0	0	0.04	0	-	0	0	0.02
S_7	0	0	0	0.04	0.06	0	-	0.02	0.27
S_8	0	0	0	0.04	0	0	0.01	-	0.02
S_9	0	0	0	0.04	0	0	0	0	-

Table 2: The sentence entailment matrix of the example article.

Id	$ConnScore$	Id	$ConnScore$
S_1	0.08	S_6	0.06
S_2	0.19	S_7	0.39
S_3	0.13	S_8	0.07
S_4	0.01	S_9	0.04
S_5	0.1		

Table 3: Connectivity Scores of the sentences of article *AP881113-0007*.

3.2 Connectivity scores

Our assumption is that entailment between sentences indicates connectivity, that – as mentioned above – is an indicator of sentence salience. More specifically, salience of a sentence is determined by the degree by which it entails other sentences in the document. We thus use the sentence entailment matrix to compute a connectivity score for each sentence by summing the entailment scores of the sentence with respect to the rest of the sentences in the document, and denote this sum as $ConnScore$. Formally, $ConnScore$ for sentence i is computed as follows.

$$ConnScore[i] = \sum_{i\neq j} SE\left[i,j\right] \quad (2)$$

Applying it to each sentence in the document, we obtain the $ConnScore_{1\times N}$ vector. The sentence connectivity scores corresponding to Table 2 are shown in Table 3.

3.3 Entailment connectivity graph construction

The more a sentence is connected, the higher its connectivity score. To adapt the scores to the wMVC algorithm, that searches for a *minimal* solution, we convert the scores into positive weights in inverted order:

$$w[i] = -ConnScore[i] + Z \quad (3)$$

$w[i]$ is the score that is assigned to the vertex of sentence i; Z is a large constant, meant to keep the scores positive. In this paper, Z has been assigned value = 100. Now, the better a sentence is connected, the lower its weight.

Given the weights, we construct an undirected weighted entailment connectivity graph, $G(V, E, w)$, for the document d. V consists of vertices for the document's sentences, and E are edges that correspond to the entailment relations between the sentences. w is the weight explained above. We create an edge between two vertices as explained below. Suppose that S_i and S_j are two sentences in d, with entailment scores $SE[i, j]$ and $SE[j, i]$ between them. We set a threshold τ for the entailment scores as the mean of all entailment values in the matrix SE. We add an edge (i, j) to G if $SE[i, j] \geqslant \tau$ OR $SE[j, i] \geqslant \tau$, i.e. if at least one of them is as high as the threshold.

Figure 2 shows the connectivity graph constructed for the example in Table 1.

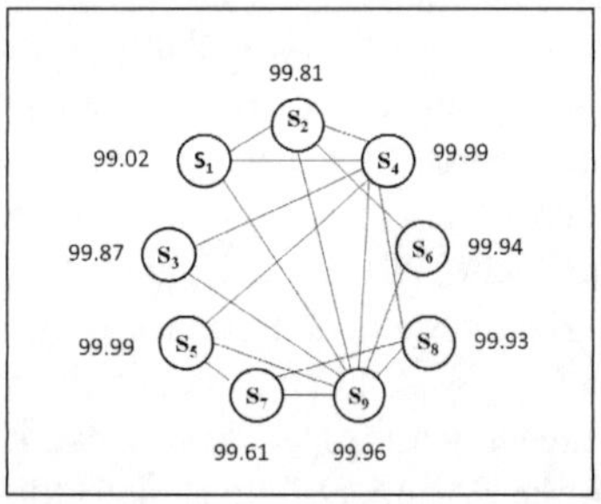

Figure 2: The Entailment connectivity graph of the considered example with associated *Score* of each node shown.

3.4 Applying WMVC

Finally, we apply the weighted minimum vertex cover algorithm to find the minimal vertex cover, which would be the document's summary. We use integer linear programming (ILP) for finding a minimum cover. This algorithm is a 2-approximation for the problem, meaning it is an efficient (polynomial-time) algorithm, guaranteed to find a solution that is no more than 2 times bigger than the optimal solution.[1] The algorithm's input is $G = (V, E, w)$, a weighted graph where each vertex $v_i \in V(1 \leq i \leq n)$ has weight w_i. Its output is a minimal vertex cover C of G, containing a subset of the vertices V. We then list these sentences as our summary, according to their original order in the document.

After applying WMVC to the graph in Figure 2, the cover C returned by the algorithm is $\{S_2, S_4, S_7, S_9\}$ (highlighted in Figure 2).

Whenever a summary is required, a word-limit on the summary is specified. We find the threshold which results with a cover that matches the word limit through binary search.

4 Experiments and results

4.1 Experimental settings

We have conducted experiments on the single-document summarization task of the *DUC 2002* dataset[2], using a random sample that contains 60 news articles picked from each of the 60 clusters available in the dataset. The target summary length limit has been set to 100 words. We used version 2.1.1 of BIUTEE (Stern and Dagan, 2012), a transformation-based TE system to compute textual entailment score between pairs of sentences.[3] BIUTEE was trained with 600 text-hypothesis pairs of the RTE-5 dataset (Bentivogli et al., 2009).

4.1.1 Baselines

We have compared our method's performance with the following re-implemented methods:

1. **Sentence selection with tf-idf**: In this baseline, sentences are ranked based on the sum of the *tf-idf* scores of all the words except stopwords they contain, where *idf* figures are computed from the dataset of 60 documents. Top ranking sentences are added to the summary one by one, until the word limit is reached.
2. **LTT**: (see Section 2)
3. **ATESC** : (see Section 2)

4.1.2 Evaluation metrics

We have evaluated the method's performance using *ROUGE* (Lin, 2004). ROUGE measures the

[1] We have used an implementation of ILP for WMVC in MATLAB, *grMinVerCover*.

[2] http://www-nlpir.nist.gov/projects/duc/data/2002_data.html

[3] Available at: http://www.cs.biu.ac.il/~nlp/downloads/biutee.

Method	P (%)	R (%)	F_1 (%)
TF-IDF	13.3	17.6	15.1
LTT	39.9	34.6	37.1
ATESC	37.7	32.5	34.9
wMVC	39.8	38.8	39.2

Table 4: *ROUGE-1* results.

Method	P (%)	R (%)	F_1 (%)
TF-IDF	7.4	9.6	8.4
LTT	18.4	15.2	16.6
ATESC	16.3	11.7	13.6
wMVC	16.7	16.8	16.8

Table 5: *ROUGE-2* results.

quality of an automatically-generated summary by comparing it to a "gold-standard", typically a human generated summary. *ROUGE-n* measures n-gram precision and recall of a candidate summary with respect to a set of *reference summaries*. We compare the system-generated summary with two reference summaries for each article in the dataset, and show the results for *ROUGE-1*, *ROUGE-2* and *ROUGE-SU4* that allows skips within n-grams. These metrics were shown to perform well for single document text summarization, especially for short summaries. Specifically, Lin and Hovy (2003) showed that *ROUGE-1* achieves high correlation with human judgments.[4]

4.2 Results

The results for *ROUGE-1*, *ROUGE-2* and *ROUGE-SU4* are shown in Tables 4, 5 and 6, respectively. For each, we show the precision (P), recall (R) and F_1 scores. Boldface marks the highest score in each table. As shown in the tables, our method achieves the best score for each of the three metrics.

4.3 Analysis

The entailment connectivity graph generated conveys information about the connectivity of sentences in the document, an important parameter for indicating the salience of a sentences.

The purpose of the wMVC is therefore to find a subset of the sentences that are well-connected and cover all the content of all the sentences. Note that merely selecting the sentences on the basis of a *greedy approach*, that picks the those sentences with the highest connectivity score, does not ensure that all edges of the graph are covered, i.e. it does not ensure that all the information is covered in the summary. In Figure 3, we illustrate the difference between wMVC (left) and a greedy algorithm (right) over our example document. The vertices selected by each algorithm are highlighted. The selected set by wMVC, $\{S_2, S_4, S_7, S_9\}$, covers all the edges in the graph. In contrast, using the greedy algorithm, the subset of vertices selected on the basis of highest scores is $\{S_2, S_3, S_7, S_8\}$. There, several edges are not covered (e.g. $(S_1 \rightarrow S_9)$).

It is therefore much more in sync with the summarization goal of finding a subset of sentences that conveys the important information of the document in a compressed manner.

[4]See (Lin, 2004) for formal definitions of these metrics.

Method	P (%)	R (%)	F_1 (%)
TF-IDF	2.2	4.2	2.9
LTT	16	11.8	13.6
ATESC	15.5	11.1	12.9
wMVC	14.1	14.2	14.2

Table 6: *ROUGE-SU4* results.

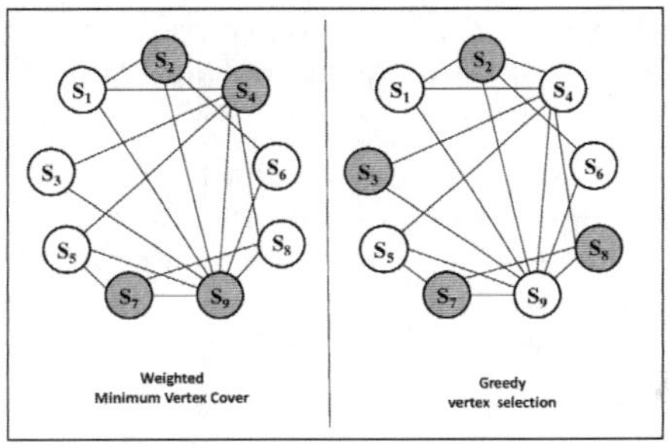

Figure 3: Minimum Vertex Cover vs. Greedy selection of sentences.

5 Conclusions and future work

The paper presents a novel method for single-document extractive summarization. We formulate the summarization task as an optimization problem and employ the weighted minimum vertex cover algorithm on a graph based on textual entailment relations between sentences. Our method has outperformed previous methods that employed TE for summarization as well as a frequency-based baseline. For future work, we wish to apply our algorithm on smaller segments of the sentences, using *partial textual entailment* Levy et al. (2013), where we may obtain more reliable entailment measurements, and to apply the same approach for multi-document summarization.

References

Regina Barzilay and Michael Elhadad. 1999. Using lexical chains for text summanzauon. In *In Inderjeet Mani and Mark T. Maybury, editors, Advances in Automatic Text Summarization*, pages 111–121, The MIT Press, 1999.

Luisa Bentivogli, Ido Dagan, Hoa Trang Dang, Danilo Giampiccolo, and Bernardo Magnini. 2009. The fifth pascal recognizing textual entailment challenge. In *Proceedings of Text Analysis Conference*, pages 14–24, Gaithersburg, Maryland USA.

Thomas H. Cormen, Charles E. Leiserson, Ronald L. Rivest, and Clifford Stein. 2001. *Introduction to Algorithms*. McGraw-Hill, New York, 2nd edition.

Gunes Erkan and Dragomir R. Radev. 2004. Lexrank: Graph-based lexical centrality as salience in text summarization. *Journal of Artificial Intellignece Research(JAIR)*, 22(1):457–479.

Michael R. Garey and David S. Johnson. 1979. *Computers and Intractability: A Guide to the Theory of NP-Completeness*. FREEMAN, New York.

Danilo Giampiccolo, Bernardo Magnini, Ido Dagan, and Bill Dolan. 2007. The third pascal recognizing textual entailment challenge. In *Proceedings of the Association for Computational Linguistics, ACL'07*, pages 1–9, Prague, Czech Republic.

Anand Gupta, Manpreet Kaur, Arjun Singh, Ashish Sachdeva, and Shruti Bhati. 2012. Analog textual entailment and spectral clustering (atesc) based summarization. In *Lecture Notes in Computer Science, Springer*, pages 101–110, New Delhi, India.

Karen Spark Jones. 2007. Automatic summarizing: The state of the art. *Information Processing and Management*, 43:1449–1481.

Omer Levy, Torsten Zesch, Ido Dagan, and Iryna Gurevych. 2013. Recognizing partial textual entailment. In *Proceedings of the Association for Computational Linguistics*, pages 17–23, Sofia, Bulgaria.

Chin-Yew Lin and Eduard Hovy. 2003. Automatic evaluation of summaries using n-gram co-occurrence statistics. In *Proceedings of the 2003 Conference of the North American Chapter of the Association for Computational Linguistics on Human Language Technology-Volume 1*, pages 71–78, Edmonta, Canada, 27 May- June 1.

Chin-Yew Lin. 2004. Rouge: A package for automatic evaluation of summaries. In *Proceedings of the Workshop on Text Summarization Branches Out*, pages 25–26, Barcelona, Spain.

Inderjeet Mani and Eric Bloedorn. 1997. Multi-document summarization by graph search and matching. In *Proceedings of the Fourteenth National Conference on Articial Intelligence (AAAI-97), American Association for Articial Intelligence*, pages 622–628, Providence, Rhode Island.

Daniel Marcu. 2008. From discourse structure to text summaries. In *Proceedings of the ACL/EACL '97, Workshop on Intelligent Scalable Text Summarization*, pages 82–88, Madrid, Spain.

Rada Mihalcea and Paul Tarau. 2004. Textrank: Bringing order into texts. In *Proceedings of EMNLP*, volume 4(4), page 275, Barcelona, Spain.

Lawrence Page, Sergey Brin, Rajeev Motwani, and Terry Winograd. 1999. The pagerank citation ranking: Bringing order to the web. *Technical Report*.

Gerard Salton, Amit Singhal, Mandar Mitra, and Chris Buckley. 1997. Automatic text structuring and summarization. *Information Processing and Management*, 33:193–207.

Asher Stern and Ido Dagan. 2012. BIUTEE: A modular open-source system for recognizing textual entailment. In *Proceedings of the ACL 2012 System Demonstrations*, pages 73–78, Jeju, Korea.

Doina Tatar, Emma Tamaianu Morita, Andreea Mihis, and Dana Lupsa. 2008. Summarization by logic seg-mentation and text entailment. In *Conference on Intelligent Text Processing and Computational Linguistics (CICLing 08)*, pages 15–26, Haifa, Israel.

Semantic Roles in Grammar Engineering

Wojciech Jaworski **Adam Przepiórkowski**
Institute of Computer Science, Polish Academy of Sciences
ul. Jana Kazimierza 5, 02-668 Warszawa
wjaworski@mimuw.edu.pl adamp@ipipan.waw.pl

Abstract

The aim of this paper is to discuss difficulties involved in adopting an existing system of semantic roles in a grammar engineering task. Two typical repertoires of semantic roles are considered, namely, VerbNet and Sowa's system. We report on experiments showing the low inter-annotator agreement when using such systems and suggest that, at least in case of languages with rich morphosyntax, an approximation of semantic roles derived from syntactic (grammatical functions) and morphosyntactic (grammatical cases) features of arguments may actually be beneficial for applications such as textual entailment.

1 Introduction

The modern notion of semantic – or thematic – roles stems from the lexical semantic work of Gruber 1965 (his *thematic relations*) and Fillmore 1968 (so-called *deep cases*), and was popularised by Jackendoff 1972, but traces of this concept may already be found in the notion of *kāraka* in the writings of the Sanskrit grammarian Pāṇini (4th century BC); see, e.g., Dowty 1991 for a historical introduction. Fillmore's deep cases are Agentive, Dative, Instrumental, Factive, Locative, Objective, as well as Benefactive, Time and Comitative, but many other sets of semantic roles may be found in the literature; for example, Dalrymple 2001, p. 206, cites – after Bresnan and Kanerva 1989 – the following ranked list of thematic roles: Agent, Benefactive, Recipient/Experiencer, Instrument, Theme/Patient, Locative.

In Natural Language Processing (NLP), one of the most popular repertoires of semantic roles is that of VerbNet (Kipper et al. 2000; http://verbs.colorado.edu/~mpalmer/projects/verbnet.html), a valence lexicon of English based on Levin's (1993) classification of verbs according to the diathesis phenomena they exhibit. The VerbNet webpage states that it contains 3769 lemmata divided into 5257 senses. There are 30 semantic roles used in VerbNet 3.2,[1] including such standard roles as Agent, Beneficiary and Instrument, but also more specialised roles such as Asset (for quantities), Material (for stuff things are made of) or Pivot (a theme more central to an event than the theme expressed by another argument). This resource is widely used in NLP, and it was one of the main lexical resources behind the Unified Lexicon of English (Crouch and King, 2005), a part of an LFG-based semantic parser (Crouch and King, 2006) employed in tasks such as question answering (Bobrow et al., 2007a) and textual entailment (Bobrow et al., 2007b).

Another system of semantic roles considered here is that developed by Sowa (2000; http://www.jfsowa.com/krbook/) for the purpose of knowledge representation in artificial intelligence. There are 18 thematic roles proposed in Sowa 2000, p. 508, including standard roles such as Agent, Recipient and Instrument, but also 4 temporal and 4 spatial roles. Unlike in case of VerbNet, there is no corpus or dictionary showing numerous examples of the acutal use of such roles – just a few examples are given (on pp. 506–510). On the other hand, principles of assigning thematic roles to arguments may be formulated as a decision tree, which should make the process of semantic role labelling more efficient.

But why should we care about semantic roles at all? From the NLP perspective, the main reason is that they are useful in tasks approximating reasoning, such as textual entailment. Take the follow-

[1]Table 2 on the VerbNet webpage lists 21 roles, of which Actor is not actually used; the 10 roles which are used but not listed there are Goal, Initial_Location (apart from Location), Pivot, Reflexive, Result, Trajectory and Value, as well as Co-Agent, Co-Patient and Co-Theme.

*Proceedings of the Third Joint Conference on Lexical and Computational Semantics (*SEM 2014)*, pages 81–86,
Dublin, Ireland, August 23-24 2014.

ing two Polish sentences, with their naïve meaning representations in (1a)–(2a):

(1) Anonim napisał artykuł na *SEM.
anonymous wrote paper for *SEM
'An anonymous person wrote a paper for *SEM.'
    a. $\exists a \exists p\, article(a) \wedge person(p) \wedge anonymous(p) \wedge write(p, a, starsem)$
    b. $\exists e \exists a \exists p\, article(a) \wedge person(p) \wedge anonymous(p) \wedge write(e) \wedge agent(e, p) \wedge patient(e, a) \wedge destination(e, starsem)$

(2) Anonim napisał artykuł.
anonymous wrote paper
'An anonymous person wrote a paper.'
    a. $\exists a \exists p\, article(a) \wedge person(p) \wedge anonymous(p) \wedge write(p, a)$
    b. $\exists e \exists a \exists p\, article(a) \wedge person(p) \wedge anonymous(p) \wedge write(e) \wedge agent(e, p) \wedge patient(e, a)$

While it is clear that (2) follows from (1), this inference is not obvious in (1a)–(2a); making such an inference would require an additional meaning postulate relating the two $write$ predicates of different arities. In contrast, when dependents of the predicate are represented via separate semantic roles, as in the neo-Davidsonian (1b)–(2b) (cf. Parsons 1990), the inference from (1b) to (2b) is straightforward and follows from general inference rules of first-order logic; nothing special needs to be said about the writing events.

Also, building on examples from Bobrow et al. 2007b, p. 20, once we know that *flies* is a possible hyponym of *travels*, we may infer *Ed travels to Boston* from *Ed flies to Boston*. Given representations employing semantic roles, e.g., $\exists e\, fly(e) \wedge agent(e, ed) \wedge destination(e, boston)$ and $\exists e\, travel(e) \wedge agent(e, ed) \wedge destination(e, boston)$, all that is needed to make this inference is a general inference schema saying that, if P is a hypernym of Q, then $\forall e\, Q(e) \rightarrow P(e)$. A more complicated set of inference schemata would be necessary if the neo-Davidsonian approach involving semantic roles were not adopted.

2 Problems with standard repertoires of semantic roles

As noted by Bobrow et al. 2007b, p. 20, standard VerbNet semantic roles may in some cases make inference more difficult. For example, in *Ed travels to Boston*, VerbNet identifies *Ed* as a Theme, while in *Ed flies to Boston* – as an Agent. The solution adopted there was to use "a backoff strategy where fewer role names are used (by projecting down role names to the smaller set)".

In order to verify the usefulness of well-known repertoires of semantic roles, we performed a usability study of the two sets of semantic roles described above. The aim of this study was to estimate how difficult it would be to create a corpus of sentences with verbs' arguments annotated with such semantic roles. For this purpose, 37 verbs were selected more or less at random and 843 instances of arguments of these verbs (in 393 sentences, but only one verb was considered in each sentence) were identified in a corpus. In two experiments, the same 7 human annotators were asked to label these arguments with VerbNet and with Sowa's semantic roles.

In both cases interannotator agreement (IAA) was below our expectations, given the fact that VerbNet comes with short descriptions of semantic roles and a corpus of illustrative examples, and that Sowa's classification could be (and was for this experiment) formalised as a decision tree. For VerbNet roles, Fleiss's κ (called *Fleiss's Multi-*π in Artstein and Poesio 2008, as it is actually a generalisation of Scott's π rather than Cohen's κ) is equal to 0.617, and for Sowa's system it is a little higher, 0.648. According to the common wisdom (reflected in Wikipedia's entry for "Fleiss' kappa"), values between 0.41 and 0.60 reflect moderate agreement and between 0.61 and 0.80 – substantial agreement. Hence, the current results could be interpreted as moderately substantial agreement. However, Artstein and Poesio 2008, p. 591, question this received wisdom and state that "only values above 0.8 ensured an annotation of reasonable quality".

This opinion is confirmed by the more detailed analysis of the distribution of (dis)agreement provided in Tab. 1. The top table gives the number of arguments for which the most commonly assigned Sowa's role was assigned by n annotators (n ranges from 2 to 7; not from 1, as there were no arguments that would be assigned 7 different roles by the 7 annotators) and the most commonly assigned VerbNet role was assigned by m annotators (m also ranges from 2 to 7). For example, the cell in the row labelled 7 and in the column labelled

		VerbNet						
		2	3	4	5	6	7	
	2	6	8	3	0	0	0	17
S	3	8	39	39	17	25	3	131
o	4	2	26	49	37	20	5	139
w	5	4	11	48	45	11	15	134
a	6	1	9	18	16	35	20	99
	7	0	3	11	47	52	210	323
		21	96	168	162	143	253	843

		VerbNet						
		2	3	4	5	6	7	
	2	0.71%	0.95%	0.36%	0.00%	0.00%	0.00%	2.02%
S	3	0.95%	4.63%	4.63%	2.02%	2.97%	0.36%	15.54%
o	4	0.24%	3.08%	5.81%	4.39%	2.37%	0.59%	16.49%
w	5	0.47%	1.30%	5.69%	5.34%	1.30%	1.78%	15.90%
a	6	0.12%	1.07%	2.14%	1.90%	4.15%	2.37%	11.74%
	7	0.00%	0.36%	1.30%	5.58%	6.17%	24.91%	38.32%
		2.49%	11.39%	19.93%	19.22%	16.96%	30.01%	100.00%

Table 1: Interannotator agreement rate for VerbNet and Sowa role systems; the top table gives numbers of arguments, the bottom table gives normalised percentages

6 contains the information that 52 arguments were such that all annotators agreed on Sowa's role and 6 agreed on a VerbNet role. The final row and the final column contain the usual marginals; e.g., out of 843 arguments, in case of Sowa's system 253 arguments were annotated unanimously, and in case of VerbNet roles – 323 arguments. The lower table gives the same information normalised to percentages. Note that for a significant percent of examples (almost 18% in case of Sowa's system and almost 14% in case of VerbNet) there is no majority decision and that the concentration of examples around the diagonal means that the lack of consensus is largely independent of the choice of the role system.

Some of the most difficult cases were discussed with annotators and the conclusion reached was that there are two main reasons for the low IAA: numerous cases where more than one role seems to be suitable for a given argument and cases where there is no suitable role at all. (In fact, as in case of LECZYĆ 'treat, cure' discussed below, it is sometimes difficult to distinguish these two reasons: more than one role seems suitable because none is clearly right.)

The first situation is caused by the fact that a distinction between the roles is often highly subjective; for example, when *a doctor is treating a girl*, is (s)he causing a structural change? The answer to this question determines the distinction between Patient and Theme in Sowa's system. It could be "no" when the doctor only prescribes some medicines, but it could be "yes" when (s)he operates her. Furthermore, some emphasis is put on volitionality in Sowa's system: the initiator of an action can be either Agent or Effector, depending on whether (s)he causes the action voluntarily or not – something that is often difficult to decide even when a context of a sentence is given.

On the other hand, the Agent role is extended in VerbNet to 'internally controlled subjects such as forces and machines', but it is easy to confuse this role with Theme. For example, in *The horse jumped over the fence*, the *horse* is – somewhat counterintuitively – marked as Theme, as it must bear the same role as in *Tom jumped the horse over the fence*, where the Agent role is already taken by *Tom*. Other commonly confused pairs are Stimulus and Theme, Topic and Theme, and Patient and Theme. Moreover, there are cases where more than one role genuinely (not as a result of confusion) matches a given argument. For example, in the Polish sentence *Ona ładuje się w foremkę, którą ktoś jej podsunął* 'She squeezes/loads herself into a/the mould that somebody offered her', the argument *w foremkę* 'into mould' can be reasonably marked as both: a spatial Destination and a functional Result.

The other common reason for interannotator disagreement is the lack of a suitable role. For example, returning to the sentence *A doctor is treating a girl*, it seems that neither of the two systems has an obvious role for the person being cured (hence the impression of potential suitability of a number of roles). In Polish sentences involving the verb LECZYĆ 'treat, cure', the object of treatment was variously marked as Agent, Beneficiary, Patient or Source when using VerbNet roles, and as Agent, Beneficiary, Experiencer, Patient, Recipient or Result when using Sowa's system. Thus, in *Zwierzę jest leczone z tych chorób* 'An animal is treated for these diseases', in the VerbNet experiment the animal was marked as Beneficiary (by 3 annotators), as Patient (×3) and as Source (×1), and in the Sowa experiment – as Beneficiary (×2), as Patient (×2), as Recipient (×2) and as Result (×1). Similarly, for *Mąż leczył się na serce*, lit. 'Husband treated himself for his heart', the husband was annotated as Agent (×2), Beneficiary (×2), Patient (×2) and Source (×1) when using VerbNet roles and as Agent (×1), Beneficiary (×2), Experiencer (×1), Patient (×2) and Recipient (×1) when using Sowa's roles.

Another major problem with the attempt to use these sets of semantic roles was a high percentage of verb occurrences with multiple arguments assigned the same semantic role. In case of Sowa's system 4.36% of sentences had this problem on the average (the raw numbers for the 7 annotators are: 2, 5, 8, 9, 17, 31, 34 out of 347 sentences with no coordination of unlikes in argument positions;[2] note the surprisingly large deviation) and in case of VerbNet – 2.47% sentences were so affected (7, 7, 8, 9, 10, 12).

On the basis of these experiments, as well as various remarks in the literature (see, e.g., the reference to Bobrow et al. 2007b at the beginning of this section), we conclude that semantic role systems such as VerbNet or Sowa's are perhaps not really well-suited for the grammar engineering task – and certainly not worth the time, effort and money needed to construct reasonably-sized corpora annotated with them – and that other approaches must be explored.

3 Syntactic approximation of semantic roles

In Jaworski and Przepiórkowski 2014 we propose to define 'semantic roles' on the basis of morphosyntactic information, including morphological cases, following the Slavic linguistic tradition stemming from the work of Roman Jakobson (see, e.g., Jakobson 1971a,b). In particular, since the broader context of the work reported here is the development of a syntactico-semantic LFG (Lexical-Functional Grammar; Bresnan 2001; Dalrymple 2001) parser for Polish, we build on the usual LFG approach of obtaining semantic representations on the basis of f-structures, i.e., non-tree-configurational syntactic representations (as opposed to more surfacy tree-configurational c-structures) containing information about predicates, grammatical functions and morphosyntactic features; this so-called description-by-analysis (DBA) approach has been adopted for German (Frank and Erk, 2004; Frank and Semecký, 2004; Frank, 2004), English (Crouch and King, 2006) and Japanese (Umemoto, 2006).

In the usual DBA approach, semantic roles are added to the resulting representations on the basis of semantic dictionaries external to LFG grammars (Frank and Semecký, 2004; Frank, 2004; Crouch and King, 2005, 2006). When such FrameNet- or VerbNet-like dictionaries are not available, grammatical function names (subject, object, etc.) are used instead of semantic roles (Umemoto, 2006). Unfortunately, this latter approach is detrimental for tasks such as textual entailment, as LFG grammatical functions represent the surface relations, so, e.g., a passivised (deep) object bears the grammatical function of (surface) subject. Other diathesis phenomena also result in different grammatical functions assigned to arguments standing in the same semantic relation to the verb, e.g., the recipient of the verb GIVE will normally be assigned a different grammatical function depending on whether it is realised as an NP (as in *John gave Mary a book*) or as a PP (*John gave a book to Mary*).

Although currently no reasonably-sized dictionaries of Polish containing semantic role information are available, we do not resort to grammatical

[2] In case of arguments realised as a coordination of unlikes, e.g., a nominal phrase and a sentential clause, annotators routinely assigned distinct semantic roles to different conjuncts, so that one argument received a number of different roles (from the same annotator) and, consequently, there were many more duplicates in the remaining $393 - 347 = 46$ sentences than in the 347 sentences free from coordination of unlikes considered here.

functions as names of semantic roles, but rather guess approximations of semantic roles on the basis of grammatical functions and morphosyntactic features. For example, subjects of active verbs are marked as R0 (the 'semantic role' approximating the Agent), but subjects of passsive verbs, as well as objects of active verbs, are marked as R1 (roughly, the Undergoer, i.e., Patient, Theme or Product).[3] Apart from grammatical functions and the voice value of the verb, also morphosyntactic features of arguments are taken into account, especially, for PP arguments, the preposition lemma and the grammatical case it governs. So, for example, both the OBJ-TH (dative NP) arguments and certain OBL (PP) arguments, e.g., those headed by the preposition DLA 'for', are translated into the R2 'semantic role', which approximates the Beneficiary and Recipient semantic roles. This results in the same semantic representations of *Papkin upolował dla Klary krokodyla* 'Papkin.NOM hunted a crocodile.ACC for Klara', lit. 'Papkin hunted for Klara crocodile', and *Papkin upolował Klarze krokodyla*, lit. 'Papkin.NOM hunted Klara.DAT crocodile.ACC'.

The advantage of this morphosyntax-based approach is that it is fully deterministic (only one 'semantic role' may be assigned to a given argument) and that it ensures high uniqueness of any 'semantic role' in the set of arguments of any verb (only 6 of the 347 sentences considered above, i.e., 1.73%, have the same 'semantic role' asigned to a couple of arguments, compared with 2.47% and 4.36% in the experiments described in this paper; see Jaworski and Przepiórkowski 2014 for additional data). The disadvantage is that sometimes wrong decisions are made; for example, OBL arguments of type Z[inst] 'with' may have one of at least three meanings: Perlative (R7), Thematic (R1) and Co-agentive (R0); in fact, the sentence *Zrób z nim porządek*, lit. 'do with him order', is ambiguous between the last two and may mean either 'Deal with him' (R1) or 'Clean up with him' (R0). However, the procedure will always assign only one of these 'roles' to such Z[inst] arguments (currently R7).

[3]We use symbols such as R0 or R1 instead of more meaningful names in order to constantly remind ourselves that we are dealing with approximations of true semantic roles; this also explains scare quotes in the term 'semantic role' when used in this approximative sense.

4 Conclusions

When developing a semantic parser, it makes sense to aim at neo-Davidsonian representations with semantic roles relating arguments to events, as such representations facilitate textual entailment and similar tasks. In this paper we reported on experiments which show that the practical usability of two popular repertoires of semantic roles in grammar engineering is limited: as the IAA is low, systems trained on corpora annotated with such semantic roles are bound to be inconsistent, limiting the usefulness of resulting semantic representations in such tasks. In case of a language that does not have a resouce such as VerbNet, the question arises then whether it makes sense to invest considerable time and effort into creating it.

In this and the accompanying paper Jaworski and Przepiórkowski 2014 we suggest an answer in the negative and propose to approximate semantic roles on the basis of syntactic and morphosyntactic information. Admittedly, this proposal is currently rather programmatic, as it is supported only with anectodal evidence. It seems plausible that the usefulness of resulting representations for textual entailment should be comparable to – or maybe even better than – that of semantic representations produced by semantic role labellers trained on rather inconsistently annotated data, but this should be quantified by further experiments.[4] If this hypothesis turns out to be true, however, the method we propose has the clear advantage of being overwhelmingly cheaper: instead of many person-years of building a resource such as VerbNet (and then training a role labeller, etc.), a couple of days of a skilled researcher are required to define and test reasonable translations from (morpho)syntax to 'semantic roles'.

References

Ron Artstein and Massimo Poesio. 2008. Inter-Coder Agreement for Computational Linguistics. *Computational Linguistics* 34(4), 555–596.

Daniel G. Bobrow, Bob Cheslow, Cleo Condoravdi, Lauri Karttunen, Tracy Holloway King,

[4]To the best of our knowledge, no testing data for such tasks are available for Polish and Polish has never been included in evaluation initiatives of this kind. The approach described here is currently employed in a large-scale grammar development effort carried out at the Institute of Computer Science, Polish Academy of Sciences, in connection with the CLARIN-PL Research Infrastructure, and we hope to further report on its usefulness in the future.

Rowan Nairn, Valeria de Paiva, Charlotte Price, and Annie Zaenen. 2007a. PARC's Bridge and Question Answering System. In *Proceedings of the GEAF07 Workshop*, pages 26–45.

Daniel G. Bobrow, Cleo Condoravdi, Richard Crouch, Valeria de Paiva, Lauri Karttunen, Tracy Holloway King, Rowan Nairn, Charlotte Price, and Annie Zaenen. 2007b. Precision-focused textual inference. In *Proceedings of the ACL–PASCAL Workshop on Textual Entailment and Paraphrasing at ACL 2007*, pages 16–21.

Joan Bresnan. 2001. *Lexical-Functional Syntax*. Blackwell Textbooks in Linguistics, Malden, MA: Blackwell.

Joan Bresnan and Jonni M. Kanerva. 1989. Locative inversion in Chicheŵa: A case study of factorization in grammar. *Linguistic Inquiry* 20(1), 1–50.

Dick Crouch and Tracy Holloway King. 2005. Unifying Lexical Resources. In *Proceedings of the Interdisciplinary Workshop on the Identification and Representation of Verb Features and Verb Classes*.

Dick Crouch and Tracy Holloway King. 2006. Semantics via f-structure rewriting. In Miriam Butt and Tracy Holloway King (eds.), *The Proceedings of the LFG'06 Conference*, Universität Konstanz, Germany: CSLI Publications.

Mary Dalrymple. 2001. *Lexical Functional Grammar*. San Diego, CA: Academic Press.

David Dowty. 1991. Thematic Proto-roles and Argument Selection. *Language* 67(3), 547–619.

Charles J. Fillmore. 1968. The Case for Case. In Emmon Bach and Robert T. Harms (eds.), *Universals in Linguistic Theory*, pages 1–88, New York: Holt, Rinehart and Winston.

Anette Frank. 2004. Generalisations over Corpus-induced Frame Assignment Rules. In Charles Fillmore, Manfred Pinkal, Collin Baker and Katrin Erk (eds.), *Proceedings of the LREC 2004 Workshop on Building Lexical Resources from Semantically Annotated Corpora*, pages 31–38, ELRA, Lisbon.

Anette Frank and Katrin Erk. 2004. Towards an LFG Syntax-Semantics Interface for Frame Semantics Annotation. In Alexander Gelbukh (ed.), *Computational Linguistics and Intelligent Text Processing (CICLing 2004)*, volume 2945 of *Lecture Notes in Computer Science*, pages 1–12, Heidelberg: Springer.

Anette Frank and Jiří Semecký. 2004. Corpus-based Induction of an LFG Syntax-Semantics Interface for Frame Semantic Processing. In Silvia Hansen-Schirra, Stefan Oepen and Hans Uszkoreit (eds.), *Proceedings of the 5th International Workshop on Linguistically Interpreted Corpora at COLING 2004*, Geneva.

Jeffrey Gruber. 1965. *Studies in Lexical Relations*. Ph. D.thesis, Massachusetts Institute of Technology.

Ray Jackendoff. 1972. *Semantic Interpretation in Generative Grammar*. Cambridge, MA: The MIT Press.

Roman O. Jakobson. 1971a. Beitrag zur allgemeinen Kasuslehre. Gesamtbedeutungen der russischen Kasus. In *Selected Writings II*, pages 23–71, The Hague: Mouton.

Roman O. Jakobson. 1971b. Morfologičeskie nabljudenija nad slavjanskim skloneniem. In *Selected Writings II*, pages 154–183, The Hague: Mouton.

Wojciech Jaworski and Adam Przepiórkowski. 2014. Syntactic Approximation of Semantic Roles. In Adam Przepiórkowski and Maciej Ogrodniczuk (eds.), *Advances in Natural Language Processing: Proceedings of the 9th International Conference on NLP, PolTAL 2014, Warsaw, Poland, September 17–19, 2014*, volume 8686 of *Lecture Notes in Artificial Intelligence*, Heidelberg: Springer.

Karin Kipper, Hoa Trang Dang, William Schuler, and Martha Palmer. 2000. Building a class-based verb lexicon using TAGs. In *Proceedings of TAG+5 Fifth International Workshop on Tree Adjoining Grammars and Related Formalisms*.

Beth Levin. 1993. *English Verb Classes and Alternations: A Preliminary Investigation*. Chicago: University of Chicago Press.

Terence Parsons. 1990. *Events in the Semantics of English: A Study in Subatomic Semantics*. Cambridge, MA: The MIT Press.

John F. Sowa. 2000. *Knowledge Representation: Logical, Philosophical, and Computational Foundations*. Pacific Grove, CA: Brooks Cole Publishing Co.

Hiroshi Umemoto. 2006. Implementing a Japanese Semantic Parser Based on Glue Approach. In *Proceedings of the 20th Pacific Asia Conference on Language, Information and Computation*, pages 418–425, Huazhong Normal University, Wuhan, China: Tsinghua University Press.

Semantic Role Labelling with minimal resources: Experiments with French

Rasoul Kaljahi[†‡], **Jennifer Foster**[†], **Johann Roturier**[‡]
[†]NCLT, School of Computing, Dublin City University, Ireland
{rkaljahi, jfoster}@computing.dcu.ie
[‡]Symantec Research Labs, Dublin, Ireland
johann_roturier@symantec.com

Abstract

This paper describes a series of French semantic role labelling experiments which show that a small set of manually annotated training data is superior to a much larger set containing semantic role labels which have been projected from a source language via word alignment. Using universal part-of-speech tags and dependencies makes little difference over the original fine-grained tagset and dependency scheme. Moreover, there seems to be no improvement gained from projecting semantic roles between direct translations than between indirect translations.

1 Introduction

Semantic role labelling (SRL) (Gildea and Jurafsky, 2002) is the task of identifying the predicates in a sentence, their semantic arguments and the roles these arguments take. The last decade has seen considerable attention paid to statistical SRL, thanks to the existence of two major hand-crafted resources for English, namely, FrameNet (Baker et al., 1998) and PropBank (Palmer et al., 2005). Apart from English, only a few languages have SRL resources and these resources tend to be of limited size compared to the English datasets.

French is one of those languages which suffer from a scarcity of hand-crafted SRL resources. The only available gold-standard resource is a small set of 1000 sentences taken from Europarl (Koehn, 2005) and manually annotated with Propbank verb predicates (van der Plas et al., 2010b). This dataset is then used by van der Plas et al. (2011) to evaluate their approach to projecting the SRLs of English sentences to their translations in French. They additionally build a large, "artificial" or automatically labelled dataset of approximately 1M Europarl sentences by projecting the SRLs from English sentences to their French translations and use it for training an SRL system.

We build on the work of van der Plas et al. (2010b) by answering the following questions: 1) *How much artificial data is needed to train an SRL system?* 2) *Is it better to use direct translations than indirect translations*, i.e. is it better to use for projection a source-target pair where the source represents the original sentence and the target represents its direct translation as opposed to a source-target pair where the source and target are both translations of an original sentence in a third language? 3) *Is it better to use coarse-grained syntactic information (in the form of universal part-of-speech tags and universal syntactic dependencies) than to use fine-grained syntactic information?* We find that SRL performance levels off after only 5K training sentences obtained via projection and that direct translations are no more useful than indirect translations. We also find that it makes very little difference to French SRL performance whether we use universal part-of-speech tags and syntactic dependencies or more fine-grained tags and dependencies.

The surprising result that SRL performance levels off after just 5K training sentences leads us to directly compare the small hand-crafted set of 1K sentences to the larger artificial training set. We use 5-fold cross-validation on the small dataset and find that the SRL performance is substantially higher (>10 F_1 in identification and classification) when the hand-crafted annotations are used.

2 Related Work

There has been relatively few works in French SRL. Lorenzo and Cerisara (2012) propose a clustering approach for verb predicate and argument labelling (but not identification). They choose

*Proceedings of the Third Joint Conference on Lexical and Computational Semantics (*SEM 2014)*, pages 87–92, Dublin, Ireland, August 23-24 2014.

VerbNet style roles (Schuler, 2006) and manually annotate sentences with them for evaluation, achieving an F_1 of 78.5.

Gardent and Cerisara (2010) propose a method for semi-automatically annotating the French dependency treebank (Candito et al., 2010) with Propbank core roles (no adjuncts). They first manually augment TreeLex (Kupść and Abeillé, 2008), a syntactic lexicon of French, with semantic roles of syntactic arguments of verbs (i.e. verb subcategorization). They then project this annotation to verb instances in the dependency trees. They evaluate their approach by performing error analysis on a small sample and suggest directions for improvement. The annotation work is however at its preliminary stage and no data is published.

As mentioned earlier, van der Plas et al. (2011) use word alignments to project the SRLs of the English side of EuroParl to its French side resulting in a large artificial dataset. This idea is based on the *Direct Semantic Transfer* hypothesis which assumes that a semantic relationship between two words in a sentence can be transferred to any two words in the translation which are aligned to these source-side words. Evaluation on their 1K manually-annotated dataset shows that a syntactic-semantic dependency parser trained on this artificial data set performs significantly better than directly projecting the labelling from its English side – a promising result because, in a real-world scenario, the English translations of the French data to be annotated do not necessarily exist.

Padó and Lapata (2009) also make use of word alignments to project SRLs from English to German. The word alignments are used to compute the semantic similarity between syntactic constituents. In order to determine the extent of semantic correspondence between English and German, they manually annotate a set of parallel sentences and find that about 72% of the frames and 92% of the argument roles exist in both sides, ignoring their lexical correspondence.

3 Datasets, SRL System and Evaluation

We use the two datasets described in (van der Plas et al., 2011) and the delivery report of the *Classic* project (van der Plas et al., 2010a). These are the gold standard set of 1K sentences which was annotated by manually identifying each verb predicate, finding its equivalent English frameset in PropBank and identifying and labelling its arguments based on the description of the frameset (henceforth known as *Classic1K*), and the synthetic dataset consisting of more than 980K sentences (henceforth known as *Classic980K*), which was created by word aligning an English-French parallel corpus (Europarl) using GIZA++ (Och and Ney, 2003) and projecting the French SRLs from the English SRLs via the word alignments. The joint syntactic-semantic parser described in (Titov et al., 2009) was used to produce the English SRLs and the dependency parses of the French side were produced using the `ISBN` parser described in (Titov and Henderson, 2007).

We use LTH (Björkelund et al., 2009), a dependency-based SRL system, in all of our experiments. This system was among the best-performing systems in the CoNLL 2009 shared task (Hajič et al., 2009) and is straightforward to use. It comes with a set of features tuned for each shared task language (English, German, Japanese, Spanish, Catalan, Czech, Chinese). We compared the performance of the English and Spanish feature sets on French and chose the former due to its higher performance (by 1 F_1 point).

To evaluate SRL performance, we use the CoNLL 2009 shared task scoring script[1], which assumes a semantic dependency between the argument and predicate and the predicate and a dummy root node and then calculates the precision (`P`), recall (`R`) and $\mathtt{F}_1$ of identification of these dependencies and classification (labelling) of them.

4 Experiments

4.1 Learning Curve

The ultimate goal of SRL projection is to build a training set which partially compensates for the lack of hand-crafted resources. van der Plas et al. (2011) report encouraging results showing that training on their projected data is beneficial over directly obtaining the annotation via projection which is not always possible. Although the quality of such automatically-generated training data may not be comparable to the manual one, the possibility of building much bigger data sets may provide some advantages. Our first experiment investigates the extent to which the size of the synthetic training set can improve performance.

We randomly select 100K sentences from *Classic980K*, shuffle them and split them into 20 sub-

[1] `https://ufal.mff.cuni.cz/conll2009-st/eval09.pl`

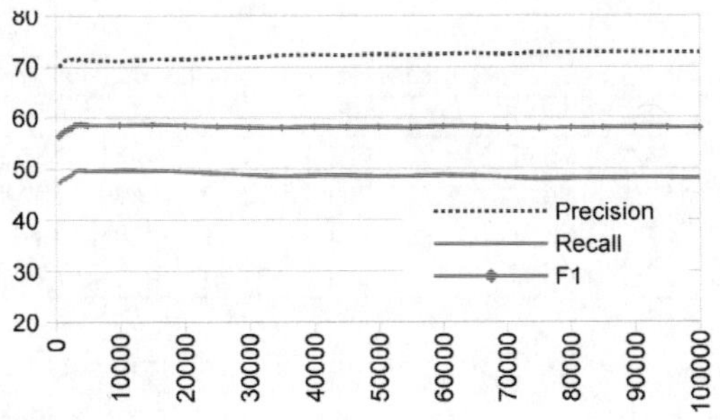

Figure 1: Learning curve with 100K training data of projected annotations

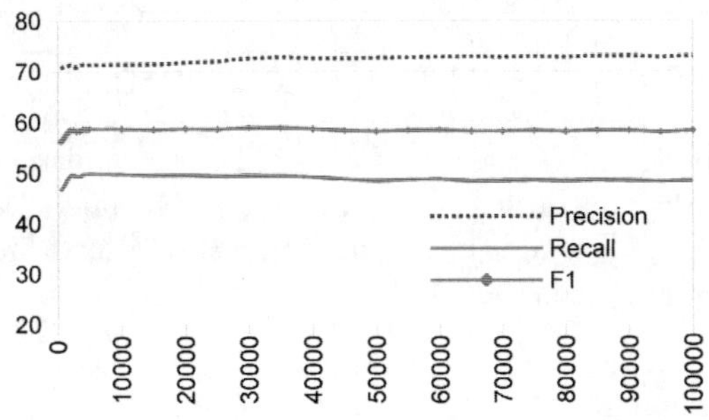

Figure 2: Learning curve with 100K training data of projected annotations on only direct translations

sets of 5K sentences. We then split the first 5K into 10 sets of 500 sentences. We train SRL models on the resulting 29 subsets using LTH. The performance of the models evaluated on *Classic1K* is presented in Fig. 1. Surprisingly, the best F_1 (58.7) is achieved by only 4K sentences, and after that the recall (and consequently F_1) tends to drop though precision shows a positive trend, suggesting that the additional sentences bring little information. The large gap between precision and recall is also interesting, showing that the projections do not have wide semantic role coverage.[2]

4.2 Direct Translations

Each sentence in Europarl was written in one of the official languages of the European Parliament and translated to all of the other languages. Therefore both sides of a parallel sentence pair can be indirect translations of each other. van der Plas et al. (2011) suggest that translation divergence may affect automatic projection of semantic roles. They therefore select for their experiments only those 276K sentences from the 980K which are direct translations between English and French. Motivated by this idea, we replicate the learning curve in Fig. 1 with another set of 100K sentences randomly selected from only the direct translations. The curve is shown in Fig. 2. There is no noticeable difference between this and the graph in Fig. 1, suggesting that the projections obtained via direct translations are not of higher quality.

4.3 Impact of Syntactic Annotation

Being a dependency-based semantic role labeller, LTH employs a large set of features based on syntactic dependency structure. This inspires us to compare the impact of different types of syntactic annotations on the performance of this system.

Based on the observations from the previous sections, we choose two different sizes of training sets. The first set contains the first 5K sentences from the original 100K, as we saw that more than this amount tends to diminish performance. The second set contains the first 50K from the original 100K, the purpose of which is to check if changing the parses affects the usefulness of adding more data. We will call these data sets *Classic5K* and *Classic50K* respectively.

Petrov et al. (2012) create a set of 12 universal part-of-speech (POS) tags which should in theory be applicable to any natural language. It is interesting to know whether these POS tags are more useful for SRL than the original set of the 29 more fine-grained POS tags used in French Treebank which we have used so far. To this end, we convert the original POS tags of the data to universal POS tags and retrain and evaluate the SRL models. The results are given in the second row of Table 1 (`OrgDep+UniPOS`). The first row of the table (`Original`) shows the performance using the original annotation. Even though the scores increase in most cases – due mostly to a rise in recall – the changes are small. It is worth noting that identification seems to benefit more from the universal POS tags.

Similar to universal POS tags, McDonald et al. (2013) introduce a set of 40 universal dependency types which generalize over the dependency structure specific to several languages. For French, they provide a new treebank, called `uni-dep-tb`, manually annotating 16,422 sentences from vari-

[2]Note that our results are not directly comparable with (van der Plas et al., 2011) because they split *Classic1K* into development and test sets, while we use the whole set for testing. We do not have access to their split.

	5K						50K					
	Identification			Classification			Identification			Classification		
	P	R	F_1	P	R	F_1	P	R	F_1	P	R	F_1
`Original`	85.95	59.64	70.42	**71.34**	49.50	**58.45**	86.67	58.07	69.54	**72.44**	48.54	58.13
`OrgDep+UniPOS`	**86.71**	**60.46**	**71.24**	71.11	**49.58**	58.43	**86.82**	58.71	**70.05**	72.30	**48.90**	**58.34**
`StdUniDep+UniPOS`	86.14	59.76	70.57	70.60	48.98	57.84	86.38	**58.90**	70.04	71.61	48.83	58.07
`CHUniDep+UniPOS`	85.98	59.21	70.13	70.66	48.66	57.63	86.47	58.26	69.61	71.74	48.34	57.76

Table 1: SRL performance using different syntactic parses with Classic 5K and 50K training sets

ous domains. We now explore the utility of this new dependency scheme in SRL.

The French universal dependency treebank comes in two versions, the first using the standard dependency structure based on basic Stanford dependencies (de Marneffe and Manning, 2008) where content words are the heads except in copula and adposition constructions, and the second which treats content words as the heads for all constructions without exemption. We use both schemes in order to verify their effect on SRL.

In order to obtain universal dependencies for our data, we train parsing models with MaltParser (Nivre et al., 2006) using the entire `uni-dep-tb`.[3] We then parse our data using these MaltParser models. The input POS tags to the parser are the universal POS tags used in `OrgDep+UniPOS`. We train and evaluate new SRL models on these data. The results are shown in the third and fourth rows of Table 1. `StdUniDept+UniPOS` is the setting using standard dependencies and `CHUDep+UPOS` using content-head dependencies.

According to the third and fourth rows in Table 1, content-head dependencies are slightly less useful than standard dependencies. The general effect of universal dependencies can be compared to those of original ones by comparing these results to `OrgDep+UniPOS` - the use of universal dependencies appears to have only a modest (negative) effect. However, we must be careful of drawing too many conclusions because in addition to the difference in dependency schemes, the training data used to train the parsers as well as the parsers themselves are different.

Overall, we observe that the universal annotations can be reliably used when the fine-grained annotation is not available. This can be especially useful for languages which lack such resources and require techniques such as cross-lingual transfer to replace them.

[3]Based on our preliminary experiments on the parsing performance, we use `LIBSVM` as learning algorithm, `nivreeager` as parsing algorithm for the standard dependency models and `stackproj` for the content-head ones.

	Identification			Classification		
	P	R	F_1	P	R	F_1
`1K`	83.76	83.00	83.37	68.40	67.78	**68.09**
`5K`	**85.94**	59.62	70.39	71.30	49.47	58.40
`1K+5K`	85.74	66.53	74.92	**71.48**	55.46	62.46
`SelfT`	83.82	**83.66**	**83.73**	67.91	**67.79**	67.85

Table 2: Average scores of 5-fold cross-validation with Classic 1K (`1K`), 5K (`5K`), 1K plus 5K (`1K+5K`) and self-training with 1K seed and 5K unlabeled data (`SelfT`)

4.4 Quality vs. Quantity

In Section 4.1, we saw that adding more data annotated through projection did not elevate SRL performance. In other words, the same performance was achieved using only a small amount of data. This is contrary to the motivation for creating synthetic training data, especially when the hand-annotated data already exist, albeit in a small size. In this section, we compare the performance of SRL models trained using manually-annotated data with SRL models trained using 5K of artificial or synthetic training data. We use the original syntactic annotations for both datasets.

To this end, we carry out a 5-fold cross-validation on *Classic1K*. We then evaluate the *Classic5K* model, on each of the 5 test sets generated in the cross-validation. The average scores of the two evaluation setups are compared. The results are shown in Table 2.

While the `5K` model achieves higher precision, its recall is far lower resulting in dramatically lower F_1. This high precision and low recall is due to the low confidence of the model trained on projected data suggesting that a considerable amount of information is not transferred during the projection. This issue can be attributed to the fact that the

Classic projection uses intersection of alignments in the two translation directions, which is the most restrictive setting and leaves many source predicates and arguments unaligned.

We next add the *Classic5K* projected data to the manually annotated training data in each fold of another cross-validation setting and evaluate the resulting models on the same test sets. The results are reported in the third row of the Table 2 (`1K+5K`). As can be seen, the low quality of the projected data significantly degrades the performance compared to when only manually-annotated data are used for training.

Finally, based on the observation that the quality of labelling using manually annotated data is higher than using the automatically projected data, we replicate `1K+5K` with the 5K data labelled using the model trained on the training subset of `1K` at each cross-validation fold. In other words, we perform a one-round self-training with this model. The performance of the resulting model evaluated in the same cross-validation setting is given in the last row of Table 2 (`SelfT`).

As expected, the labelling obtained by models trained on manual annotation are more useful than the projected ones when used for training new models. It is worth noting that, unlike with the `1K+5K` setting, the balance between precision and recall follows that of the `1K` model. In addition, some of the scores are the highest among all results, although the differences are not significant.

4.5 How little is too little?

In the previous section we saw that using a manually annotated dataset with as few as 800 sentences resulted in significantly better SRL performance than using projected annotation with as many as 5K sentences. This unfortunately indicates the need for human labour in creating such resources. It is interesting however to know the lower bound of this requirement. To this end, we reverse our cross-validation setting and train on 200 and test on 800 sentences. We then compare to the `5K` models evaluated on the same 800 sentence sets at each fold. The results are presented in Table 3. Even with only 200 manually annotated sentences, the performance is considerably higher than with 5K sentences of projected annotations. However, as one might expect, compared to when 800 sentences are used for training, this small model performs significantly worse.

	Identification			Classification		
	P	R	F_1	P	R	F_1
`1K`	82.34	**79.61**	**80.95**	64.14	**62.01**	**63.06**
`5K`	**85.95**	59.64	70.42	**71.34**	49.50	58.45

Table 3: Average scores of 5-fold cross-validation with Classic 1K (`1K`) and 5K (`5K`) using 200 sentences for training and 800 for testing at each fold

5 Conclusion

We have explored the projection-based approach to SRL by carrying out experiments with a large set of French semantic role labels which have been automatically transferred from English. We have found that increasing the number of these artificial projections that are used in training an SRL system does not improve performance as might have been expected when creating such a resource. Instead it is better to train directly on what little gold standard data is available, even if this dataset contains only 200 sentences. We suspect that the disappointing performance of the projected dataset originates in the restrictive way the word alignments have been extracted. Only those alignments that are in the intersection of the English-French and French-English word alignment sets are retained resulting in low SRL recall. Recent preliminary experiments show that less restrictive alignment extraction strategies including extracting the union of the two sets or source-to-target alignments lead to a better recall and consequently F_1 both when used for direct projection to the test data or for creating the training data and then applying the resulting model to the test data.

We have compared the use of universal POS tags and dependency labels to the original, more fine-grained sets and shown that there is only a little difference. However, it remains to be seen whether this finding holds for other languages or whether it will still hold for French when SRL performance can be improved. It might also be interesting to explore the combination of universal dependencies with fine-grained POS tags.

Acknowledgments

This research has been supported by the Irish Research Council Enterprise Partnership Scheme (EPSPG/2011/102) and the computing infrastructure of the CNGL at DCU. We thank Lonneke van der Plas for providing us the Classic data. We also thank the reviewers for their helpful comments.

References

Collin F. Baker, Charles J. Fillmore, and John B. Lowe. 1998. The berkeley framenet project. In *Proceedings of the 36th ACL*, pages 86–90.

Anders Björkelund, Love Hafdell, and Pierre Nugues. 2009. Multilingual semantic role labeling. In *Proceedings of the Thirteenth Conference on Computational Natural Language Learning: Shared Task*, pages 43–48.

Marie Candito, Benot Crabbé, and Pascal Denis. 2010. Statistical french dependency parsing: treebank conversion and first results. In *Proceedings of LREC'2010*.

Marie-Catherine de Marneffe and Christopher D. Manning. 2008. The stanford typed dependencies representation. In *Proceedings of the COLING Workshop on Cross-Framework and Cross-Domain Parser Evaluation*.

Claire Gardent and Christophe Cerisara. 2010. Semi-Automatic Propbanking for French. In *TLT9 - The Ninth International Workshop on Treebanks and Linguistic Theories*.

Daniel Gildea and Daniel Jurafsky. 2002. Automatic labeling of semantic roles. *Computational Linguistics*, 28(3):245–288.

Jan Hajič, Massimiliano Ciaramita, Richard Johansson, Daisuke Kawahara, Maria Antònia Martí, Lluís Màrquez, Adam Meyers, Joakim Nivre, Sebastian Padó, Jan Štěpánek, Pavel Straňák, Mihai Surdeanu, Nianwen Xue, and Yi Zhang. 2009. The conll-2009 shared task: Syntactic and semantic dependencies in multiple languages. In *Proceedings of the Thirteenth Conference on Computational Natural Language Learning: Shared Task*, pages 1–18.

Philipp Koehn. 2005. Europarl: A Parallel Corpus for Statistical Machine Translation. In *Conference Proceedings: the tenth Machine Translation Summit*, pages 79–86.

Anna Kupść and Anne Abeillé. 2008. Growing treelex. In *Proceedings of the 9th International Conference on Computational Linguistics and Intelligent Text Processing*, CICLing'08, pages 28–39.

Alejandra Lorenzo and Christophe Cerisara. 2012. Unsupervised frame based semantic role induction: application to french and english. In *Proceedings of the ACL 2012 Joint Workshop on Statistical Parsing and Semantic Processing of Morphologically Rich Languages*, pages 30–35.

Ryan McDonald, Joakim Nivre, Yvonne Quirmbach-Brundage, Yoav Goldberg, Dipanjan Das, Kuzman Ganchev, Keith Hall, Slav Petrov, Hao Zhang, Oscar Täckström, Claudia Bedini, Núria Bertomeu Castelló, and Jungmee Lee. 2013. Universal dependency annotation for multilingual parsing. In *Proceedings of the 51st Annual Meeting of the Association for Computational Linguistics (Volume 2: Short Papers)*, pages 92–97.

Joakim Nivre, Johan Hall, and Jens Nilsson. 2006. Maltparser: A data-driven parser-generator for dependency parsing. In *In Proceedings of LREC*.

Franz Josef Och and Hermann Ney. 2003. A systematic comparison of various statistical alignment models. *Computational Linguistics*, 29(1):19–51.

Sebastian Padó and Mirella Lapata. 2009. Cross-lingual annotation projection of semantic roles. *J. Artif. Int. Res.*, 36(1):307–340.

Martha Palmer, Daniel Gildea, and Paul Kingsbury. 2005. The proposition bank: An annotated corpus of semantic roles. *Computational Linguistics*, 31(1):71–106.

Slav Petrov, Dipanjan Das, and Ryan McDonald. 2012. A universal part-of-speech tagset. In *Proceedings of LREC*, May.

Karin Kipper Schuler. 2006. *VerbNet: A Broad-Coverage, Comprehensive Verb Lexicon*. Ph.D. thesis, University of Pennsylvania.

Ivan Titov and James Henderson. 2007. A latent variable model for generative dependency parsing. In *Proceedings of the 10th International Conference on Parsing Technologies*, pages 144–155.

Ivan Titov, James Henderson, Paola Merlo, and Gabriele Musillo. 2009. Online projectivisation for synchronous parsing of semantic and syntactic dependencies. In *In Proceedings of the Internation Joint Conference on Artificial Intelligence (IJCAI)*, pages 1562–1567.

Lonneke van der Plas, James Henderson, and Paola Merlo. 2010a. D6. 2: Semantic role annotation of a french-english corpus.

Lonneke van der Plas, Tanja Samardžić, and Paola Merlo. 2010b. Cross-lingual validity of propbank in the manual annotation of french. In *Proceedings of the Fourth Linguistic Annotation Workshop*, LAW IV '10, pages 113–117.

Lonneke van der Plas, Paola Merlo, and James Henderson. 2011. Scaling up automatic cross-lingual semantic role annotation. In *Proceedings of the 49th Annual Meeting of the Association for Computational Linguistics: Human Language Technologies*, pages 299–304.

Compositional Distributional Semantics Models in Chunk-based Smoothed Tree Kernels

Nghia The Pham
University of Trento
thenghia.pham@unitn.it

Lorenzo Ferrone
University of Rome "Tor Vergata"
lorenzo.ferrone@gmail.com

Fabio Massimo Zanzotto
University of Rome "Tor Vergata"
fabio.massimo.zanzotto@uniroma2.it

Abstract

The field of compositional distributional semantics has proposed very interesting and reliable models for accounting the distributional meaning of simple phrases. These models however tend to disregard the syntactic structures when they are applied to larger sentences. In this paper we propose the *chunk-based smoothed tree kernels* (CSTKs) as a way to exploit the syntactic structures as well as the reliability of these compositional models for simple phrases. We experiment with the recognizing textual entailment datasets. Our experiments show that our CSTKs perform better than basic compositional distributional semantic models (CDSMs) recursively applied at the sentence level, and also better than syntactic tree kernels.

1 Introduction

A clear interaction between syntactic and semantic interpretations for sentences is important for many high-level NLP tasks, such as question-answering, textual entailment recognition, and semantic textual similarity. Systems and models for these tasks often use classifiers or regressors that exploit convolution kernels (Haussler, 1999) to model both interpretations.

Convolution kernels are naturally defined on spaces where there exists a similarity function between terminal nodes. This feature has been used to integrate distributional semantics within tree kernels. This class of kernels is often referred to as *smoothed tree kernels* (Mehdad et al., 2010; Croce et al., 2011), yet, these models only use distributional vectors for words.

Compositional distributional semantics models (CDSMs) on the other hand are functions mapping text fragments to vectors (or higher-order tensors) which then provide a distributional meaning for simple phrases or sentences. Many CDSMs have been proposed for simple phrases like non-recursive noun phrases or verbal phrases (Mitchell and Lapata, 2008; Baroni and Zamparelli, 2010; Clark et al., 2008; Grefenstette and Sadrzadeh, 2011; Zanzotto et al., 2010). Non-recursive phrases are often referred to as chunks (Abney, 1996), and thus, CDSMs are good and reliable models for chunks.

In this paper, we present the *chunk-based smoothed tree kernels* (CSTK) as a way to merge the two approaches: the smoothed tree kernels and the models for compositional distributional semantics. Our approach overcomes the limitation of the smoothed tree kernels which only use vectors for words by exploiting reliable CDSMs over chunks. CSTKs are defined over a chunk-based syntactic subtrees where terminal nodes are words or word sequences. We experimented with CSTKs on data from the recognizing textual entailment challenge (Dagan et al., 2006) and we compared our CSTKs with other standard tree kernels and standard recursive CDSMs. Experiments show that our CSTKs perform better than basic compositional distributional semantic models (CDSMs) recursively applied at the sentence level and better than syntactic tree kernels.

The rest of the paper is organized as follows. Section 2 describes the CSTKs. Section 3 reports on the experimental setting and on the results. Finally, Section 4 draws the conclusions and sketches the future work.

2 Chunk-based Smoothed Tree Kernels

This section describes the new class of kernels. We first introduce the notion of the chunk-based syntactic subtree. Then, we describe the recursive formulation of the class of kernels. Finally, we introduce the basic CDSMs we use and we introduce two instances of the class of kernels.

*Proceedings of the Third Joint Conference on Lexical and Computational Semantics (*SEM 2014)*, pages 93–98, Dublin, Ireland, August 23-24 2014.

2.1 Notation and preliminaries

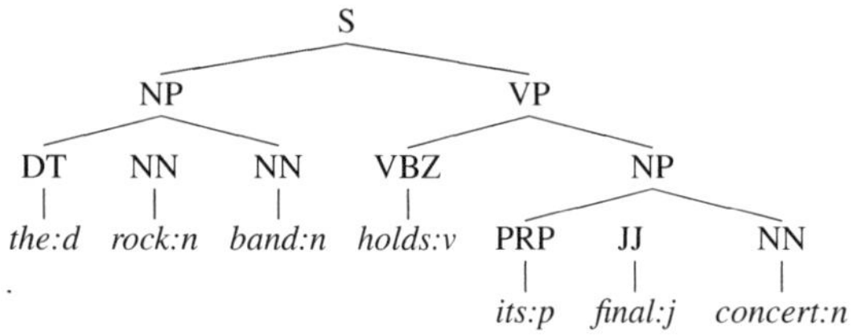

Figure 1: Sample Syntactic Tree

A *Chunk-based Syntactic Sub-Tree* is a subtree of a syntactic tree where each non-terminal node dominating a contiguous word sequence is collapsed into a chunk and, as usual in chunks (Abney, 1996), the internal structure is disregarded. For example, Figure 2 reports some chunk-based syntactic subtrees of the tree in Figure 1. Chunks are represented with a pre-terminal node dominating a triangle that covers a word sequence. The first subtree represents the chunk covering the second NP and the node dominates the word sequence *its:d final:n concert:n.* The second subtree represents the structure of the whole sentence and one chunk, that is the first NP dominating the word sequence *the:d rock:n band:n.* The third subtree again represents the structure of the whole sentence split into two chunks without the verb.

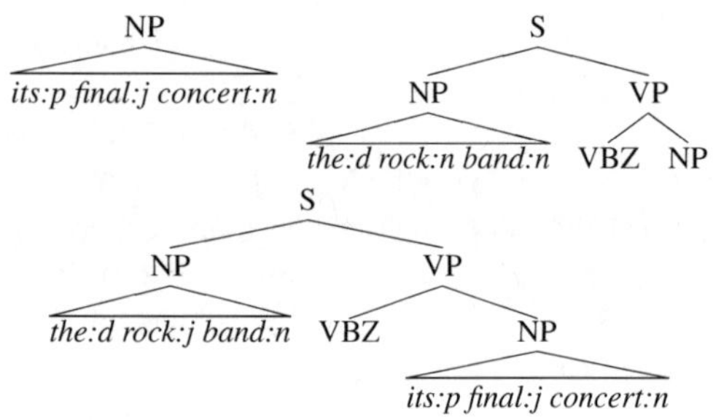

Figure 2: Some Chunk-based Syntactic Sub-Trees of the tree in Figure 1

In the following sections, generic trees are denoted with the letter t and $N(t)$ denotes the set of non-terminal nodes of tree t. Each non-terminal node $n \in N(t)$ has a label s_n representing its syntactic tag. As usual for constituency-based parse trees, pre-terminal nodes are nodes that have a single terminal node as child. Terminal nodes of trees are words denoted with *w:pos* where w is the actual token and *pos* is its postag. The structure of these trees is represented as follows. Given a tree t, $c_i(n)$ denotes i-th child of a node n in the set of nodes $N(t)$. The production rule headed in node n is $\mathsf{prod}(n)$, that is, given the node n with m children, $\mathsf{prod}(n)$ is:

$$\mathsf{prod}(n) = s_n \rightarrow s_{c_1(n)} \dots s_{c_m(n)}$$

Finally, for a node n in $N(t)$, the function $d(n)$ generates the word sequence dominated by the non-terminal node n in the tree t. For example, *d(VP)* in Figure 1 is *holds:v its:p final:j concert:n.*

Chunk-based Syntactic Sub-Trees (CSSTs) are instead denoted with the letter τ. Differently from trees t, CSSTs have terminal nodes that can represent subsequences of words of the original sentence. The explicit syntactic structure of a CSST is the structure not falling in chunks and it is represented as $\mathsf{s}(\tau)$. For example, $\mathsf{s}(\tau_3)$ is:

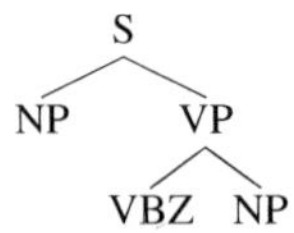

where τ_3 is the third subtree of Figure 2.

Given a tree t, the set $\mathcal{S}(t)$ is defined as the set containing all the relevant CSSTs of the tree t. As for the tree kernels (Collins and Duffy, 2002), the set $\mathcal{S}(t)$ contains all CSSTs derived from the subtrees of t such that if a node n belongs to a subtree t_s, all the siblings of n in t belongs to t_s. In other words, productions of the initial subtrees are complete. A CSST is obtained by collapsing in a single terminal nodes a contiguous sequence of words dominated by a single non-terminal node. For example:

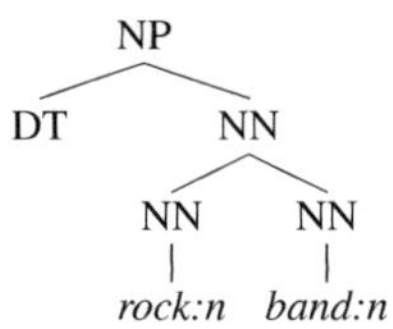

is collapsed into:

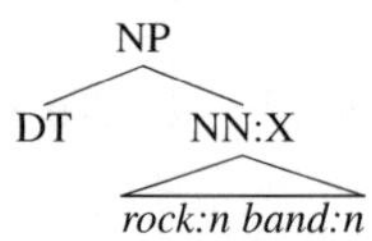

Finally, $\vec{w_n} \in \mathbb{R}^m$ represent the *distributional* vectors for words w_n and $f(w_1 \dots w_k)$ represents a compositional distributional semantics model applied to the word sequence $w_1 \dots w_k$.

2.2 Smoothed Tree Kernels on Chunk-based Syntactic Trees

As usual, a tree kernel, although written in a recursive way, computes the following general equation:

$$K(t_1, t_2) = \sum_{\substack{\tau_i \in S(t_1) \\ \tau_j \in S(t_2)}} \lambda^{|N(\tau_i)|+|N(\tau_j)|} K_F(\tau_i, \tau_j) \quad (1)$$

In our case, the basic similarity $K_F(t_i, t_j)$ is defined to take into account the syntactic structure and the distributional semantic part. Thus, we define it as follows in line with what done with several other smoothed tree kernels:

$$K_F(\tau_i, \tau_j) = \delta(\mathsf{s}(\tau_i), \mathsf{s}(\tau_j)) \prod_{\substack{a \in PT(\tau_i) \\ b \in PT(\tau_j)}} \langle f(a), f(b) \rangle$$

where $\delta(\mathsf{s}(\tau_i), \mathsf{s}(\tau_j))$ is the Kroneker's delta function between the the structural part of two chunk-based syntactic subtrees, $PT(\tau)$ are the nodes in τ directly covering a chunk or a word, and $\langle \vec{x}, \vec{y} \rangle$ is the cosine similarity between the two vectors $\vec{x}$ and $\vec{y}$. For example, given the chunk-based subtree τ_3 in Figure 2 and

$\tau_4 =$ 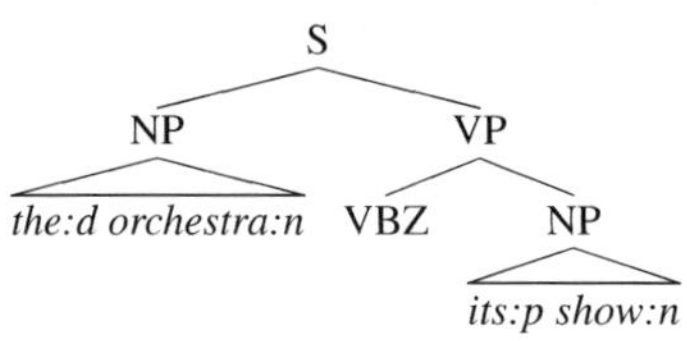

the similarity $K_F(\tau_3, \tau_4)$ is: $\langle f(\textit{the:d orchestra:n}), f(\textit{the:d rock:n band:n}) \rangle \cdot \langle f(\textit{its:p show:n}), f(\textit{its:p final:j concert:n}) \rangle$.

The recursive formulation of the Chunk-based Smoothed Tree Kernel (CSTK) is a bit more complex but very similar to the recursive formulation of the syntactic tree kernels:

$$K(t_1, t_2) = \sum_{\substack{n_1 \in N(t_1) \\ n_2 \in N(t_2)}} C(n_1, n_2) \quad (2)$$

where $C(n_1, n_2) =$

$$\begin{cases} \langle f(d(n_1)), f(d(n_2)) \rangle \text{ if } \mathit{label}(n_1) = \mathit{label}(n_2) \\ \quad \text{and } \mathsf{prod}(n_1) \neq \mathsf{prod}(n_2) \\ \langle f(d(n_1)), f(d(n_2)) \rangle \\ \quad + \prod_{j=1}^{nc(n_1)} (1 + C(c_j(n_1), c_j(n_2))) \\ \quad - \prod_{j=1}^{nc(n_1)} \langle f(d(c_j(n_1))), f(d(c_j(n_2))) \rangle \\ \quad \text{if } n_1, n_2 \text{ are not pre-terminals and} \\ \quad \mathsf{prod}(n_1) = \mathsf{prod}(n_2) \\ 0 \text{ otherwise} \end{cases}$$

where $nc(n_1)$ is the lenght of the production $\mathsf{prod}(n_1)$.

2.3 Compositional Distributional Semantic Models and two Specific CSTKs

To define specific CSTKs, we need to introduce the basic compositional distributional semantic models (CDSMs). We use two CDSMs: the Basic Additive model (BA) and teh Full Additive model (FA). We thus define two specific CSTKs: the CSTK+BA that is based on the basic additive model and the CSTK+FA that is based on the full additive model. We describe the two CDSMs in the following.

The Basic Additive model (BA) (introduced in (Mitchell and Lapata, 2008)) computes the distibutional semantics vector of a pair of words $a = a_1 a_2$ as:

$$ADD(a_1, a_2) = \alpha \vec{a_1} + \beta \vec{a_2}$$

where α and β weight the first and the second word of the pair. The basic additive model for word sequences $s = w_1 \ldots w_k$ is recursively defined as follows:

$$f_{BA}(s) = \begin{cases} \vec{w_1} & \text{if } k = 1 \\ \alpha \vec{w_1} + \beta f_{BA}(w_2 \ldots w_k) & \text{if } k > 1 \end{cases}$$

The Full Additive model (FA) (used in (Guevara, 2010) for adjective-noun pairs and (Zanzotto et al., 2010) for three different syntactic relations) computes the compositional vector $\vec{a}$ of a pair using two linear tranformations A_R and B_R respectively applied to the vectors of the first and the second word. These matrices generally only depends on the syntactic relation R that links those two words. The operation follows:

$$f_{FA}(a_1, a_2, R) = A_R \vec{a_1} + B_R \vec{a_2}$$

	RR					RRTWS				
	RTE1	RTE2	RTE3	RTE5	Average	RTE1	RTE2	RTE3	RTE5	Average
Add	0.541	0.496	0.507	0.520	0.516	0.560	0.538	0.643	0.578	0.579
FullAdd	0.512	0.516	0.507	0.569	0.526	0.571	0.608	0.643	0.643	0.616
TK	0.561	0.552	0.531	0.54	0.546	0.608	0.627	0.648	0.630	0.628
CSTK+BA	0.553	0.545	0.562	0.568	$0.557^{\dagger}$	0.626	0.616	0.648	0.628	$0.629^{\dagger}$
CSTK+FA	0.543	0.550	0.574	0.576	**0.560**†	0.628	0.616	0.652	0.630	**0.631**†

Table 1: Task-based analysis: Accuracy on Recognizing Textual Entailment († is different from both ADD and FullADD with a stat.sig. of $p > 0.1$.)

The full additive model for word sequences $s = w_1 \dots w_k$, whose node has a production rule $s \rightarrow s_{c_1} \dots s_{c_m}$ is also defined recursively:

$$f_{FA}(s) = \begin{cases} \vec{w_1} & \text{if } k = 1 \\ A_{vn}\vec{V} + B_{vn} f_{FA}(NP) & \\ \quad \text{if } s \rightarrow V\ NP & \\ A_{an}\vec{A} + B_{an} f_{FA}(N) & \\ \quad \text{if } s \rightarrow A\ N & \\ \sum f_{FA}(s_{c_i}) & \text{otherwise} \end{cases}$$

where A_{vn}, B_{vn} are matrices used for verb and noun phrase interaction, and A_{an}, B_{an} are used for adjective, noun interaction.

3 Experimental Investigation

3.1 Experimental set-up

We experimented with the Recognizing Textual Entailment datasets (RTE) (Dagan et al., 2006). RTE is the task of deciding whether a long text T entails a shorter text, typically a single sentence, called hypothesis H. It has been often seen as a classification task (see (Dagan et al., 2013)). We used four datasets: RTE1, RTE2, RTE3, and RTE5, with the standard split between training and testing. The dev/test distribution for RTE1-3, and RTE5 is respectively 567/800, 800/800, 800/800, and 600/600 T-H pairs.

Distributional vectors are derived with DISSECT (Dinu et al., 2013) from a corpus obtained by the concatenation of ukWaC (wacky.sslmit.unibo.it), a mid-2009 dump of the English Wikipedia (en.wikipedia.org) and the British National Corpus (www.natcorp.ox.ac.uk), for a total of about 2.8 billion words. We collected a 35K-by-35K matrix by counting co-occurrence of the 30K most frequent content lemmas in the corpus (nouns, adjectives and verbs) and all the content lemmas occurring in the datasets within a 3 word window. The raw count vectors were transformed into positive Pointwise Mutual Information scores and reduced to 300 dimensions by Singular Value Decomposition. This setup was picked without tuning, as we found it effective in previous, unrelated experiments.

We built the matrices for the full additive models using the procedure described in (Guevara, 2010). We considered only two relations: the Adjective-Noun and Verb-Noun. The full additive model falls back to the basic additional model when syntactic relations are different from these two.

To build the final kernel to learn the classifier, we followed standard approaches (Dagan et al., 2013), that is, we exploited two models: a model with only a rewrite rule feature space (RR) and a model with the previous space along with a token-level similarity feature (RRTWS). The two models use our CSTKs and the standard TKs in the following way as kernel functions: (1) $RR(p_1, p_2) = \kappa(t_1^a, t_2^a) + \kappa(t_1^b, t_2^b)$; (2) $RRTWS(p_1, p_2) = \kappa(t_1^a, t_2^a) + \kappa(t_1^b, t_2^b) + (TWS(a_1, b_1) \cdot TWS(a_2, b_2) + 1)^2$ where TWS is a weighted token similarity (as in (Corley and Mihalcea, 2005)).

3.2 Results

Table 1 shows the results of the experiments, the table is organised as follows: columns 2-6 report the accuracy of the RTE systems based on rewrite rules (RR) and columns 7-11 report the accuracies of RR systems along with token similarity (RRTS). We compare five differente models: ADD is the Basic Additive model with parameters $\alpha = \beta = 1$ (as defined in 2.3) applied to the words of the sentence (without considering its tree structure), the same is done for the Full Additive (FullADD), defined as in 2.3. The Tree Kernel (TK) as defined in (Collins and Duffy, 2002) are applied to the constituency-based tree representation of the tree, without the intervening collapsing step described in 2.2. These three models are the baseline against which we compare the CSTK models where the collapsing procedure is done via Basic Additive (CSTK + BA, again with $\alpha = \beta = 1$) and FullAdditive (CSTK + FA), as described in section 2.2, again, with the aforementioned restriction on the relation considered. For RR models we have that CSTK+BA and CSTK+FA both achieve higher accuracy than ADD and FullAdd, with a statistical significante greater than 93.7%, as computed with the sign test. Specifically we have that CSTK+BA has an average accuracy 7.94% higher than ADD and 5.89% higher than FullADD, while CSTK+FA improves on ADD and FullADD by 8.52% and 6.46%, respectively. The same trend is visible for the RRTS model, again both models are statistically better than ADD and FullADD, in this case we have that CSTK+BA is 8.63% more accurate then ADD and 2.11% more than FullADD, CSTK+FA is respectively 8.98% and 2.43% more accurate than ADD and FullADD. As for the TK models we have that both CSTK models achieve again an higher average accuracy: for RR models CSTK+BA and CSTK+FA are respectively 2.01% and 0.15% better than TK, while for RRTS models the number are 2.54% and 0.47%. These results though are not statistically significant, as is the difference between the two CSTK models themselves.

4 Conclusions and Future Work

In this paper, we introduced a novel sub-class of the convolution kernels in order exploit reliable compositional distributional semantic models along with the syntactic structure of sentences. Experiments show that this novel subclass, namely, the Chunk-based Smoothed Tree Kernels (CSTKs), are a promising solution, performing significantly better than a naive recursive application of the compositional distributional semantic models. We experimented with CSTKS equipped with the basic additive and the full additive CDSMs but these kernels are definitely open to all the CDSMs.

Acknowledgments

We acknowledge ERC 2011 Starting Independent Research Grant n. 283554 (COMPOSES).

References

Steven Abney. 1996. Part-of-speech tagging and partial parsing. In G.Bloothooft K.Church, S.Young, editor, *Corpus-based methods in language and speech*. Kluwer academic publishers, Dordrecht.

Marco Baroni and Roberto Zamparelli. 2010. Nouns are vectors, adjectives are matrices: Representing adjective-noun constructions in semantic space. In *Proceedings of the 2010 Conference on Empirical Methods in Natural Language Processing*, pages 1183–1193, Cambridge, MA, October. Association for Computational Linguistics.

Stephen Clark, Bob Coecke, and Mehrnoosh Sadrzadeh. 2008. A compositional distributional model of meaning. *Proceedings of the Second Symposium on Quantum Interaction (QI-2008)*, pages 133–140.

Michael Collins and Nigel Duffy. 2002. New ranking algorithms for parsing and tagging: Kernels over discrete structures, and the voted perceptron. In *Proceedings of ACL02*.

Courtney Corley and Rada Mihalcea. 2005. Measuring the semantic similarity of texts. In *Proc. of the ACL Workshop on Empirical Modeling of Semantic Equivalence and Entailment*, pages 13–18. Association for Computational Linguistics, Ann Arbor, Michigan, June.

Danilo Croce, Alessandro Moschitti, and Roberto Basili. 2011. Structured lexical similarity via convolution kernels on dependency trees. In *Proceedings of the Conference on Empirical Methods in Natural Language Processing*, EMNLP '11, pages 1034–1046, Stroudsburg, PA, USA. Association for Computational Linguistics.

Ido Dagan, Oren Glickman, and Bernardo Magnini. 2006. The pascal recognising textual entailment challenge. In Quionero-Candela et al., editor, *LNAI 3944: MLCW 2005*, pages 177–190. Springer-Verlag, Milan, Italy.

Ido Dagan, Dan Roth, Mark Sammons, and Fabio Massimo Zanzotto. 2013. *Recognizing Textual Entailment: Models and Applications*. Synthesis Lectures on Human Language Technologies. Morgan & Claypool Publishers.

Georgiana Dinu, Nghia The Pham, and Marco Baroni. 2013. DISSECT: DIStributional SEmantics Composition Toolkit. In *Proceedings of ACL (System Demonstrations)*, pages 31–36, Sofia, Bulgaria.

Edward Grefenstette and Mehrnoosh Sadrzadeh. 2011. Experimental support for a categorical compositional distributional model of meaning. In *Proceedings of the Conference on Empirical Methods in Natural Language Processing*, EMNLP '11, pages 1394–1404, Stroudsburg, PA, USA. Association for Computational Linguistics.

Emiliano Guevara. 2010. A regression model of adjective-noun compositionality in distributional semantics. In *Proceedings of the 2010 Workshop on GEometrical Models of Natural Language Semantics*, pages 33–37, Uppsala, Sweden, July. Association for Computational Linguistics.

David Haussler. 1999. Convolution kernels on discrete structures. Technical report, University of California at Santa Cruz.

Yashar Mehdad, Alessandro Moschitti, and Fabio Massimo Zanzotto. 2010. Syntactic/semantic structures for textual entailment recognition. In *Human Language Technologies: The 2010 Annual Conference of the North American Chapter of the Association for Computational Linguistics*, HLT '10, pages 1020–1028, Stroudsburg, PA, USA. Association for Computational Linguistics.

Jeff Mitchell and Mirella Lapata. 2008. Vector-based models of semantic composition. In *Proceedings of ACL-08: HLT*, pages 236–244, Columbus, Ohio, June. Association for Computational Linguistics.

Fabio Massimo Zanzotto, Ioannis Korkontzelos, Francesca Fallucchi, and Suresh Manandhar. 2010. Estimating linear models for compositional distributional semantics. In *Proceedings of the 23rd International Conference on Computational Linguistics (COLING)*, August,.

Generating Simulations of Motion Events from Verbal Descriptions

James Pustejovsky
Computer Science Dept.
Brandeis University
Waltham, MA USA
jamesp@cs.brandeis.edu

Nikhil Krishnaswamy
Computer Science Dept.
Brandeis University
Waltham, MA USA
nkrishna@brandeis.edu

Abstract

In this paper, we describe a computational model for motion events in natural language that maps from linguistic expressions, through a dynamic event interpretation, into three-dimensional temporal simulations in a model. Starting with the model from (Pustejovsky and Moszkowicz, 2011), we analyze motion events using temporally-traced Labelled Transition Systems. We model the distinction between *path*- and *manner*-motion in an operational semantics, and further distinguish different types of manner-of-motion verbs in terms of the mereo-topological relations that hold throughout the process of movement. From these representations, we generate minimal models, which are realized as three-dimensional simulations in software developed with the game engine, *Unity*. The generated simulations act as a conceptual "debugger" for the semantics of different motion verbs: that is, by testing for consistency and informativeness in the model, simulations expose the presuppositions associated with linguistic expressions and their compositions. Because the model generation component is still incomplete, this paper focuses on an implementation which maps directly from linguistic interpretations into the Unity code snippets that create the simulations.

1 Introduction

Semantic interpretation requires access to both knowledge about words and how they compose. As the linguistic phenomena associated with lexical semantics have become better understood, several assumptions have emerged across most models of word meaning. These include the following:

(1) a. Lexical meaning involves some sort of "componential analysis", either through predicative primitives or a system of types.
b. The selectional properties of predicators can be explained in terms of these components;
c. An understanding of event semantics and the different role of event participants seems crucial for modeling linguistic utterances.

As a starting point in lexical semantic analysis, a standard methodology in both theoretical and computational linguistics is to identify features in a corpus that differentiate the data in meaningful ways; meaningful in terms of prior theoretical assumptions or in terms of observably differentiated behaviors. Combining these strategies we might, for instance, take a theoretical constraint that we hope to justify through behavioral distinctions in the data. An example of this is the theoretical claim that motion verbs can be meaningfully divided into two classes: *manner*- and *path*-oriented predicates (Talmy, 1985; Jackendoff, 1983; Talmy, 2000). These constructions can be viewed as encoding two aspects of meaning: *how* the movement is happening and *where* it is happening. The former strategy is illustrated in (2a) and the latter in (2b) (where m indicates a manner verb, and p indicates a path verb).

(2) a. The ball rolled$_m$.
b. The ball crossed$_p$ the room.

With both of the verb types, adjunction can make reference to the missing aspect of motion, by introducing a path (as in (3a)) or the manner of movement (in (3b)).

(3) a. The ball rolled$_m$ across the room.
b. The ball crossed$_p$ the room rolling.

Differences in syntactic distribution and grammatical behavior in large datasets, in fact, correlate

*Proceedings of the Third Joint Conference on Lexical and Computational Semantics (*SEM 2014)*, pages 99–109,
Dublin, Ireland, August 23-24 2014.

fairly closely with the theoretical claims made by linguists using small introspective datasets.

The path-manner classification is a case where there are data-derived distinctions that correlate nicely with theoretically inspired predictions. More often than not, however, lexical semantic distinctions are formal stipulations in a linguistic model, that often have no observable correlations to data. For example, an examination of the *manner of movement* class from Levin (1993) illustrates this point. The verbs below are all Levin-class manner of motion verbs:

(4) MANNER OF MOTION VERBS: drive, walk, run, crawl, fly, swim, drag, slide, hop, roll

Assuming the two-way distinction between path and manner predication of motion mentioned above, these verbs do, in fact, tend to pattern according to the latter class in the corpus. Given that they are all manner of motion verbs, however, any data-derived distinctions that emerge within this class will have to be made in terms of additional syntactic or semantic dimensions. While it is most likely possible to differentiate, for example, the verbs *slide* from *roll*, or *walk* from *hop* in the corpus, given enough data, it is important to realize that conceptual and theoretical modeling is often necessary to reveal the factors that semantically distinguish such linguistic expressions, in the first place.

We argue that this problem can be approached with the use of minimal model generation. As Blackburn and Bos (2008) point out, theorem proving (essentially type satisfaction of a verb in one class as opposed to another) provides a "negative handle" on the problem of determining consistency and informativeness for an utterance, while model building provides a "positive handle" on both. For our concerns, simulation construction provides a positive handle on whether two manner of motion processes are distinguished in the model. Further, the simulation must specify *how* they are distinguished, the analogue to informativeness.

In this paper, we argue that traditional lexical modeling can benefit greatly from examining how semantic interpretations are contextually and conceptually grounded. We explore a dynamic interpretation of the lexical semantic model developed in Generative Lexicon Theory (Pustejovsky, 1995; Pustejovsky et al., 2014). Specifically, we are interested in using model building (Blackburn and Bos, 2008; Konrad, 2004; Gardent and Konrad, 2000) and simulation generation (Coyne and Sproat, 2001; Siskind, 2011) to reveal the conceptual presuppositions inherent in natural language expressions. In this paper, we focus our attention on motion verbs, in order to distinguish between manner and path motion verbs, as well as to model mereotopological distinctions within the manner class.

2 Situating Motion in Space and Time

The interpretation of motion in language has been one of the most researched areas in linguistics and Artificial Intelligence (Kuipers, 2000; Freksa, 1992; Galton, 2000; Levinson, 2003; Mani and Pustejovsky, 2012). Because of their grammatical and semantic import, linguistic interest in identifying where events happen has focused largely on motion verbs and the role played by paths. Jackendoff (1983), for example, elaborates a semantics for motion verbs incorporating explicit reference to the *path* traversed by the mover, from source to destination (goal) locations. Talmy (1983) develops a similar conceptual template, where the path followed by the *figure* is integral to the conceptualization of the motion against a *ground*. Hence, the path can be identified as the central element in defining the location of the event (Talmy, 2000). Related to this idea, both Zwarts (2005) and Pustejovsky and Moszkowicz (2011) develop mechanisms for dynamically creating the path traversed by a mover in a manner of motion predicate, such as *run* or *drive*. Starting with this approach, the localization of a motion event, therefore, is at least minimally associated with the path created by virtue of the activity.

In addition to capturing the spatial trace of the object in motion, several researchers have pointed out that identifying the shape of the path during motion is also critical for fully interpreting the semantics of movement. Eschenbach et al. (1999) discusses the orientation associated with the trajectory, something they refer to as *oriented curves*. Motivated more by linguistic considerations, Zwarts (2006) introduces the notion of an *event shape*, which is the trajectory associated with an event in space represented by a path. He defines a shape function, which is a partial function assigning unique paths to those events involving motion or extension in physical space. This work suggests that the localization of an event makes reference to orientational as well as configurational factors, a view that is pursued in Pustejovsky (2013b). This forces us to look at the various spatio-temporal regions associated with the event participants, and the interactions between them.

These issues are relevant to our present concerns, because in order to construct a simulation, a motion event must be embedded within an appropriate minimal embedding space. This must sufficiently enclose the event localization, while optionally including room enough for a frame of reference visualization of the event (the viewer's perspective). We return to this issue later in the paper when constructing our simulation from the semantic interpretation associated with motion events.

3 Modeling Motion in Language

3.1 Theoretical Assumptions

The advantage of adopting a dynamic interpretation of motion is that we can directly distinguish path predication from manner of motion predication in an operational semantics (Miller and Charles, 1991; Miller and Johnson-Laird, 1976) that maps nicely to a simulation environment. Models of processes using updating typically make reference to the notion of a state transition (van Benthem, 1991; Harel, 1984). This is done by distinguishing between formulae, ϕ, and programs, π. A formula is interpreted as a classical propositional expression, with assignment of a truth value in a specific model. We will interpret specific models by reference to specific states. A state is a set of propositions with assignments to variables at a specific index. Atomic programs are input/output relations ($[\![\pi]\!] \subseteq S \times S$), and compound programs are constructed from atomic ones following rules of dynamic logic (Harel et al., 2000).

For the present discussion, we represent the dynamics of actions in terms of Labeled Transition Systems (LTSs) (van Benthem, 1991).[1] An LTS consists of a triple, $\langle S, Act, \rightarrow \rangle$, where: S is the set of states; Act is a set of actions; and $\rightarrow$ is a total transition relation: $\rightarrow \subseteq S \times Act \times S$. An action, $\alpha \in Act$, provides the labeling on an arrow, making it explicit what brings about a state-to-state transition. As a shorthand for $(e_1, \alpha, e_2) \in \rightarrow$, we will also use $e_1 \xrightarrow{\alpha} e_2$. If reference to the state content (rather than state name) is required for interpretation purposes (van Benthem et al., 1994), then as shorthand for $(\{\phi\}_{e_1}, \alpha, \{\neg\phi\}_{e_2}) \in \rightarrow$, we use, $\boxed{\phi}_{e_1} \xrightarrow{\alpha} \boxed{\neg\phi}_{e_2}$. Finally, when referring to temporally-indexed states in the model, where $e_i@i$ indicates the state e_i interpreted at time i, as shorthand for $(\{\phi\}_{e_1@i}, \alpha, \{\neg\phi\}_{e_2@i+1}) \in \rightarrow$, we will use, $\boxed{\phi}^{i}_{e_1} \xrightarrow{\alpha} \boxed{\neg\phi}^{i+1}_{e_2}$, as described in Pustejovsky (2013).

3.2 Distinguishing Path and Manner Motion

We will assume that change of location of an object can be viewed as a special instance of a first-order program, which we will refer to as ν (Pustejovsky and Moszkowicz, 2011).[2]

(5) $x := y$ (ν-transition, where $loc(z)$ is value being updated)
"x assumes the value given to y in the next state."
$\langle \mathcal{M}, (i, i+1), (u, u[x/u(y)]) \rangle \models x := y$
iff $\langle \mathcal{M}, i, u \rangle \models loc(z) = x \wedge \langle \mathcal{M}, i+1, u[x/u(y)] \rangle \models loc(z) = y$

Given a simple transition, a *process* can be viewed as simply an iteration of ν (Fernando, 2009). However, as (Pustejovsky, 2013a) points out, since most manner motion verbs in language are actually directed processes, simple decompositions into change-of-location are inadequate. That is, they are guarded transitions where the test is not just non-coreference, but makes reference to values on a scale, C, and ensures that it continues in an order-preserving change through the iterations. When this test references the values on a scale, C, we call this a *directed ν-transition ($\vec{\nu}$)*, e.g., $x \preccurlyeq y$, $x \succcurlyeq y$:

(6) $\vec{\nu} =_{df} \overset{C?}{\curvearrowleft}{e_i} \xrightarrow{\nu} e_{i+1}$.

(7) $\boxed{loc(z) = x}_{e_0} \xrightarrow{\vec{\nu}} \boxed{loc(z) = y_1}_{e_1} \xrightarrow{\vec{\nu}} \ldots$
$\boxed{loc(z) = y_n}_{e_n}$

This now provides us with our dynamic interpretation of directed manner of motion verbs, such as *slide*, *swim*, *roll*, where we have an iteration of assignments of locations, undistinguished except

[1]This is consistent with the approach developed in (Fernando, 2009; Fernando, 2013). This approach to a dynamic interpretation of change in language semantics is also inspired by Steedman (2002).

[2]Cf. Groenendijk and Stokhof (1990) for dynamic updating, and Naumann (2001) for a related analysis.

that the values are order-preserving according to a scalar constraint.

This is quite different from the dynamic interpretation of path predicates. Following (Galton, 2004; Pustejovsky and Moszkowicz, 2011), path predicates such as *arrive* and *leave* make reference to a "distinguished location", not an arbitrary location. For example, *the ball enters the room* is satisified when the distinguished location, D, (the room) is successfully tested as the location for the moving object. That is, the location is tested against the current location for an object $((loc(x) \neq D)?)$, and retested until it is satisfied $((loc(x) = D)?)$.

(8)
$$\boxed{loc(z) = x}_{e_0} \overset{(loc(x)\neq D)?}{\curvearrowleft} \xrightarrow{\vec{\nu}} \boxed{loc(z) = y_1}_{e_1} \overset{(loc(x)\neq D)?}{\curvearrowleft} \xrightarrow{\vec{\nu}} \ldots$$
$$\overset{(loc(x)=D)?}{\curvearrowleft} \boxed{loc(z) = y_n}_{e_n}$$

While beyond the scope of the present discussion, it is worth noting that the model of event structure adopted here for motion verbs fits well with most of the major semantic and syntactic phenomena associated with event classes and Aktionsarten.[3]

3.3 Mereotopological Distinctions in Manner

Given the formal distinction between path and manner predicates as described above, let us examine how to differentiate meaning within the manner class. Levin (1993) differentiates this class in terms of argument alternation patterns, and identifies the following verb groupings: ROLL, RUN, EPONYMOUS VEHICLE, WALTZ, ACCOMPANY, and CHASE verbs. While suggestive, these distinctions are only partially useful towards actually teasing apart the semantic dimensions along which we identify the contributing factors of manner.

Mani and Pustejovsky (2012) suggest a different strategy involving the identification of semantic parameters that clearly differentiate verb senses from each other within this class. One parameter exploited quite extensively within the motion class involves the mereotopological contraints that inhere throughout the movement of the object (Randell et al., 1992; Asher and Vieu, 1995; Galton, 2000). Using this parameter, we are able to distinguish several of Levin's classes of manner

[3]Cf. (Pustejovsky, 2013a) and (Krifka, 1992).

as well as some novel ones, as described in (9), where a class is defined by the constraints that hold throughout the event (where EC is "externally connected", and DC is "disconnected").

(9) For Figure (F) relative to Ground (G):
a. EC(F,G), throughout motion:
b. DC(F,G), throughout motion:
c. EC(F,G) followed by DC(F,G), throughout motion:
d. Sub-part(F',F), EC(F',G) followed by DC(F',G), throughout motion:
e. Containment of F in a Vehicle (V).

For example, consider the semantic distinction between the verbs *slide* and *hop* or *bounce*. When the latter are employed in *induced (directed) motion* constructions (Levin, 1993; Jackendoff, 1996), they take on the meaning of manner of motion verbs. Distinguishing between a sliding and hopping motion involves inspecting the next-state content in the motion n-gram: namely, there is a continuous satisfaction of EC(F,G) throughout the motion for *slide* and a toggling effect (on-off) for the predicates *bounce* and *hop*, as shown in (10).

(10)
$$\boxed{loc(z) = x}_{e_0} \overset{\neg DC(x,G)?}{\curvearrowleft} \xrightarrow{\vec{\nu}} \boxed{loc(z) = y_1}_{e_1} \overset{DC(x,G)?}{\curvearrowleft} \xrightarrow{\vec{\nu}}$$
$$\overset{\neg DC(x,G)?}{\curvearrowleft} \boxed{loc(z) = y_2}_{e_2}$$

With the surface as the *ground* argument, these verbs are defined in terms of two transitions.[4]

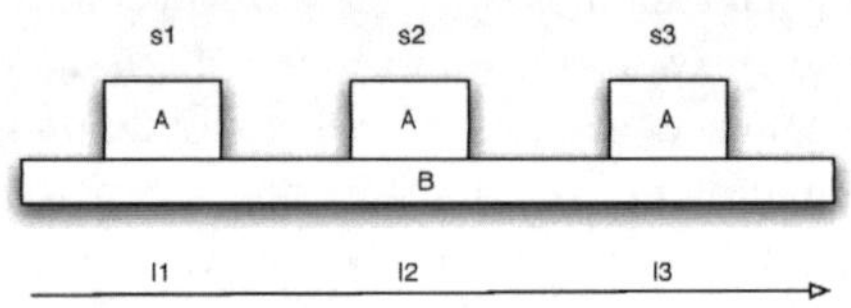

Figure 1: Slide Motion

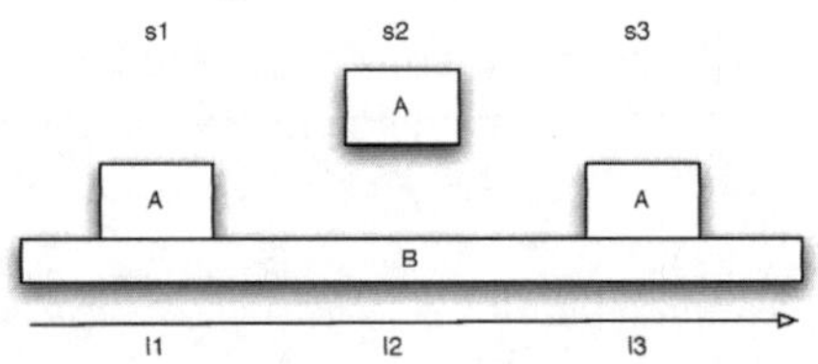

Figure 2: Hop Motion

[4]Many natural language predicates require reference to at least three states. These include the semelfactives mentioned above, as well as *blink* and iterative uses of *knock* and *clap* (Vendler, 1967; Dowty, 1979; Rothstein, 2008).

Distinguishing between a sliding motion and a rolling motion is also fairly straightforward. We have the entailments that result from each kind of motion, given a set of initial conditions, as in the following short sentence describing the motion of a ball relative to a floor (the domain for our event simulations).

- *The ball slid.*: At the termination of the action, object `ball` has moved relative to a surface in a manner that is `[+translate]`. That is, the movement is a translocation across absolute space, but other attributes (such as the ball's orientation) do not change.

- *The ball rolled.*: At the termination of the action, object `ball` has moved relative to a surface in a manner that is `[+translate]` *and* `[+rotate]`. Here, the translocation across space is preserved, with the addition of an orientation change.

We can further decompose these features, casting the `[+translate]` in terms of the translation's dimensionality. For both *the ball slid* and *the ball rolled*, it is required that the ball remain in the contact with the relevant surface, thus we can enforce a `[-3-dimensional]` constraint on the `[+translate]` feature. Thus, we arrive at the following differentiating semantic constraints for these verbs: (a) *slide*, `[+translate]`, `[-3-dimensional]`; (b) *roll*, `[+translate]`, `[-3-dimensional]`, `[+rotate]`. This is illustrated below over three states of execution.

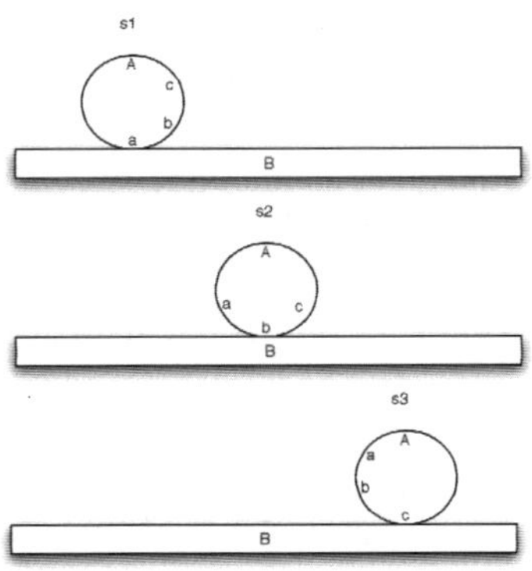

Figure 3: Roll Motion

In our approach to conceptual modeling, we hypothesize that between the members of any pair of motion verbs, there exists at least one distinctive feature of physical motion that distinguishes the two predicates. While this may be too strong, it is helpful in our use of simulations for debugging the lexical semantics of linguistic expressions.[5] In order to quantify the qualitative distinctions between motion predicates and identify the precise primitive components of a motion verb, we build a real-time simulation, within which the individual features of a single motion verb can be defined and isolated in three-dimensional space.

The idea of constructing simulations from linguistic utterances is, of course, not new. There are two groups of researchers who have developed related ideas quite extensively: simulation theorists, working in the philosophy of mind, such as Alvin Goldman and Robert Gordon; and cognitive scientists and linguists, such as Jerry Feldman, Ron Langacker, and Ben Bergen. According to Goldman (1989), simulation provides a process-driven theory of mind and mental attribution, differing from the theory-driven models proposed by Churchland and others (Churchland, 1991). From the cognitive linguistics tradition, simulation semantics has come to denote the mental instantiation of an interpretation of any linguistic utterance (Feldman, 2006; Bergen et al., 2007; Bergen, 2012). While these communities do not seem to reference each other, it is clear from our perspective, that they are both pursuing similar programs, where distinct linguistic utterances correspond to generated models that have differentiated structures and behaviors (Narayanan, 1999; Siskind, 2011; Goldman, 2006).

4 Simulations as Minimal Models

The approach to simulation construction introduced in the previous section is inspired by work in minimal model generation (Blackburn and Bos, 2008; Konrad, 2004). Type satisfaction in the compositional process mirrors the theorem proving component, while construction of the specific model helps us distinguish what is inherent in the different manner of motion events. This latter aspect is the "positive handle", (Blackburn and Bos, 2008) which demonstrates the informativeness of a distinction in our simulation.

Simulation software must be able to map a predicate to a known behavior, its arguments to objects in the scene, and then prompt those objects to execute the behavior. A simple input sentence needs

[5] Obviously, true synonyms in the lexicon would not be distinguishable in a model.

to be tagged and parsed and transformed into predicate/argument representation, and from there into a dynamic event structure, as in (Pustejovsky and Moszkowicz, 2011). The event structure is interpreted as the transformation executed over the object or objects in each frame, and then rendered.

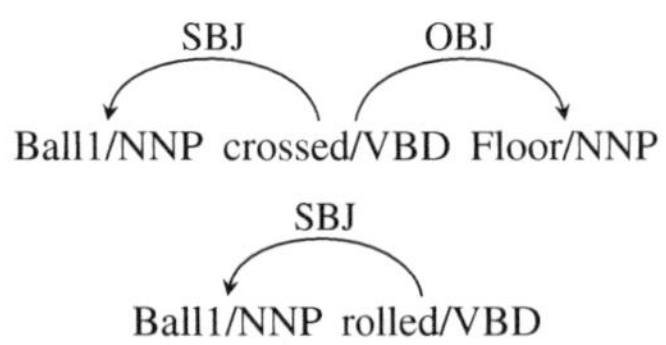

Table 1: Dependency parses for *Ball1 crossed Floor* (top) and *Ball1 rolled* (bottom).

We currently use only proper names to refer to objects in the scene, to simplify model generation, hence *Ball1* and *Floor*. This facilitates easy object identification in this prototype development stage.

Given a tagged and dependency parsed sentence, we can the transform the parse into a predicate formula, using the root of the parse as the predicate, the subject as a singleton first argument, and all objects as an optional stack of subsequent arguments.

1. *pred* := *cross* 2. *x* := *Ball1* 3. *y*.push(*Floor*)	1. *pred* := *roll* 2. *x* := *Ball1*
cross(*Ball1*,[*Floor*])	*roll*(*Ball1*)

Table 2: Transformation to predicate formula for *Ball1 crossed Floor* and *Ball1 rolled.*

The resulting predicates are represented in Table 3 as expressions in Dynamic Interval Temporal Logic (DITL) (Pustejovsky and Moszkowicz, 2011), which are equivalent to the LTS expressions used above.

cross(Ball1,Floor)
$loc(Ball1) := y,\ target(Ball1) := z;\ b := y;$ $(y := w;\ y \neq w;\ d(b,y) < d(b,w),$ $d(b,z) > d(z,w),\ IN(y,Floor))^+$
roll(Ball1)
$loc(Ball1) := y,\ rot(Ball1) := z;\ b_{loc} := y,$ $b_{rot} := z;\ (y := w;\ y \neq w;\ d(b_{loc},y) < d(b_{loc},w),$ $IN(y,Floor))^+,\ (z := v;\ z \neq v;\ z\text{-}b_{rot} < v\text{-}b_{rot})^+$

Table 3: DITL expressions for *Ball1 crossed Floor* and *Ball1 rolled.*

The DITL expression forms the basis of the coded behavior. The first two initialization steps are coded into the behavior's start function while the the third, Kleene iterated step, is encoded in the behavior's update function.

5 Generating Simulations

We use the freely-available game engine, *Unity*, (Goldstone, 2009) to handle all underlying graphics processing, and limited our object library to simple primitive shapes of spheroids, rectangular prisms, and planes. For every instance of an object, the game engine maintains a data structure for the object's virtual representation. Table 4 shows the data structure for `Entity`, the superclass of all movable objects.

Entity:

position: 3-vector	rotation: 3-vector
scale: 3-vector	transform: Matrix
collider = [center: 3-vector; min: 3-vector; max: 3-vector; radius: float]	geometry: Mesh
currentBehavior: Behavior	

Table 4: Data structure of motion-capable entities.

The `position` and `scale` of the object are represented as 3-vectors of floating point numbers. The `rotation` is represented as the Euler angles of the object's current rotation, also a 3-vector. This 3-vector is computed as a quaternion for rendering purposes. The `transform` matrix composes the position, scale, and quaternion rotation into the complete transformation applied to the object at any given frame. The `geometry` is a mesh. The points, edges, faces, and texture attributes that comprise the mesh are all immutable at the moment so the mesh type is considered atomic for our purposes. The `collider` contains the coordinates of the center of the object, minimum and maximum extents of the object's boundaries, and radius of the boundaries (for spherical objects).

Behaviors can only be executed over `Entity` instances, so we also provide each one with a `currentBehavior` property, referencing the code to be executed over the object every frame that said behavior is being run. This code performs a transformation over the object at every step, generating a new state in a dynamic model of the event denoted by the a given predicate. Thus, the event[6] is decomposed into frame-by-frame transformations representing the ν-transition from Section 3.2.

We generate example simulations of behaviors in a sample environment, shown in Figure 4, that

[6]These events are linguistic events, and not the same as "events" as used in software development or with event handlers.

consists of a sealed four-walled room that contains a number of primitive objects.

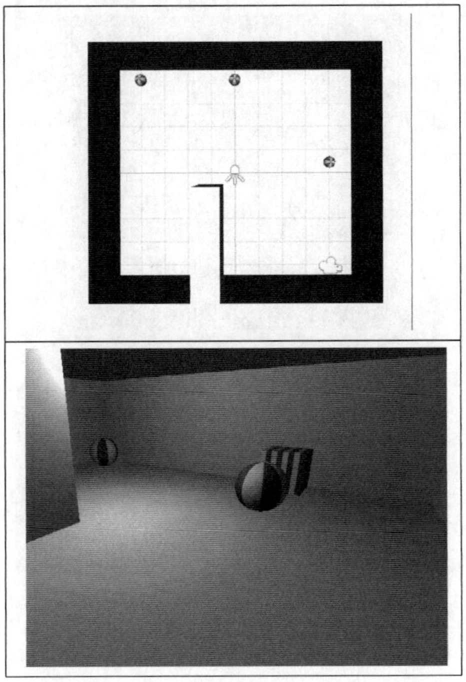

Figure 4: Sample environment in top-down and perspective views.

The behaviors currently coded into our software map directly from DITL to the simulation. The various parts of the DITL formula that describes a given behavior are coded into the behavior's start or update functions in Unity. Below is one such C# code snippet: the per-frame transformation for *roll*.

(11)
```
transform.rotation = new Vector3(
  0.0,0.0,transform.rotation.z+
  (rotSpeed*deltaTime));
transform.position = new Vector3(
  transform.position.x-radius*
  deltaTime,transform.position.y,
  transform.position.z);
```

This "translates" the DITL expression $(y := w;\ y \neq w;\ d(b_{loc},y) < d(b_{loc},w))^{+}$, $(z := v;\ z \neq v;\ z\text{-}b_{rot} < v\text{-}b_{rot}),IN(y,Floor)^{+}$ while explicitly calculating the value of the precise differences in location and rotation between each frame or time step. The variables `moveSpeed`, `rotSpeed` and `radius` are given explicit value. `deltaTime` refers to the time elapsed between frames.

Translating a DITL formula into executable code makes evident the differences in minimal verb pairs, such as *the ball (or box) rolled* and *the ball (or box) slid*. When an object rolls, one area on the object must remain in contact with the supporting surface, and that area must be adjacent to the area contacting the surface in the previous time step. When an object slides, *the same* area on the object must contact the supporting surface. Compare the per-frame transformation for *slide* below to the given transformation for *roll*.

(12)
```
transform.position = new Vector3(
transform.position.x-radius*deltaTime,
 transform.position.y,
transform.position.z);
```

This maps the DITL expression $(y := w;\ y \neq w;\ d(b_{loc},y) < d(b_{loc},w),IN(y,Floor))^{+}$. Here, the object's location changes along a path leading away from the start location, but does not rotate as in *roll*.

DITL expressions and their coded equivalents can also be composed into new, more specific motions. The *cross* formula from Section 4 can be composed with that for *roll* to describe a "roll across" motion.

In a model, a path verb such as *cross* does not necessarily need an explicit manner of motion specified. In a simulation, the manner needs to be given a value, requiring the composition of the path verb (e.g., *cross*) with one of a certain subsets of manner verbs specifying *how* the object moves relative to the supporting surface. Below are DITL expressions and code implementations for two *cross* predicates, the first a cross motion while sliding, the second a cross motion while rolling.

(13) $loc(Ball1) := y,\ target(Ball1) := z;\ b := y;\ (y := w;\ y \neq w;\ d(b,y) < d(b,w),\ d(b,z) > d(z,w),\ IN(y,Floor))^{+}$

```
offset = transform.position-
 destination;
offset = Vector3.Normalize(offset);
transform.position = new Vector3(
 transform.position.x-offset.x*
 radius*deltaTime,
 transform.position.y,
 transform.position.z-
 offset.z*radius*deltaTime);
```

At each frame, the distance between the object's current position and its previously computed destination is computed again, and the update moves the object away from its current position ($d(b,y) < d(b,w)$) toward the destination ($d(b,z) > d(z,w)$). Since no other manner of motion is specified, the object does not turn or rotate as it moves, but simply "slides."

(14) $loc(Ball1) := y$, $target(Ball1) := z$; $b := y$; ($y := w$; $y \neq w$; $d(b_{loc},y) < d(b_{loc},w)$, $d(b_{loc},z) > d(z,w)$, ($u := v$; $u \neq v$; $u\text{-}b_{rot} < v\text{-}b_{rot}$), $IN(y,Floor))^{+}$

```
offset = transform.position-
 destination;
offset = Vector3.Normalize(offset);
transform.rotation = new Vector3(
 0.0,arccos(offset.z)*(360/PI*2),
 transform.rotation.z+
 (rotSpeed*deltaTime));
transform.position = new Vector3(
 transform.position.x-offset.x*
 radius*deltaTime,
 transform.position.y,
 transform.position.z-offset.z*
 radius*deltaTime);
```

Here the update is the same as above, but with the introduction of the rolling motion. In both code snippets, the non-changing value of `transform.position.y` implicitly maps the IN RCC condition in the DITL formulas, and keeps the moving object attached to the floor.

If there exists a behavior corresponding to the predicate (by name) on an entity bearing the name of the predicate's first (subject) argument, the transformation encoded in that behavior is performed over the entity until an end condition specific to the behavior is met. The resulting animated motion depicts the manner of motion denoted by the predicate. Given a predicate of arity greater than 1, the simulator tries to prompt a behavior on the first argument that can be run using parameters of the subsequent arguments.

A *cross* behavior, for example, divides the supporting surface into regions and attempts to move the crossing object from one region to the the opposite region. In figure 5, the bounds of *Floor* completely surround the bounds of *Ball2* (IN(*Ball2*,*Floor*) in RCC8). This configuration makes it possible for the simulation to compute a motion moving the *Ball2* object from one side of the *Floor* to the other.

The left side of figure 5 shows a ball rolling and a box sliding, a depiction of two predicates: *Box1 slid* and *Ball1 rolled*. The right side depicts *Ball2 crossed Floor* (from the rear center to the front center). The starting state of each scene is overlaid semi-transparently while the in-progress state is fully opaque.

6 Discussion and Conclusion

In this paper, we describe a model for mapping natural language motion expressions into a 3D simulation environment. Our strategy has been to use minimal simulation generation as a conceptual debugging tool, in order to tease out the semantic differences between linguistic expressions; specifically those between verbs that are members of conventionally homogeneous classes, according to linguistic analysis.

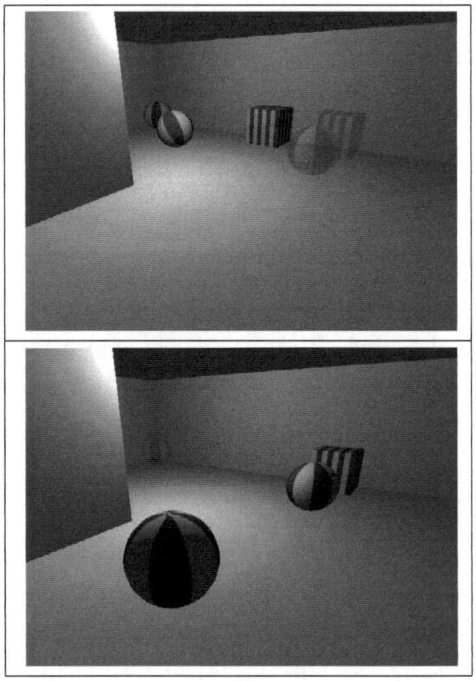

Figure 5: *Roll* and *slide* motions in progress (top), and *cross* motion in progress (bottom).

It should be pointed out that our goal is different from WordsEye (Coyne and Sproat, 2001). While we are interested in using simulation generation to differentiate semantic distinctions in both lexical classes and compositional constructions, the goal behind WordsEye is to provide an enhanced interface to allow non-specialists create 3D scenes without being familiar with special software models for everyday objects and relations. There are obvious synergies between these two goals that can be pursued.

The simulations we create provide *an* interpretation of the given motion predicate over the given entity, but not the *only* interpretation. Just as Coyne et al. (2010) does for static objects in the WordsEye system, we must apply some implicit constraints to our motion predicates to allow them to be visually simulated. For instance, in the *roll* and *slide* examples given in Figure 5, both objects are moving in the same direction–parallel to the back wall of the room object. Had the objects been moving perpendicular to the back wall or in any other direction, as long as they remained in contact with the floor at all times, the simulated motion would still be considered a "roll" (if rotating around an axis parallel to the floor), or a "slide" (if not), regardless of what the precise direction of motion is. Minimal pairs in a model have to be compared and contrasted in a discriminative way, and thus in modeling a *slide* predicate versus a *roll* predicate, knowing that the distinction is one of rotation parallel to the surface is enough to distinguish the two predicates in a model.

In a simulation, the discriminative process requires that the two contrasting behaviors look different, and as such, the simulation software must be able to completely render a scene for each frame from behavior start to behavior finish, and so every variable for every object being rendered must have an assigned value, including the position of the object from frame to frame. If these values are left unspecified, the software either fails to compile or throws an exception. Thus, we are forced to arbitrarily choose a direction of motion (as well as direction of rotation, speed of rotation, speed of motion, etc.). As long as all non-changing variables are kept consistent between a minimal pair of behaviors, we can evaluate the quantitative and qualitative differences between the values that do change. As simulations require values to be assigned to variables that can be left unspecified in an ordinary modeling process, simulations expose presuppositions about the semantics of motion verbs and of compositions that would not be necessary in a model alone.

In order to evaluate the appropriateness of a given simulation, we are currently experimenting with a strategy often used in classification and annotation tasks, namely *pairwise similarity judgments* (Rumshisky et al., 2012; Pustejovsky and Rumshisky, 2014). This involves presenting a user with a simple discrimination task that has a reduced cognitive load, comparing the similarity of the example to the target instances. In the present context, a subject is shown a specific simulation resulting from the translation from textual input, through DITL, to the visualization. A set of activity or event descriptions is given, and the subject is then asked to select which best describes the simulation shown; e.g., "Is this a sliding?", "Is this a rolling?". The results of this experiment are presently being evaluated.

The system is currently in the prototype stage and needs to be expanded in three main areas: object library, parsing pipeline, and predicate handling. Our object and behavior libraries are currently limited to geometric primitives and the motions that can be applied over them. While *roll*, *slide*, and *cross* behaviors can be scripted for spheres and cubes and shapes derived from them, a predicate like *walk* cannot be supported on the current infrastructure. Thus, we intend to expand the object library to include more complex inanimate objects (tables, chairs, or other household objects) as well as animate objects. Having an object library containing forms capable of executing greater numbers of predicates will allow us to implement those predicates.

The parsing pipeline described in Section 4 is only partially implemented, with the only completed parts being the latter stages, relating a formulas to a scripted behavior and its arguments. We intend to expand the parsing pipeline to include all the steps described in this paper: taking input as a simple natural language sentence, tagging and parsing it to extract the constituent parts of a predicate/argument representation, and using that output to prompt a behavior in software as a dynamic event structure. More robust parsing will afford us the opportunity to expand the diversity of predicates that the software can handle as well (McDonald and Pustejovsky, 2014). While currently limited to unary and binary predicates, we need to extend the capability to ternary predicates and predicates of greater arity, including the use of adjunct phrases and indirect objects. We are in the process of developing an implementation that uses Boxer (Curran et al., 2007) so that we can create first-order models from the dynamic expressions used here.

Acknowledgements

We would like to thank David McDonald for comments and discussion. We would also like to thank the reviewers for several substantial suggestions for improvements and clarifications to the paper. All remaining errors are of course the responsibilities of the authors. This work was supported in part by the Department of the Navy, Office of Naval Research under grant N00014-13-1-0228. Any opinions, findings, and conclusions or recommendations expressed in this material are those of the authors and do not necessarily reflect the views of the Office of Naval Research.

References

Nicholas Asher and Laure Vieu. 1995. Towards a geometry of common sense: a semantics and a complete axiomatisation of merotopology. In *Proceedings of IJCAI95*, Montreal, Canada.

Benjamin K. Bergen, Shane Lindsay, Teenie Matlock, and Srini Narayanan. 2007. Spatial and linguistic aspects of visual imagery in sentence comprehension. *Cognitive Science*, 31(5):733–764.

Benjamin K Bergen. 2012. *Louder than words: The new science of how the mind makes meaning*. Basic Books.

Patrick Blackburn and Johan Bos. 2008. Computational semantics. *THEORIA. An International Journal for Theory, History and Foundations of Science*, 18(1).

Paul M Churchland. 1991. Folk psychology and the explanation of human behavior. *The future of folk psychology: Intentionality and cognitive science*, pages 51–69.

Bob Coyne and Richard Sproat. 2001. Wordseye: an automatic text-to-scene conversion system. In *Proceedings of the 28th annual conference on Computer graphics and interactive techniques*, pages 487–496. ACM.

Bob Coyne, Owen Rambow, Julia Hirschberg, and Richard Sproat. 2010. Frame semantics in text-to-scene generation. In *Knowledge-Based and Intelligent Information and Engineering Systems*, pages 375–384. Springer.

James Curran, Stephen Clark, and Johan Bos. 2007. Linguistically motivated large-scale nlp with c&c and boxer. In *Proceedings of the 45th Annual Meeting of the Association for Computational Linguistics Companion Volume Proceedings of the Demo and Poster Sessions*, pages 33–36, Prague, Czech Republic, June. Association for Computational Linguistics.

David R Dowty. 1979. *Word meaning and Montague grammar: The semantics of verbs and times in generative semantics and in Montague's PTQ*, volume 7. Springer.

C. Eschenbach, C. Habel, L. Kulik, et al. 1999. Representing simple trajectories as oriented curves. In *FLAIRS-99, Proceedings of the 12th International Florida AI Research Society Conference*, pages 431–436.

Jerome Feldman. 2006. *From molecule to metaphor: A neural theory of language*. MIT press.

Tim Fernando. 2009. Situations in ltl as strings. *Information and Computation*, 207(10):980–999.

Tim Fernando. 2013. Segmenting temporal intervals for tense and aspect. In *The 13th Meeting on the Mathematics of Language*, page 30.

Christian Freksa. 1992. *Using orientation information for qualitative spatial reasoning*. Springer.

Antony Galton. 2000. *Qualitative Spatial Change*. Oxford University Press, Oxford.

Antony Galton. 2004. Fields and objects in space, time, and space-time. *Spatial Cognition and Computation*, 4(1).

Claire Gardent and Karsten Konrad. 2000. Interpreting definites using model generation. *Journal of Language and Computation*, 1(2):193–209.

Alvin I Goldman. 1989. Interpretation psychologized*. *Mind & Language*, 4(3):161–185.

Alvin I Goldman. 2006. *Simulating minds: The philosophy, psychology, and neuroscience of mindreading*. Oxford University Press.

Will Goldstone. 2009. *Unity Game Development Essentials*. Packt Publishing Ltd.

Jeroen Groenendijk and Martin Stokhof. 1990. Dynamic predicate logic. *Linguistics and Philosophy*, 14:39–100.

David Harel, Dexter Kozen, and Jerzy Tiuyn. 2000. *Dynamic Logic*. The MIT Press, 1st edition.

David Harel. 1984. Dynamic logic. In M. Gabbay and F. Gunthner, editors, *Handbook of Philosophical Logic, Volume II: Extensions of Classical Logic*, page 497?604. Reidel.

Ray Jackendoff. 1983. *Semantics and Cognition*. MIT Press.

Ray Jackendoff. 1996. The proper treatment of measuring out, telicity, and perhaps even quantification in english. *Natural Language & Linguistic Theory*, 14(2):305–354.

Karsten Konrad. 2004. *Model generation for natural language interpretation and analysis*, volume 2953. Springer.

Manfred Krifka. 1992. Thematic relations as links between nominal reference and temporal constitution. *Lexical matters*, 2953.

Benjamin Kuipers. 2000. The spatial semantic hierarchy. *Artificial Intelligence*, 119(1):191–233.

Beth Levin. 1993. *English verb class and alternations: a preliminary investigation*. University of Chicago Press.

S.C. Levinson. 2003. *Space in Language and Cognition: Explorations in Cognitive Diversity*. Language, culture, and cognition. Cambridge University Press.

Inderjeet Mani and James Pustejovsky. 2012. *Interpreting Motion: Grounded Representations for Spatial Language*. Oxford University Press.

David McDonald and James Pustejovsky. 2014. On the representation of inferences and their lexicalization. In *Advances in Cognitive Systems*, volume 3.

G. Miller and W. Charles. 1991. Contextual correlates of semantic similarity. *Language and Cognitive Processes*, 6(1):1–28.

George A Miller and Philip N Johnson-Laird. 1976. *Language and perception*. Belknap Press.

Srinivas Narayanan. 1999. Reasoning about actions in narrative understanding. *IJCAI*, 99:350–357.

Ralf Naumann. 2001. Aspects of changes: a dynamic event semantics. *Journal of semantics*, 18:27–81.

James Pustejovsky and Jessica Moszkowicz. 2011. The qualitative spatial dynamics of motion. *The Journal of Spatial Cognition and Computation*.

James Pustejovsky and Anna Rumshisky. 2014. Deep semantic annotation with shallow methods. LREC Tutorial, May.

James Pustejovsky, Anna Rumshisky, Olga Batiukova, and Jessica Moszkowicz. 2014. Annotation of compositional operations with glml. In Harry Bunt, editor, *Computing Meaning*, pages 217–234. Springer Netherlands.

J. Pustejovsky. 1995. *The Generative Lexicon*. Bradford Book. Mit Press.

James Pustejovsky. 2013a. Dynamic event structure and habitat theory. In *Proceedings of the 6th International Conference on Generative Approaches to the Lexicon (GL2013)*, pages 1–10. ACL.

James Pustejovsky. 2013b. Where things happen: On the semantics of event localization. In *Proceedings of ISA-9: International Workshop on Semantic Annotation*.

David Randell, Zhan Cui, and Anthony Cohn. 1992. A spatial logic based on regions and connections. In Morgan Kaufmann, editor, *Proceedings of the 3rd Internation Conference on Knowledge Representation and REasoning*, pages 165–176, San Mateo.

Susan Rothstein. 2008. Two puzzles for a theory of lexical aspect: Semelfactives and degree achievements. *Event structures in linguistic form and interpretation*, 5:175.

Anna Rumshisky, Nick Botchan, Sophie Kushkuley, and James Pustejovsky. 2012. Word sense inventories by non-experts. In *LREC*, pages 4055–4059.

Jeffrey Mark Siskind. 2011. Grounding the lexical semantics of verbs in visual perception using force dynamics and event logic. *arXiv preprint arXiv:1106.0256*.

Mark Steedman. 2002. Plans, affordances, and combinatory grammar. *Linguistics and Philosophy*, 25(5-6):723–753.

Leonard Talmy. 1983. How language structures space. In Herbert Pick and Linda Acredolo, editors, *Spatial Orientation: Theory, Research, and Application*. Plenum Press.

Leonard Talmy. 1985. Lexicalization patterns: semantic structure in lexical forms. In T. Shopen, editor, *Language typology and semantic description Volume 3:*, pages 36–149. Cambridge University Press.

Leonard Talmy. 2000. *Towards a cognitive semantics*. MIT Press.

Johan van Benthem, Jan van Eijck, and Vera Stebletsova. 1994. Modal logic, transition systems and processes. *Journal of Logic and Computation*, 4(5):811–855.

Johannes Franciscus Abraham Karel van Benthem. 1991. Logic and the flow of information.

Z. Vendler. 1967. *Linguistics in philosophy*. Cornell University Press Ithaca.

J. Zwarts. 2005. Prepositional aspect and the algebra of paths. *Linguistics and Philosophy*, 28(6):739–779.

J. Zwarts. 2006. Event shape: Paths in the semantics of verbs.

See No Evil, Say No Evil: Description Generation from Densely Labeled Images

Mark Yatskar [1*] my89@cs.washington.edu

Michel Galley[2] mgalley@microsoft.com

Lucy Vanderwende[2] lucyv@microsoft.com

Luke Zettlemoyer[1] lsz@cs.washington.edu

[1]Computer Science & Engineering
University of Washington
Seattle, WA, 98195, USA

[2]Microsoft Research
One Microsoft Way
Redmond, WA, 98052, USA

Abstract

This paper studies generation of descriptive sentences from densely annotated images. Previous work studied generation from automatically detected visual information but produced a limited class of sentences, hindered by currently unreliable recognition of activities and attributes. Instead, we collect human annotations of objects, parts, attributes and activities in images. These annotations allow us to build a significantly more comprehensive model of language generation and allow us to study what visual information is required to generate human-like descriptions. Experiments demonstrate high quality output and that activity annotations and relative spatial location of objects contribute most to producing high quality sentences.

1 Introduction

Image descriptions compactly summarize complex visual scenes. For example, consider the descriptions of the image in Figure 1, which vary in content but focus on the women and what they are doing. Automatically generating such descriptions is challenging: a full system must understand the image, select the relevant visual content to present, and construct complete sentences. Existing systems aim to address all of these challenges but use visual detectors for only a small vocabulary of words, typically nouns, associated with objects that can be reliably found.[1] Such systems are blind

Five young people on the street, two sharing a bicycle.
Several young people are walking near parked vehicles.
Three girls with large handbags walking down the sidewalk.
Three women walk down a city street, as seen from above.
Three young woman walking down a sidewalk looking up.

Figure 1: An annotated image with human generated sentence descriptions. Each bounding polygon encompasses one or more objects and is associated with a count and text labels.This image has 9 high level objects annotated with over 250 textual labels.

to much of the visual content needed to generate complete, human-like sentences.

In this paper, we instead study generation with more complete visual support, as provided by human annotations, allowing us to develop more comprehensive models than previously considered. Such models have the dual benefit of (1) providing new insights into how to construct more human-like sentences and (2) allowing us to perform experiments that systematically study the contribution of different visual cues in generation, suggesting which automatic detectors would be most beneficial for generation.

In an effort to approximate relatively complete visual recognition, we collected manually labeled representations of objects, parts, attributes and activities for a benchmark caption generation dataset that includes images paired with human authored

*This work was conducted at Microsoft Research.

[1]While object recognition is improving (ImageNet accuracy is over 90% for 1000 classes) progress in activity recognition has been slower; the state of the art is below 50% mean average precision for 40 activity classes (Yao et al., 2011).

*Proceedings of the Third Joint Conference on Lexical and Computational Semantics (*SEM 2014)*, pages 110–120, Dublin, Ireland, August 23-24 2014.

descriptions (Rashtchian et al., 2010).[2] As seen in Figure 1, the labels include object boundaries and descriptive text, here including the facts that the children are "riding" and "walking" and that they are "young." Our goal is to be as exhaustive as possible, giving equal treatment to all objects. For example, the annotations in Figure 1 contain enough information to generate the first three sentences and most of the content in the remaining two. Labels gathered in this way are a type of feature norms (McRae et al., 2005), which have been used in the cognitive science literature to approximate human perception and were recently used as a visual proxy in distributional semantics (Silberer and Lapata, 2012). We present the first effort, that we are aware of, for using feature norms to study image description generation.

Such rich data allows us to develop significantly more comprehensive generation models. We divide generation into choices about which visual content to select and how to realize a sentence that describes that content. Our approach is grammar-based, feature-rich, and jointly models both decisions. The content selection model includes latent variables that align phrases to visual objects and features that, for example, measure how visual salience and spatial relationships influence which objects are mentioned. The realization approach considers a number of cues, including language model scores, word specificity, and relative spatial information (e.g. to produce the best spatial prepositions), when producing the final sentence. When used with a reranking model, including global cues such as sentence length, this approach provides a full generation system.

Our experiments demonstrate high quality visual content selection, within 90% of human performance on unigram BLEU, and improved complete sentence generation, nearly halving the difference from human performance to two baselines on 4-gram BLEU. In ablations, we measure the importance of different annotations and visual cues, showing that annotation of activities and relative bounding box information between objects are crucial to generating human-like description.

2 Related Work

A number of approaches have been proposed for constructing sentences from images, including copying captions from other images (Farhadi et al., 2010; Ordonez et al., 2011), using text surrounding an image in a news article (Feng and Lapata, 2010), filling visual sentence templates (Kulkarni et al., 2011; Yang et al., 2011; Elliott and Keller, 2013), and stitching together existing sentence descriptions (Gupta and Mannem, 2012; Kuznetsova et al., 2012). However, due to the lack of reliable detectors, especially for activities, many previous systems have a small vocabulary and must generate many words, including verbs, with no direct visual support. These problems also extend to video caption systems (Yu and Siskind, 2013; Krishnamoorthy et al., 2013).

The Midge algorithm (Mitchell et al., 2012) is most closely related to our approach, and will provide a baseline in our experiments. Midge is syntax-driven but again uses a small vocabulary without direct visual support for every word. It outputs a large set of sentences to describe all triplets of recognized objects in the scene, but does not include a content selection model to select the best sentence. We extend Midge with content and sentence selection rules to use it as a baseline.

The visual facts we annotate are motivated by research in machine vision. Attributes are a good intermediate representation for categorization (Farhadi et al., 2009). Activity recognition is an emerging area in images (Li and Fei-Fei, 2007; Yao et al., 2011; Sharma et al., 2013) and video (Weinland et al., 2011), although less studied than object recognition. Also, parts have been widely used in object recognition (Felzenszwalb et al., 2010). Yet, no work tests the contribution of these labels for sentence generation.

There is also a significant amount of work on other grounded language problems, where related models have been developed. Visual referring expression generation systems (Krahmer and Van Deemter, 2012; Mitchell et al., 2013; FitzGerald et al., 2013) aim to identify specific objects, a sub-problem we deal with when describing images more generally. Other research generates descriptions in simulated worlds and, like this work, uses feature rich models (Angeli et al., 2010), or syntactic structures like PCFGs (Chen et al., 2010; Konstas and Lapata, 2012) but does not combine the two. Finally, Zitnick and Parikh (2013) study sentences describing clipart scenes. They present a number of factors influencing overall descriptive quality, several of which we use in sentence generation for the first time.

[2] Available at : http://homes.cs.washington.edu/~my89/

3 Dataset

We collected a dataset of richly annotated images to approximate gold standard visual recognition. In collecting the data, we sought a visual annotation with sufficient coverage to support the generation of as many of the words in the original image descriptions as possible. We also aimed to make it as visually exhaustive as possible—giving equal treatment to all visible objects. This ensures less bias from annotators' perception about which objects are important, since one of the problems we would like to solve is content selection. This dataset will be available for future experiments.

We built on the dataset from (Rashtchian et al., 2010) which contained 8,000 Flickr images and associated descriptions gathered using Amazon Mechanical Turk (MTurk). Restricting ourselves to Creative Commons images, we sampled 500 images for annotation.

We collected annotations of images in three stages using MTurk, and assigned each annotation task to 3-5 workers to improve quality through redundancy (Callison-Burch, 2009). Below we describe the process for annotating a single image.

Stage 1: We prompted five turkers to list *all* objects in an image, ignoring objects that are parts of larger objects (e.g., the arms of a person), which we collected later in Stage 3. This list also included groups, such as crowds of people.

Stage 2: For each unique object label from Stage 1, we asked two turkers to draw a polygon around the object identified.[3] In cases where the object is a group, we also asked for the number of objects present (1-6 or many). Finally, we created a list of all references to the object from the first stage, which we call the *Object* facet.

Stage 3: For each object or group, we prompted three turkers to provide descriptive phrases of:

- *Doing* – actions the object participates in, e.g. "jumping."
- *Parts* – physical parts e.g. "legs", or other items in the possession of the object e.g. "shirt."
- *Attributes* – adjectives describing the object, e.g. "red."
- *Isa* – alternative names for a object e.g. "boy", "rider."

Figure 1 shows more examples for objects in a labeled image.[4] We refer to all of these annotations, including the merged *Object* labels, as facets. These labels provide feature norms (McRae et al., 2005), which have recently used as a visual proxy in distributional semantics (Silberer and Lapata, 2012; Silberer et al., 2013) but have not been previous studied for generation. This annotation of 500 images (2500 sentences) yielded over 4000 object instances and 100,000 textual labels.

4 Approach

Given such rich annotations, we can now develop significantly more comprehensive generation models. In this section, we present an approach that first uses a generative model and then a reranker. The generative model defines a distribution over content selection and content realization choices, using diverse cues from the image annotations. The reranker trades off our generative model score, language model score (to encourage fluency), and length to produce the final sentence.

Generative Model We want to generate a sentence $\vec{w} = \langle w_1 \dots w_n \rangle$ where each word $w_i \in V$ comes from a fixed vocabulary V. The vocabulary V includes all 2700 words used in descriptive sentences in the training set.[5]

The model conditions on an annotated image I that contains a set of objects O, where each object $o \in O$ has a bounding polygon and a number of facets containing string labels. To model the naming of specific objects, words w_i can be associated with alignment variables a_i that range over O. One such variable is introduced for each head noun in the sentence. Figure 2 shows alignment variable settings with colors that match objects in the image. Finally, as a byproduct of the hierarchical generative process, we construct an undirected dependency tree $\vec{d}$ over the words in $\vec{w}$.

The complete generative model defines the probability $p(\vec{w}, \vec{a}, \vec{d} \mid I)$ of a sentence $\vec{w}$, word alignments $\vec{a}$, and undirected dependency tree $\vec{d}$, given the annotated input image I. The overall process unfolds recursively, as seen in Figure 3.

[3] We modified LabelMe (Torralba et al., 2010).

[4] In the experiments, Parts and Isa facets do not improve performance, so we do not use them in the final model. Isa is redundant with the Object facet, as seen in Figure 1. Also parts like clothing, were often annotated as separate objects.

[5] We do not generate from image facets directly, because only 20% of the sentences in our data can be produced like this. Instead, we develop features which consider the similarity between labels in the image and words in the vocabulary.

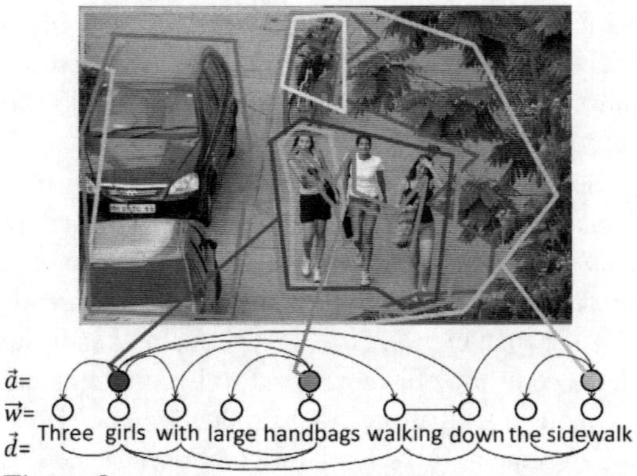

Figure 2: One path through the generative model and the Bayesian network it induces. The first row of colored circles are alignment variables to objects in the image. The second row is words, generated conditioned on alignments.

The main clause is produced by first selecting the subject alignment a_s followed by the subject word w_s. It then chooses the verb and optionally the object alignment a_o and word w_o. The process then continues recursively, modifying the subject, verb, and object of the sentence with noun and prepositional modifiers. The recursion begins at Step 2 in Figure 3. Given a parent word w and that word's relevant alignment variable a, the model creates attachments where w is the grammatical head of subsequently produced words. Choices about whether to create noun modifiers or prepositional modifiers are made in steps (a) and (b). The process chooses values for the alignment variables and then chooses content words, adding connective prepositions in the case of prepositional modifiers. It then chooses to end or submits new word-alignment pairs to be recursively modified.

Each line defines a decision that must be made according to a local probability distribution. For example, Step 1.a defines the probability of aligning a subject word to various objects in the image. The distributions are maximum entropy models, similar to previous work (Angeli et al., 2010), using features described in the next section. The induced undirected dependency tree $\vec{d}$ has an edge between each word and the previously generated word (or the input word w in Steps 2.a.i and 2.a.ii, when no previous word is available). Figure 2 shows a possible output from the process, along with the Bayesian network that encodes what each decision was conditioned on during generation.

Learning We learn the model from data $\{(\vec{w}_i, \vec{d}_i, I_i) \mid i = 1 \ldots m\}$ containing sentences $\vec{w}_i$, dependency trees $\vec{d}_i$, computed with the Stanford parser (de Marneffe et al., 2006), and images

1. for a main clause (d,e are optional), select:
   (a) subject a_s alignment from $p_a(a)$.
   (b) subject word w_s from $p_n(w \mid a_s, \vec{d}_c)$
   (c) verb word w_v from $p_v(w \mid a_s, \vec{d}_c)$
   (d) object alignment a_o from $p_a(a' \mid a_s, w_v, \vec{d}_c)$
   (e) object word w_o from $p_n(w \mid a_o, \vec{d}_c)$
   (f) end with p_{stop} or go to (2) with (w_s, a_s)
   (g) end with p_{stop} or go to (2) with (w_v, a_s)
   (h) end with p_{stop} or go to (2) with (w_o, a_o)
2. for a (word, alignment) (w', a) (a,b are optional):
   (a) if w' not verb: modify w' with noun, select:
      i. modifier word w_n from $p_n(w \mid a, \vec{d}_c)$.
      ii. end with p_{stop} or go to (2) with (a_m, w_n)
   (b) modify w' with preposition, select:
      i. preposition word w_p
         if w' not a verb: from $p_p(w \mid a, \vec{d}_c)$
         else: from $p_p(w \mid a, w_v, \vec{d}_c)$
      ii. object alignment a_p from $p_a(a' \mid a, w_p, \vec{d}_c)$
      iii. object word w_n from $p_n(w \mid a_p, \vec{d}_c)$.
      iv. end with p_{stop} or go to (2) with (a_p, w_n)

Figure 3: Generative process for producing words $\vec{w}$, alignments $\vec{a}$ and dependencies $\vec{d}$. Each distribution is conditioned on the partially complete path through generative process $\vec{d}_c$ to establish sentence context. The notation p_{stop} is short hand for $p_{stop}(STOP|\vec{w}, \vec{d}_c)$ the stopping distribution.

I_i. The dependency trees define the path that was taken through the generative process in Figure 3 and are used to create a Bayesian network for every sentence, like in Figure 2. However, object alignments $\vec{a}_i$ are latent during learning and we must marginalize over them.

The model is trained to maximize the conditional marginal log-likelihood of the data with regularization:

$$\mathcal{L}(\theta) = \sum_i \log \sum_{\vec{a}} p(\vec{a}, \vec{w}_i, \vec{d}_i \mid I_i; \theta) - r|\theta|^2$$

where θ is the set of parameters and r is the regularization coefficient. In essence, we maximize the likelihood of every sentence's observed Bayesian network, while marginalizing over content selection variables we did not observe.

Because the model only includes pairwise dependencies between the hidden alignment variables $\vec{a}$, the inference problem is quadratic in the number of objects and non-convex because $\vec{a}$ is unobserved. We optimize this objective directly with L-BFGS, using the junction-tree algorithm to compute the sum and the gradient.[6]

[6]To compute the gradient, we differentiate the recurrence in the junction-tree algorithm by applying the product rule.

Inference To describe an image, we need to maximize over word, alignment, and the dependency parse variables:

$$\arg\max_{\vec{w},\vec{a},\vec{d}} p(\vec{w},\vec{a},\vec{d} \mid I)$$

This computation is intractable because we need to consider all possible sentences, so we use beam search for strings up to a fixed length.

Reranking Generating directly from the process in Figure 3 results in sentences that may be short and repetitive because the model score is a product of locally normalized distributions. The reranker takes as input a candidate list c, for an image I, as decoded from the generative model. The candidate list includes the top-k scoring hypotheses for each sentence length up to a fixed maximum. A linear scoring function is used for reranking optimized with MERT (Och, 2003) to maximize BLEU-2.

5 Features

We construct indicator features to capture variation in usage in different parts of the sentence, types of objects that are mentioned, visual salience, and semantic and visual coordination between objects. The features are included in the maximum entropy models used to parameterize the distributions described in Figure 3. Whenever possible, we use WordNet Synsets (Miller, 1995) instead of lexical features to limit over-fitting.

Features in the generative model use tests for local properties, such as the identity of a synset of a word in WordNet, conjoined with an identifier that indicates context in the generative process.[7] Generative model features indicate (1) visual and semantic information about objects in distributions over alignments (content selection) and (2) preferences for referring to objects in distributions over words (content realization). Features in the reranking model indicate global properties of candidate sentences. Exact formulas for computing the features are in the appendix.

Visual features, such as an object's position in the image, are used for content selection. Pairwise visual information between two objects, for example the bounding box overlap between objects or the relative position of the two objects, is included in distributions where selection of an alignment variable conditions on previously generated alignments. For verbs (Step 1.d in Figure 3) and prepositions (Step 2.b.ii), these features are conjoined with the stem of the connective.

Semantic types of objects are also used in content selection. We define semantic types by finding synsets of labels in objects that correspond to high level types, a list motivated by the animacy hierarchy (Zaenen et al., 2004).[8] Type features indicate the type of the object referred to by an alignment variable as well as the cross product of types when an alignment variable is on conditioning side of a distribution (e.g. Step 1.d). Like above, in the presence of a connective word, these features are conjoined with the stem of the connective.

Content realization features help select words when conditioning on chosen alignments (e.g. Step 1.b). These features include the identity of the WordNet synset corresponding to a word, the word's depth in the synset hierarchy, the language model score for adding that word[9] and whether the word matches labels in facets corresponding to the object referenced by an alignment variable.

Reranking features are primarily used to overcome issues of repetition and length in the generative distributions, more commonly used for alignment, than to create sentences. We use only four features: length, the number of repetitions, generative model score, and language model score.

6 Experimental Setup

Data We used 70% of the data for training (1750 sentences, 350 images), 15% for development, and 15% for testing (375 sentences, 75 images).

Parameters The regularization parameter was set on the held out data to $r = 8$. The reranker candidate list included the top 500 sentences for each sentence length up to 15 and weights were optimized with Z-MERT (Zaidan, 2009).

Metrics Our evaluation is based on BLEU-n (Papineni et al., 2001), which considers all n-grams up to length n. To assess human performance using BLEU, we score each of the five references against the four other ones and finally average the five BLEU scores. In order to make these results comparable to BLEU scores for our model

[7] For example, in Figure 2 the context for the word "sidewalk" would be "word,syntactic-object,verb,preposition" indicating it is a word, in the syntactic object of a preposition, which was attached to a verb modifying prepositional phrase.

[8] For example, human, animal, artifact (a human created object), natural body (trees, water, ect.), or natural artifact (stick, leaf, rock).

[9] We use tri-grams with Kneser-Ney smoothing over the 1 million caption data set (Ordonez et al., 2011).

and baselines, we perform the same five-fold averaging when computing BLEU for each system.

We also compute accuracy for different syntactic positions in the sentence. We look at a number of categories: the main clause's components (S,V,O), prepositional phrase components, the preposition (Pp) and their objects (Po) and noun modifying words (N), including determiners. Phrases match if they have an exact string match and share context identifiers as defined in the features sections.

Human Evaluation Annotators rated sentences output by our full model against either human or a baseline system generated descriptions. Three criteria were evaluated: grammaticality, which sentence is more complete and well formed; truthfulness, which sentence is more accurately capturing something true in the image; and salience, which sentence is capturing important things in the image while still being concise. Two annotators annotated all test pairs for all criteria for a given pair of systems. Six annotators were used (none authors) and agreement was high (Cohen's kappa = 0.963, 0.823 and 0.703 for grammar, truth and salience).

Machine Translation Baseline The first baseline is designed to see if it is possible to generate good sentences from the facet string labels alone, with no visual information. We use an extension of phrase-based machine translation techniques (Och et al., 1999). We created a virtual bitext by pairing each image description (the target sentence) with a sequence[10] of visual identifiers (the source "sentence") listing strings from the facet labels. Since phrases produced by turkers lack many of the functions words needed to create fluent sentences, we added one of 47 function words either at the start or the end of each output phrase.

The translation model included standard features such as language model score (using our caption language model described previously), word count, phrase count, linear distortion, and the count of deleted source words. We also define three features that count the number of *Object*, *Isa*, and *Doing* phrases, to learn a preference for types of phrases. The feature weights are tuned with MERT (Och, 2003) to maximize BLEU-4.

Midge Baseline As described in related work, the Midge system creates a set of sentences to describe everything in an input image. These sentences must all be true, but do not have to select the same content that a person would. It can be adapted to our task by adding object selection and sentence ranking rules. For object selection, we choose the three most frequently named objects in the scene according to a background corpus of image descriptions. For sentence selection, we take all sentences within one word of the average length of a sentence in our corpus, 11, and select the one with best Midge generation score.

[10]We defined a consistent ordering of visual identifiers and set the distortion limit of the phrase-based decoder to infinity.

	BL-1	BL-2	BL-3	BL-4
Human	61.0	42.0	27.8	18.3
Full Model	**57.1**	**35.7**	**18.3**	**9.5**
MT Baseline	39.8	23.6	13.2	6.1
Midge Baseline	43.5	20.2	9.4	0.0

Table 1: Results for the test set for the BLEU1-4 metrics.

Grammar	Full	Other	Equal
Full vs **Human**	7.65	19.4	72.94
Full vs MT	6.47	5.29	88.23
Full vs Midge	40.59	15.88	43.53
Truth	Full	Other	Equal
Full vs **Human**	0.59	67.65	31.76
Full vs MT	30.0	10.59	59.41
Full vs Midge	51.76	27.71	23.53
Salience	Full	Other	Equal
Full vs **Human**	8.82	88.24	2.94
Full vs MT	51.76	16.47	31.77
Full vs Midge	71.18	14.71	14.12

Table 2: Human evaluation of our Full-Model in heads up tests against Human authored sentences and baseline systems, the machine translation baseline (MT) and the Midge inspired baseline. **Bold** indicates the better system. Other is not the Full system. Equal indicates neither sentence is better.

7 Results

We report experiments for our generation pipeline and ablations that remove data and features.

Overall Performance Table 1 shows the results on the test set. The full model consistently achieves the highest BLEU scores. Overall, these numbers suggest strong content selection by getting high recall for individual words (BLEU-1), but fall further behind human performance as the length of the n-gram grows (BLEU-2 through BLEU-4). These number match our perception that the model is learning to produce high quality sentences, but does not always describe all of the important aspects of the scene or use exactly the expected wording. Table 4 presents example output, which we will discuss in more detail shortly.

Model	BL-1	BL-2	BL-3	BL-4	S	V	O	Pp	Po	N
Human	64.7	46.0	31.5	20.1	-	-	-	-	-	-
Full-Model	**59.0**	36.9	**19.3**	**10.5**	**64.9**	**40.4**	36.8	50.0	20.7	69.1
– doing	51.1	32.6	16.9	9.2	63.2	15.8	10.5	45.5	**21.6**	69.7
– count	55.4	33.5	16.0	8.5	59.6	35.1	15.4	**53.7**	19.5	66.7
– properties	57.8	**37.2**	18.8	10.0	61.4	36.8	36.8	47.1	20.7	**73.5**
– visual	56.7	35.1	18.9	9.4	**64.9**	36.8	**50.0**	41.8	15.3	71.6
– pairwise	56.9	35.5	16.5	8.2	**64.9**	**40.4**	45.5	42.4	21.2	70.9

Table 3: Ablation results on development data using BLEU1-4 and reporting match accuracy for sentence structures.

S: A girl playing a guitar in the grass

R: A woman with a nylon stringed guitar is playing in a field

S: A man playing with two dogs in the water

R: A man is throwing a log into a waterway while two dogs watch

S: Two men playing with a bench in the grass

R: Nine men are playing a game in the park, shirts versus skins

S: Three kids sitting on a road

R: A boy runs in a race while onlookers watch

Table 4: Two good examples of output (top), and two examples of poor performance (bottom). Each image has two captions, the system output **S** and a human reference **R**.

Human Evaluation Table 2 presents the results of a human evaluation. The full model outperforms all baselines on every measure, but is not always competitive with human descriptions. It performs the best on grammaticality, where it is judged to be as grammatical as humans. However, surprisingly, in many cases it is also often judged equal to the other baselines. Examination of baseline output reveals that the MT baseline often generates short sentences, having little chance of being judged ungrammatical. Furthermore, the Midge baseline, like our system, is a syntax-based system and therefore often produces grammatical sentences. Although our system performs well with respect to the baselines on truthfulness, often the system constructs sentences with incorrect prepositions, an issue that could be improved with better estimates of 3-d position in the image. On truthfulness, the MT baseline is comparable to our system, often being judged equal, because its output is short. Our system's strength is salience, a factor the baselines do not model.

Data Ablation Table 3 shows annotation ablation experiments on the development set, where we remove different classes of data labels to measure the performance that can be achieved with less visual information. In all cases, the overall behavior of the system varies, as it tries to learn to compensate for the missing information.

Ablating actions is by far the most detrimental. Overall BLEU score suffers and prediction accuracy of the verb (V) degrades significantly causing cascading errors that affect the object of the verb (O). Removing count information affects noun attachment (N) performance. Images where determiner use is important or where groups of objects are best identified by the number (for example, three dogs) are difficult to describe naturally. Finally, we see a tradeoff when removing properties. There is an increase in noun modifier accuracy (N) but a decrease in content selection quality (BL-1), showing recall has gone down. In essence, the approach learns to stop trying to generate adjectives and other modifiers that would rely on the missing properties. The difference in BLEU score with the Full-Model is small, even without these modifiers, because there often still exists a a short output with high accuracy.

Feature Ablation The bottom two rows in Table 3 show ablations of the visual and pairwise features, measuring the contribution of the visual information provided by the bounding box annotations. The ablated visual information includes bounding-box positions and relative pairwise visual information. The pairwise ablation removes the ability to model any interactions between objects, for example, relative bounding box or pairwise object type information.

Overall, prepositional phrase accuracy is most affected. Ablating visual features significantly impacts accuracy of prepositional phrases (Pp and Po), affecting the use of preposition words the most, and lowering fluency (BL-4). Precision in the object of the verb (O) rises; the model makes $\sim 50\%$ fewer predictions in that position than the Full-Model because it lacks features to coordinate subject and object of the verb. Ablating pairwise features has similar results. While the model corrects errors in the object of the preposition (Po) with the addition of visual features, fluency is still worse than Full-Model, as reflected by BL-4.

Qualitative Results Table 4 has examples of good and bad system output. The first two images are good examples, including both system output (**S**) and a human reference (**R**). The second two contain lower quality outputs. Overall, the model captures common ways to refer to people and scenes. However, it does better for images with fewer sentient objects because content selection is less ambiguous.

Our system does well at finding important objects. For example, in the first good image, we mention the guitar instead of the house, both of which are prominent and have high overlap with the woman. In the second case, we identify that both dogs and humans tend to be important actors in scenes but poorly identify their relationship.

The bad examples show difficult scenes. In the first description the broad context is not identified, instead focusing on the bench (highlighted in red). The second example identifies a weakness in our annotation: it encodes contradictory groupings of the people. The groupings covers all of the children, including the boy running, and many subsets of the people near the grass. This causes ambiguity and our methods cannot differentiate them, incorrectly mentioning just the children and picking an inappropriate verb (one participant in the group is not sitting). Improved annotation of groups would enable the study of generation for more complex scenes, such as these.

8 Conclusion

In this work we used dense annotations of images to study description generation. The annotations allowed us to not only develop new models, better capable of generating human-like sentences, but also to explore what visual information is crucial for description generation. Experiments showed that activity and bounding-box information is important and demonstrated areas of future work. In images that are more complex, for example multiple sentient objects, object grouping and reference will be important to generating good descriptions. Issues of this type can be explored with annotations of increasing complexity.

Appendix A

This appendix describes the feature templates for the generative model in greater detail.

Features in the generative model conjoin indicators for local tests, such as $\mathbf{STEM}(w)$ which indicates the stem of a word w, with a global contextual identifier $\mathbf{CONTEXT}(v, d)$ that indicates properties of the generation history, as described in detail below. Table 5 provides a reference for which feature templates are used in the generative model distributions, as defined in Figure 3.

8.1 Feature Templates

$\mathbf{CONTEXT}(n, d)$ is an indicator for a contextual identifier for a variable n in the model depending on the dependency structure d. There is an indicator for all combinations of the type of n (alignment or word), the position of n (subject, syntactic object, verb, noun-modifier, or preposition), the position of the earliest variable along the path to generate n, and the type of attachment to that variable (noun or prepositional modifier). For example, in Figure 2 the context for the word "sidewalk" would be "word,syntactic-object,verb,preposition" indicating it is a word, the object of a preposition, whose path was along a verb modifying prepositional phrase.[11]

$\mathbf{TYPE}(a)$ indicates the high level type of an object referred to by alignment variable a. We use synsets to define high level types including human, animal, artifact, natural artifact and various synsets that capture scene information,[12] a list motivated by the animacy hierarchy (Zaenen et al., 2004). Each object is assigned a type by finding the synset for its name (object facet), and tracing the hypernym structure in Wordnet to find the appropriate class, if one exists. Additionally, the type indicates whether the object is a group or not. For example, in Figure 2, the blue polygon has type "person,group", or the red bike polygon has type "artifact,single."

[11]Similarly "large" is "word,noun,subject,preposition" while "girls" is special cased to "word,subject,root" because it has no initial attachment. The alignment variable above the word handbags is "alignment,syntactic-object,subject,preposition" because it an alignment variable, is in the syntactic object position of a preposition and can be located by following a subject attached pp.

[12]WordNet divides these into synsets expressing water, weather, nature and a few more.

Feature Family	Included In	Steps
$\textbf{CONTEXT}(a', \vec{d_c}) \otimes$ $\{\textbf{TYPE}(a'), \textbf{MENTION}(a', do), \textbf{MENTION}(a', obj), \textbf{VISUAL}(a')\}$	$p_a(a' \mid \vec{d_c})$ $p_a(a' \mid a, w, \vec{d_c})$	1.a, 1.d, 2.b.ii
$\textbf{CONTEXT}(a', \vec{d_c}) \otimes \{\textbf{TYPE}(a) \otimes \textbf{TYPE}(a'), \textbf{VISUAL2}(a, a')\}$	$p_a(a' \mid a, w, \vec{d_c})$	1.d, 2.b.i
$\textbf{CONTEXT}(a', \vec{d_c}) \otimes$ $\{\textbf{TYPE}(a) \otimes \textbf{TYPE}(a') \otimes \textbf{STEM}(w), \textbf{VISUAL2}(a, a') \otimes \textbf{STEM}(w)\}$	$p_a(a' \mid a, w, \vec{d_c})$	1.d, 2.b.i
$\textbf{CONTEXT}(a, \vec{d_c}) \otimes$ $\{\textbf{WORDNET}(w), \textbf{MATCH}(w, a), \textbf{SPECIFICITY}(w, a),$ $\textbf{ADJECTIVE}(w, a), \textbf{DETERMINER}(w, a)\}$	$p_n(w \mid a, \vec{d_c})$	1.b, 1.e, 2.a.i 2.b.ii
$\textbf{CONTEXT}(a, \vec{d_c}) \otimes \{\textbf{MATCH}(w, a), \textbf{TYPE}(a) \otimes \textbf{STEM}(w)\}$	$p_v(w \mid a, \vec{d_c})$	1.c
$\textbf{CONTEXT}(a', \vec{d_c}) \otimes \textbf{TYPE}(a) \otimes \textbf{STEM}(w_p)$	$p_p(w \mid a, \vec{d_c})$ $p_p(w \mid a, w_v, \vec{d_c})$	2.b.i
$\textbf{CONTEXT}(a', \vec{d_c}) \otimes \textbf{STEM}(w_v) \otimes \textbf{STEM}(w)$	$p_p(w \mid a, w_v, \vec{d_c})$	2.b.i

Table 5: Feature families and distributions that include them. $\otimes$ indicates the cross-product of the indicator features. Distributions are listed more than once to indicate they use multiple feature families.

$\textbf{VISUAL}(a)$ returns indicators for visual facts about the object that a aligns to. There is an indicator for two quantities: (1) overlap of object's polygon with every horizontal third of the image, as a fraction of the object's area, and (2) the object's distance to the center of the image as fraction of the diagonal of the image. Each quantity, v, is put into three overlapping buckets: if $v > .1$, if $v > .5$, and if $v > .9$.

$\textbf{VISUAL2}(a, a')$ indicates pairwise visual facts about two objects. There is an indicator for the following quantities bucketed: the amount of overlap between the polygons for a and a' as a fraction of the size of a's polygon, the distance between the center of the polygon for a and a' as a fraction of image's diagonal, and the slope between the center of a and a'. Each quantity, v, is put into three overlapping buckets: if $v > .1$, if $v > .5$, and if $v > .9$. There is an indicator for the relative position of extremities a and a': whether the rightmost point of a is further right than a''s rightmost or leftmost point, and the same for top, left, and bottom.

$\textbf{WORDNET}(w)$ returns indicators for all hypernyms of a word w. The two most specific synsets are not used when there at least 8 options.

$\textbf{MENTION}(a, \textit{facet})$ returns the union of the $\textbf{WORDNET}(w)$ features for all words w in the facet *facet* for the object referred to alignment a.

$\textbf{ADJECTIVE}(w, a)$ indicates four types of features specific to adjective usage. If $\textbf{MENTION}(w, \textit{Attributes})$ is not empty, indicate : (1) the satellite adjective synset of w in Wordnet, (2) the head adjective synset of w in Wordnet, (3) the head adjective synset conjoined with $\textbf{TYPE}(a)$, and (4) the number of times there exists a label in the Attributes facet of a that has the same head adjective synset as w.

$\textbf{DETERMINER}(w, a)$ indicates four determiner specific features. If w is a determiner, then indicate : (1) the identity of w conjoined with the count (the label for numerosity) of a, (2) the identity of w conjoined with an indicator for if the count of a is greater than one, (3) the identity of w conjoined with $\textbf{TYPE}(a)$ and (4) the frequency with which w appears before its head word in the Flikr corpus (Ordonez et al., 2011).

$\textbf{MATCH}(w, a)$, indicates all *facets* of object a that contain words with the same stem as w.

$\textbf{SPECIFICITY}(w, a)$ is an indicator of the specificity of the word w when referring to the object aligned to a. Indicates the relative depth of w in Wordnet, as compared to all words w' where $\textbf{MATCH}(w', a)$ is not empty. The depth is bucketed into quintiles.

$\textbf{STEM}(w)$ returns the Porter2 stem of w.[13]

The distribution for stopping, $p_{stop}(STOP \mid \vec{d_c}, \vec{w})$, contains two types of features. (1) Structural features indicating for the number of times a contextual identifier has appeared so far in the derivation and (2) mention features indicating the types of objects mentioned.[14] To compute mention features, we consider all possible types of objects, t, then there is an indicator for: (1) if $\exists o, \exists w \in \vec{w} : \textbf{MATCH}(w, o) \neq \emptyset \wedge \textbf{TYPE}(o) = t$, (2) whether $\exists o, \nexists w \in \vec{w} : \textbf{MATCH}(w, o) \neq \emptyset \wedge \textbf{TYPE}(o) = t$ and (3) if (1) does not hold but (2) does.

Acknowledgments This work is partially funded by DARPA CSSG (D11AP00277) and ARO (W911NF-12-1-0197). We thank L. Zitnick, B. Dolan, M. Mitchell, C. Quirk, A. Farhadi, B. Russell for helpful conversations. Also, L. Zilles, Y. Atrzi, N. FitzGerald, T. Kwiatkowski and reviewers for comments.

[13] http://snowball.tartarus.org/algorithms/english/stemmer.html

[14] Object mention features cannot contain $\vec{a}$ because that creates large dependencies in inference for learning.

References

Gabor Angeli, Percy Liang, and Dan Klein. 2010. A simple domain-independent probabilistic approach to generation. In *Empirical Methods in Natural Language Processing (EMNLP)*.

Chris Callison-Burch. 2009. Fast, cheap, and creative: Evaluating translation quality using Amazon's Mechanical Turk. In *EMNLP*, pages 286–295, August.

David L. Chen, Joohyun Kim, and Raymond J. Mooney. 2010. Training a multilingual sportscaster: Using perceptual context to learn language. *JAIR*, 37:397–435.

Marie-Catherine de Marneffe, Bill MacCartney, Christopher D Manning, et al. 2006. Generating typed dependency parses from phrase structure parses. In *LREC*, volume 6, pages 449–454.

Desmond Elliott and Frank Keller. 2013. Image Description using Visual Dependency Representations. In *EMNLP*.

Ali Farhadi, Ian Endres, Derek Hoiem, and David Forsyth. 2009. Describing objects by their attributes. In *Computer Vision and Pattern Recognition, 2009. CVPR 2009. IEEE Conference on*, pages 1778–1785. IEEE.

Ali Farhadi, Mohsen Hejrati, Mohammad Amin Sadeghi, Peter Young, Cyrus Rashtchian, Julia Hockenmaier, and David Forsyth. 2010. Every picture tells a story: Generating sentences from images. In *Proceedings of the 11th European conference on Computer Vision*, ECCV'10, pages 15–29.

Pedro F Felzenszwalb, Ross B Girshick, David McAllester, and Deva Ramanan. 2010. Object detection with discriminatively trained part-based models. *Pattern Analysis and Machine Intelligence, IEEE Transactions on*, 32(9):1627–1645.

Yansong Feng and Mirella Lapata. 2010. How many words is a picture worth? Automatic caption generation for news images. In *ACL*, pages 1239–1249.

Nicholas FitzGerald, Yoav Artzi, and Luke Zettlemoyer. 2013. Learning distributions over logical forms for referring expression generation. In *EMNLP*.

Ankush Gupta and Prashanth Mannem. 2012. From image annotation to image description. In *NIPS*, volume 7667, pages 196–204.

Ioannis Konstas and Mirella Lapata. 2012. Concept-to-text generation via discriminative reranking. In *ACL*, pages 369–378.

Emiel Krahmer and Kees Van Deemter. 2012. Computational generation of referring expressions: A survey. *Computational Linguistics*, 38(1):173–218.

Niveda Krishnamoorthy, Girish Malkarnenkar, Raymond Mooney, Kate Saenko, and Sergio Guadarrama. 2013. Generating natural-language video descriptions using text-mined knowledge. *Procedings of AAAI*, 2013(2):3.

G. Kulkarni, V. Premraj, S. Dhar, S. Li, Y. Choi, A.C. Berg, and T.L. Berg. 2011. Baby talk: Understanding and generating simple image descriptions. In *Computer Vision and Pattern Recognition (CVPR)*, pages 1601–1608.

Polina Kuznetsova, Vicente Ordonez, Alexander C Berg, Tamara L Berg, and Yejin Choi. 2012. Collective generation of natural image descriptions. In *ACL*, pages 359–368.

Li-Jia Li and Li Fei-Fei. 2007. What, where and who? Classifying events by scene and object recognition. In *ICCV*, pages 1–8. IEEE.

Ken McRae, George S. Cree, Mark S. Seidenberg, and Chris Mcnorgan. 2005. Semantic feature production norms for a large set of living and nonliving things. *Behavior Research Methods*, 37(4):547–559.

George A Miller. 1995. WordNet: a lexical database for english. *Communications of the ACM*, 38(11):39–41.

Margaret Mitchell, Xufeng Han, Jesse Dodge, Alyssa Mensch, Amit Goyal, Alex Berg, Kota Yamaguchi, Tamara Berg, Karl Stratos, and Hal Daumé, III. 2012. Midge: Generating image descriptions from computer vision detections. In *EACL*, pages 747–756.

Margaret Mitchell, Kees van Deemter, and Ehud Reiter. 2013. Generating expressions that refer to visible objects. In *Proceedings of NAACL-HLT*, pages 1174–1184.

F. Och, C. Tillmann, and H. Ney. 1999. Improved alignment models for statistical machine translation. In *Proc. of the Joint Conf. of Empirical Methods in Natural Language Processing and Very Large Corpora*, pages 20–28.

Franz Josef Och. 2003. Minimum error rate training in statistical machine translation. In *ACL*, pages 160–167.

Vicente Ordonez, Girish Kulkarni, and Tamara L. Berg. 2011. Im2Text: Describing images using 1 million captioned photographs. In *NIPS*, pages 1143–1151.

Kishore Papineni, Salim Roukos, Todd Ward, and Wei-Jing Zhu. 2001. BLEU: a method for automatic evaluation of machine translation. In *Proc. of ACL*.

C. Rashtchian, P. Young, M. Hodosh, and J. Hockenmaier. 2010. Collecting image annotations using Amazon's Mechanical Turk. In *Proceedings of the NAACL HLT 2010 Workshop on Creating Speech and Language Data with Amazon's Mechanical Turk*, pages 139–147.

Gaurav Sharma, Frédéric Jurie, Cordelia Schmid, et al. 2013. Expanded parts model for human attribute and action recognition in still images. In *CVPR*.

Carina Silberer and Mirella Lapata. 2012. Grounded models of semantic representation. In *EMNLP*, July.

Carina Silberer, Vittorio Ferrari, and Mirella Lapata. 2013. Models of semantic representation with visual attributes. In *ACL*, pages 572–582.

Antonio Torralba, Bryan C Russell, and Jenny Yuen. 2010. LabelMe: Online image annotation and applications. *Proceedings of the IEEE*, 98(8):1467–1484.

Daniel Weinland, Remi Ronfard, and Edmond Boyer. 2011. A survey of vision-based methods for action representation, segmentation and recognition. *Computer Vision and Image Understanding*, 115(2):224–241.

Yezhou Yang, Ching Lik Teo, Hal Daumé III, and Yiannis Aloimonos. 2011. Corpus-guided sentence generation of natural images. In *Empirical Methods in Natural Language Processing*.

Bangpeng Yao, Xiaoye Jiang, Aditya Khosla, Andy Lai Lin, Leonidas J. Guibas, and Li Fei-Fei. 2011. Action recognition by learning bases of action attributes and parts. In *ICCV*, Barcelona, Spain, November.

Haonan Yu and Jeffrey Mark Siskind. 2013. Grounded language learning from video described with sentences. In *Proceedings of the 51st Annual Meeting of the Association for Computational Linguistics*, volume 1, pages 53–63.

Annie Zaenen, Jean Carletta, Gregory Garretson, Joan Bresnan, Andrew Koontz-Garboden, Tatiana Nikitina, M Catherine O'Connor, and Tom Wasow. 2004. Animacy encoding in English: why and how. In *ACL Workshop on Discourse Annotation*, pages 118–125.

Omar F. Zaidan. 2009. Z-MERT: A fully configurable open source tool for minimum error rate training of machine translation systems. *The Prague Bulletin of Mathematical Linguistics*, 91:79–88.

C. Lawrence Zitnick and Devi Parikh. 2013. Bringing semantics into focus using visual abstraction. In *CVPR*.

Extracting Latent Attributes from Video Scenes Using Text as Background Knowledge

Anh Tran, Mihai Surdeanu, Paul Cohen
University of Arizona
{trananh, msurdeanu, prcohen}@email.arizona.edu

Abstract

We explore the novel task of identifying latent attributes in video scenes, such as the mental states of actors, using only large text collections as background knowledge and minimal information about the videos, such as activity and actor types. We formalize the task and a measure of merit that accounts for the semantic relatedness of mental state terms. We develop and test several largely unsupervised information extraction models that identify the mental states of human participants in video scenes. We show that these models produce complementary information and their combination significantly outperforms the individual models as well as other baseline methods.

1 Introduction

"Labeling a narrowly avoided vehicular manslaughter as *approach(car, person)* is missing something."[1] The recognition of activities, participants, and objects in videos has advanced considerably in recent years (Li et al., 2010; Poppe, 2010; Weinland et al., 2011; Yang and Ramanan, 2011; Ng et al., 2012). However, identifying latent attributes of scenes, such as the mental states of human participants, has not been addressed. Latent attributes matter: If a video surveillance system detects one person chasing another, the response from law enforcement should be radically different if the people are happy (e.g., children playing) or afraid and angry (e.g., a person running from an assailant).

Attributes that are latent in visual representations are often explicit in textual representations. This suggests a novel method for inferring latent attributes: Use explicit features of videos to query text corpora, and from the resulting texts extract attributes that are latent in the videos, such as mental states. The contributions of this work are:

1: We formalize the novel task of latent attribute identification from video scenes, focusing on the identification of actors' mental states. The input for the task is contextual information about the scene, such as detections about the activity (e.g., chase) and actor types (e.g., policeman or child), and the output is a distribution over mental state labels. We show that gold standard annotations for this task can be reliably generated using crowd sourcing. We define a novel evaluation measure, called *constrained weighted similarity-aligned* F_1 score, that accounts for both the differences between mental state distributions and the semantic relatedness of mental state terms (e.g., partial credit is given for *irate* when the target is *angry*).

2: We propose several robust and largely unsupervised information extraction (IE) models for identifying the mental state labels of human participants in a scene, given solely the activity and actor types: a lexical semantic (LS) model that extracts mental state labels that are highly similar to the context of the scene in a latent, conceptual vector space; and an information retrieval (IR) model that identifies labels commonly appearing in sentences related to the explicit scene context. We show that these models are complementary and their combination performs better than either model, alone.

3: Furthermore, we show that an event-centric model that focuses on the mental state labels of the participants in the relevant event (identified using syntactic patterns and coreference resolution) outperforms the above shallower models.

[1] James Donlon, former manager of DARPA's Mind's Eye program, personal communication.

*Proceedings of the Third Joint Conference on Lexical and Computational Semantics (*SEM 2014)*, pages 121–131, Dublin, Ireland, August 23-24 2014.

2 Related Work

As far as we know, the task proposed here is novel. We can, however, review work relevant to each part of the problem and our solution. Mental state inference is often formulated as a classification problem, where the goal is to predict target mental state labels based on low-level sensory input data. Most solutions try to learn classification models based on large amounts of training data, while some require human engineering of domain knowledge. Hidden Markov Models (HMMs) and Dynamic Bayesian Networks (DBNs) are popular representations because they can model the temporal evolution of mental states. For instance, the mental states of students can be inferred from unintentional body gestures using a DBN (Abbasi et al., 2009). Likewise, an HMM can also be used to model the emotional states of humans (Liu and Wang, 2011). Some solutions combine HMMs and DBNs in a Bayesian inference framework to yield a multi-layer representation that can do real-time inference of complex mental and emotional states (El Kaliouby and Robinson, 2004; Baltrusaitis et al., 2011). Our work differs from these approaches in several ways: It is mostly unsupervised, multi-modal, and requires little training.

Relevant video processing technology includes object detection (e.g., (Felzenszwalb et al., 2008)), person detection, and pose detection (e.g., (Yang and Ramanan, 2011)). Many tracking algorithms have been developed, such as group tracking (McKenna et al., 2000), tracking by learning appearances (Ramanan et al., 2007), and tracking in 3D space (Giebel et al., 2004; Brau et al., 2013). For human action recognition, current state-of-the-art techniques are capable of achieving near perfect performance on the commonly used KTH Actions dataset (Schuldt et al., 2004) and high performance rates on other more challenging datasets (O'Hara and Draper, 2012; Sadanand and Corso, 2012).

To extract mental state information from texts, one might use any or all of the technologies of natural language processing, so a complete review of relevant technologies is impossible, here. Of immediate relevance is the work of de Marneffe et al. (2010), which identified the latent meaning behind scalar adjectives (e.g., which ages people have in mind when talking about "little kids"). The authors learned these meanings by extracting scalars, such as children's ages, that were commonly collocated with phrases, such as "little kids," in web documents. Mohtarami et al. (2011) tried to infer yes/no answers from indirect yes/no question-answer pairs (IQAPs) by predicting the uncertainty of sentiment adjectives in indirect answers. Their method employs antonyms, synonyms, word sense disambiguation as well as the semantic association between the sentiment adjectives that appear in the IQAP to assign a degree of certainty to each answer. Sokolova and Lapalme (2011) further showed how to learn a model for predicting the opinions of users based on their written contents, such as reviews and product descriptions, on the Web. Gabbard et al. (2011) found that coreference resolution can significantly improve the recall rate of relations extraction without much expense to the precision rate.

Our work builds on these efforts by combining information retrieval, lexical semantics, and event extraction to extract latent scene attributes.

3 Data

For the experiments in this paper, we focus solely on videos containing chase scenes. Chases often invoke clear mental state inferences, and depending on context can suggest very different mental state distributions for the actors involved.

3.1 Video Corpus

We compiled a video dataset of 26 chase videos found on the Web. Of these, five involve police officers, seven involve children, four show sports-related scenes, and twelve describe different chase scenarios involving civilian adults (two videos involve children playing sports). The average duration of the dataset is 8.8 seconds with a range of $[4, 18]$. Most videos involve a single chaser and a single chasee (a person being chased) while a few have several chasers and/or chasees.

For each video, we used Amazon Mechanical Turk (MTurk) to identify both the actors and their mental states. Each worker was asked to view a video in its entirety before answering some questions about the scene. We give no prior training to the workers. The questions were carefully phrased to apply to all participants of a particular role, for example all chasers (if there are more than one). We also ask obvious validation questions about the participants in each role (e.g., are the chasers running towards the camera?) and use the answers to these questions to filter out poor responses. In general, we found that most responses were good and only a few incomplete submissions were rejected.

In the first experiment, we asked MTurk workers to select the actor types and various other detections from a predefined list of tags. This labeling task is a proxy for a computer vision detection system that functions at a human level of performance. Indeed, we restricted the actor type labels to a set that can be reasonably expected from automatic detection algorithms: *person*, *police officer*, *child*, and (non-human) *object*. For instance, police officers often wear distinctive color uniforms that can be learned using the Felzenszwalb detector (Felzenszwalb et al., 2008), whereas children can be reliably differentiated by their heights under a 3D-tracking model (Brau et al., 2013). Each video was annotated by three different workers and the union of their annotations is produced. The overall accuracy of the annotation was excellent. The MTurk workers correctly identified the important actors in every video.

Next, we collected a gold standard list of mental state labels for each video by asking MTurk workers to identify *all* applicable mental state adjectives for the actors involved. We used a text-box to allow for free-form input. Studies have shown that people of different cultures can perceive emotions very differently, and having forced choice options cannot always capture their true perception (Gendron et al., 2014). Therefore, we did not restrict the response of the workers in any way. Workers could abstain from answering if they felt the video was too ambiguous. Each video was evaluated by ten different workers. We converted each term provided to the closest adjective form if possible. Terms with no equivalent adjective forms were left in place. On rare occasions, workers provided sentence descriptions despite being asked for single-word adjectives. These sentences were either removed, or collapsed into a single word if appropriate. The overall quality of the annotations was good and generally followed common intuition. Asides from the frequently used terms, we also received some colorful (yet informative) descriptions, like *incredulous* and *vindictive*. In general, chases involving police scenarios often contained violent and angry states while chases involving children received more cheerful labels. There were unexpected descriptions, such as *annoy* for a playful chase between two children. Upon review of the video, we agreed that one child did indeed look annoyed. Thus, the resulting descriptions were subjective, but very few were hard to rationalize. By aggregating the answers from the workers, we generated a gold standard distribution of mental state terms for each video.[2]

3.2 Text Corpus

The text corpus used for our models is the English Gigaword 5th Edition corpus[3], made available by the Linguistics Data Consortium and indexed by Lucene[4]. It is a comprehensive archive of newswire text data (approximately 26 GB), acquired over several years. It is in this corpus that we expect to find mental state terms cued by contextual information from videos.

4 Neighborhood Models

We developed several individual models based on the *neighborhood paradigm*, that is, the hypothesis that relevant mental state labels will appear "near" text cued by the visual features of a scene.

The models take as input the *context* extracted from a video scene, defined simply as a list of "activity and actor-type" tuples (e.g., (*chase*, *police*)). Multiple actor types will result in multiple tuples for a video. The actors can be either a person, a policeman, a child, or a (non-human) object. If the detections describe the actor as both a person and a child, or a person and a policeman, we automatically remove the *person* label as it is a WordNet (Miller, 1995) hypernym of both *child* and *policeman*. For each human actor type, we further increase our coverage by retrieving the synonym set (synset) of its most frequent sense (i.e., sense #1) from WordNet. For example, a chase involving a policeman would generate the following tuples: (*chase*, *policeman*) and (*chase*, *officer*).

We call these *query tuples* because they are used to query text for sentences that – if all goes well – will contain relevant mental state labels.

Given query tuples, our models use an initial seed set of 160 mental state adjectives to produce a single distribution over mental state labels, referred to as the *response distribution*, for each video. The seed set is compiled from popular mental and emotional state dictionaries, including the Profile of Mood States (POMS) (McNair et al., 1971) and Plutchik's wheel of emotion. We

[2] All videos and annotations are available at: `http://trananh.github.io/vlsa`

[3] Linguistics Data Consortium catalog no. LDC2011T07

[4] Apache Lucene: `http://lucene.apache.org`

Source	Example Mental State Labels
POMS	alert, annoyed, energetic, exhausted, helpful, sad, terrified, unworthy, weary, etc.
Plutchik	angry, disgusted, fearful, joyful/joyous, sad, surprised, trusting, etc.
Others	agitated, competitive, cynical, disappointed, excited, giddy, happy, inebriated, violent, etc.

Table 1: The initial seed set contains 160 mental state labels, compiled from different sources like the popular Profile of Mood States dictionary and Plutchik's wheel of emotion.

also included frequently used labels gathered from synsets found in WordNet (see Table 1 for examples). Note that the gold standard annotations produced by MTurk workers (Sec. 3) was not a source for this set, nor was it restricted to these terms.

4.1 Back-off Interpolation in Vector Space

Our first model uses the recurrent neural network language model (RNNLM) of Mikolov et al. (2013) to project both mental state labels and query tuples into a latent conceptual space. Similarity is then trivially computed as the cosine similarity between these vectors. In all of our experiments, we used a RNNLM computed over the Gigaword corpus with 600-dimensional vectors.

For this vector space (*vec*) model, we separate the query tuples into different levels of back-off context. The first level includes the set of activity types as singleton context tuples, e.g., (*chase*), while the second level includes all (*activity*, *actor*) context tuples. Hence, each query tuple will yield two different context tuples, one for each back-off level. For each context tuple with multiple terms, such as (*chase*, *policeman*), we find the vector representation for the context by aggregating the vectors representing the search terms:

$$vec(\textit{chase}, \textit{policeman}) = vec(\textit{chase}) + vec(\textit{policeman}) \, .$$

The vector representation for a singleton context tuple is just the vector of the single search term. We then calculate the distance of each mental state label m to the normalized vector representation of the context tuple by computing the cosine similarity score between the two vectors:

$$cos(\Theta_m) = \frac{vec(m) \cdot vec(\textit{context tuple})}{||vec(m)||\;||vec(\textit{context tuple})||} \, .$$

The hypothesis here is that mental state labels that are related to the search context will have a RNNLM vector that is closer to the context tuple vector, resulting in a high cosine similarity score. Because the number of latent dimensions is relatively small (when compared to vocabulary size), cosine similarity scores in this latent space tend to be close. To further separate these scores, we raise them to an exponential power:

$$score(m) = e^{cos(\Theta_m)+1} - 1 \, .$$

The processing of each context tuple yields 160 different scores, one for each mental state label. We normalize these scores to form a single distribution of scores for each context tuple. The distributions are then integrated into a single distribution representative of the complete activity as follows: (a) the distributions at each context back-off level are averaged to generate a single distribution per level – for the second level (which includes activity and actor types), it means distributions for all (*activity*, *actor*) tuples are averaged, whereas the first level only has a single distribution from the singleton activity tuple (*chase*); and (b) distributions for the different levels are linearly interpolated, similar to the back-off strategy of (Collins, 1997). Let e_1 and e_2 represent the weights of some mental state label m from the average distribution at the first and second level, respectively. Then the interpolated distribution score e for m is:

$$e = \lambda e_1 + (1 - \lambda) e_2 \, .$$

Compiling the distribution scores for each m produces the final distribution representing the activity modeled. We prune this final distribution by taking the top ranked items that make up some γ proportion of the distribution. We delay the discussion of how γ is tuned to Section 6. The final pruned distribution is normalized to produce the response distribution.

4.2 Sentence Co-occurrence with Deleted Interpolation

Our second model, the *sent* model, extracts mental state labels based on the likelihood that they appear in sentences cued by query tuples. For each tuple, we estimate the conditional probability that we will see a mental state label m in a sentence, where m is from the seed set, given that we already observed the desired activity and actor type in the same sentence: $P(m|\textit{activity}, \textit{actor})$. In this case, we refer to the sentence length as the neighborhood window. Furthermore, all terms must appear as the correct part-of-speech (POS): m must appear as an adjective or verb, the activity as a verb, and the actor as a noun. (Mental state adjectives are allowed to appear as verbs because some are often mis-tagged as verbs; e.g., agitated, determined, welcoming.) We used Stanford's CoreNLP toolkit for tokenization and POS tagging.[5]

Note that this probability is similar to a trigram probability in POS tagging, except the triples need not form an ordered sequence but must appear in the same sentence and under the correct POS tag. Unfortunately, we cannot always compute this trigram probability directly from the corpus because there might be too few instances of each trigram to compute a probability reliably. As is common, we instead estimate it as a linear interpolation of unigrams, bigrams, and trigrams. We define the maximum likelihood probabilities $\hat{P}$, derived from relative frequencies f, for the unigrams, bigrams, and trigrams as follows:

$$\hat{P}(m) = \frac{f(m)}{N}$$

$$\hat{P}(m|\mathit{activity}) = \frac{f(m, \mathit{activity})}{f(\mathit{activity})}$$

$$\hat{P}(m|\mathit{activity}, \mathit{actor}) = \frac{f(m, \mathit{activity}, \mathit{actor})}{f(\mathit{activity}, \mathit{actor})}$$

for all mental state labels m, activities, and actor types in our queries. N is the total number of tokens in the corpus. The aforementioned POS requirement is enforced: $f(m)$ is the number of occurrences of m as an adjective or verb. We define $\hat{P} = 0$ if the corresponding numerator and denominator are zero. The desired trigram probability is then estimated as:

$$P(m|\mathit{activity}, \mathit{actor}) = \lambda_1 \hat{P}(m) + \lambda_2 \hat{P}(m|\mathit{activity}) + \lambda_3 \hat{P}(m|\mathit{activity}, \mathit{actor}) .$$

As $\lambda_1 + \lambda_2 + \lambda_3 = 1$, P represents a probability distribution. We use the deleted interpolation algorithm (Brants, 2000) to estimate one set of lambda values for the model, based on all trigrams.

For each query tuple generated in a video, 160 different trigrams are computed, one for each mental state label in the seed set, resulting in 160 conditional probability scores. We normalize these scores into a single distribution – the mental state distribution for that query tuple. We then combine all resulting distributions, one from each query tuple, and take the average to produce a single distribution over mental state labels for the video. As before, we prune this distribution by taking the top-ranked items that cover a large fraction γ of total probability. The pruned distribution is renormalized to yield the final response distribution.

[5] `http://nlp.stanford.edu/software/corenlp.shtml`.

4.3 Event-centric with Deleted Interpolation

The *sent* model has two limitations. On one hand, it is too sparse: the single sentence neighborhood window is too small to reliably estimate the frequencies of trigrams for the probabilities of mental state terms. On the other hand, it may be too lenient, as it extracts all mental state mentions appearing in the same sentence with the activity, or event, under consideration, regardless if they apply to this event or not. We address these limitations next with an event-centric model (*event*).

Intuitively, the *event* model focuses on the mental state labels of event participants. Formally, these mental state terms are extracted as follows:

1: We identify event participants (or actors). We do this by analyzing the syntactic dependencies of sentences containing the target verb (e.g., *chase*) to find the subject and object. In most cases, the nominal subject of the verb *chase* is the chaser and the direct object is the person being chased. We implemented additional patterns to model passive voice and other exceptions. We used Stanford's CoreNLP toolkit for syntactic dependency parsing and the downstream coreference resolution.

2: Once the phrases that point to actors are identified, we identify all mentions of these actors in the entire document by traversing the coreference chains containing the phrases extracted in the previous step. The sentences traversed in the chains define the neighborhood area for this model.

3: Lastly, we identify the mental state terms of event participants using a second set of syntactic patterns. First, we inspect several copulative verbs, such as to *be* and *feel*, and extract mental state labels from these structures if the corresponding subject is one of the mentions detected above. Second, we search for mental states along adjectival modifier relations, where the head is an actor mention. For all patterns, we make sure to filter for only mental state complements belonging to the initial seed list. The same POS restriction as in the other models also applies. We increment the joint frequency f for the n-gram once for each neighborhood that properly contain all search terms from the n-gram in the correct POS.

The *event* model addresses both limitations of the *sent* model: it avoids the lenient extraction of mental state labels by focusing on labels associated with event participants; it addresses sparsity by considering all mentions of event participants in a document.

To understand the impact of this model, we compare it against two additional baselines. The first baseline investigates the importance of focusing on mental state terms associated with event participants. This model, called *coref*, implements the first two steps of the above algorithm, but instead of extracting only mental state terms associated with event actors (last step), it considers all mentions appearing anywhere in the coreference neighborhood. That is, all unique sentences traversed by the relevant coreference chains are first pieced together to define a single neighborhood for a given document; then the relative joint frequencies of n-grams are computed by incrementing f once for each neighborhood that contains all terms with correct POS tags.

The second baseline analyzes the importance of coreference resolution to our problem. This model is similar to *sent*, with the modification that it increases the size of the neighborhood window to include the immediate neighbors of target sentences that contain activity labels. We call this the *win-n* model: The window around a target verb contains $2n + 1$ sentences. We build the context neighborhood by concatenating all target sentences and their windows together for a given document. This defines a single neighborhood for each document. This contrasts with the *sent* model, in which the neighborhood is defined for each sentence containing the activity label in the document, resulting in several possible neighborhoods in a document. The joint frequency f for each n-gram – where $n > 1$ – is computed similarly with the *coref* model: it is incremented once for each neighborhood that contains all the terms from the n-gram in the correct POS. Frequencies for unigrams are computed similar to *sent*.

As before, 160 different trigrams are generated for each query tuple, one for each mental state label in the seed set, resulting in 160 conditional probability scores. We similarly combine these scores and generate a single pruned distribution as the response for each of the model above.

G	(irate, 0.8), (afraid, 0.2)
R_1	(angry, 0.6), (mad, 0.4)
R_2	(irate, 0.2), (afraid, 0.8)
R_3	(mad, 0.4), (irate, 0.4), (scared, 0.2)

Table 2: We show an example gold standard distribution G and several candidate response distributions to be matched against G. Here, R_3 best matches the shape and meaning of G, because (*irate, mad*) and (*afraid, scared*) are close synonyms. R_2 appears to match G semantically, but matches its shape poorly. R_1 misses one of the mental state labels, *afraid*, but contains labels that are semantically close to the weightiest term in G.

4.4 Ensemble Model

We combined the results from the *event* and *vec* models to produce an ensemble model (*ens*) which, for a mental state label m, returns the average of m's scores according to the response distributions of the two individual models.

5 Evaluation Measures

Let R denote the response distribution over mental state labels produced for a single video by one of the models described in the previous section, and let G denote the gold standard distribution produced for the same video by MTurk workers. If R is similar to G then our models produce similar mental state terms as the workers. There are many ways to compare distributions (e.g., KL distance, chi-square statistics) but these give bad results when distributions are sparse. More importantly, for our purposes, the measures that compare the shapes of distributions do not allow semantic comparisons at the level of distribution elements. Suppose R assigns high scores to *angry* and *mad*, only, while G assigns a high score to *happy*, only. Clearly, R is wrong. But if instead G had assigned a high score to *irate*, only, then R would be more right than wrong because, at the level of the individual elements, *angry* and *mad* are similar to *irate* but not similar to *happy*.

We describe a series of measures, starting with the familiar F_1 score, and discuss their applicability. To illustrate the effectiveness of each measure, we will use the examples shown in Table 2.

5.1 F_1 Score

The F_1 *score* measures the similarity between two sets of elements, R and G. $F_1 = 1$ when $R = G$

and $F_1 = 0$ when R and G share no elements. F_1 is the harmonic mean of *precision* and *recall*:

$$precision = \frac{|R \cap G|}{|R|}, \quad recall = \frac{|R \cap G|}{|G|}, \tag{1}$$

$$F_1 = 2 \cdot \frac{precision \cdot recall}{precision + recall}. \tag{2}$$

The F_1 score penalizes the responses in Table 3 that include semantically similar labels to those in G, and fails to reflect the weights of the labels in G and R.

5.2 Similarity-Aligned F_1 Score

Although the standard F_1 does not immediately fit our needs, it is a good starting point. We can incorporate the semantic similarity of distribution elements by generalizing the formulas for precision and recall as follows:

$$\begin{aligned} precision &= \frac{1}{|R|} \sum_{r \in R} \max_{g \in G} \sigma(r, g), \\ recall &= \frac{1}{|G|} \sum_{g \in G} \max_{r \in R} \sigma(r, g), \end{aligned} \tag{3}$$

where $\sigma \in [0, 1]$ is a function that yields the similarity between two elements. The standard F_1 has:

$$\sigma(r, g) = \begin{cases} 1, & \text{if } r = g \\ 0, & \text{otherwise} \end{cases},$$

but clearly σ can be defined to take values proportional to the similarity of r and g. We can choose from a wide range of semantic similarity and relatedness measures that are based on WordNet (Pedersen et al., 2004). The recent RNNLM of Mikolov opens the door to even more similarity measures based on vector space representations of words (Mikolov et al., 2013). After experimentations, we settled on one proposed by Hirst and St-Onge (1998). It represents two lexicalized concepts as semantically close if their WordNet synsets are connected by a path that is not too long and that "does not change direction too often" (Hirst and St-Onge, 1998). We chose this metric because it has a finite range, accommodates numerous POS pairs, and works well in practice.

Given the generalized precision and recall formulas in Eq 3, our *similarity-aligned* (SA) F_1 score can be computed in the usual way, as the harmonic mean of precision and recall (Eq 2).

SA-F_1 is inspired by the Constrained Entity-Aligned F-Measure (CEAF) metric proposed by (Luo, 2005) for coreference resolution. CEAF computes an optimal one-to-one mapping between subsets of reference and system entities before it computes recall, precision and F. Similarly, SA-F_1 finds optimal mappings between the labels of the two sets based on σ (this is what the max terms in Eq 3 do). Table 3 shows that SA-F_1 correctly rewards the use of synonyms. The high scores given to R_2, however, indicate that it does not measure the similarity between distribution shapes.

	F_1			SA-F_1			CWSA-F_1		
	p	r	f_1	p	r	f_1	p	r	f_1
$\mathcal{R}_1$	0	0	0	1	.5	$\frac{2}{3}$	1	.8	.89
$\mathcal{R}_2$	1	1	1	1	1	1	.4	.4	.4
$\mathcal{R}_3$	$\frac{1}{3}$	.5	.4	1	1	1	1	1	1

Table 3: The precision (p), recall (r), and F_1 (f_1) scores under various evaluation models are presented for the examples from Table 2. Suppose that $\sigma(irate, angry) = \sigma(irate, mad) = \sigma(afraid, scared) = 1$, with σ of any two identical strings being 1, and σ of all other pairs are 0.

5.3 Constrained Weighted Similarity-Aligned F_1 Score

Let $R(r)$ and $G(r)$ be the probabilities of label r in the R and G distributions, respectively. Let $\sigma_S^*(\ell)$ denote the best similarity score achievable when comparing elements from set S to ℓ using the similarity function σ. That is, $\sigma_S^*(\ell) = \max_{e \in S} \sigma(\ell, e)$. We can easily weight $\sigma_S^*(\ell)$ by the probability of ℓ. For example, we might redefine precision as $\sum_{r \in R} R(r) \cdot \sigma_G^*(r)$. However, this would not account for the probability of r in the gold standard distribution, G.

An analogy might help here: Suppose we have an unknown "mystery bag" of 100 colored pencils that we will try to match with a "response bag" of pencils. If we fill our response bag with 100 crimson pencils, while the mystery bag contains only 25 crimson pencils, then our precision score should get points only for the first 25 pencils, while the remaining 75 in the response bag should not be rewarded. For recall, the reward given for each color in the mystery bag is capped by the number of pencils of that color in the response bag. The analogy is complete when we consider that crimson pencils should perhaps be partially rewarded when matched by cardinal, rose or cerise pencils. In other words, a similarity measure should account for an accumulated mass of synonyms. Let $M_S(\ell)$ denote the subset of terms from S that have the *best* similarity score to ℓ:

$$M_S(\ell) = \{e \mid \sigma(\ell, e) = \sigma^*_S(\ell), \forall e \in S\} .$$

We define new forms of precision and recall as:

$$p = \sum_{r \in R} \min\left(R(r), \sum_{e \in M_G(r)} G(e) \right) \sigma^*_G(r) ,$$

$$r = \sum_{g \in G} \min\left(G(g), \sum_{e \in M_R(g)} R(e) \right) \sigma^*_R(g) . \tag{4}$$

The resulting *constrained weighted similarity-aligned* (CWSA) F_1 score is the harmonic mean of these new precision and recall scores. Table 3 shows that CWSA-F_1 yields the most intuitive evaluation of the response distributions, down-weighting R_2 in favor of R_3 and R_1.

6 Experimental Procedure

As described in Section 3, MTurk workers annotated 26 videos by identifying the actor types and mental state labels for each video. The actor types become query tuples of the form (*activity*, *actor*) and the mental state labels are compiled into one probability distribution over labels for each video, designated G. The query tuples were provided to our neighborhood models (Sec. 4), which returned a response distribution over mental state labels for each video, designated R.

We selected four videos of the 26 to calibrate the prune parameters γ and the interpolation parameters λ (Sec. 4). One of these videos contains children, one has police involvement, and two contain adults. We asked additional MTurk workers to annotate these videos, yielding an independent set of annotations to be used solely for calibration.

The experimental question is, how well does G match R for each video?

7 Results & Discussions

We report the average performance of our models along with two additional baseline methods in Table 4. The naïve baseline method *unif* simply binds R to the initial seed set of 160 mental state labels with uniform probability, while the stronger *freq* baseline uses the occurrence frequency distribution of the labels from the Gigaword corpus (note that only occurrences tagged as adjectives or verbs were counted). All average improvements of the ensemble model over the baseline models are significant ($p < 0.01$). Significance tests were one-tailed and were based on nonparametric bootstrap resampling with $10,000$ iterations.

	F_1			CWSA-F_1		
	p	r	f_1	p	r	f_1
unif	.107	**.750**	.187	.284	.289	.286
freq	.107	**.750**	.187	.362	.352	.355
sent	.194	.293	.227	.366	.376	.368
vec	.226	.145	.175	.399	.392	.393
coref	**.264**	.251	.253	.382	.461	.416
event	.231	.303	.256	.446	.488	.463
ens	.259	.296	**.274**	**.488**	**.517**	**.500**

Table 4: The average evaluation performance across 26 different chase videos are shown against 2 different baselines for all proposed models. Bold font indicates the best score in a given column.

Using the classical F_1 measure, the *coref* model scored highest on precision, while the ensemble method did best on F_1. Not surprisingly, no model can top the baseline methods on recall as both baselines use the entire seed set of 160 terms. Even so, the average recall for the baselines were only $.750$, which means that the initial seed set did not include words that were used by the MTurk annotators. As we've mentioned, the classical F_1 is misleading because it does not credit synonyms. For example, in one movie, one of our models was rewarded once for matching the label *angry* and penalized six times for also reporting *irate*, *enraged*, *raging*, *upset*, *furious*, and *mad*. Frequently, our models were penalized for using the terms *scared* and *afraid* instead of *fearful*.

Under the CWSA-F_1 evaluation measure, which correctly accounts for both synonyms and label probabilities, our ensemble model performed best. The average CWSA-F_1 score of the ensemble model improves upon the simple uniform baseline *unif* by almost 75%, and over the stronger *freq* baseline by over 40%. The ensemble method also outperforms each individual method in all measured scores. These improvements were also found to be significant. This strongly suggests that the *vec* and *event* models are complementary, and not entirely redundant. Furthermore, Table 4 shows that the *event* model performs considerably better than *coref*. This result emphasizes the importance of focusing on the mental state labels of event participants rather than considering all mental state terms collocated in the same sentence with an actor or action verb.

Models	CWSA-F1	Versus *coref*	p-value
win-0	0.388682	−0.027512	0.0067
win-1	0.415328	−0.000866	0.4629
win-2	0.399777	−0.016417	0.0311
win-3	0.392832	−0.023362	0.0029

Table 5: The average CWSA-F_1 scores for the *win-n* model with different window parameters are shown in comparison to the *coref* model. The *coref* model outperformed all tested configurations, though the difference is not significant for $n = 1$. The p-value based on the average differences were obtained using one-tailed nonparametric bootstrap resampling with $10,000$ iterations.

Table 5 explores the effectiveness of coreference resolution in expanding the neighborhood area. The *coref* model outperformed the simple windowing method under every tested configuration. However, the improvement over windowing with $n = 1$ is not significant. This can be explained by fact that immediately neighboring sentences are more likely to be related. Moreover, since newswire articles tend to be short, the neighborhoods generated by *win-1* tend to be similar to those generated by *coref*. In general, *coref* does not do worse than a simple windowing method and has the bonus advantage of providing references to the actors of interest for downstream processes.

In Table 6, we show the performance results based on the types of chase scenarios happening in the videos. The average scores under the uniform baseline *unif* for chase videos involving children and sporting events are lower than for police and other chases. This suggests that our seed set of 160 mental state labels is biased towards the latter types of events, and is not as fit to describe chases involving children.

On average, videos involving police officers show the biggest improvement in the CWSA-F_1 scores over the *unif* baseline (+0.2693), whereas videos involving children received the lowest gain (+0.1517). We believe this is the effect of the Gigaword text corpus, which is a comprehensive archive of newswire text, and thus is heavily biased towards high-speed and violent chases involving the police. The Gigaword corpus is not the place to find children happily chasing each other. Similarly, sports-related chases, which are also news-worthy, have a higher gain than children's videos on average.

Categories	Unif	Ensemble	Gain
children	0.2082	0.3599	+0.1517
police	**0.3313**	**0.6006**	**+0.2693**
sports	0.2318	0.4126	+0.1808
others	0.3157	0.5457	+0.2300

Table 6: The average CWSA-F_1 scores for the ensemble model are shown in comparison to the uniform baseline method, categorize by video types.

8 Conclusion and Future Work

We introduced the novel task of identifying latent attributes in video scenes, specifically the mental states of actors in chase scenes. We showed that these attributes can be identified by using explicit features of videos to query text corpora, and from the resulting texts extract attributes that are latent in the videos. We presented several largely unsupervised methods for identifying distributions of actors' mental states in video scenes. We defined a similarity measure, CWSA-F_1, for comparing distributions of mental state labels that accounts for both semantic relatedness of the labels and their probabilities in the corresponding distributions. We showed that very little information from videos is needed to produce good results that significantly outperform baseline methods.

In the future, we plan to add more detection types. Additional contextual information from videos (e.g., scene locations) should help improve performance, especially on tougher videos (e.g., videos involving children chases). Moreover, we believe that the initial seed set of mental state labels can be learned simultaneously with the extraction patterns of the *event* model using a mutual bootstrapping method, similar to that of (Riloff and Jones, 1999).

Currently, our experiments assume one distribution of mental state labels for each video. They do not distinguish between the mental states of the chaser and chasee, while in reality these participants may be in very different states of mind. Our *event* model is capable of making this distinction and we will test its performance on this task in the future. We also plan to test the effectiveness of our models with actual computer vision detectors. As a first approximation, we will simulate the noisy nature of detectors by degrading the quality of annotated data. Using artificial noise on ground-truth data, we can simulate the performance of real detectors and test the robustness of our models.

References

Abdul Rehman Abbasi, Matthew N. Dailey, Nitin V. Afzulpurkar, and Takeaki Uno. 2009. Student mental state inference from unintentional body gestures using dynamic Bayesian networks. *Journal on Multimodal User Interfaces*, 3(1-2):21–31, December.

Tadas Baltrusaitis, Daniel McDuff, Ntombikayise Banda, Marwa Mahmoud, Rana el Kaliouby, Peter Robinson, and Rosalind Picard. 2011. Real-time inference of mental states from facial expressions and upper body gestures. In *Face and Gesture 2011*, pages 909–914. IEEE, March.

Thorsten Brants. 2000. TnT: A statistical part-of-speech tagger. In *Proceedings of the sixth conference on Applied natural language processing*, pages 224–231, Morristown, NJ, USA. Association for Computational Linguistics.

Ernesto Brau, Jinyan Guan, Kyle Simek, Luca Del Pero, Colin Reimer Dawson, and Kobus Barnard. 2013. Bayesian 3D Tracking from monocular video. In *The IEEE International Conference on Computer Vision (ICCV)*, December.

Michael Collins. 1997. Three generative, lexicalised models for statistical parsing. In *Proceedings of the 35th annual meeting on Association for Computational Linguistics -*, pages 16–23, Morristown, NJ, USA. Association for Computational Linguistics.

R. El Kaliouby and P. Robinson. 2004. Real-Time Inference of Complex Mental States from Facial Expressions and Head Gestures. In *2004 Conference on Computer Vision and Pattern Recognition Workshop*, pages 154–154. IEEE.

Pedro Felzenszwalb, David McAllester, and Deva Ramanan. 2008. A discriminatively trained, multiscale, deformable part model. In *2008 IEEE Conference on Computer Vision and Pattern Recognition*, pages 1–8. IEEE, June.

Ryan Gabbard, Marjorie Freedman, and RM Weischedel. 2011. Coreference for learning to extract relations: yes, Virginia, coreference matters. In *Proceedings of the 49th Annual Meeting of the Association for Computational Linguistics: Human Language Technologies: short papers - Volume 2*, pages 288–293.

Maria Gendron, Debi Roberson, Jacoba Marieta van der Vyver, and Lisa Feldman Barrett. 2014. Cultural relativity in perceiving emotion from vocalizations. *Psychological science*, 25(4):911–20, April.

J Giebel, DM Gavrila, and C Schnörr. 2004. A bayesian framework for multi-cue 3d object tracking. In *Computer Vision-ECCV 2004*, pages 241–252.

Graeme Hirst and D St-Onge. 1998. Lexical chains as representations of context for the detection and correction of malapropisms. In Christiane Fellbaum, editor, *WordNet: An Electronic Lexical Database (Language, Speech, and Communication)*, pages 305–332. The MIT Press.

LJ Li, Hao Su, L Fei-Fei, and EP Xing. 2010. Object bank: A high-level image representation for scene classification & semantic feature sparsification. In *Advances in Neural Information Processing Systems*.

Zhilei Liu and Shangfei Wang. 2011. Emotion recognition using hidden Markov models from facial temperature sequence. In *ACII'11 Proceedings of the 4th international conference on Affective computing and intelligent interaction - Volume Part II*, pages 240–247.

Xiaoqiang Luo. 2005. On coreference resolution performance metrics. In *Proceedings of the conference on Human Language Technology and Empirical Methods in Natural Language Processing - HLT '05*, pages 25–32, Morristown, NJ, USA. Association for Computational Linguistics.

MC De Marneffe, CD Manning, and Christopher Potts. 2010. "Was it good? It was provocative." Learning the meaning of scalar adjectives. In *Proceedings of the 48th Annual Meeting of the Association for Computational Linguistics*, pages 167–176.

Stephen J. McKenna, Sumer Jabri, Zoran Duric, Azriel Rosenfeld, and Harry Wechsler. 2000. Tracking Groups of People. *Computer Vision and Image Understanding*, 80(1):42–56, October.

D M McNair, M Lorr, and L F Droppleman. 1971. Profile of Mood States (POMS).

Tomas Mikolov, Kai Chen, Greg Corrado, and Jeffrey Dean. 2013. Efficient estimation of word representations in vector space. *arXiv preprint arXiv:1301.3781*, pages 1–12.

George A. Miller. 1995. WordNet: a lexical database for English. *Communications of the ACM*, 38(11):39–41, November.

Mitra Mohtarami, Hadi Amiri, Man Lan, and Chew Lim Tan. 2011. Predicting the uncertainty of sentiment adjectives in indirect answers. In *Proceedings of the 20th ACM international conference on Information and knowledge management - CIKM '11*, page 2485, New York, New York, USA. ACM Press.

CB Ng, YH Tay, and BM Goi. 2012. Recognizing human gender in computer vision: a survey. *PRICAI 2012: Trends in Artificial Intelligence*, 7458:335–346.

S O'Hara and B. A. Draper. 2012. Scalable action recognition with a subspace forest. In *2012 IEEE Conference on Computer Vision and Pattern Recognition*, pages 1210–1217. IEEE, June.

Ted Pedersen, S Patwardhan, and J Michelizzi. 2004. WordNet::Similarity: measuring the relatedness of concepts. In *Proceedings of the Nineteenth National Conference on Artificial Intelligence (AAAI-04)*, pages 1024–1025, San Jose, CA.

Ronald Poppe. 2010. A survey on vision-based human action recognition. *Image and Vision Computing*, 28(6):976–990, June.

Deva Ramanan, David a Forsyth, and Andrew Zisserman. 2007. Tracking people by learning their appearance. *IEEE transactions on pattern analysis and machine intelligence*, 29(1):65–81, January.

E Riloff and R Jones. 1999. Learning dictionaries for information extraction by multi-level bootstrapping. In *Proceedings of the sixteenth national conference on Artificial intelligence (AAAI-1999)*, pages 474–479.

S. Sadanand and J. J. Corso. 2012. Action bank: A high-level representation of activity in video. In *2012 IEEE Conference on Computer Vision and Pattern Recognition*, pages 1234–1241. IEEE, June.

C Schuldt, I Laptev, and B Caputo. 2004. Recognizing human actions: a local SVM approach. In *Proceedings of the 17th International Conference on Pattern Recognition, 2004. ICPR 2004.*, pages 32–36 Vol.3. IEEE.

M. Sokolova and G. Lapalme. 2011. Learning opinions in user-generated web content. *Natural Language Engineering*, 17(04):541–567, March.

Daniel Weinland, Remi Ronfard, and Edmond Boyer. 2011. A survey of vision-based methods for action representation, segmentation and recognition. *Computer Vision and Image Understanding*, 115(2):224–241, February.

Yi Yang and Deva Ramanan. 2011. Articulated pose estimation with flexible mixtures-of-parts. In *CVPR 2011*, pages 1385–1392. IEEE, June.

Using Text Segmentation Algorithms for the Automatic Generation of E-Learning Courses

Can Beck, Alexander Streicher and Andrea Zielinski
Fraunhofer IOSB
Karlsruhe, Germany
{can.beck, alexander.streicher,
andrea.zielinski}@iosb.fraunhofer.de

Abstract

With the advent of e-learning, there is a strong demand for tools that help to create e-learning courses in an automatic or semi-automatic way. While resources for new courses are often freely available, they are generally not properly structured into easy to handle units. In this paper, we investigate how state of the art text segmentation algorithms can be applied to automatically transform unstructured text into coherent pieces appropriate for e-learning courses. The feasibility to course generation is validated on a test corpus specifically tailored to this scenario. We also introduce a more generic training and testing method for text segmentation algorithms based on a Latent Dirichlet Allocation (LDA) topic model. In addition we introduce a scalable random text segmentation algorithm, in order to establish lower and upper bounds to be able to evaluate segmentation results on a common basis.

1 Introduction

The creation of e-learning courses is generally a time consuming effort. However, separating text into topically cohesive segments can help to reduce this effort whenever textual content is already available but not properly structured according to e-learning standards. Since these segments textually describe the content of learning units, automatic pedagogical annotation algorithms could be applied to categorize them into introductions, descriptions, explanations, examples and other pedagogical meaningful concepts (K.Sathiyamurthy & T.V.Geetha, 2011).

Course designers generally assume that learning content is composed of small inseparable learning objects at the micro level which in turn are wrapped into Concept Containers (CCs) at the macro level. This approach is followed, e.g., in the Web-Didactic approach by Swertz et al. (2013) where CCs correspond to chapters in a book and Knowledge Objects (KOs) correspond to course pages. To automate the partition of an unstructured text source into appropriate segments for the macro and micro level we applied different text segmentation algorithms (segmenters) on each level.

To evaluate the segmenters in the described scenario, we created a test corpus based on featured Wikipedia articles. For the macro level we exploit sections from different articles and the corresponding micro structure consists of subsequent paragraphs from these sections. On the macro level the segmenter TopicTiling (TT) by Riedl and Biemann (2012) is used. It is based on a LDA topic model which we train based on the articles from Wikipedia to extract a predefined number of different topics. On the micro level, the segmenter BayesSeg (BS) is applied (Eisenstein & Barzilay, 2008).

We achieved overall good results measured in three different metrics over a baseline approach, i.e., a scalable random segmenter, that indicate

*Proceedings of the Third Joint Conference on Lexical and Computational Semantics (*SEM 2014)*, pages 132–140,
Dublin, Ireland, August 23-24 2014.

text segmentation algorithms are ready to be applied to facilitate the creation of e-learning courses.

This paper is organized as follows: Section 2 gives an overview of related work on automatic course generation as well as text segmentation applications. In the main sections 3 and 4 we describe our approach and evaluation results on our corpus. In the last section we summarize the presented findings and give an outlook on further research needed for the automatic generation of e-learning courses.

2 Related Work

Automatic course generation can roughly be divided into two different areas. One is concerned with generation from existing courses and is mainly focused on adaption to the learner or instructional plans see Lin et al. (2009), Capuno et al. (2009) and Tan et al. (2010). The other area is the course creation itself on which we focus on in this paper.

Since the publication of the segmenter TextTiling by Hearst (1997) at least a dozen different segmenters have been developed. They can be divided into linear and hierarchical segmenters. Linear segmenters process the text sequentially sentence by sentence. Hierarchical segmenters first process the whole text and extract topics with varying granularities. These topics are then agglomerated based on a predefined criterion.

Linear segmenters have been developed by Kan et al. (1998) and Galley et al. (2003). One of the first probabilistic algorithms has been introduced by Utiyama and Isahara (2001). LDA based approaches were first described by Sun et al. (2008) and improved by Misra et al. (2009). The newest LDA based segmenter is TT. It performs linear text segmentation based on a pretrained LDA topic model and calculates the similarity between segments (adjacent sentences) to measure text coherence on the basis of a topic vector representation using cosine similarity. For reasons of efficiency, only the most frequent topic ID is assigned to each word in the sentence, using Gibbs sampling.

Hierarchical text segmentation algorithms were first introduced by Yaari (1997). The latest approach by Eisenstein (2008) uses a generative Bayesian model BS for text segmentation, assuming that a) topic shifts are likely to occur at points marked by cue phrases and b) a linear discourse structure. Each sentence in the document is modeled by a language model associated with a segment. The algorithm then calculates the maximum likelihood estimates of observing the whole sequence of sentences at selected topic boundaries.

The applications of text segmentation algorithms range from information retrieval (Huang, et al., 2002) to topic tracking and segmentation of multi-party conversations (Galley, et al., 2003).

Similar to our work Sathiyamurthy and Geetha (2011) showed how LDA based text segmentation algorithms combined with hierarchical domain ontology and pedagogical ontology can be applied to content generation for e-learning courses. They focussed on the segmentation of existing e-learning material in the domain of computer science and introduced new metrics to measure the segmentation results with respect to concepts from the ontologies. Our work focusses on the appropriate segmentation of unstructured text instead of existing e-learning material. Although the usage of domain models is an interesting approach the availability of such models is very domain dependent. We rely on the LDA model parameters and training to accomplish a word to topic assignment.

Rather than introducing new aspects such as pedagogical concepts we investigated the general usability of segmentation algorithms with focus on the macro and micro structure which is characteristic for most e-learning content.

3 Automatic Generation of E-Learning Courses

The main objective is to provide e-learning course designers with a tool to efficiently organize existing textual content for new e-learning courses. This can be done by the application of text segmenters that automatically generate the basic structure of the course. The intended web-didactic conform two-level structure differentiates between macro and micro levels. The levels have different requirements with respect to thematic coherence: the CCs are thematically rather independent and the KOs within each CC need to be intrinsically coherent but still separable.

We chose the linear LDA-based segmenter TT to find the boundaries between CCs. The LDA-based topic model can be trained on content which is topically related to the target course. This approach gives the course creator flexibility in the generation of the macro level structure by either adjusting the training documents or by changing the number and size of topics that should be extracted for the topic model.

On the micro level we did not use TT. The training of an appropriate LDA model would have to be done for every CC separately since they are thematically relatively unrelated. Apart from that the boundaries between the KOs should be an optimal division for a given number of expected boundaries. The reason for this is that the length of KOs should be adapted to the intended skill and background of the learners. This is why we decided to use the hierarchical segmenter BS.

3.1 Application Setting and Corpus

To evaluate segmenters many different corpora have been created. The most commonly used corpus was introduced by Choi (2000). It is based on the Brown Corpus and contains 700 samples, each containing a fixed number of sentences from 10 different news texts, which are randomly chosen from the Brown Corpus. Two other widely tested corpora were introduced by Galley et al. (2003). Both contain 500 samples, one with concatenated texts from the Wall Street Journal (WSJ) and the other with concatenated texts from the Topic Detection and Tracking (TDT) corpus (Strassel, et al., 2000). A standard for the segmentation of speech is the corpus from the International Computer Science Institute (ICSI) by Janin et al. (2003). A medical text book has been used by Eisenstein and Barzilay (2008). The approaches to evaluate segmenters are always similar: they have to find the boundaries in artificially concatenated texts.

We developed our own dataset because we wanted to use text that potentially could be used as a basis for creating e-learning courses. We therefore need samples which, on the one hand, have relatively clear topic boundaries on the macro level and, on the other hand resemble the differences in number of topics and inter-topic cohesion on the micro level.

We based our corpus on 530 featured[1] articles from 6 different categories of the English Wikipedia. It can be assumed that Wikipedia articles are often the source for learning courses. We used featured articles because the content structure is very consistent and clear, i.e., sections and paragraphs are well defined.

The corpus is divided into a macro and micro dataset in the following manner: The macro dataset contains 1200 samples. Each sample is a concatenation of paragraphs from 6-8 different sections from featured articles. Each topic in a sample consists of 3-6 subsequent paragraphs from a randomly selected section. We propose that one paragraph describes one KO. One CC contains all KOs which are from the same section in the article. Thus, one sample from the macro dataset contains 6-8 CCs, each containing 3-6 KOs. The segmentation task is to find the topic boundaries between the CCs. The macro dataset is quite similar in structure to the Choi-Corpus.

The micro dataset is extracted from the macro dataset. It contains 8231 samples, where each sample contains all KOs from one CC of the macro dataset. The segmentation task is to find the topic boundaries between the KOs, i.e, subsequent paragraphs of one section, see Figure 1.

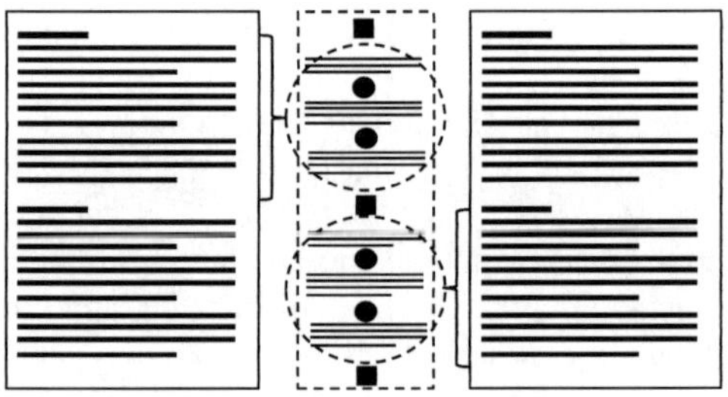

Figure 1: Schema for corpus samples: left and right Wikipedia articles with sections and paragraphs, in the middle three samples, dashed rectangle is a macro sample and dashed circles are micro samples. Filled squares indicate topic boundaries in the macro sample and filled circles in the micro samples.

All texts in our corpus are stemmed and stopwords are removed with the NLP-Toolkit for Python (Bird, et al., 2009) using an adapted variant[2] of the keyword extraction method by Kim et al. (2013).

The macro and micro dataset themselves are divided into multiple subsets to evaluate the stability of the segmenters when the number of sentences per topic or the number of topics per sample have changed. The detailed configuration is shown in Table 1 and 2. Each subset is identified by the number of CCs per sample and the number of KOs per CC (the subset is denoted as #CC_#KO). Subsets of the micro dataset are identified by a single value which is the number

[1] http://en.wikipedia.org/wiki/Wikipedia:Featured_articles

[2] https://gist.github.com/alexbowe/879414

of KOs per sample (#KO). In Table 1 the identifier *R* means that the number of CCs or KOs is not the same for all samples, it is chosen randomly from the set depicted by curly brackets.

ID	CCs per sample	KOs per CC	mean sentences per CC
7_3	7	3	20
7_4	7	4	27
7_5	7	5	33
7_6	7	6	40
7_R	7	{3,4,5,6}	30
R_R	{6,7,8}	{3,4,5,6}	30

Table 1: Macro dataset and its subsets each with 200 samples.

ID	KOs per sample	mean sentences per KO
3	3	9
4	4	8
5	5	7
6	6	7

Table 2: Micro dataset and its subsets.

The important difference between the macro and micro dataset is that every subset of the macro dataset contains a constant number of topics which differ in number of sentences per topic between 20 and 40, except the subset *R_R* which contains a random number of topics between 6 and 8. In contrast, each micro-level subset differs in number of topics but not significantly in the number of sentences per topic.

This difference between the datasets allows us to focus on the different level-specific aspects. On the macro dataset we can evaluate the stability of TT over topics with highly varying lengths and on the micro dataset we can evaluate BS when the number of strongly coherent topics changes.

3.2 Text Segmentation Metrics

The performance of a segmenter cannot simply be measured by false positive and false negative boundaries compared to the true boundaries because, if the predicted boundary is only one sentence away from the true boundary this could still be very close, e.g., if the next true topic boundary is 30 sentences away. Thus, the relative proximity to true boundaries should also be considered. There is an ongoing discussion about what kind of metric is appropriate to measure the performance of segmenters (Fournier & Inkpen, 2012). Most prominent and widely used are WindowDiff *wd* (Pevzner & Hearst, 2002) and the probabilistic metric *pk* (Beeferman, et al., 1999). The basic principle is to slide a window of fixed size over the segmented text, i.e., fixed number of words or sentences, and assess whether the sentences on the edges are correctly segmented with respect to each other. Both metrics *wd* and *pk* are penalty metrics, therefore lower values indicate better segmentations. The problem with these metrics is that they strongly depend on the arbitrarily defined window size parameter and do not penalize all error types equally, e.g., *pk* penalizes false negatives more than false positives and *wd* penalizes false positive and negative boundaries more at the beginning and end of the text (Lamprier, et al., 2007). Because of that we also used a rather new metric called BoundarySimilarity *b*. This metric is parameter independent and has been developed by Fournier and Inkpen (2013) to solve the mentioned deficiencies. Since *b* measures the similarity between the boundaries, higher values indicate better segmentations. We used the implementations of *wd*, *pk* and *b* by Fournier[3] (*wd* and *pk* with default parameters).

3.3 LDA Topic Model Training

Riedl and Biemann evaluated TT on the Choi-Corpus based on a 10-fold cross validation. Thus, the LDA topic model was generated with 90% of the samples and TT then tested on the remaining 10% of the samples. The 700 samples in the Choi-Corpus are only concatenations of 1111 different excerpts from the Brown Corpus and each sample contains 10 of these excepts it is clear that there are just not enough excerpts to make sure that the samples in the training set do not contain any excerpt that is also part of some samples in the testing set.

That is one reason why we do not use the same approach since we want to make sure that training and testing sets are truly disjoint to evaluate TT on the macro dataset. The other reason is that the topic structure generated by TT should be based on an LDA topic model with topics extracted from documents which are thematically related to certain parts of the course that is to be created without using its text source.

[3] https://github.com/cfournie/segmentation.evaluation

We train the LDA topic model to extract topics from the real Wikipedia articles. This model is then used to evaluate TT on the macro dataset and not the Wikipedia articles. This approach has consequences for the LDA topic model training and respective TT testing sets, since the LDA training set contains real articles and the TT test set contains the samples from the macro dataset. Because training and testing set should truly be disjoint we cannot train with any article that is part of a sample from the test set. Because each test sample from the macro dataset contains parts of 6 to 8 articles, the training set is reduced by a large factor, even with little test set size, which is shown for different number of folds (k) for cross validation in Table 3.

k	Test Set Size	Training Set Size
10	120±0 Samples (10% of the macro dataset)	139±7 featured Articles (26% of all articles)
20	60±0 Samples (5% of the macro dataset)	267±8 featured Articles (51% of all articles)
30	40±0 Samples (3% of the macro dataset)	338±7 featured Articles (64% of all articles)

Table 3: Mean size and standard deviation of truly disjunctive LDA training and respective TT testing set.

If we truly separate training and testing sets and train the LDA topic model with real articles a 10-fold cross validation leads to very small training sets (only 26% of all articles are used), which is why we also used higher folds to evaluate the results of TT on the macro dataset.

4 Evaluation Results

We evaluated TT on the macro dataset without providing the number of boundaries. On the micro dataset we evaluated BS with the expected number of boundaries provided. We also implemented a scalable random segmenter (RS) to compare TT and BS against some algorithm with interpretable performance. The interpretation of the values in any metric even with respect to different metrics is very difficult without comparison to another segmenter. For every true boundary in a document, RS predicts a boundary drawn from a normally distributed set around the true boundary with scalable standard deviation σ. Thus smaller values for σ result in better segmentations because the probability of selecting the true boundary increases, e.g., for $\sigma = 2$, more than 68% of all predicted boundaries are at most 2 sentences away from the true boundary and more than 99% of all predicted boundaries are located within a range of 6 sentences from it. But whether 6 sentences is a large or small distance should depend on the average topic size. We therefore relate the performance of RS to the mean number of sentence per topic by defining σ in percentages of that number as shown in the table below.

Distance from True Boundary:	Standard Deviation
very close	σ = 0% - 5%
close	σ = 5% -15%
large	σ = 15% - 30%

Table 4: Defined performance of RS for different standard deviations σ, given in percentage of mean sentences per topic.

To give an example, the subset *7_6* of the macro dataset has an average of 40 sentences per topic, therefore RS with σ=15% means that it is set to 6 which is 15% of 40. This is defined as a medium performance in Table 4 because 68% of the boundaries predicted are within a range of 6 sentences from the true boundaries and 99% within 18 sentences.

One important difference between the macro and micro dataset is that all subsets of the macro dataset have 7 topics, differing in length, except for subset *R_R* where this number is only slightly varied (Table 1). In contrast, all topics subsets of the micro dataset have roughly the same number of sentences but highly differ in the number of topics (Table 2). We therefore do not compare the performance of BS and TT since they are evaluated on quite different datasets designed for testing different types of segmentation tasks relevant to course generation, as explained earlier. We compare both to RS for different standard deviations σ.

4.1 Results for TopicTiling on the Macro Dataset

For the LDA topic model training we used the following default parameters: `alpha=0.5, beta=0.1,ntopics=100,niters=1000,` `twords=20,savestep=100,` for details we refer to (Griffiths & Steyvers, 2004). To compare TT's performance for different folds of the macro dataset we optimized the window parameter which has to be set for TT, it specifies the number of sentences to the left and to the right of the current position *p* between two sentences that are used to calculate the coherence score between these sentences (Riedl & Biemann, 2012). The performance for TT has been best with window sizes between 9 and 11 for all metrics as shown in Figure 2. As expected, higher folds increase TT's overall performance especially with respect to metric *b* (Figure 3). This is due to the larger training set sizes of the LDA topic model.

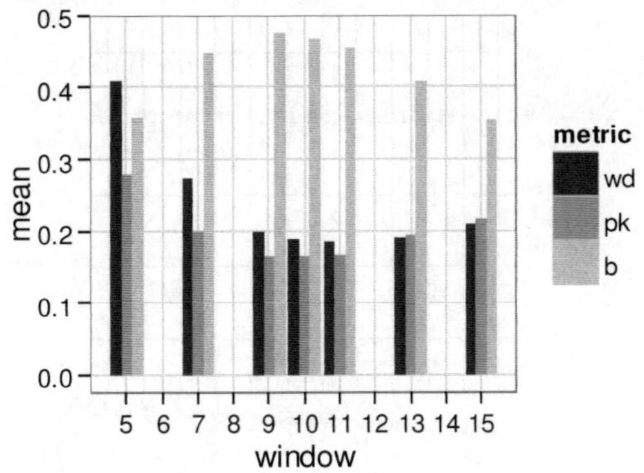

Figure 2: TT performance for different window sizes with 30-fold cross validation.

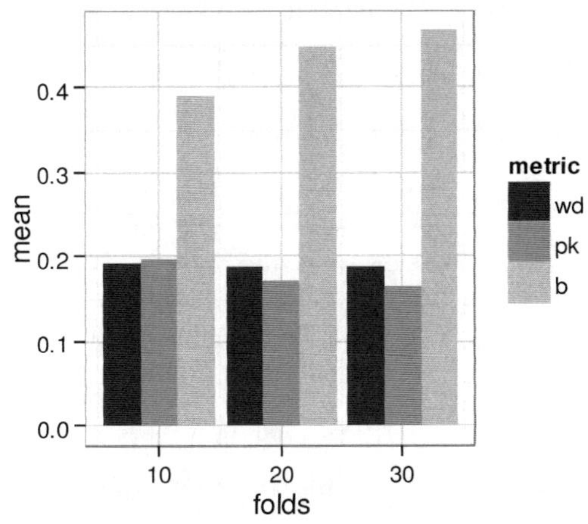

Figure 3: TT performance for different folds and window size set to 9.

In general smaller window sizes increase the number of predicted boundaries. The optimal window size is between 9 and 11 and we would expect the measures for 5 and 15 to be similar (Figure 2). This is only the case for metric *b*, the metrics *wd* and *pk* seem to penalize false positives more than false negatives. This would be a contradiction to the findings of Lamprier et al. (2007) since they actually found the opposite to be true. This behaviour is explained by the non-linear relation between the window parameter and number of predicted boundaries by TT as shown in Figure 4.

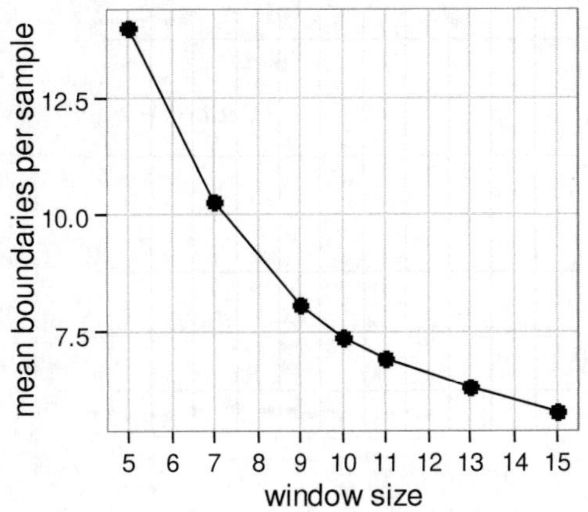

Figure 4: Mean number of predicted boundaries by TT for different window sizes and an LDA topic model trained with 30 folds.

Another important finding is the stability of TT's performance over different window sizes (from 9 to 11). This is important since a very sensitive behaviour would be very difficult to handle for course creators because they would have to estimate this parameter in advance.

For the following detailed evaluation TT window size is set to 9 because of the best overall results with respect to metric *b* and 30-fold cross validation. The detailed performance with respect to metric *wd*, *pk* and *b* of TT compared to RS with different standard deviations σ is shown in Figure 5 i), ii) and iii).

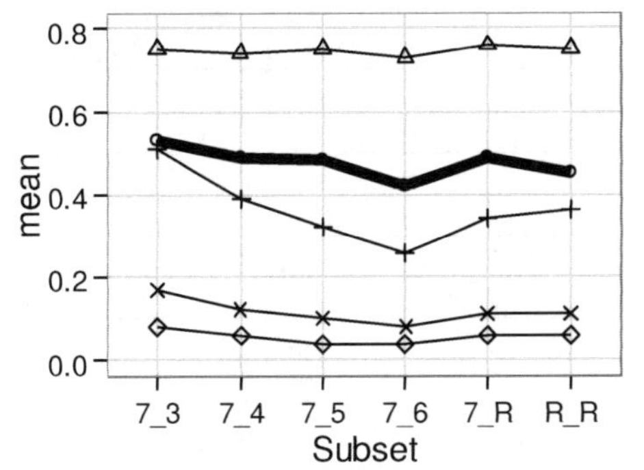

i. TT measured with metric *b*.

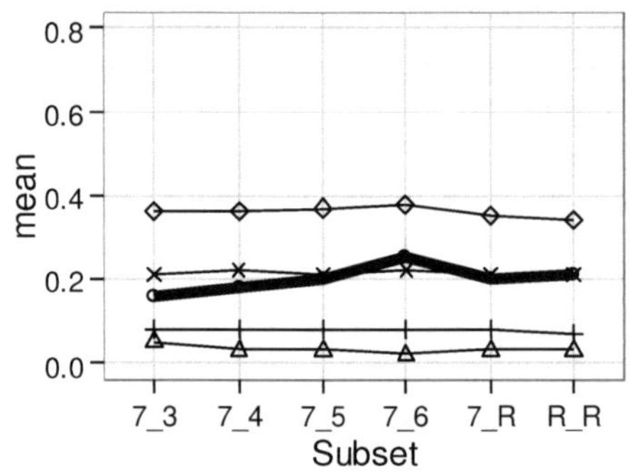

ii. TT measured with metric *wd*.

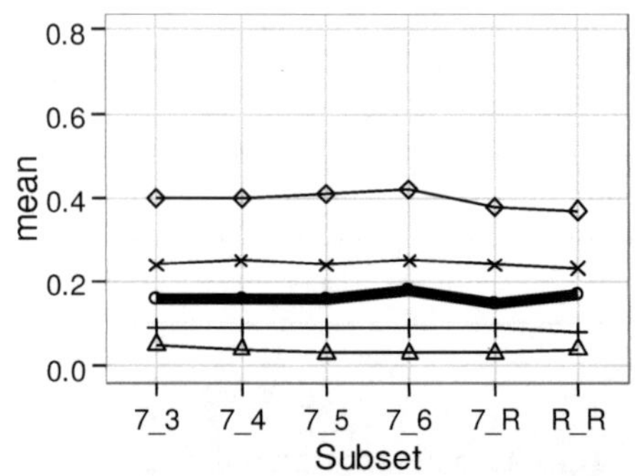

iii. TT measured with metric *pk*.

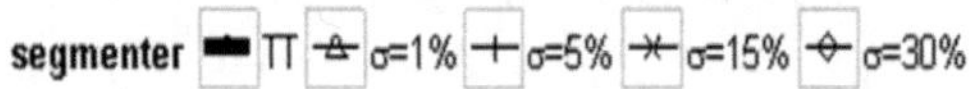

Figure 5: Performance of TT on the macro dataset.

First of all we want to point out that the graphs of RS for different values of σ are ordered as expected by all metrics. Lower percentages indicate better results. And with respect to metric *wd* and *pk* the performance for each σ is nearly constant over all subsets, which indicates that the metrics correctly consider the relative distance of a predicted boundary from the true boundary by using the mean number of sentences per topic. In metric *b* only the RS with σ=30%, 15% and 5% are constant. For σ=5% there is a strong decrease in performance for subsets with more sentences per topic.

The overall performance of TT is between that of RS for σ=1% and σ=15%, except for subset *7_6* with respect to metric *wd*. With respect to metric *b* TT even predicts *very close* boundaries. In all metrics TT has the worst results on subset *7_6*, which has the largest number of sentences per topic (see Table 1). This is due to TT's window parameter which influences the number of predicted boundaries as shown in Figure 4.

4.2 Results for BayesSeg on the Micro Dataset

BS does not need any training or parameter fitting, since it is provided with the number of expected segments. We therefore used the default parameter settings.

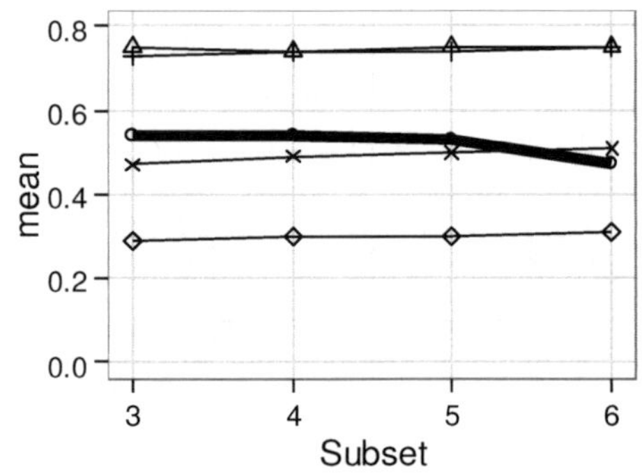

i. BS measured with metric *b*.

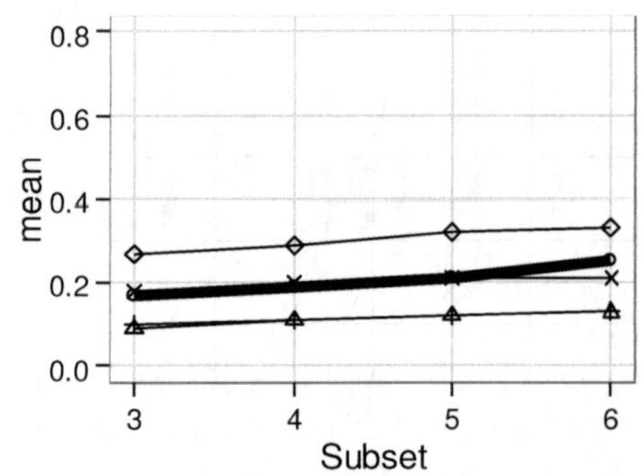

ii. BS measured with metric *wd*.

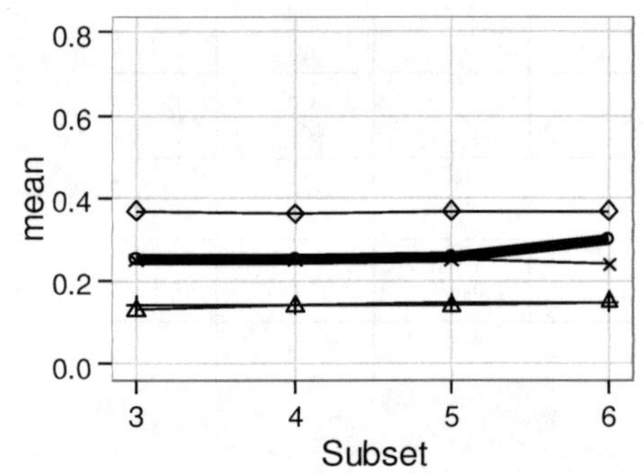

iii. BS measured with metric *pk*.

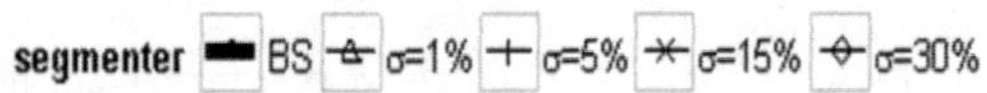

Figure 6: Performance of BS on the micro dataset.

As expected, the performance of RS is decreasing for higher values of σ in all metrics (Figure 6 i), ii), iii)). For metric *wd* and *pk* the increasing number of topics leads to slightly increasing penalties for constant values of σ, which clearly indicates that the metrics do not treat all errors equally, as repeatedly pointed out. Metric *b* treats errors equally over increasing number of topics for RS. BS predicts with respect to all metrics *close* boundaries since it is better than RS with σ=15% except on subset *6* (Table 4). With an increasing number of topics BS is getting worse in all metrics.

Comparing the measures of metric *b* for macro and micro dataset it seems that it handles increasing numbers of topics better than increasing size of topics. On the micro dataset the results with respect to all metrics are far more similar than the once on the macro dataset, where the differences are very large. Since we are only interested in comparative measures of the performance of the segmenters and RS, which has shown to be a very useful approach to interpret segmentation results, we leave detailed explanations of the metrics behaviours itself to further research.

5 Conclusion

We demonstrated that text segmentation algorithms can be applied to the generation of e-learning courses. We use a web-didactic approach that is based on a flat two-level hierarchical structure. A new corpus has been compiled based on featured articles from the English Wikipedia that reflects this kind of course structure. On the broader macro level we applied the linear LDA-based text segmentation algorithm TopicTiling without providing the expected number of boundaries. The LDA topic model is usually trained with concatenated texts from the very same dataset TopicTiling is tested on. We showed that it is very difficult to ensure that the two sets are always truly disjoint. The reason is that concatenated texts normally always have identical parts. This problem is solved by applying a different training and testing method.

The more fine grained micro level was segmented using BayesSeg, a hierarchical algorithm which we provided with the expected number of boundaries.

We used three different evaluation metrics and presented a scalable random segmentation algorithm to establish upper and lower bounds for baseline comparison. The results, especially on the macro level, demonstrate that text segmentation algorithms have evolved enough to be used for the automatic generation of e-learning courses.

An interesting aspect of future research would be the application and creation of real e-learning content. Based on the textual segments, summarization and question generation algorithms as well as automatic replacement with appropriate pictures and videos instead of text could be used to finally evaluate an automatically generated e-learning course with real learners.

Regarding text segmentation in general, future research especially needs to address the difficult task of transparently and equally measuring the performance of segmentation algorithms. Our results, i.e., the ones from the random segmentation algorithm, indicate that there are still unsolved issues regarding the penalization of false positives and false negatives when the number of topics or sentences per topic is changed.

Reference

Beeferman, D., Berger, A. & Lafferty, J., 1999. Statistical Models for Text Segmentation. *Mach. Learn.*, #feb#, 34(1-3), pp. 177-210.

Bird, S., Klein, E. & Loper, E., 2009. *Natural Language Processing with Python.* s.l.:O'Reilly Media.

Capuano, N. et al., 2009. LIA: an intelligent advisor for e-learning. *Interactive Learning Environments,* 17(3), pp. 221-239.

Choi, F. Y. Y., 2000. *Advances in Domain Independent Linear Text Segmentation.* Stroudsburg, PA, USA, Association for Computational Linguistics, pp. 26-33.

Eisenstein, J. & Barzilay, R., 2008. *Bayesian Unsupervised Topic Segmentation.* Honolulu, Hawaii, Association for Computational Linguistics, pp. 334-343.

Fournier, C., 2013. *Evaluating Text Segmentation using Boundary Edit Distance.* Stroudsburg, PA, USA, Association for Computational Linguistics, p. To appear.

Fournier, C. & Inkpen, D., 2012. *Segmentation Similarity and Agreement.* Montreal, Canada, Association for Computational Linguistics, pp. 152-161.

Galley, M., McKeown, K., Fosler-Lussier, E. & Jing, H., 2003. *Discourse Segmentation of Multi-party Conversation.* Stroudsburg, PA, USA, Association for Computational Linguistics, pp. 562-569.

Griffiths, T. L. & Steyvers, M., 2004. Finding scientific topics. *Proceedings of the National Academy of Sciences,* April, 101(Suppl. 1), pp. 5228-5235.

Hearst, M. A., 1997. TextTiling: Segmenting Text into Multi-paragraph Subtopic Passages. *Comput. Linguist.*, #mar#, 23(1), pp. 33-64.

Huang, X. et al., 2002. *Applying Machine Learning to Text Segmentation for Information Retrieval.* s.l.:s.n.

Janin, A. et al., 2003. *The ICSI Meeting Corpus.* s.l., s.n., pp. I-364--I-367 vol.1.

Kan, M.-Y., Klavans, J. L. & McKeown, K. R., 1998. *Linear Segmentation and Segment Significance.* s.l., s.n., pp. 197-205.

Kim, S., Medelyan, O., Kan, M.-Y. & Baldwin, T., 2013. Automatic keyphrase extraction from scientific articles. *Language Resources and Evaluation,* 47(3), pp. 723-742.

Lamprier, S., Amghar, T., Levrat, B. & Saubion, F., 2007. *On Evaluation Methodologies for Text Segmentation Algorithms.* s.l., s.n., pp. 19-26.

Lin, Y.-T., Cheng, S.-C., Yang, J.-T. & Huang, Y.-M., 2009. An Automatic Course Generation System for Organizing Existent Learning Objects Using Particle Swarm Optimization. In: M. Chang, et al. Hrsg. *Learning by Playing. Game-based Education System Design and Development.* s.l.:Springer Berlin Heidelberg, pp. 565-570.

Misra, H., Yvon, F., Jose, J. M. & Cappe, O., 2009. *Text Segmentation via Topic Modeling: An Analytical Study.* New York, NY, USA, ACM, pp. 1553-1556.

Pevzner, L. & Hearst, M. A., 2002. A Critique and Improvement of an Evaluation Metric for Text Segmentation. *Comput. Linguist.*, #mar#, 28(1), pp. 19-36.

Riedl, M. & Biemann, C., 2012. *TopicTiling: A Text Segmentation Algorithm Based on LDA.* Stroudsburg, PA, USA, Association for Computational Linguistics, pp. 37-42.

Strassel, S., Graff, D., Martey, N. & Cieri, C., 2000. *Quality Control in Large Annotation Projects Involving Multiple Judges: The Case of the TDT Corpora.* s.l., s.n.

Sun, Q., Li, R., Luo, D. & Wu, X., 2008. *Text Segmentation with LDA-based Fisher Kernel.* Stroudsburg, PA, USA, Association for Computational Linguistics, pp. 269-272.

Swertz, C. et al., 2013. *A Pedagogical Ontology as a Playground in Adaptive Elearning Environments..* s.l., GI, pp. 1955-1960.

Tan, X., Ullrich, C., Wang, Y. & Shen, R., 2010. *The Design and Application of an Automatic Course Generation System for Large-Scale Education.* s.l., s.n., pp. 607-609.

Utiyama, M. & Isahara, H., 2001. *A Statistical Model for Domain-independent Text Segmentation.* Stroudsburg, PA, USA, Association for Computational Linguistics, pp. 499-506.

Yaari, Y., 1997. *Segmentation of Expository Texts by Hierarchical Agglomerative Clustering.* s.l.:s.n.

Cognitive Compositional Semantics using Continuation Dependencies

William Schuler
Department of Linguistics
The Ohio State University
schuler@ling.osu.edu

Adam Wheeler
Department of Linguistics
The Ohio State University
wheeler@ling.osu.edu

Abstract

This paper describes a graphical semantic representation based on bottom-up 'continuation' dependencies which has the important property that its vertices define a usable set of discourse referents in working memory even in contexts involving conjunction in the scope of quantifiers. An evaluation on an existing quantifier scope disambiguation task shows that non-local continuation dependencies can be as reliably learned from annotated data as representations used in a state-of-the-art quantifier scope resolver, suggesting that continuation dependencies may provide a natural representation for scope information.

1 Introduction

It is now fairly well established that at least shallow semantic interpretation informs parsing decisions in human sentence processing (Tanenhaus et al., 1995; Brown-Schmidt et al., 2002), and recent evidence points to incremental processing of quantifier implicatures as well (Degen and Tanenhaus, 2011). This may indicate that inferences about the meaning of quantifiers are processed directly in working memory. Human working memory is widely assumed to store events (including linguistic events) as re-usable activation-based states, connected by a durable but rapidly mutable weight-based memory of cued associations (Marr, 1971; Anderson et al., 1977; Murdock, 1982; McClelland et al., 1995; Howard and Kahana, 2002). Complex dependency structures can therefore be stored in this associative memory as graphs, with states as vertices and cued associations as directed edges (e.g. Kintsch, 1988). This kind of representation is necessary to formulate and evaluate algorithmic claims (Marr, 1982) about cued associations and working memory use in human sentence processing (e.g. van Schijndel and Schuler, 2013). But accounting for syntax and semantics in this way must be done carefully in order to preserve linguistically important distinctions. For example, positing spurious local dependencies in filler-gap constructions can lead to missed integrations of dependency structure in incremental processing, resulting in weaker model fitting (van Schijndel et al., 2013). Similar care may be necessary in cases of dependencies arising from anaphoric coreference or quantifier scope.

Unfortunately, most existing theories of compositional semantics (Montague, 1973; Barwise and Cooper, 1981; Bos, 1996; Baldridge and Kruijff, 2002; Koller, 2004; Copestake et al., 2005) are defined at the *computational* level (Marr, 1982), employing beta reduction over complete or underspecified lambda calculus expressions as a precise description of the language processing task to be modeled, not at the *algorithmic* level, as a model of human language processing itself. The structured expressions these theories generate are not intended to represent re-usable referential states of the sort that could be modeled in current theories of associative memory. As such, it should not be surprising that structural adaptations of lambda calculus expressions as referential states exhibit a number of apparent deficiencies:

First, representations based on lambda calculus expressions lack topologically distinguishable referents for sets defined in the context of outscoping quantifiers. For example, a structural adaptation of a lambda calculus expression for the sentence *Every line contains two numbers,* shown in Figure 1a (adapted from Koller, 2004), contains referents for the set of all document lines ($\mathbf{s_L}$) and for the set of all numbers ($\mathbf{s_N}$) which can be identified by cued associations to predicate constants like N , but it is not clear how a referent for the set of numbers in document lines can be distinguished from a referent for the set of numbers

*Proceedings of the Third Joint Conference on Lexical and Computational Semantics (*SEM 2014)*, pages 141–150,
Dublin, Ireland, August 23-24 2014.

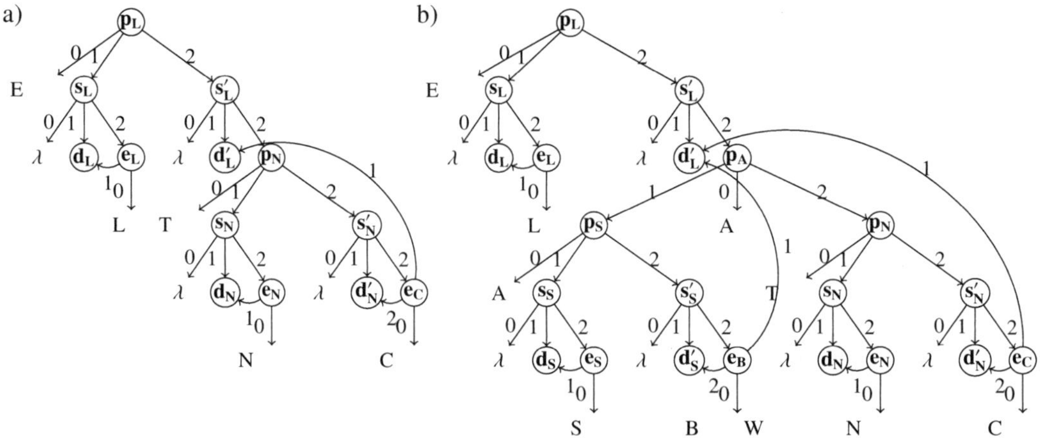

$$\text{c) } (\text{E}\quad \mathbf{p_L}\, \mathbf{s_L}\, \mathbf{s'_L}) \wedge (\text{S}\quad \mathbf{s_L}\, \mathbf{d_L}\, \mathbf{e_L}) \wedge (\text{L}\quad \mathbf{e_L}\, \mathbf{d_L}) \wedge (\text{S}\quad \mathbf{s'_L}\, \mathbf{d'_L}\, \mathbf{p_N}) \wedge$$

$$(\text{T}\quad \mathbf{p_N}\, \mathbf{s_N}\, \mathbf{s'_N}) \wedge (\text{S}\quad \mathbf{s_N}\, \mathbf{d_N}\, \mathbf{e_N}) \wedge (\text{N}\quad \mathbf{e_N}\, \mathbf{d_N}) \wedge (\text{S}\quad \mathbf{s'_N}\, \mathbf{d'_N}\, \mathbf{e_C}) \wedge (\text{C}\quad \mathbf{e_C}\, \mathbf{d'_L}\, \mathbf{d'_N})$$

Figure 1: Semantic dependency graph in a 'direct' (top-down) style, adapted from a disambiguated representation of Koller (2004), excluding quantifiers over eventualities. The semantic dependency structure for the sentence *Every line contains two numbers* (a), with flat logical form (c), is not a subgraph of the semantic dependency structure for *Every line begins with a space and contains two numbers* (b), because the structure is interrupted by the explicit conjunction predicate 'A '.

in *each* document line ($\mathbf{s'_N}$) using local topological features of the dependency graph, as would be required to accurately recall assertions about total or average quantities of numbers in document lines.[1]

Second, graphs based on traditional lambda calculus representations do not model conjuncts as subgraphs of conjunctions. For example, the graphical representation of the sentence *Every line begins with a space and contains two numbers* shown in Figure 1b does not contain the graphical representation of the sentence *Every line contains two numbers* shown in Figure 1a as a connected subgraph. Although one might expect a query about a conjunct to be directly answerable from a knowledge base containing the conjoined representation, the pattern of dependencies that make up the conjunct in a graphical representation of a lambda calculus expression does not match those in the larger conjunction.

Finally, representations based on lambda calculus expressions contain vertices that do not seem to correspond to viable discourse referents. For example, following the sentence *Every line contains two numbers,* using the lambda expression shown in Figure 1b, $\mathbf{d_L}$ may serve as a referent of *it* in *but it has only one underscore,* $\mathbf{s_N}$ may serve as a referent of *they* in *but they are not negative,* $\mathbf{e_C}$ may serve as a referent of *that* in *but that was before it was edited,* and $\mathbf{p_L}$ may serve as a referent of *that* in *but the compiler doesn't enforce that,* but it is not clear what if anything would naturally refer to the internal conjunction $\mathbf{p_A}$. Predications over such conjunctions (e.g. *Kim believes that every line begins with a space and contains*

[1]This graph matching can be implemented in a vectorial model of associative memory by comparing the (e.g. cosine) similarity of superposed vectors resulting from cueing incoming and outgoing dependencies with all possible labels in increasingly longer paths from one or more constant vector states (e.g. vectors for predicate constants). This graph matching does not necessarily preclude the introduction of monotonicity constraints from matched quantifiers. For example, *More than two perl scripts work,* can entail *More than two scripts work,* using a subgraph in the first argument, but *Fewer than two scripts work,* can entail *Fewer than two perl scripts work,* using a supergraph in the first argument. This consideration is similar to those observed in representations based on natural logic (MacCartney and Manning, 2009) which also uses low-level matching to perform some kinds of inference, but representations based on natural logic typically exclude other forms of inference, whereas the present model does not.

This matching also assumes properties of nuclear scope variables are inherited from associated restrictor variables, e.g. through a set of dependencies from nuclear scope sets to restrictor sets not shown in the figure. This assumption will be revisited in Section 3.

two numbers) are usually predicated at the outer proposition $\mathbf{p}_{\mathrm{L}}$, and in any case do not have truth values that are independent of the same predication at each conjunct. One of the goals of Minimal Recursion Semantics (Copestake et al., 2005) was to eliminate similar kinds of superfluous conjunction structure.

Fortunately, lambda calculus expressions like those shown in Figure 1 are not the only way to represent compositional semantics of sentences. This paper defines a graphical semantic dependency representation that can be translated into lambda calculus, but has the important property that its vertices define a usable set of discourse referents in working memory even in contexts involving conjunction in the scope of quantifiers. It does this by reversing the direction of dependencies from parent-to-child subsumption in a lambda-calculus tree to a representation similar to the inside-out structure of function definitions in a continuation-passing style (Barker, 2002; Shan and Barker, 2006)[2] so that sets are defined in terms of their context, and explicit 'A ' predicates are no longer required, leaving nothing to get in the way of an exact pattern match.[3] The learnability of the non-local continuation dependencies involved in this representation is then evaluated on an existing quantifier scope disambiguation task using a dependency-based statistical scope resolver, with results comparable to a state-of-the-art unrestricted graph-based quantifier scope resolver (Manshadi et al., 2013).

2 Continuation Dependencies

This paper explores the use of a bottom-up dependency representation, inspired by the inside-out structure of function definitions in a continuation-passing style (Barker, 2002; Shan and Barker, 2006), which creates discourse referents for sets that are associated with particular scoping contexts. This dependency representation preserves the propositions, sets, eventualities, and ordinary discourse referents of a 'direct' representation (the **p**, **s**, **e**, and **d** nodes in Figure 1), but replaces the downward dependencies departing set referents with upward dependencies to context sets (highlighted in Figure 2).

Figures 1c and 2c also show flat logical forms composed of *elementary predications*, adapted from Kruijff (2001) and Copestake et al. (2005), for the sentence *Every line contains two numbers,* which are formed by identifying the function associated with the predicate constant (e.g. C) that is connected to each proposition or eventuality referent (e.g. $\mathbf{e}_{\mathrm{C}}$) by a dependency labeled '0', then applying that function to this referent, followed by the list of arguments connected to this referent by functions numbered '1' and up: e.g. (C $\mathbf{e}_{\mathrm{C}}\ \mathbf{d}'_{\mathrm{L}}\ \mathbf{d}'_{\mathrm{N}}$). These dependencies can also be defined by numbered dependency functions $\mathbf{f}_n$ from source instance j to destination instance i, notated $(\mathbf{f}_n\ j) = i$. This notation will be used in Section 4 to define constraints in the form of equations. For example, the subject (first argument) of a lexical item may be constrained to be the subject (first argument) of that item's sentential complement (second argument), as in an instance of subject control, using the dependency equation $(\mathbf{f}_1\ i) = (\mathbf{f}_1\ (\mathbf{f}_2\ i))$.

Since continuation dependencies all flow up the tree, any number of conjuncts can impinge upon a common outscoping continuation, so there is no longer any need for explicit conjunction nodes. The representation is also attractive in that it locally distinguishes queries about, say, the cardinality of the set of numbers in each document line (S $\mathbf{s}'_{\mathrm{N}}\ \mathbf{d}'_{\mathrm{N}}\ \mathbf{s}'_{\mathrm{L}}$) from queries about the cardinality of the set of numbers in general (S $\mathbf{s}'_{\mathrm{N}}\ \mathbf{d}'_{\mathrm{N}}\ \mathbf{s}'_{\bot}$) which is crucial for successful inference by pattern matching. Finally, connected sets of continuation dependencies form natural 'scope graphs' for use in graph-based disambiguation algorithms (Manshadi and Allen, 2011; Manshadi et al., 2013), which will be used to evaluate this representation in Section 6.

3 Mapping to Lambda Calculus

It is important for this representation not only to have attractive graphical subsumption properties, but also to be sufficiently expressive to define corresponding expressions in lambda calculus. When continuation dependencies are filled in, the resulting dependency structure can be trans-

[2]This representation also has much in common with generalized Skolem terms of Steedman (2012), which also represent dependencies to outscoped terms, but here continuation dependencies are applied to all quantifiers, including universals.

[3]This also holds for explicit disjunction predicates, which can be cast as conjunction through application of de Morgan's law and manipulation of the polarity of adjacent quantifiers. For example, *Every line begins with at least one space or contains at least two numbers,* is equivalent to *No line begins with fewer than one space and contains fewer than two numbers.*

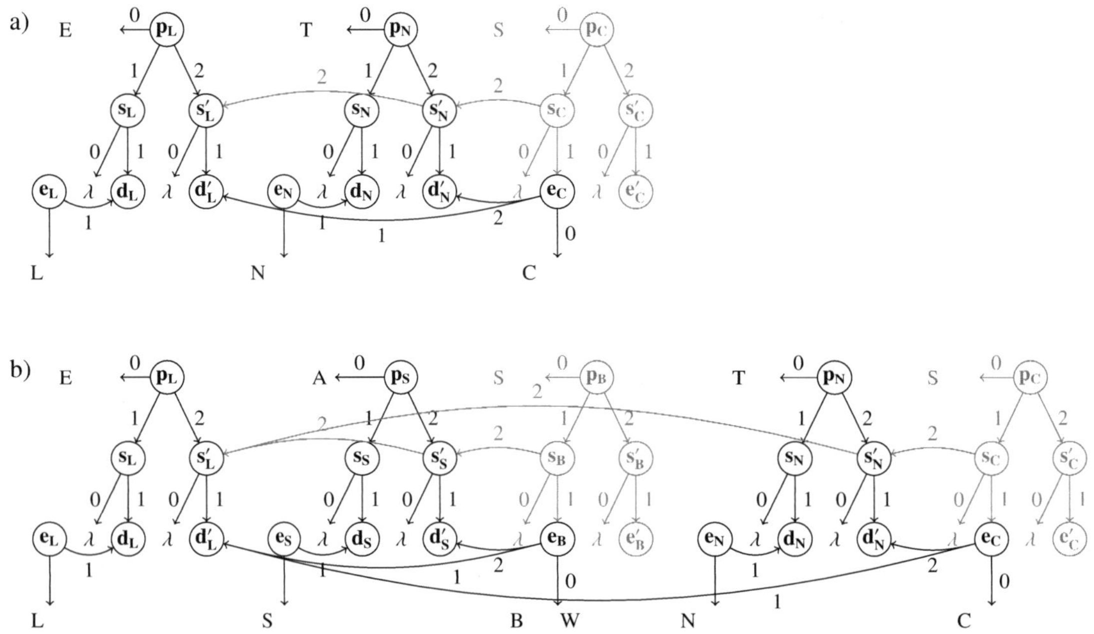

c) $(\mathrm{E}\quad \mathbf{p_L\, s_L\, s'_L}) \wedge (\mathrm{S}\quad \mathbf{s_L\, d_L\, s_\perp}) \wedge (\mathrm{L}\quad \mathbf{e_L\, d_L}) \wedge (\mathrm{S}\quad \mathbf{s'_L\, d'_L\, s_\perp}) \wedge$
$(\mathrm{T}\quad \mathbf{p_N\, s_N\, s'_N}) \wedge (\mathrm{S}\quad \mathbf{s_N\, d_N\, s_\perp}) \wedge (\mathrm{N}\quad \mathbf{e_N\, d_N}) \wedge (\mathrm{S}\quad \mathbf{s'_N\, d'_N\, s'_L}) \wedge (\mathrm{C}\quad \mathbf{e_C\, d'_L\, d'_N})$

Figure 2: Semantic dependency graph in a 'continuation-passing' (bottom-up) style, including quantifiers over eventualities for verbs (in gray). The semantic dependency structure for the sentence *Every line contains two numbers* (a), with flat logical form (c), is now contained by the semantic dependency structure for *Every line begins with a space and contains two numbers* (b).

lated into a lambda calculus expression by a deterministic algorithm which traverses sequences of continuation dependencies and constructs accordingly nested terms in a manner similar to that defined for DRT (Kamp, 1981). This graphical representation can be translated into lambda calculus by representing the source graph as a set Γ of elementary predications $(f\ i_0\ ..\ i_N)$ and the target as a set Δ of translated lambda calculus expressions, e.g. $(\lambda_i\ (h_f\ i_0\ ..\ i\ ..\ i_N))$. The set Δ can then be derived from Γ using the following natural deduction rules:[4]

- Initialize Δ with lambda terms (sets) that have no outscoped sets in Γ:

$$\frac{\Gamma, (\mathrm{S}\quad s\ i\ \_\ \_)\ ;\ \Delta}{\Gamma, (\mathrm{S}\quad s\ i\ \_\ \_)\ ;\ (\lambda_i\ \mathrm{T}\quad), \Delta}\ (\mathrm{S}\quad \_\ \_\ s\ \_) \notin \Gamma$$

- Add constraints to appropriate sets in Δ:

$$\frac{\Gamma, (f\ i_0\ ..\ i\ ..\ i_N)\ ;\ (\lambda_i\ o), \Delta}{\Gamma\ ;\ (\lambda_i\ o \wedge (h_f\ i_0\ ..\ i\ ..\ i_N)), \Delta}\ i_0 \in E$$

- Add constraints of supersets as constraints on subsets in Δ:

$$\frac{\begin{array}{l}\Gamma, (\mathrm{S}\quad s\ i\ \_\ \_), (\mathrm{S}\quad s'\ i'\ s''\ s)\ ;\\ (\lambda_i\ o \wedge (h_f\ i_0\ ..\ i\ ..\ i_N)), (\lambda_{i'}\ o'), \Delta\end{array}}{\begin{array}{l}\Gamma, (\mathrm{S}\quad s\ i\ \_\ \_), (\mathrm{S}\quad s'\ i'\ s''\ s)\ ;\\ (\lambda_i\ o \wedge (h_f\ i_0\ ..\ i\ ..\ i_N)),\\ \qquad (\lambda_{i'}\ o' \wedge (h_f\ i_0\ ..\ i'\ ..\ i_N)), \Delta\end{array}}$$

- Add quantifiers over completely constrained sets in Δ:

$$\frac{\begin{array}{l}\Gamma, (\mathrm{S}\quad s\ i\ \_\ \_), (f\ p\ s'\ s''),\\ \quad (\mathrm{S}\quad s'\ i'\ s\ \_), (\mathrm{S}\quad s''\ i''\ s'\ s')\ ;\\ (\lambda_i\ o), (\lambda_{i'}\ o'), (\lambda_{i''}\ o''), \Delta\end{array}}{\begin{array}{l}\Gamma, (\mathrm{S}\quad s\ i\ \_\ \_)\ ;\\ (\lambda_i\ o \wedge (h_f\ (\lambda_{i'}\ o')\ (\lambda_{i''}\ o''))), \Delta\end{array}}\ \begin{array}{l}p \in P,\\ (f'..\ i'..) \notin \Gamma,\\ (f''..\ i''..) \notin \Gamma.\end{array}$$

For example, the graph in Figure 2 can be translated into the following lambda calculus expression (including quantifiers over eventualities in the source graph, to eliminate unbound variables):

[4]Here, set predications are defined with an additional final argument position, which is defined to refer in a nuclear scope set to the restrictor set that is its sibling, and in a restrictor set to refer to $\mathbf{s}_\perp$.

$$
\begin{array}{lllll}
(\mathrm{E} & (\lambda_{d_L}\mathrm{S} & (\lambda_{e_L}\mathrm{L} & e_L\, d_L)) & \\
 & (\lambda_{d'_L}\mathrm{T} & (\lambda_{d_N}\mathrm{S} & (\lambda_{e_N}\mathrm{N} & e_N\, d_N)) \\
 & & (\lambda_{d'_N}\mathrm{S} & (\lambda_{e_C}\mathrm{C} & e_C\, d'_L\, d'_N))))
\end{array}
$$

4 Derivation of Syntactic and Semantic Dependencies

The semantic dependency representation defined in this paper assumes semantic dependencies other than those representing continuations are derived compositionally by a categorial grammar. In particular, this definition assumes a Generalized Categorial Grammar (GCG) (Bach, 1981; Oehrle, 1994), because it can be used to distinguish argument and modifier compositions (from which restrictor and nuclear scope sets are derived in a tree-structured continuation graph), and because large GCG-annotated corpora defined with this distinction are readily available (Nguyen et al., 2012). GCG category types $c \in C$ each consist of a primitive category type $u \in U$, typically labeled with the part of speech of the head of a category (e.g. **V**, **N**, **A**, etc., for phrases or clauses headed by verbs, nouns, adjectives, etc.), followed by one or more unsatisfied dependencies, each consisting of an operator $o \in O$ (**-a** and **-b** for adjacent argument dependencies preceding and succeeding a head, **-c** and **-d** for adjacent conjunct dependencies preceding and succeeding a head, **-g** for filler-gap dependencies, **-r** for relative pronoun dependencies, and some others), each followed by a dependent category type from C. For example, the category type for a transitive verb would be **V-aN-bN**, since it is headed by a verb, and has unsatisfied dependencies to satisfied noun-headed categories preceding and succeeding it (for the subject and direct object noun phrase, respectively). This formulation has the advantage for semantic dependency calculation that it distinguishes modifier and argument attachment. Since the semantic representation described in this paper makes explicit distinctions between restrictor sets and scope sets (which is necessary for coherent interpretation of quantifiers) it is necessary to consistently apply predicate-argument constraints to discourse referents in the nuclear scope set of a quantifier and modifier-modificand constraints to discourse referents in the restrictor set of a quantifier. For example, in Sentence 1:

(1) Everything is [**A-aN** open].

the predicate *open* constrains the nuclear scope set of *every*, but in Sentence 2:

(2) Everything [**A-aN** open] is finished.

the predicate *open* constrains the restrictor set. These constraints can be consistently applied in the argument and modifier attachment rules of a GCG.

Like a Combinatory Categorial Grammar (Steedman, 2000), a GCG defines syntactic dependencies for compositions that are determined by the number and kind of unsatisfied dependencies of the composed category types. These are similar to dependencies for subject, direct object, preposition complement, etc., of Stanford dependencies (de Marneffe et al., 2006), but are reduced to numbers based on the order of the associated dependencies in the category type of the lexical head.

These syntactic dependencies are then associated with semantic dependencies, with the referent of a subject associated with the first argument of an eventuality, the referent of a direct object associated with the second argument, and so on, for all verb forms other than passive verbs. In the case of passive verbs, the referent of a subject is associated with the second argument of an eventuality, the referent of a direct object associated with the third argument, and so on.

In order to have a consistent treatment of argument and modifier attachment across all category types, and also in order to model referents of verbs as eventualities which can be quantified by adverbs like *never, once, twice,* etc. (Parsons, 1990), it is desirable for eventualities associated with verbs to also be quantified. Outgoing semantic dependencies to arguments of eventualities are then applied as constraints to the discourse referent variable of the restrictor sets of these quantifiers. Incoming dependencies to eventualities and other discourse referents used as modificands of modifiers are also applied as constraints to discourse referent variables of restrictor sets, but incoming dependencies to discourse referents used as arguments of predicates are applied as constraints to discourse referent variables of nuclear scope sets. This assignment to restrictor or nuclear scope sets depends on the context of the relevant (argument or modifier attachment) parser operation, so associations between syntactic and semantic dependencies must be left partially undefined in lexical entries. Lexical entries are therefore defined with separate syntactic and semantic dependencies, using even numbers for syntactic dependencies from lexical items, and odd numbers for

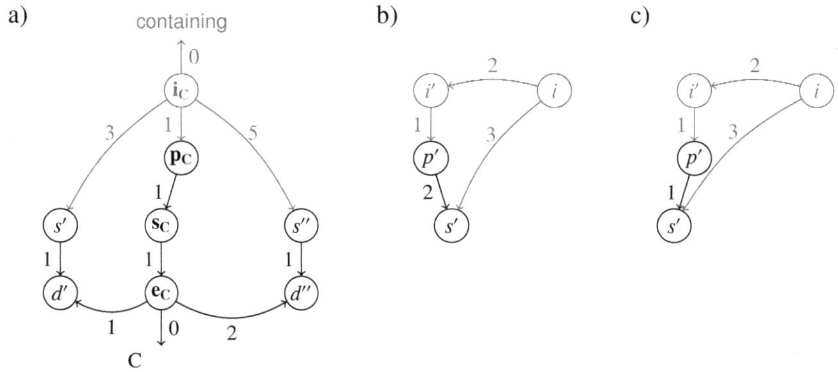

Figure 3: Example lexical semantic dependencies for the verb *containing* (a), and dependency equations for argument attachment (b) and modifier attachment (c) in GCG deduction rules. Lexical dependencies are shown in gray. Even numbered edges departing lexical items denote lexical syntactic dependencies, and odd numbered edges departing lexical items are lexical semantic dependencies. Argument attachments constrain semantic arguments to the nuclear scope sets of syntactic arguments, and modifier attachments constrain semantic arguments to the restrictor sets of syntactic arguments.

semantic dependencies from lexical items. For example, a lexical mapping for the finite transitive verb *contains* might be associated with the predicate C   , and have the discourse referent of its first lexical semantic argument $(\mathbf{f_1}\ (\mathbf{f_3}\ i))$ associated with the first argument of the eventuality discourse referent of the restrictor set of its proposition $(\mathbf{f_1}\ (\mathbf{f_1}\ (\mathbf{f_1}\ (\mathbf{f_1}\ i))))$, and the discourse referent of its second lexical semantic argument $(\mathbf{f_1}\ (\mathbf{f_5}\ i))$ associated with the second argument of the eventuality discourse referent of the restrictor set of its proposition $(\mathbf{f_2}\ (\mathbf{f_1}\ (\mathbf{f_1}\ (\mathbf{f_1}\ i))))$:

$$\begin{aligned}\text{contains} \Rightarrow \mathbf{V\text{-}aN\text{-}bN} : \lambda_i\, &(\mathbf{f_0}\ i)=\mathsf{contains}\\ &\wedge (\mathbf{f_0}\ (\mathbf{f_1}\ (\mathbf{f_1}\ (\mathbf{f_1}\ i))))=\mathrm{C}\\ &\wedge (\mathbf{f_1}\ (\mathbf{f_1}\ (\mathbf{f_1}\ (\mathbf{f_1}\ i))))=(\mathbf{f_1}\ (\mathbf{f_3}\ i))\\ &\wedge (\mathbf{f_2}\ (\mathbf{f_1}\ (\mathbf{f_1}\ (\mathbf{f_1}\ i))))=(\mathbf{f_1}\ (\mathbf{f_5}\ i))\end{aligned}$$

A graphical representation of these dependencies is shown in Figure 3a. These lexical semantic constraints are then associated with syntactic dependencies by grammar rules for argument and modifier attachment, as described below.

4.1 Inference rules for argument attachment

In GCG, as in other categorial grammars, inference rules for argument attachment apply functors of category c-**a**d or c-**b**d to preceding or succeeding arguments of category d:

$$d:g \quad c\text{-}\mathbf{a}d:h \Rightarrow c:(\mathbf{f}_{c\text{-}\mathbf{a}d}\ g\ h) \qquad \text{(Aa)}$$

$$c\text{-}\mathbf{b}d:g \quad d:h \Rightarrow c:(\mathbf{f}_{c\text{-}\mathbf{b}d}\ g\ h) \qquad \text{(Ab)}$$

where $\mathbf{f}_{u\varphi_1\ldots\varphi_n}$ are composition functions for $u \in U$ and $\varphi \in \{\text{-}\mathbf{a}, \text{-}\mathbf{b}, \text{-}\mathbf{c}, \text{-}\mathbf{d}\} \times C$, which connect the lexical item $(\mathbf{f}_{2n}\ i)$ of a preceding child function g as the $2n^{\text{th}}$ argument of lexical item i of a succeeding child function h, or vice versa:

$$\begin{aligned}\mathbf{f}_{u\varphi_{1..n\text{-}1}\text{-}\mathbf{a}d} &\stackrel{\text{def}}{=} \lambda_{g\,h\,i}\,(g\ (\mathbf{f}_{2n}\ i)) \wedge (h\ i)\\ &\quad \wedge (\mathbf{f}_{2n+1}\ i)=(\mathbf{f_2}\ (\mathbf{f_1}\ (\mathbf{f}_{2n}\ i))) \qquad \text{(1a)}\end{aligned}$$

$$\begin{aligned}\mathbf{f}_{u\varphi_{1..n\text{-}1}\text{-}\mathbf{b}d} &\stackrel{\text{def}}{=} \lambda_{g\,h\,i}\,(g\ i) \wedge (h\ (\mathbf{f}_{2n}\ i))\\ &\quad \wedge (\mathbf{f}_{2n+1}\ i)=(\mathbf{f_2}\ (\mathbf{f_1}\ (\mathbf{f}_{2n}\ i))) \qquad \text{(1b)}\end{aligned}$$

as shown in Figure 3b. This associates the lexical semantic argument of the predicate $(\mathbf{f}_{2n+1}\ i)$ with the nuclear scope of the quantifier proposition associated with the syntactic argument $(\mathbf{f_2}\ (\mathbf{f_1}\ (\mathbf{f}_{2n}\ i)))$. For example, the following inference attaches a subject to a verb:

$$\dfrac{\dfrac{\text{every line}}{\mathbf{N}:\lambda_i\,(\mathbf{f_0}\ i)=\mathsf{line}\ ..} \quad \dfrac{\text{contains two numbers}}{\mathbf{V\text{-}aN}:\lambda_i\,(\mathbf{f_0}\ i)=\mathsf{contains}\ ..}}{\begin{array}{c}\mathbf{V}:\lambda_i\,(\mathbf{f_0}\ (\mathbf{f_2}\ i))=\mathsf{line}\ ..\ \wedge (\mathbf{f_0}\ i)=\mathsf{contains}\ ..\\ \wedge (\mathbf{f_3}\ i)=(\mathbf{f_2}\ (\mathbf{f_1}\ (\mathbf{f_2}\ i)))\end{array}}\ \text{Aa}$$

4.2 Inference rules for modifier attachment

This grammar also uses distinguished inference rules for modifier attachment. Inference rules for modifier attachment apply preceding or succeeding modifiers of category u-**a**d to modificands of category c, for $u \in U$ and $c, d \in C$:

$$u\text{-}\mathbf{a}d:g \quad c:h \Rightarrow c:(\mathbf{f}_{\mathrm{PM}}\ g\ h) \qquad \text{(Ma)}$$

$$c:g \quad u\text{-}\mathbf{a}d:h \Rightarrow c:(\mathbf{f}_{\mathrm{SM}}\ g\ h) \qquad \text{(Mb)}$$

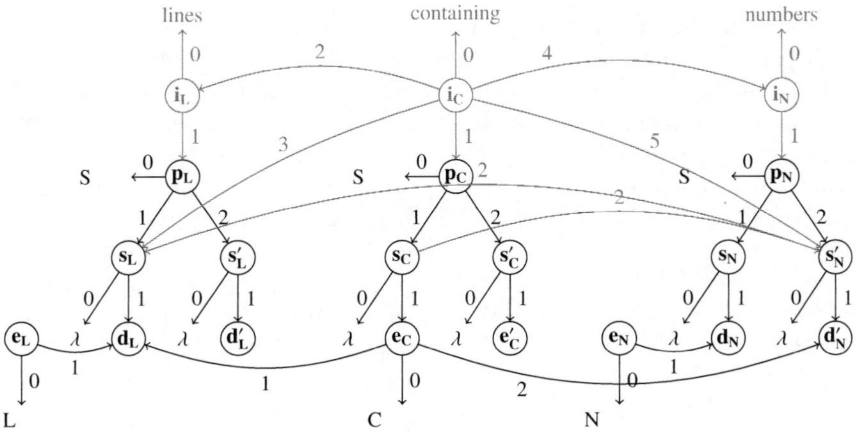

Figure 4: Compositional analysis of noun phrase *lines containing numbers* exemplifying both argument attachment (to *numbers*) and modifier attachment (to *lines*). Lexical dependencies are shown in gray, and continuation dependencies (which do not result from syntactic composition) are highlighted.

where $\mathbf{f}_{\text{PM}}$ and $\mathbf{f}_{\text{SM}}$ are category-independent composition functions for preceding and succeeding modifiers, which return the lexical item of the argument (j) rather than of the predicate (i):

$$\mathbf{f}_{\text{PM}} \stackrel{\text{def}}{=} \lambda_{g\,h\,j}\, \exists_i\, (\mathbf{f}_2\; i){=}j \wedge (g\; i) \wedge (h\; j) \wedge (\mathbf{f}_3\; i){=}(\mathbf{f}_1\; (\mathbf{f}_1\; (\mathbf{f}_2\; i))) \tag{2a}$$

$$\mathbf{f}_{\text{SM}} \stackrel{\text{def}}{=} \lambda_{g\,h\,j}\, \exists_i\, (\mathbf{f}_2\; i){=}j \wedge (g\; j) \wedge (h\; i) \wedge (\mathbf{f}_3\; i){=}(\mathbf{f}_1\; (\mathbf{f}_1\; (\mathbf{f}_2\; i))) \tag{2b}$$

as shown in Figure 3c. This allows categories for predicates to be re-used as modifiers. Unlike argument attachment, modifier attachment associates the lexical semantic argument of the modifier ($\mathbf{f}_{2n+1}\; i$) with the restrictor of the quantifier proposition of the modificand ($\mathbf{f}_1\; (\mathbf{f}_1\; (\mathbf{f}_{2n}\; i))$). For example, the following inference attaches an adjectival modifier to the quantifier proposition of a noun phrase:

$$\dfrac{\dfrac{\text{every line}}{\mathbf{N}{:}\lambda_i\, (\mathbf{f}_0\; i){=}\text{line}\,..} \quad \dfrac{\text{containing two numbers}}{\mathbf{A\text{-}aN}{:}\lambda_i\, (\mathbf{f}_0\; i){=}\text{containing}\,..}}{\mathbf{N}: \lambda_i\, (\mathbf{f}_0\; i){=}\text{line}\,.. \wedge \exists_j\, (\mathbf{f}_0\; j){=}\text{containing}\,.. \wedge (\mathbf{f}_2\; j){=}i \wedge (\mathbf{f}_3\; j){=}(\mathbf{f}_1\; (\mathbf{f}_1\; (\mathbf{f}_2\; j)))}\;\text{Mb}$$

An example of argument and modifier attachment is shown in Figure 4.

5 Estimation of Scope Dependencies

Semantic dependency graphs obtained from GCG derivations as described in Section 4 are scopally underspecified. Scope disambiguations must then be obtained by specifying continuation dependencies from every set referent to some other set referent (or to a null context, indicating a top-level set). In a sentence processing model, these non-local continuation dependencies would be incrementally calculated in working memory in a manner similar to coreference resolution.[5] However, in this paper, in order to obtain a reasonable estimate of the learnability of such a system, continuation dependencies are assigned post-hoc by a statistical inference algorithm.

The disambiguation algorithm first defines a partition of the set of reified set referents into sets $\{s, s', s''\}$ of reified set referents s whose discourse referent variables ($\mathbf{f}_1\; s$) are connected by semantic dependencies. For example, $\mathbf{s}_{\text{L}}$, $\mathbf{s}_{\text{C}}$ and $\mathbf{s}'_{\text{N}}$ in Figure 4 are part of the same partition, but $\mathbf{s}'_{\text{L}}$ is not.

Scope dependencies are then constructed from these partitions using a greedy algorithm which starts with an arbitrary set from this partition in

[5]Like any other dependency, a continuation dependency may be stored during incremental processing when both its cue (source) and target (destination) referents have been hypothesized. For example, upon processing the word *numbers* in the sentence *Every line contains two numbers*, a continuation dependency may be stored from the nuclear scope set associated with this word to the nuclear scope set of the subject *every line*, forming an in-situ interpretation with some amount of activation (see Figure 4), and with some (probably smaller) amount of activation, a continuation dependency may be stored from the nuclear scope set of this subject to the nuclear scope set of this word, forming an inverted interpretation. See Schuler (2014) for a model of how sentence processing in associative memory might incrementally store dependencies like these as cued associations.

the dependency graph, then begins connecting it, selecting the highest-ranked referent of that partition that is not yet attached and designating it as the new highest-scoping referent in that partition, attaching it as the context of the previously highest-scoping referent in that partition if one exists. This proceeds until:

1. the algorithm reaches a restrictor or nuclear scope referent with a sibling (superset or subset) nuclear scope or restrictor referent that has not yet served as the highest-scoping referent in its partition, at which point the algorithm switches to the partition of that sibling referent and begins connecting that; or

2. the algorithm reaches a restrictor or nuclear scope referent with a sibling nuclear scope or restrictor referent that *is* the highest-scoping referent in its partition, in which case it connects it to its sibling with a continuation dependency from the nuclear scope referent to the restrictor referent and merges the two siblings' partitions.

In this manner, all set referents in the dependency graph are eventually assembled into a single tree of continuation dependencies.

6 Evaluation

This paper defines a graphical semantic representation with desirable properties for storing sentence meanings as cued associations in associative memory. In order to determine whether this representation of continuation dependencies is reliably learnable, the set of test sentences from the QuanText corpus (Manshadi et al., 2011) was automatically annotated with these continuation dependencies and evaluated against the associated set of gold-standard quantifier scopes. The sentences in this corpus were collected as descriptions of text editing tasks using unix tools like sed and awk, collected from online tutorials and from graduate students asked to write and describe example scripts. Gold-standard scoping relations in this corpus are specified over bracketed sequences of words in each sentence. For example, the sentence *Print every line that starts with a number* might be annotated:

Print [$_1$ *every line*] *that starts with* [$_2$ *a number*] .
scoping relations: 1 > 2

meaning that the quantifier over *lines*, referenced in constituent 1, outscopes the quantifier over *numbers*, referenced in constituent 2. In order to isolate the learnablility of the continuation dependencies described in this paper, both training and test sentences of this corpus were annotated with hand-corrected GCG derivations which are then used to obtain semantic dependencies as described in Section 4. Continuation dependencies are then inferred from these semantic dependencies using the algorithm described in Section 5. Gold-standard scoping relations are considered successfully recalled if a restrictor ($\mathbf{f_1}$ ($\mathbf{f_1}$ i)) or nuclear scope ($\mathbf{f_2}$ ($\mathbf{f_1}$ i)) referent of any lexical item i within the outscoped span is connected by a sequence of continuation dependencies (in the appropriate direction) to any restrictor or nuclear scope referent of any lexical item within the outscoping span.

First, the algorithm was run without any lexicalization on the 94 non-duplicate sentences of the QuanText test set. Results of this evaluation are shown in the third line of Table 1 using the per-sentence complete recall accuracy ('AR') defined by Manshadi et al. (2013).

The algorithm was then run using bilexical weights based on the frequencies $\tilde{\mathsf{F}}(h, h')$ with which a word h' occurs as a head of a category outscoped by a category headed by word h in the 350-sentence training set of the QuanText corpus. For example, since quantifiers over *lines* are often outscoped by quantifiers over *files* in the training data, the system learns to rank continuation dependencies to referents associated with the word *lines* ahead of continuation dependencies to referents associated with the word *files* in bottom-up inference. These lexical features may be particularly helpful because continuation dependencies are generated only between directly adjacent sets. Results for scope disambiguation using these rankings are shown in the fourth line of Table 1. This increase is statistically significant ($p = 0.001$ by two-tailed McNemar's test). This significance for local head-word features on continuation dependencies shows that these dependencies can be reliably learned from training examples, and suggests that continuation dependencies may be a natural representation for scope information.

Interestingly, effects of lexical features for quantifiers (the word *each*, or definite/indefinite distinctions) were not substantial or statistically significant, despite the relatively high frequencies

System	AR
Manshadi and Allen (2011) baseline	63%
Manshadi et al. (2013)	72%
This system, w/o lexicalized model	61%
This system, w. lexicalized model	72%

Table 1: Per-sentence complete recall accuracy ('AR') of tree-based algorithm as compared to Manshadi and Allen (2011) and Manshadi et al. (2013) on explicit NP chunks in the QuanText test set, correcting for use of gold standard trees as described in footnote 19 of Manshadi et al. (2013).

of the words *each* and *the* in the test corpus (occurring in 16% and 68% of test sentences, respectively), which suggests that these words may often be redundant with syntactic and head-word constraints. Results using preferences that rank referents quantified by the word *each* after other referents achieve a numerical increase in accuracy over a model with no preferences (up 5 points, to 66%), but it is not statistically significant (p = .13). Results using preferences that rank referents quantified by the word *the* after other referents achieve a numerical increase in accuracy over a model with no preferences (up 1 point, to 62%), but this is even less significant (p = 1). Results are even weaker in combination with head-word features (up 1 point, to 73%, for *each*; down two points, to 70%, for *the*). This suggests that world knowledge (in the form of head-word information) may be more salient to quantifier scope disambiguation than many intuitive linguistic preferences.

7 Conclusion

This paper has presented a graphical semantic dependency representation based on bottom-up continuation dependencies which can be translated into lambda calculus, but has the important property that its vertices define a usable set of discourse referents in working memory even in contexts involving conjunction in the scope of quantifiers. An evaluation on an existing quantifier scope disambiguation task shows that non-local continuation dependencies can be as reliably learned from annotated data as representations used in a state-of-the-art quantifier scope resolver. This suggests that continuation dependencies may be a natural representation for scope information.

Continuation dependencies as defined in this paper provide a local representation for quantificational context. This ensures that graphical representations match only when their quantificational contexts match. When used to guide a statistical or vectorial representation, it is possible that this local context will allow certain types of inference to be defined by simple pattern matching, which could be implemented in existing working memory models. Future work will explore the use of this graph-based semantic representation as a basis for vectorial semantics in a cognitive model of inference during sentence processing.

8 Acknowledgements

The authors would like to thank Mehdi Manshadi for assistance in obtaining the QuanText corpus. The authors would also like to thank Erhard Hinrichs, Craige Roberts, the members of the OSU LLIC Reading Group, and the three anonymous *SEM reviewers for their helpful comments about this work.

References

James A. Anderson, Jack W. Silverstein, Stephen A. Ritz, and Randall S. Jones. 1977. Distinctive features, categorical perception and probability learning: Some applications of a neural model. *Psychological Review*, 84:413–451.

Emmon Bach. 1981. Discontinuous constituents in generalized categorial grammars. *Proceedings of the Annual Meeting of the Northeast Linguistic Society (NELS)*, 11:1–12.

Jason Baldridge and Geert-Jan M. Kruijff. 2002. Coupling CCG and hybrid logic dependency semantics. In *Proceedings of the 40th Annual Meeting of the Association for Computational Linguistics (ACL 2002)*, Philadelphia, Pennsylvania.

Chris Barker. 2002. Continuations and the nature of quantification. *Natural Language Semantics*, 10:211–242.

Jon Barwise and Robin Cooper. 1981. Generalized quantifiers and natural language. *Linguistics and Philosophy*, 4.

Johan Bos. 1996. Predicate logic unplugged. In *Proceedings of the 10th Amsterdam Colloquium*, pages 133–143.

Sarah Brown-Schmidt, Ellen Campana, and Michael K. Tanenhaus. 2002. Reference resolution in the wild: Online circumscription of referential domains in a natural interactive problem-solving task. In *Proceedings of the 24th Annual Meeting of the Cognitive Science Society*, pages 148–153, Fairfax, VA, August.

Ann Copestake, Dan Flickinger, Carl Pollard, and Ivan Sag. 2005. Minimal recursion semantics: An introduction. *Research on Language and Computation*, pages 281–332.

Marie-Catherine de Marneffe, Bill MacCartney, and Christopher D. Manning. 2006. Generating typed dependency parses from phrase structure parses. In *Proceedings of LREC 2006*.

Judith Degen and Michael K. Tanenhaus. 2011. Making inferences: The case of scalar implicature processing. In *Proceedings of the 33rd Annual Conference of the Cognitive Science Society*, pages 3299–3304.

Marc W. Howard and Michael J. Kahana. 2002. A distributed representation of temporal context. *Journal of Mathematical Psychology*, 45:269–299.

Hans Kamp. 1981. A theory of truth and semantic representation. In Jeroen A. G. Groenendijk, Theo M. V. Janssen, and Martin B. J. Stokhof, editors, *Formal Methods in the Study of Language: Mathematical Centre Tracts 135*, pages 277–322. Mathematical Center, Amsterdam.

Walter Kintsch. 1988. The role of knowledge in discourse comprehension: A construction-integration model. *Psychological review*, 95(2):163–182.

Alexander Koller. 2004. *Constraint-based and graph-based resolution of ambiguities in natural language*. Ph.D. thesis, Universität des Saarlandes.

Geert-Jan M. Kruijff. 2001. *A Categorial-Modal Architecture of Informativity: Dependency Grammar Logic and Information Structure*. Ph.D. thesis, Charles University.

Bill MacCartney and Christopher D. Manning. 2009. An Extended Model of Natural Logic. In *Proceedings of the Eighth International Conference on Computational Semantics*, IWCS-8 '09, pages 140–156. Association for Computational Linguistics.

Mehdi Manshadi and James F. Allen. 2011. Unrestricted quantifier scope disambiguation. In *Graph-based Methods for Natural Language Processing*, pages 51–59.

Mehdi Manshadi, James F. Allen, and Mary Swift. 2011. A corpus of scope-disambiguated english text. In *Proceedings of ACL*, pages 141–146.

Mehdi Manshadi, Daniel Gildea, and James F. Allen. 2013. Plurality, negation, and quantification: Towards comprehensive quantifier scope disambiguation. In *Proceedings of ACL*, pages 64–72.

David Marr. 1971. Simple memory: A theory for archicortex. *Philosophical Transactions of the Royal Society (London) B*, 262:23–81.

David Marr. 1982. *Vision. A Computational Investigation into the Human Representation and Processing of Visual Information*. W.H. Freeman and Company.

J. L. McClelland, B. L. McNaughton, and R. C. O'Reilly. 1995. Why there are complementary learning systems in the hippocampus and neocortex: Insights from the successes and failures of connectionist models of learning and memory. *Psychological Review*, 102:419–457.

Richard Montague. 1973. The proper treatment of quantification in ordinary English. In J. Hintikka, J.M.E. Moravcsik, and P. Suppes, editors, *Approaches to Natural Langauge*, pages 221–242. D. Riedel, Dordrecht. Reprinted in R. H. Thomason ed., *Formal Philosophy*, Yale University Press, 1994.

B.B. Murdock. 1982. A theory for the storage and retrieval of item and associative information. *Psychological Review*, 89:609–626.

Luan Nguyen, Marten van Schijndel, and William Schuler. 2012. Accurate unbounded dependency recovery using generalized categorial grammars. In *Proceedings of the 24th International Conference on Computational Linguistics (COLING '12)*, pages 2125–2140, Mumbai, India.

Richard T. Oehrle. 1994. Term-labeled categorial type systems. *Linguistics and Philosophy*, 17(6):633–678.

Terence Parsons. 1990. *Events in the Semantics of English*. MIT Press.

William Schuler. 2014. Sentence processing in a vectorial model of working memory. In *Fifth Annual Workshop on Cognitive Modeling and Computational Linguistics (CMCL 2014)*.

Chung-chieh Shan and Chris Barker. 2006. Explaining crossover and superiority as left-to-right evaluation. *Linguistics and Philosophy*, 29:91–134.

Mark Steedman. 2000. *The syntactic process*. MIT Press/Bradford Books, Cambridge, MA.

Mark Steedman. 2012. *Taking Scope - The Natural Semantics of Quantifiers*. MIT Press.

Michael K. Tanenhaus, Michael J. Spivey-Knowlton, Kathy M. Eberhard, and Julie E. Sedivy. 1995. Integration of visual and linguistic information in spoken language comprehension. *Science*, 268:1632–1634.

Marten van Schijndel and William Schuler. 2013. An analysis of frequency- and recency-based processing costs. In *Proceedings of NAACL-HLT 2013*. Association for Computational Linguistics.

Marten van Schijndel, Luan Nguyen, and William Schuler. 2013. An analysis of memory-based processing costs using incremental deep syntactic dependency parsing. In *Proceedings of CMCL 2013*. Association for Computational Linguistics.

Vagueness and Learning: A Type-Theoretic Approach

Raquel Fernández
Institute for Logic, Language and Computation
University of Amsterdam
raquel.fernandez@uva.nl

Staffan Larsson
Department of Philosophy, Linguistics and Theory of Science
University of Gothenburg
sl@ling.gu.se

Abstract

We present a formal account of the meaning of vague scalar adjectives such as '*tall*' formulated in Type Theory with Records. Our approach makes precise how perceptual information can be integrated into the meaning representation of these predicates; how an agent evaluates whether an entity counts as tall; and how the proposed semantics can be learned and dynamically updated through experience.

1 Introduction

Traditional semantic theories such as those described in Partee (1989) and Blackburn and Bos (2005) offer precise accounts of the truth-conditional content of linguistic expressions, but do not deal with the connection between meaning, perception and learning. One can argue, however, that part of getting to know the meaning of linguistic expressions consists in learning to identify the individuals or the situations that the expressions can describe. For many concrete words and phrases, this identification relies on perceptual information. In this paper, we focus on characterising the meaning of vague scalar adjectives such as '*tall*', '*dark*', or '*heavy*'. We propose a formal account that brings together notions from traditional formal semanticswith perceptual information, which allows us to specify how a logic-based interpretation function is determined and modified dynamically by experience.

The need to integrate language and perception has been emphasised by researchers working on the generation and resolution of referring expressions (Kelleher et al., 2005; Reiter et al., 2005; Portet et al., 2009) and, perhaps even more strongly, on the field of robotics, where grounding language on perceptual information is critical to allow artificial agents to autonomously acquire and verify beliefs about the world (Siskind, 2001; Steels, 2003; Roy, 2005; Skocaj et al., 2010). Most of these approaches, however, do not build on theories of formal semantics for natural language. Here we choose to formalise our account in a theoretical framework known as Type Theory with Records (TTR), which has been shown to be suitable for formalising classic semantic aspects such as intensionality, quantification, and negation (Cooper, 2005a; Cooper, 2010; Cooper and Ginzburg, 2011) as well as less standard phenomena such as linguistic interaction (Ginzburg, 2012; Purver et al., 2014), perception and action (Dobnik et al., 2013), and semantic coordination and learning (Larsson, 2009). In this paper we use TTR to put forward an account of the semantics of vague scalar predicates like '*tall*' that makes precise how perceptual information can be integrated into their meaning representation; how an agent evaluates whether an entity counts as tall; and how the proposed semantics for these expressions can be learned and dynamically updated through language use.

We start by giving a brief overview of TTR and explaining how it can be used for classifying entities as being of particular types integrating perceptual information. After that, in Section 3, we describe the main properties of vague scalar predicates. Section 4 presents a probabilistic TTR formalisation of the meaning of '*tall*', which captures its context-dependence and its vague character. In Section 5, we then offer an account of how that meaning representation is acquired and updated with experience. Finally, in Section 6 we discuss related work, before concluding in Section 7.

*Proceedings of the Third Joint Conference on Lexical and Computational Semantics (*SEM 2014)*, pages 151–159, Dublin, Ireland, August 23-24 2014.

2 Meaning as Classification in TTR

In this section we give a brief and hence inevitably partial introduction to Type Theory with Records. For more comprehensive introductions, we refer the reader to Cooper (2005b) and Cooper (2012).

2.1 Type Theory with Records: Main Notions

As in any type theory, the most central notion in TTR is that of a judgement that an object a is of type T, written as $a : T$. In TTR judgements are seen as fundamentally related to perception, in the sense that perceiving inherently involves categorising what we perceive. Some common *basic types* in TTR are Ind (the type of individuals) and $\mathbb{R}^+$ (the type of positive real numbers). All basic types are members of a special type Type. Given types T_1 and T_2, we can create the *function type* $T_1 \rightarrow T2$ whose domain are objects of type T_1 and whose range are objects of type T_2. Types can also be constructed from predicates and objects $P(a_1, \ldots, a_n)$. Such types are called *ptypes* and correspond roughly to propositions in first order logic. In TTR, propositions are types of *proofs*, where proofs can be a variety of things, from situations to sensor readings (more on this below).

Next, we introduce *records* and *record types*. These are structured objects made up of pairs $\langle l, v\rangle$ of labels and values that are displayed in a matrix:

(1) a. A record type:

$$\begin{bmatrix} \ell_1 : T_1 \\ \ell_2 : T_2(\ell_1) \\ \ldots \\ \ell_n : T_n(\ell_1, \ell_2, \ldots, \ell_{n-1}) \end{bmatrix}$$

b. A record: $r = \begin{bmatrix} \ell_1 = a_1 \\ \ell_2 = a_2 \\ \ldots \\ \ell_n = a_n \\ \ldots \end{bmatrix}$

Record r in (1b) is of the record type in (1a) if and only if $a_1 : T_1$, $a_2 : T_2(a_1)$, ..., and $a_n : T_n(a_1, a_2, \ldots, a_{n-1})$. Note that the record may contain more fields but would still be of type (1a) if the typing condition holds. Records and record types can be nested so that the value of a label is itself a record (or record type). We can use *paths* within a record or record type to refer to specific bits of structure: for instance, we can use $r.\ell_2$ to refer to a_2 in (1b).

As can be seen in (1a), the labels $\ell_1, \ldots \ell_n$ in a record type can be used elsewhere to refer to the values associated with them. This is a common way of constructing ptypes where the arguments of a predicate are entities that have been introduced before in the record type. A sample record and record type are shown in (2).

(2) $\begin{bmatrix} \text{x} & = a \\ \text{c}_{man} & = \text{prf(man}(a)) \\ \text{c}_{run} & = \text{prf(run}(a)) \end{bmatrix} : \begin{bmatrix} \text{x} & : \text{Ind} \\ \text{c}_{man} & : \text{man(x)} \\ \text{c}_{run} & : \text{run(x)} \end{bmatrix}$

In (2), a is an entity of type individual and $\text{prf}(P)$ is used as a placeholder for proofs of ptypes P. In the record type above, the ptypes man(x) and run(x) constructed from predicates are *dependent* on x (introduced earlier in the record type).

2.2 Perceptual Meaning

Larsson (2013) proposes a system formalised in TTR where some perceptual aspects of meaning are represented using *classifiers*. For example, the meaning of '*right*' (as in '*to the right of*') involves a two-input perceptron classifier $\kappa_{right}(w, t, r)$, specified by a weight vector w and a threshold t, which takes as input a context r including an object x and a position-sensor reading sr_{pos}. The sensor reading consists of a vector containing two real numbers representing the space coordinates of x. The classifier classifies x as either being to the right on a plane or not.[1]

(3) if $r : \begin{bmatrix} \text{x} & : \text{Ind} \\ \text{sr}_{pos} & : \text{RealVector} \end{bmatrix}$, then

$$\kappa_{right}(w, t, r) = \begin{cases} \text{right}(r.\text{x}) & \text{if } (r.\text{sr}_{pos} \cdot w) > t \\ \neg\ \text{right}(r.\text{x}) & \text{otherwise} \end{cases}$$

As output we get a record type containing either a ptype right(x) or its negation, ¬ right(x). Larsson (2013) proposes that readings from sensors may count as proofs of such ptypes. A classifier can be used for judging x as being of a particular type on the grounds of perceptual information. A perceptual proof for right(x) would thus include the output from the position sensor that is directed towards x. Here, this output would be the space coordinates of x.

3 Vague Scalar Predicates

Scalar predicates such as '*tall*', '*long*' and '*expensive*', also called "relative gradable adjectives" (Kennedy, 2007), are interpreted with respect to a

[1] We are here assuming that we have a definition of dot product for TTR vectors a:RealVector$_n$ and b:RealVector$_n$ such that $a \cdot b = \Sigma_{i=1}^n a_i b_i = a_1 b_1 + a_2 b_2 + \ldots + a_n b_n$. We also implicitly assume that the weight vector and the sensor reading vector have the same dimensionality.

scale, i.e., a dimension such as height, length, or cost along which entities for which the relevant dimension is applicable can be ordered. This makes scalar predicates compatible with degree morphology, like comparative and superlative morphemes (*'taller than'*, *'the longest'*) and intensifier morphemes such as *'very'* or *'quite'*. In this paper, our focus is on the so-called *positive form* of these adjectives (e.g. *'tall'* as opposed to *'taller'* or *'tallest'*).

A property that distinguishes the positive form from the comparative and the superlative forms is its *context-dependance*. To take a common example: If Sue's height is 180cm, she may be appropriately described as a tall woman, but probably not as a tall basketball player. Thus, what counts as tall can vary from context to context, with the most relevant contextual parameter being a *comparison class* relative to which the adjective is interpreted (e.g., the set of women, the set of basketball players, etc.). In addition to being context-dependent, positive-form scalar predicates are also *vague*, in the sense that they give rise to *borderline cases*, i.e., entities for which it is unclear whether the predicate holds or not.

Vagueness is certainly a property that affects most natural language expressions, not only scalar adjectives. However, scalar adjectives have a relatively simple semantics (they are often uni-dimensional) and thus constitute a perfect case-study for investigating the properties and effects of vagueness on language use. Gradable adjectives have received a high amount of attention in the formal semantics literature. It is common to distinguish between two main approaches to their semantics: delineation-based and degree-based approaches. The delineation approach is associated with the work of Klein (1980), who proposes that gradable adjectives denote partial functions dependent on a comparison class. They partition the comparison class into three disjoint sets: a positive extension, a negative extension, and an extension gap (entities for which the predicate is neither true nor false). In contrast, degree-based approaches assume a measure function m mapping individuals x to degrees on a particular scale (degrees of height, degrees of darkness, etc.) and a *standard of comparison* or *degree threshold* θ (again, dependent on a comparison class) such that x belongs to the adjective's denotation if $m(x) > \theta$ (Kamp, 1975; Pinkal, 1979; Pinkal, 1995; Barker, 2002; Kennedy and McNally, 2005; Kennedy, 2007; Solt, 2011; Lassiter, 2011).

We build on degree approaches but adopt a perception-based perspective and take a step further to formalise how the meaning of these predicates can be learned and constantly updated through language use.

4 A Perceptual Semantics for *'Tall'*

To exemplify our approach, we will use the scalar predicate *'tall'* throughout.

4.1 Context-sensitivity

We first focus on capturing the context-dependence of relative scalar predicates. For this we define a type T_{ctxt} as follows:

(4) $$\mathrm{T}_{ctxt} = \begin{bmatrix} \mathrm{c} & : & \mathrm{Type} \\ \mathrm{x} & : & \mathrm{c} \\ \mathrm{h} & : & \mathbb{R}^+ \end{bmatrix}$$

The *context* (*ctxt*) of a scalar predicate like *'tall'* is a record of the type in (4), which includes: a type c (typically a subtype of Ind) representing the comparison class; an individual x within the comparison class (the argument of tall); a perceived measure on the relevant scale(s), in this case the perceived height h of x expressed as a positive real number.

The context presupposes the acquisition of sensory input from the environment. In particular, it assumes that an agent using such a representation is able to classify the entity in focus x as being of type c and is able to use some height sensor to obtain an estimate of x's height (the value of h is the sensor reading). We thus forgo the inclusion of an abstract measure function in the representation. In an artificial agent, this may be accomplished by image processing software for detecting and measuring objects in a digital image.

Besides the *ctxt*, we also assume a standard threshold of tallness θ_{tall} of the type given in (5). θ_{tall} is a function from a type specifying a comparison class to a height value, which corresponds to a tallness threshold for that comparison class. (In Section 5 we will discuss how such a threshold may be computed.)

(5) $\theta_{tall} : \mathrm{Type} \rightarrow \mathbb{R}^+$

The meaning of *'tall'* involves a *classifier* for tallness, κ_{tall}, of the following type:

(6) $\kappa_{tall} : (\mathrm{Type} \rightarrow \mathbb{R}^+, \mathrm{T}_{ctxt}) \rightarrow \mathrm{Type}$

We define this classifier as a one-input perceptron that compares the perceived height h of an individual x to the relevant threshold θ determined by a comparison class c. Thus, if θ : Type $\rightarrow \mathbb{R}^+$ and $r : \mathrm{T}_{ctxt}$, then:

$$\kappa_{tall}(\theta, r) = \begin{cases} \mathrm{tall}(r.\mathrm{x}) & \text{if } r.\mathrm{h} > \theta(r.\mathrm{c}) \\ \neg\mathrm{tall}(r.\mathrm{x}) & \text{otherwise} \end{cases}$$

Simplifying somewhat, we can represent the meaning of '*tall*', **tall**, as a record specifying the type of context (T_{ctxt}) where an utterance of '*tall*' can be made, the parameter of the tallness classifier (the threshold θ), and a function f which is applied to the context to produce the content of '*tall*'.

(7)
$$\textbf{tall} = \begin{bmatrix} \mathrm{T}_{ctxt} = \begin{bmatrix} \mathrm{c} & : & \mathrm{Type} \\ \mathrm{x} & : & \mathrm{c} \\ \mathrm{h} & : & \mathbb{R}^+ \end{bmatrix} \\ \theta \quad = \theta_{tall} \\ \mathrm{f} \quad = \lambda r : \mathrm{T}_{ctxt}. \\ \qquad \begin{bmatrix} \mathrm{sit} = r \\ \mathrm{sit\text{-}type} = \begin{bmatrix} \mathrm{c}_{tall} : \kappa_{tall}(\theta, r) \end{bmatrix} \end{bmatrix} \end{bmatrix}$$

The output of the function f is an Austinian proposition (Cooper, 2005b): a judgement that a situation (sit, represented as a record r of type T_{ctxt}), is of a particular type (specified in sit-type). In the case of **tall**, the context of utterance (which instantiates r) is judged to be of the type where there is an individual x which is either tall or not tall, according to the output of the classifier κ_{tall}. The context of utterance in the sit field will include the height-sensor reading, which means that the sensor reading is part of the proof of the sit-type indicating that x is tall (or not, as the case may be).

Thus, to decide whether to refer to some individual x as tall or to evaluate someone else's utterance describing x as tall, an agent applies the function **tall**.f to the current situation, represented as a record $r : T_{ctxt}$. As an example, let us consider a situation that includes the context in (8), resulting from observing John Smith as being 1.88 meters tall (assuming this is our scale of tallness):

$$\text{(8)}\quad ctxt = \begin{bmatrix} \mathrm{c} & = & \mathrm{Human} \\ \mathrm{x} & = & \mathrm{john\_smith} \\ \mathrm{h} & = & 1.88 \end{bmatrix}$$

Let us assume that given the comparison class Human, $\theta_{tall}(\mathrm{Human}) = 1.87$. In this case, **tall**.f(*ctxt*) will compute as shown in (9). The resulting Austinian proposition corresponds to the agent's judgement that the situation in sit is one where John Smith counts as tall.

$$\text{(9)}\quad \lambda r : \mathrm{T}_{ctxt}. \begin{bmatrix} \mathrm{sit} = r \\ \mathrm{sit\text{-}type} = \begin{bmatrix} \mathrm{c}_{tall} : \kappa_{tall}(\theta_{tall}, r) \end{bmatrix} \end{bmatrix}$$
$$\left(\begin{bmatrix} \mathrm{c} & = & \mathrm{Human} \\ \mathrm{x} & = & \mathrm{john\_smith} \\ \mathrm{h} & = & 1.88 \end{bmatrix} \right) =$$
$$\begin{bmatrix} \mathrm{sit} = \begin{bmatrix} \mathrm{c} & = & \mathrm{Human} \\ \mathrm{x} & = & \mathrm{john\_smith} \\ \mathrm{h} & = & 1.88 \end{bmatrix} \\ \mathrm{sit\text{-}type} = \begin{bmatrix} \mathrm{c}_{tall} : \mathrm{tall(john\_smith)} \end{bmatrix} \end{bmatrix}$$

4.2 Vagueness

According to the above account, '*tall*' has a precise interpretation: given a degree of height and a comparison class, the threshold sharply determines whether tall applies or not. There are several ways in which one can account for vagueness—amongst others, by introducing perceptual uncertainty (possibly inaccurate sensor readings). Here, in line with Lassiter (2011), we opt for substituting the precise threshold with a noisy, probabilistic threshold. We consider the threshold to be a normal random variable, which can be represented by the parameters of its Gaussian distribution, the mean μ and the standard deviation σ (the noise width).[2]

To incorporate this modification into our approach, we update the tallness classifier κ_{tall} we had defined in (6) so that it now takes as parameters μ_{tall} and σ_{tall}, both of them dependent on the comparison class and hence of type Type $\rightarrow \mathbb{R}^+$. The output of the classifier is now a probability rather than a ptype such as $\mathrm{tall}(x)$ or $\neg\mathrm{tall}(x)$. Before indicating how this probability is computed, we give the type of the vague version of the classifier in (10) and the vague representation of the meaning of '*tall*' in (11).

$$\text{(10)}\quad \kappa_{tall} : (\mathrm{Type} \rightarrow \mathbb{R}^+, \mathrm{Type} \rightarrow \mathbb{R}^+, \mathrm{T}_{ctxt}) \rightarrow [0, 1]$$

(11)
$$\textbf{tall} = \begin{bmatrix} \mathrm{T}_{ctxt} = \begin{bmatrix} \mathrm{c} & : & \mathrm{Type} \\ \mathrm{x} & : & \mathrm{c} \\ \mathrm{h} & : & \mathbb{R}^+ \end{bmatrix} \\ \mu \quad = \mu_{tall} \\ \sigma \quad = \sigma_{tall} \\ \mathrm{f} \quad = \lambda r : \mathrm{T}_{ctxt}. \\ \qquad \begin{bmatrix} \mathrm{sit} = r \\ \mathrm{sit\text{-}type} = \begin{bmatrix} \mathrm{c}_{tall} : \mathrm{tall}(r.\mathrm{x}) \end{bmatrix} \\ \mathrm{prob} = \kappa_{tall}(\sigma, \mu, r) \end{bmatrix} \end{bmatrix}$$

---

[2] Which noise function may be the most appropriate is an empirical question we do not tackle in this paper. Our choice of Gaussian noise follows Schmidt et al. (2009)—see Section 5.1.

The output of the function **tall**.f is now a *probabilistic* Austinian proposition (Cooper et al., 2014). Like before, the proposition expresses a judgement that a situation sit is of a particular type. But here the judgement is probabilistic—it encodes the belief of an agent concerning the likelihood that sit is of a type where x counts as tall.

Since we take the noisy threshold to be a normal random variable, given a particular μ and σ, we can calculate the probability that the height r.h of individual r.x counts as tall as follows:

$$\kappa_{tall}(\mu, \sigma, r) = \frac{1}{2}\left[1 + \text{erf}\left(\frac{r.\text{h} - \mu(r.\text{c})}{\sigma(r.\text{c})\sqrt{2}}\right)\right]$$

Here erf is the error function, defined as[3]

$$\text{erf}(x) = \frac{2}{\sqrt{\pi}}\int_{t=0}^{x} e^{-t^2}\text{d}t$$

The error function defines a sigmoid shape (see Figure 1), in line with the upward monotonicity of '*tall*'. The output of $\kappa_{tall}(\mu, \sigma, r)$ corresponds to the probability that h will exceed the normal random threshold with mean μ and deviation σ.

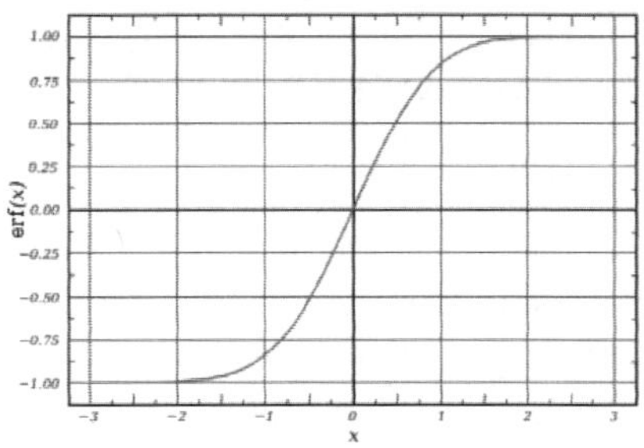

Figure 1: Plot of the error function.

Let us consider an example. Assume that we have $\mu_{tall}(\text{Human}) = 1.87$ and $\sigma_{tall}(\text{Human}) = 0.05$ (see Section 5.1 below for justification of the latter value). Let's also assume the same *ctxt* as above in (8). In this case, **tall**.f(*ctxt*) will compute as in (12), given that

$$\kappa_{tall}(\mu_{tall}, \sigma_{tall}, \begin{bmatrix}\text{c=Human}\\ \text{x=john\_smith}\\ \text{h=1.88}\end{bmatrix}) =$$

$$\frac{1}{2}\left[1 + \text{erf}\left(\frac{1.88 - 1.87}{0.05\sqrt{2}}\right)\right] = 0.579$$

[3]For an explanation of this standard definition, see `http://en.wikipedia.org/wiki/Error_function`, which is the source of the graph in Figure 1.

(12) $$\lambda r : \text{T}_{ctxt}. \begin{bmatrix}\text{sit} = r\\ \text{sit-type} = \begin{bmatrix}\text{c}_{tall} : \text{tall}(r.\text{x})\end{bmatrix}\\ \text{prob} = \kappa_{tall}(\mu_{tall}, \sigma_{tall}, r)\end{bmatrix}$$

$$(\begin{bmatrix}\text{c} & = & \text{Human}\\ \text{x} & = & \text{john\_smith}\\ \text{h} & = & 1.88\end{bmatrix}) =$$

$$\begin{bmatrix}\text{sit} = \begin{bmatrix}\text{c} & = & \text{Human}\\ \text{x} & = & \text{john\_smith}\\ \text{h} & = & 1.88\end{bmatrix}\\ \text{sit-type} = \begin{bmatrix}\text{c}_{tall} : \text{tall(john\_smith)}\end{bmatrix}\\ \text{prob} = 0.579\end{bmatrix}$$

This probability can now be used in further probabilistic reasoning, to decide whether to refer to an individual x as tall, or to evaluate someone else's utterance describing x is tall. For example, an agent may map different probabilities to different adjective qualifiers of tallness to yield compositional phrases such as '*sort of tall*', '*quite tall*', '*very tall*', '*extremely tall*', etc. The meanings of these composed adjectival phrases could specify probability ranges trained independently. Compositionality for vague perceptual meanings, and the interaction between compositionality and learning, is an exciting area for future research.[4]

5 Learning from Language Use

In this section we consider possibilities for computing the noisy threshold we have introduced in the previous section and discuss how such a threshold and the probabilistic judgements it gives rise to are updated with language use.

5.1 Computing the Noisy Threshold

We assume that agents keep track of judgements made by other agents. More concretely, for a vague scalar predicate like '*tall*', we assume that an agent will have at its disposal a set of *observations* consisting of entities of a particular type T (a comparison class such as *Human*) that have been judged to be tall, together with their observed heights. Judgements of tallness may vary across individuals—indeed, such variation (both inter- and intra-individual) is a hallmark of vague predicates. We use Ω^T_{tall} to refer to the set of heights of those entities $x : T$ that have been considered tall by some individual. From this agent-specific set of observations, which is constantly updated as the agent is exposed to new judgements by other individuals, we want to compute a noisy threshold,

[4]See Larsson (2013) for a sketch of compositionality for perceptual meaning.

which the agent uses to make her own judgements of tallness, as specified in (11).

Different functions can be used to compute μ_{tall} and σ_{tall} from Ω^{T}_{tall}. What constitutes an appropriate function is an empirical matter and what the most suitable function is possibly varies across predicates (what may apply to '*tall*' may not be suitable for '*dark*' or '*expensive*', for example). Hardly any work has been done on trying to identify how the threshold is computed from experience. A notable exception, however, is the work of Schmidt et al. (2009), who collect judgements of people asked to indicate which items are tall given distributions of items of different heights. Schmidt and colleagues then propose different probabilistic models to account for the data and compare their output to the human judgements. They explore two types of models: threshold-based models and category-based or cluster models. The best performing models within these two types perform equally well and the study does not identify any advantages of one type over the other one. Since we have chosen threshold models as our case-study, we focus our attention on those here.

Each of the threshold models tested by Schmidt et al. (2009) corresponds to a possible way of computing the mean μ_{tall} of a noisy threshold from a set of observations. The best performing threshold model in their study is the *relative height by range* model, where (in our notation):

(13) relative height by range (RH-R): $\mu_{tall}(T) = \max(\Omega^{T}_{tall}) - k \cdot (\max(\Omega^{T}_{tall}) - \min(\Omega^{T}_{tall}))$

Here $\max(\Omega^{T}_{tall})$ and $\min(\Omega^{T}_{tall})$ stand for the maximum and the minimum height, respectively, of the items that have been judged to be tall by some individual. According to this threshold model, any item within the top $k\%$ of the range of heights that have been judged to be tall counts as tall. The model includes two parameters, k and a noise-width parameter that in our approach corresponds to σ_{tall}. Schmidt et al. (2009) report that the best fit of their data was obtained with $k = 29\%$ and $\sigma_{tall} = 0.05$.

5.2 Updating Vague Meanings

We now want to specify how the vague meaning of '*tall*' is updated as an agent is exposed to new judgements via language use. Our setting so far offers a straightforward solution to this: If a new entity $x : T$ with height h is referred to as tall, the agent adds h to its set of observations Ω^{T}_{tall} and recomputes μ_{tall}(Human), for instance using RH-R as defined in (13). If RH-H is used, ideally the value of k and σ_{tall} should be (re)estimated from Ω^{T}_{tall}. For the sake of simplicity, however, here we will assume that these two parameters take the values experimentally validated by Schmidt et al. (2009) and are kept constant. An update to μ_{tall} will take place if it is the case that $h > \max(\Omega^{T}_{tall})$ or $h < \min(\Omega^{T}_{tall})$. This in turn will trigger un update to the probability outputted by κ_{tall}.

As an example, let us assume that our initial set of observations is $\Omega^{Human}_{tall} = \{1.87, 1.92, 1, 90, 1.75, 1.80\}$ (recall this corresponds to the perceived heights of individuals that have been described as tall by some agent). This means that $\max(\Omega^{Human}_{tall}) = 1.92$ and $\min(\Omega^{Human}_{tall}) = 1.75$. Hence, given (13):

(14) $\mu_{tall}(\text{Human}) =$
$1.92 - 0.29 \cdot (1.92 - 1.75) = 1.87$

Let's assume we now make an observation where a person of height 1.72 is judged to be tall. This will mean that the set of observations is now $\Omega^{Human}_{tall} = \{1.87, 1.92, 1, 90, 1.75, 1.80, 1.72\}$ and consequently $\min(\Omega^{Human}_{tall}) = 1.72$, which yields an updated mean of the noisy threshold:

(15) $\mu_{tall}(\text{Human}) =$
$1.92 - 0.29 \cdot (1.92 - 1.72) = 1.862$

If we were to re-evaluate John Smith's tallness in light of this observation, we would get a new probability 0.64 that he is tall (in contrast to the earlier probability of 0.579 given in (12)).

5.3 Possible Extensions

The set of observations Ω^{Human}_{tall} can be derived from a set of Austinian propositions corresponding to instances where people have been judged to be tall. To update from an Austinian proposition p we simply add p.sit.h to Ω^{tall}_{Human} and recompute $\mu_{tall}(p.\text{c})$. Note that we are here treating these Austinian propositions as non-probabilistic. This seems to make sense since an addressee does not have direct access to the probability associated with the judgement of the speaker. If we were to take these probabilities into account (for instance, the use of a hedge in '*sort of tall*' may be used to make inferences about such probabilities), and if those probabilities are not always 1, we would need a different way of computing μ_{tall} than the one specified so far.

Somewhat related to the point above, note that in our approach we treat all judgements equally, i.e., we do not distinguish between possible different levels of trustworthiness amongst speakers. An agent who is told that an entity with height h is tall adds that observation to its knowledge base without questioning the reliability of the speaker. This is clearly a simplification. For instance, there is developmental evidence showing that children are more sensitive to reliable speakers than to unreliable ones during language acquisition (Scofield and Behrend, 2008).

6 Other Approaches

Within the literature in formal semantics, Lassiter (2011) has put forward a proposal that extends in interesting ways earlier work by Barker (2002) and shares some aspects with the account we have presented here. Operating in a probabilistic version of classical possible-worlds semantics, Lassiter assumes a probability distribution over a set of possible worlds and a probability distribution over a set of possible languages. Each possible language represents a precise interpretation of a predicate like '*tall*': $\textbf{tall}_1 = \lambda x.x$'s height $\geq$ 5'6"; $\textbf{tall}_2 = \lambda x.x$'s height $\geq$ 5'7"; and so forth. Lassiter thus treats "metalinguistic belief" (representing an agent's knowledge of the meaning of words) in terms of probability distributions over precise languages. Since each precise interpretation of '*tall*' includes a given threshold, this can be seen as defining a probability distribution over possible thresholds, similarly to the noisy threshold we have used in our account. Lassiter, however, is not concerned with learning.

Within the computational semantics literature, DeVault and Stone (2004) describe an implemented system in a drawing domain that is able to interpret and execute instructions including vague scalar predicates such as '*Make a small circle*'. Their approach makes use of degree-based semantics, but does not take into account comparison classes. This is possible in their drawing domain since the kind of geometric figures it includes (squares, rectangles, circles) do not have intrinsic expected properties (size, length, etc). Their focus is on modelling how the threshold for a predicate such as '*small*' is updated during an interaction with the system given the local discourse context. For instance, if the initial context just contains a square, the size of that square is taken to be the standard of comparison for the predicate '*small*'. The user's utterance '*Make a small circle*' is then interpreted as asking for a circle of an arbitrary size that is smaller than the square.

In our characterisation of the context-sensitivity of vague gradable adjectives in Section 4.1, we have focused on their dependence on general comparison classes corresponding to types of entities (such as Human, Woman, etc) with expected properties such as height. Thus, in contrast to DeVault and Stone (2004), who focus on the local context of discourse, we have focused on what could be called the *global* context (an agent's experience regarding types of entities and their expected properties). How these two types of context interact remains an open question, which we plan to explore in our future work (see Kyburg and Morreau (2000), Kemp et al. (2007), and Fernández (2009) for pointers in this direction).

7 Conclusions and future work

Traditional formal semantics theories postulate a fixed, abstract interpretation function that mediates between natural language expressions and the world, but fall short of specifying how this function is determined or modified dynamically by experience. In this paper we have presented a characterisation of the semantics of vague scalar predicates such as '*tall*' that clarifies how their context-dependent meaning and their vague character are connected with perceptual information, and we have also shown how this low-level perceptual information (here, real-valued readings from a height sensor) connects to high level logical semantics (ptypes) in a probabilistic framework. In addition, we have put forward a proposal for explaining how the meaning of vague scalar adjectives like '*tall*' is dynamically updated through language use.

Tallness is a function of a single value (height), and is in this sense a uni-dimensional predicate. Indeed, most linguistic approaches to vagueness focus on uni-dimensional predicates such as '*tall*'. However, many vague predicates are *multi-dimensional*, including nouns for positions ('*above*'), shapes ('*hexagonal*'), and colours ('*green*'), amongst many others. Together with compositionality (mentioned at the end of Section 4.2), generalisation of the present account to multi-dimensional vague predicates is an interesting area of future development.

Acknowledgements

The first author acknowledges the support of the Netherlands Organisation for Scientific Research (NWO) and thanks the Centre for Language Technology at the University of Gothenburg for generously funding research visits that led to the work presented in this paper. The second author acknowledges the support of Vetenskapsrådet, project 2009-1569, Semantic analysis of interaction and coordination in dialogue (SAICD); the Department of Philosophy, Linguistics, and Theory of Science; and the Centre for Language Technology at the University of Gothenburg.

References

Chris Barker. 2002. The dynamics of vagueness. *Linguistics & Philosophy*, 25(1):1–36.

Patrick Blackburn and Johan Bos. 2005. *Representation and Inference for Natural Language: A First Course in Computational Semantics*. CSLI Publications.

Robin Cooper and Jonathan Ginzburg. 2011. Negation in dialogue. In *Proceedings of the 15th Workshop on the Semantics and Pragmatics of Dialogue (SemDial 2011)*, Los Angeles (USA).

Robin Cooper, Simon Dobnik, Shalom Lappin, and Staffan Larsson. 2014. A probabilistic rich type theory for semantic interpretation. In *Proceedings of the EACL Workshop on Type Theory and Natural Language Semantics (TTNLS)*.

Robin Cooper. 2005a. Austinian truth, attitudes and type theory. *Research on Language and Computation*, 3(4):333–362, December.

Robin Cooper. 2005b. Austinian truth, attitudes and type theory. *Research on Language and Computation*, 3:333–362.

Robin Cooper. 2010. Generalized quantifiers and clarification content. In Paweł Łupkowski and Matthew Purver, editors, *Aspects of Semantics and Pragmatics of Dialogue. SemDial 2010, 14th Workshop on the Semantics and Pragmatics of Dialogue*, Poznań. Polish Society for Cognitive Science.

Robin Cooper. 2012. Type theory and semantics in flux. In Ruth Kempson, Nicholas Asher, and Tim Fernando, editors, *Handbook of the Philosophy of Science*, volume 14: Philosophy of Linguistics. Elsevier BV. General editors: Dov M. Gabbay, Paul Thagard and John Woods.

David DeVault and Matthew Stone. 2004. Interpreting vague utterances in context. In *Proceedings of the 20th International Conference on Computational Linguistics (COLING'04)*, pages 1247–1253.

Simon Dobnik, Robin Cooper, and Staffan Larsson. 2013. Modelling language, action, and perception in type theory with records. In *Constraint Solving and Language Processing*, Lecture Notes in Computer Science, pages 70–91. Springer.

Raquel Fernández. 2009. Salience and feature variability in definite descriptions with positive-form vague adjectives. In *Workshop on the Production of Referring Expressions: Bridging the gap between computational and empirical approaches to reference (CogSci'09)*.

Jonathan Ginzburg. 2012. *The Interactive Stance*. Oxford University Press.

Hans Kamp. 1975. Two theories of adjectives. In E. Keenan, editor, *Formal Semantics of Natural Language*, pages 123–155. Cambridge University Press.

John Kelleher, Fintan Costello, and Josef van Genabith. 2005. Dynamically structuring, updating and interrelating representations of visual and linguistic discourse context. *Artificial Intelligence*, 167(1):62–102.

Charles Kemp, Amy Perfors, and Joshua B. Tenenbaum. 2007. Learning overhypotheses with hierarchical bayesian models. *Developmental Science*, 10(3):307–321.

Christopher Kennedy and Louise McNally. 2005. Scale structure, degree modification, and the semantics of gradable predicates. *Language*, pages 345–381.

Christopher Kennedy. 2007. Vagueness and grammar: The semantics of relative and absolute gradable adjectives. *Linguistics and Philosophy*, 30(1):1–45.

Ewan Klein. 1980. A semantics for positive and comparative adjectives. *Linguistics and Philosophy*, 4:1–45.

Alice Kyburg and Michael Morreau. 2000. Fitting words: Vague language in context. *Linguistics and Philosophy*, 23:577–597.

Staffan Larsson. 2009. Detecting and learning from lexical innovation in dialogue: a ttr account. In *Proceedings of the 5th International Conference on Generative Approaches to the Lexicon*.

Staffan Larsson. 2013. Formal semantics for perceptual classification. *Journal of Logic and Computation*.

Dan Lassiter. 2011. Vagueness as probabilistic linguistic knowledge. In R. Nowen, R. van Rooij, U. Sauerland, and H. C. Schmitz, editors, *Vagueness in Communication*. Springer.

Barbara Partee. 1989. Possible worlds in model-theoretic semantics: A linguistic perspective. In S. Allen, editor, *Possible Worlds in Humanities, Arts and Sciences*, pages 93–123. Walter de Gruyter.

Manfred Pinkal. 1979. Semantics from different points of view. In R. Bäurle, U. Egli, and A. von Stechow, editors, *How to Refer with Vague Descriptions*, pages 32–50. Springer-Verlag.

Manfred Pinkal. 1995. *Logic and lexicon: the semantics of the indefinite*, volume 56 of *Studies in Linguistics and Philosophy*. Springer.

François Portet, Ehud Reiter, Albert Gatt, Jim Hunter, Somayajulu Sripada, Yvonne Freer, and Cindy Sykes. 2009. Automatic generation of textual summaries from neonatal intensive care data. *Artificial Intelligence*, 173(7):789–816.

Matthew Purver, Julian Hough, and Eleni Gregoromichelaki. 2014. Dialogue and compound contributions. In A. Stent and S. Bangalore, editors, *Natural Language Generation in Interactive Systems*. Cambridge University Press.

Ehud Reiter, Somayajulu Sripada, Jim Hunter, Jin Yu, and Ian Davy. 2005. Choosing words in computer-generated weather forecasts. *Artificial Intelligence*, 167(1):137–169.

Deb Roy. 2005. Semiotic schemas: A framework for grounding language in action and perception. *Artificial Intelligence*, 167(1):170–205.

L.A. Schmidt, N.D. Goodman, D. Barner, and J.B. Tenenbaum. 2009. How tall is tall? compositionality, statistics, and gradable adjectives. In *Proceedings of the 31st annual conference of the cognitive science society*.

Jason Scofield and Douglas A Behrend. 2008. Learning words from reliable and unreliable speakers. *Cognitive Development*, 23(2):278–290.

Jeffrey Mark Siskind. 2001. Grounding the lexical semantics of verbs in visual perception using force dynamics and event logic. *Journal of Artificial Intelligence Research*, (15):31–90.

Danijel Skocaj, M Janicek, Matej Kristan, Geert-Jan M Kruijff, Aleš Leonardis, Pierre Lison, Alen Vrecko, and Michael Zillich. 2010. A basic cognitive system for interactive continuous learning of visual concepts. In *Proceeding of the Workshop on Interactive Communication for Autonomous Intelligent Robots*, pages 30–36.

Stephanie Solt. 2011. Notes on the comparison class. In *Vagueness in communication*, pages 189–206. Springer.

Luc Steels. 2003. Evolving grounded communication for robots. *Trends in cognitive sciences*, 7(7):308–312.

Contrasting Syntagmatic and Paradigmatic Relations: Insights from Distributional Semantic Models

Gabriella Lapesa[3,1]
[1]Universität Osnabrück
Institut für
Kognitionswissenschaft
glapesa@uos.de

Stefan Evert[2]
[2]FAU Erlangen-Nürnberg
Professur für
Korpuslinguistik
stefan.evert@fau.de

Sabine Schulte im Walde[3]
[3]Universität Stuttgart
Institut für Maschinelle
Sprachverarbeitung
schulte@ims.uni-stuttgart.de

Abstract

This paper presents a large-scale evaluation of bag-of-words distributional models on two datasets from priming experiments involving syntagmatic and paradigmatic relations. We interpret the variation in performance achieved by different settings of the model parameters as an indication of which aspects of distributional patterns characterize these types of relations. Contrary to what has been argued in the literature (Rapp, 2002; Sahlgren, 2006) – that bag-of-words models based on second-order statistics mainly capture paradigmatic relations and that syntagmatic relations need to be gathered from first-order models – we show that second-order models perform well on both paradigmatic and syntagmatic relations if their parameters are properly tuned. In particular, our results show that size of the context window and dimensionality reduction play a key role in differentiating DSM performance on paradigmatic vs. syntagmatic relations.

1 Introduction

Distributional takes on the representation and acquisition of word meaning rely on the assumption that words with similar meaning tend to occur in similar contexts: this assumption, known as *distributional hypothesis*, has been first proposed by Harris (1954). Distributional Semantic Models (henceforth, DSMs) are computational models that operationalize the distributional hypothesis; they produce semantic representations for words in the form of distributional vectors recording patterns of co-occurrence in large samples of language data (Sahlgren, 2006; Baroni and Lenci, 2010; Turney and Pantel, 2010). Comparison between distributional vectors allows the identification of shared contexts as an empirical correlate of the semantic similarity between the target words. As noted in Sahlgren (2008), the notion of semantic similarity applied in distributional approaches to meaning is an easy target of criticism, as it is employed to capture a wide range of semantic relations, such as synonymy, antonymy, hypernymy, up to topical relatedness.

The study presented in this paper contributes to the debate concerning the nature of the semantic representations built by DSMs, and it does so by comparing the performance of several DSMs in a classification task conducted on priming data and involving paradigmatic and syntagmatic relations. Paradigmatic relations hold between words that occur in similar contexts; they are also called relations *in absentia* (Sahlgren, 2006) because paradigmatically related words do not co-occur. Examples of paradigmatic relations are *synonyms* (e.g., *frigid–cold*) and *antonyms* (e.g., *cold–hot*). Syntagmatic relations hold between words that co-occur (relations *in praesentia*) and therefore exhibit a similar distribution across contexts. Typical examples of syntagmatic relations are phrasal associates (e.g., *help–wanted*) and syntactic collocations (e.g., *dog–bark*).

Distributional modeling has already tackled the issue of paradigmatic and syntagmatic relations (Sahlgren, 2006; Rapp, 2002). Key contributions of the present work are the scope of its evaluation (in terms of semantic relations and model parameters) and the new perspective on paradigmatic vs. syntagmatic models provided by our results.

Concerning the scope of the evaluation, this is the first study in which the comparison involves such a wide range of semantic relations (*paradigmatic:* synonyms, antonyms and co-hyponyms; *syntagmatic:* syntactic collocations, backward and forward phrasal associates). Moreover, our evaluation covers a large number of DSM parameters: source corpus, size and direction of the context window, criteria for feature selection, feature

*Proceedings of the Third Joint Conference on Lexical and Computational Semantics (*SEM 2014)*, pages 160–170,
Dublin, Ireland, August 23-24 2014.

weighting, dimensionality reduction and index of distributional relatedness. We consider the variation in performance achieved by different parameter settings as a cue towards characteristic aspects of specific relations (or groups of relations).

Our work also differs from previous studies (Sahlgren, 2006; Rapp, 2002) in its focus on second-order models. We aim to show that they are able to capture both paradigmatic and syntagmatic relations with appropriate parameter settings. In addition, this focus provides a uniform experimental design for the evaluation. For example, parameters like window size and directionality apply to bag-of-words DSMs and collocation lists but not to term-context models; dimensionality reduction, whose effect has not yet been explored systematically in the context of syntagmatic and paradigmatic relations, is not applicable to collocation lists.

This paper is structured as follows. Section 2 summarizes previous work. Section 3 describes the experimental setup, in terms of task, datasets and evaluated parameters. Section 4 introduces our model selection methodology. Section 5 presents the results of our evaluation study. Section 6 summarizes main findings and sketches ongoing and future work.

2 Previous Work

In this section we discuss previous work relevant to the distributional modeling of paradigmatic and syntagmatic relations. For space constraints, we focus only on two studies (Rapp, 2002; Sahlgren, 2006) in which the two classes of relations are compared at a global level, and not on studies that are concerned with specific semantic relations, e.g., *synonymy* (Edmonds and Hirst, 2002; Curran, 2003), *hypernymy* (Weeds et al., 2004; Lenci and Benotto, 2012) or syntagmatic predicate preferences (McCarthy and Carroll, 2003; Erk et al., 2010), etc.

In previous studies, the comparison of syntagmatic and paradigmatic relations has been implemented in terms of an opposition between different classes of corpus-based models: term-context models (words as targets, documents or context regions as features) vs. bag-of-words models (words as targets and features) in Sahlgren (2006); collocation lists vs. bag-of-words models in Rapp (2002). Given the high terminological variation in the literature, in this paper we will adopt the labels *syntagmatic* and *paradigmatic* to characterize different types of semantic relations, and we will use the labels *first-order* and *second-order* to characterize corpus-based models with respect to the kind of co-occurrence information they encode. We will refer to collocation lists and term-document DSMs as *first-order models*, and to bag-of-words DSMs as *second-order models*[1].

Rapp (2002) integrates first-order (co-occurrence lists) and second-order (bag-of-words DSMs) information to distinguish syntagmatic and paradigmatic relations. Under the assumption that paradigmatically related words will be found among the closest neighbors of a target word in the DSM space and that paradigmatically and syntagmatically related words will be intermingled in the list of collocates of the target word, Rapp proposes to exploit a comparison of the most salient collocates and the nearest DSM neighbors to distinguish between the two types of relations.

Sahlgren (2006) compares term-context and bag-of-words DSMs in a number of tasks involving syntagmatic and paradigmatic relations. First, a comparison between the thesaurus entries for target words (containing both paradigmatically and syntagmatically related words) and neighbors in the distributional spaces is conducted. It shows that, while term-context DSMs produce both syntagmatically and paradigmatically related words, the nearest neighbors in a bag-of-words DSM mainly provide paradigmatic information. Bag-of-words models also performed better than term-context models in predicting association norms, in the TOEFL multiple-choice synonymy task and in the prediction of antonyms (although the difference in performance was less significant here). Last, word neighborhoods are analysed in terms of their part-of-speech distribution. Sahlgren (2006) observes that bag-of-words spaces contain more neighbors with the same part of speech as the target than term-context spaces. He concludes that bag-of-words spaces privilege paradigmatic relations, based on the assumption that paradigmatically related word pairs belong to the same part of speech, while this is not necessarily the case for syntagmatically related word pairs.

[1]Term-document models encode first-order information because dot products between row vectors are related to co-occurrence counts of the corresponding words (within documents). More precisely, for a binary term-document matrix, cosine similarity is identical to the square root of the MI^2 association measure. Please note that our terminology differs from that of Schütze (1998) and Peirsman et al. (2008).

Summing up, in both Rapp (2002) and Sahlgren (2006) it is claimed that second-order models perform poorly in predicting syntagmatic relations. However, neither of those studies involves datasets containing *exclusively syntagmatic relations*, as the evaluation focuses either on paradigmatic relations (TOEFL multiple choice test, antonymy test) or on resources containing both types of relations (thesauri, association norms).

3 Experimental Setting

3.1 Evaluation Task and Data

In this study, bag-of-words DSMs are evaluated on two datasets containing experimental items from two priming studies. Each item is a word triple (target, consistent prime, inconsistent prime) with a particular semantic relation between target and consistent prime. Following previous work on modeling priming effects as a comparison between prime-target pairs (McDonald and Brew, 2004; Padó and Lapata, 2007; Herdağdelen et al., 2009), we evaluate our models in a classification task. The goal is to identify the consistent prime on the basis of its distributional relatedness to the target: if a particular DSM (i.e., a certain parameter combination) is sensitive to a specific relation (or group of relations), we expect the consistent primes to be closer to the target in semantic space than the inconsistent ones.

The first dataset is derived from the **Semantic Priming Project** (SPP) (Hutchison et al., 2013). To the best of our knowledge, our study represents the first evaluation of bag-of-words DSMs on items from this dataset. The original data consist of 1661 word triples (target, consistent prime, inconsistent prime) collected within a large-scale project aiming at characterizing English words in terms of a set of lexical and associative/semantic characteristics, along with behavioral data from visual lexical decision and naming studies[2]. We manually discarded all triples containing proper nouns, adverbs or inflected words. We then selected five subsets involving different semantic relations, namely: **synonyms** (SYN), 436 triples (example of a consistent prime and target: *frigid–cold*); **antonyms** (ANT): 135 triples (e.g., *hot–cold*); **cohyponyms** (COH): 159 triples (e.g., *table–chair*); **forward phrasal associates** (FPA): 144 triples (e.g., *help–wanted*); **backward phrasal associates** (BPA): 89 triples (e.g., *wanted–help*).

The second priming dataset is the **Generalized Event Knowledge** dataset (henceforth GEK), already evaluated in Lapesa and Evert (2013): a collection of 402 triples (target, consistent prime, inconsistent prime) from three priming studies conducted to demonstrate that event knowledge is responsible for facilitation of the processing of words that denote events and their participants. The first study was conducted by Ferretti et al. (2001), who found that verbs facilitate the processing of nouns denoting prototypical participants in the depicted event and of adjectives denoting features of prototypical participants. The study covered five thematic relations: agent (e.g., *pay–customer*), patient, feature of the patient, instrument, location. The second study (McRae et al., 2005) focussed on priming from nouns to verbs. It involved four relations: agent (e.g., *reporter–interview*), patient, instrument, location. The third study (Hare et al., 2009) investigated priming from nouns to nouns, referring to participants of the same event or the event itself. The dataset involves seven relations: event-people (e.g., *trial–judge*), event-thing, location-living, location-thing, people-instrument, instrument-people, instrument-thing.

In the presentation of our results we group synonyms with antonyms and cohyponyms from SPP as paradigmatic relations, and the entire GEK dataset with backward and forward phrasal associates from SPP as syntagmatic relations.

3.2 Evaluated Parameters

DSMs evaluated in this paper belong to the class of bag-of-words models. We defined a large vocabulary of target words (27522 lemma types) containing all the items from the evaluated datasets as well as items from other state-of-the-art evaluation studies (Baroni and Lenci, 2010; Baroni and Lenci, 2011). Context words were filtered by part-of-speech (nouns, verbs, adjectives, and adverbs). Distributional models were built using the UCS toolkit[3] and the `wordspace` package for R[4]. The following parameters have been evaluated:

- **Source corpus** (abbreviated as *corpus* in plots 1-4): We compiled DSMs from three corpora often used in DSM evaluation studies and that

[2]The dataset is available at http://spp.montana.edu/

[3]http://www.collocations.de/software.html

[4]http://r-forge.r-project.org/projects/wordspace/

differ in both size and quality: British National Corpus[5], ukWaC, and WaCkypedia_EN[6].

- **Size of the context window** (*win.size*): As this parameter quantifies the amount of shared context involved in the computation of similarity, we expect it to be crucial in determining whether syntagmatic or paradigmatic relations are captured. We therefore use a finer granularity for window size than Lapesa and Evert (2013): 1, 2, 4, 8 and 16 words.
- **Directionality of the context window** (*win.direction*): When collecting co-occurrence information from the source corpora, we use either a directed window (i.e., separate frequency counts for co-occurrences of a context term to the left and to the right of the target term) or an undirected window (i.e., no distinction between left and right context when collecting co-occurrence counts).
- **Context selection**: From the full co-occurrence matrix collected as described above, we select dimensions (columns) according to the following parameters:
  - **Criterion for context selection** (*criterion*): We select the top-ranked dimensions either according to marginal frequency (i.e., we use the most frequent words as context terms) or number of nonzero co-occurrence counts (i.e., we use the context terms that co-occur with the highest number of targets).
  - **Number of context dimensions** (*context.dim*): We select the top-ranked 5000, 10000, 20000, 50000 or 100000 dimensions, according to the criterion above.
- **Feature scoring** (*score*): Co-occurrence counts are weighted using one of the following association measures: frequency, Dice coefficient, simple log-likelihood, Mutual Information, t-score, z-score or tf.idf.[7]
- **Feature transformation** (*transformation*): A transformation function may be applied to reduce the skewness of feature scores. Possible transformations are: none, square root, logarithmic and sigmoid.
- **Distance metric** (*metric*): We apply cosine distance (i.e., angle between vectors) or Manhattan distance.
- **Dimensionality reduction**: We apply singular value decomposition in order to project distributional vectors to a relatively small number of latent dimensions and compare the results to the unreduced runs[8]. For the SVD-based models, there are two additional parameters:
  - **Number of latent dimensions** (*red.dim*): Whether to use the first 100, 300, 500, 700 or 900 latent dimensions from the SVD analysis.
  - **Number of skipped dimensions** (*dim.skip*): When selecting latent dimensions, we optionally skip the first 50 or 100 SVD components. This parameter was inspired by Bullinaria and Levy (2012), who found that discarding the initial components of the reduced matrix, i.e. the SVD components with highest variance, improves evaluation results.
- **Index of distributional relatedness** (*rel.index*): We propose two alternative ways of quantifying the degree of relatedness between two words *a* and *b* represented in a DSM. The first option (and standard in distributional modeling) is to compute the *distance* (cosine or Manhattan) between the vectors of *a* and *b*. The second option, proposed in this work, is based on *neighbor rank*, i.e. we determine the rank of the target among the nearest neighbors of each prime. We expect that the target will occur in a higher position among the neighbors of the consistent prime than among those of the inconsistent prime. Since this corresponds to a lower numeric rank value for the consistent prime, we can treat neighbor rank as a measure of dissimilarity. Neighbor rank is particularly interesting as an index of relatedness because, unlike a distance metric, it can capture asymmetry effects[9].

4 Methodology

In our evaluation study, we tested all the possible combinations of the parameters listed in section

[5]http://www.natcorp.ox.ac.uk/

[6]Both ukWaC and WaCkypedia_EN are available at: wacky.sslmit.unibo.it/doku.php?id=corpora

[7]See Evert (2008) for a description of these measures and details on the calculation of association scores. Note that we compute "sparse" versions of the association measures (where negative values are clamped to zero) in order to preserve the sparseness of the co-occurrence matrix.

[8]For efficiency reasons, we use randomized SVD (Halko et al., 2009) with a sufficiently high oversampling factor to ensure a good approximation.

[9]Note that our use of neighbor rank is fully consistent with the experimental design (primes are shown before targets). See Lapesa and Evert (2013) for an analysis of the performance of neighbor rank as a predictor of priming and discussion of the implications of using rank in cognitive modeling.

3.2, resulting in a total of 537600 different model runs (33600 in the setting without dimensionality reduction, 504000 in the dimensionality-reduced setting). The models were generated and evaluated on a large HPC cluster within approx. 4 weeks.

Our methodology for model selection follows the proposal of Lapesa and Evert (2013), who consider DSM parameters as predictors of model performance. We analyze the influence of individual parameters and their interactions using general linear models with performance (percent accuracy) as a dependent variable and the model parameters as independent variables, including all two-way interactions. Analysis of variance – which is straightforward for our full factorial design – is used to quantify the importance of each parameter or interaction. Robust optimal parameter settings are identified with the help of effect displays (Fox, 2003), which marginalize over all the parameters not shown in a plot and thus allow an intuitive interpretation of the effect sizes of categorical variables irrespective of the dummy coding scheme.

For each dataset, a separate linear model was fitted. The results are reported and compared in section 5. Table 1 lists the global goodness-of-fit (R^2) on each dataset, for the reduced and unreduced runs. Despite some variability across relations and between unreduced and reduced runs, the R^2 values are always high ($\geq 75\%$), showing that the linear model explains a large part of the observed performance differences. It is therefore justified to base our analysis on the linear models.

Relation	Dataset	Unreduced	Reduced
Syntagmatic	GEK	93%	87%
Syntagmatic	FPA	90%	79%
Syntagmatic	BPA	88%	77%
Paradigmatic	SYN	92%	85%
Paradigmatic	COH	89%	75%
Paradigmatic	ANT	89%	76%

Table 1: Evaluation, Global R^2

5 Results

In this section, we present the results of our study. We begin by looking at the distribution of accuracy for different datasets, and by comparing reduced and unreduced experimental runs in terms of minimum, maximum and mean performance.

The results displayed in table 2 show that dimensionality reduction with SVD improves the performance of the models for all datasets but GEK. We conclude that the information lost by applying SVD reduction (namely, meaningful distributional features, which are replaced by the generalization encoded in the reduced dimensions) is irrelevant to other tasks, but crucial for modeling the relations in the GEK dataset. This interpretation is consistent with the detrimental effect of SVD in tasks involving vector composition reported in the literature (Baroni and Zamparelli, 2010).

Relation	Dataset	Unreduced			Reduced		
		Min	Max	Mean	Min	Max	Mean
Syntagmatic	GEK	54.8	98.4	86.6	48.0	97.0	80.8
Syntagmatic	FPA	41.0	98.0	82.3	43.0	98.6	82.1
Syntagmatic	BPA	49.4	97.7	83.8	41.6	98.9	83.9
Paradigmatic	SYN	54.8	98.4	86.6	57.3	99.0	88.2
Paradigmatic	COH	49.0	100.0	92.6	54.3	100.0	94.0
Paradigmatic	ANT	69.6	100.0	94.2	57.8	100.0	94.3

Table 2: Distribution of Accuracy

5.1 Importance of Parameters

To obtain further insights into DSM performance we explore the effect of specific model parameters, comparing syntagmatic vs. paradigmatic relations and reduced vs. unreduced runs.

In order to establish a ranking of the parameters according to their importance wrt. model performance, we use a feature ablation approach. The ablation value for a given parameter is the proportion of variance (R^2) explained by this parameter together with all its interactions, corresponding to the reduction in adjusted R^2 of the linear model fit if the parameter were left out. In other words, it allows us to find out whether a certain parameter has a substantial effect on model performance (on top of all other parameters). Figures 1 to 4 display the feature ablation values of all the evaluated parameters in the unreduced and reduced setting, for paradigmatic and syntagmatic relations. Parameters are ranked according to their average feature ablation values in each setting.

Two parameters, namely **feature score** and **feature transformation**, are consistently crucial in determining DSM performance, both in reduced and unreduced runs, and for both paradigmatic and syntagmatic relations. In the next section we will show that it is possible to identify optimal (or nearly optimal) values for those parameters that are constant across relations.

A comparison of figures 1 and 2 with figures 3 and 4 allows us to identify parameters that lose or gain explanatory power when SVD comes into play. Feature ablation shows that the effect of the **index of distributional relatedness** is substantially smaller in the SVD-reduced runs, but this parameter still plays an important role. On the other hand, two parameters gain explanatory power in a

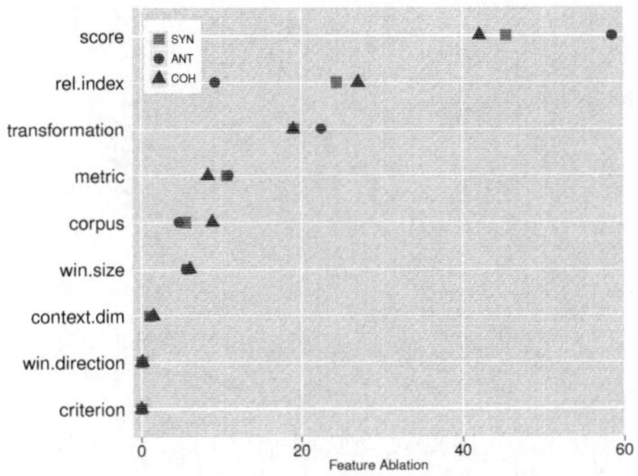

Figure 1: Paradigmatic, unreduced

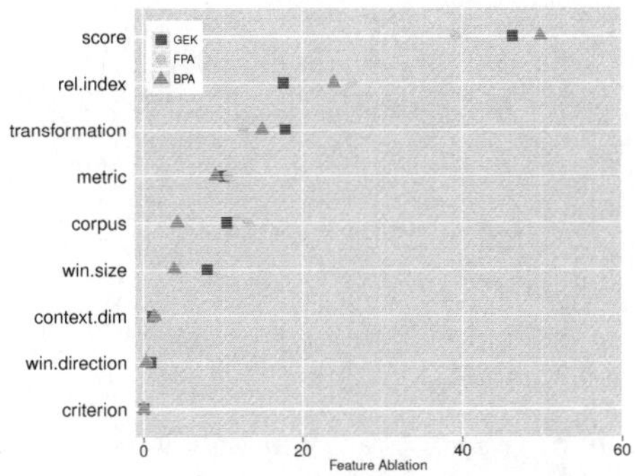

Figure 2: Syntagmatic, unreduced

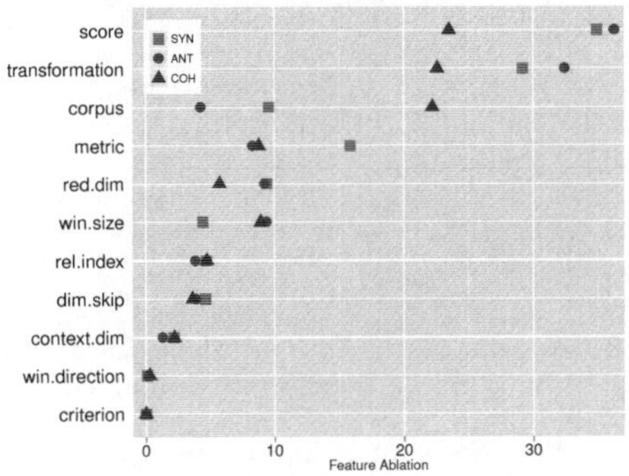

Figure 3: Paradigmatic, reduced

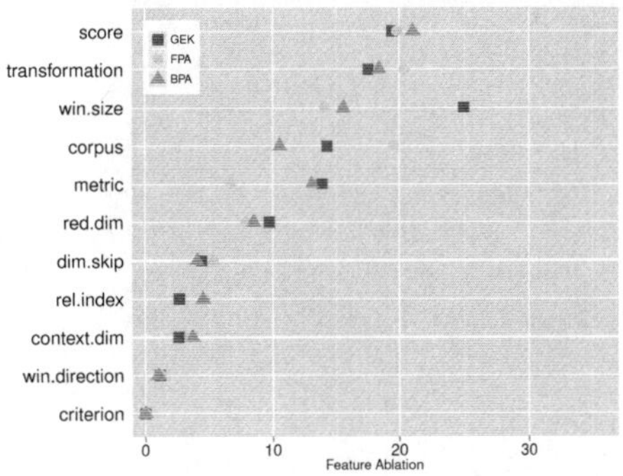

Figure 4: Syntagmatic, reduced

SVD-reduced setting: the **size of the context window** and the **source corpus**. Optimal values are discussed in section 5.2.

Three parameters consistently have little or no explanatory power: **directionality of the context window**, **criterion for context selection** and **number of context dimensions**.

We conclude this section by comparing relations within groups. Within paradigmatic relations, we note a significant drop in explanatory power for the **relatedness index** when it comes to antonyms. Within syntagmatic relations, the **size of the context window** appears to be more crucial on the GEK dataset than it is for FPA and BPA: in the next section, the analysis of the best choices for this parameter will provide a clue for the interpretation of this opposition.

5.2 Best Parameter Values

In this section, we identify the best parameter values for syntagmatic and paradigmatic relations by inspecting partial effects plots[10]. Our discussion starts from the parameters that contribute to the leading topic of this paper, namely the comparison between syntagmatic and paradigmatic relations: window size, parameters related to dimensionality reduction, and relatedness index.

As already anticipated in the feature ablation analysis, the **size of the context window** plays a crucial role in contrasting syntagmatic and paradigmatic relations, as well as different relations within those general groups. The plots in figures 5 and 6 display its partial effect for paradigmatic relations in the unreduced and reduced settings, respectively. The plots in figures 7 and 8 display its partial effect for syntagmatic relations. When no dimensionality reduction is involved, a very small context window (i.e., one word) is sufficient for all paradigmatic relations, and DSM performance decreases as soon as we enlarge the context window. The picture changes when applying dimensionality reduction: a 4-word window is a robust choice for all paradigmatic relations (although ANT show a further increase in performance with an 8-word window), even in the SYN task that is traditionally associated with very small windows of 1 or 2 words (cf. Sahlgren (2006)).

A significant interaction between window size and number of skipped dimensions (not shown for reasons of space) sheds further light on this matter. Without skipping SVD dimensions, the reduced models achieve optimal performance for a 2-word window and degrade more (COH) or less (ANT)

[10]The partial effect plots in figures 5 to 12 display parameter values on the x-axis and their effect size in terms of predicted accuracy on the y-axis (see section 4 for more details concerning the calculation of effect size).

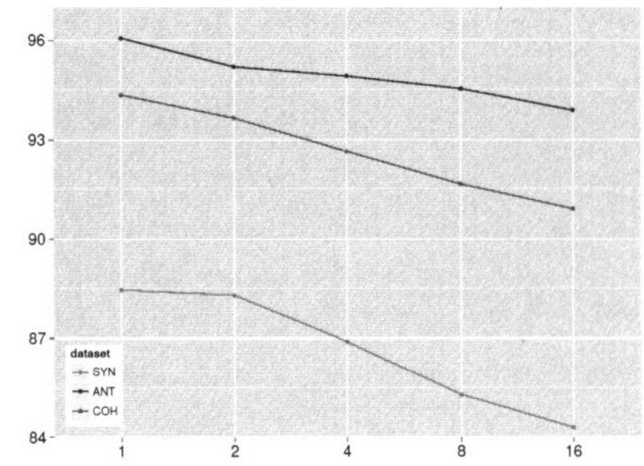

Figure 5: Window, paradigmatic, unreduced

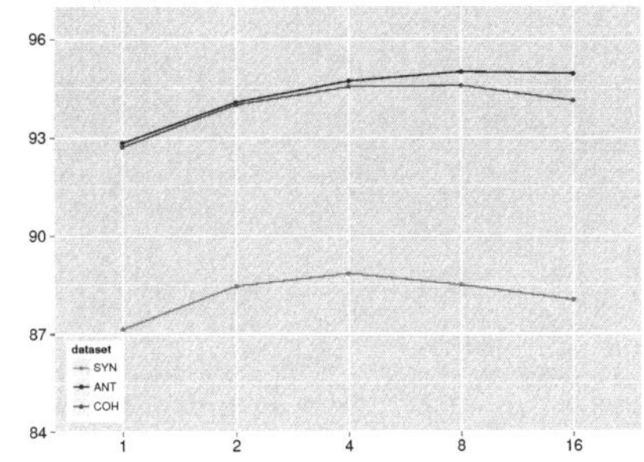

Figure 6: Window, paradigmatic, reduced

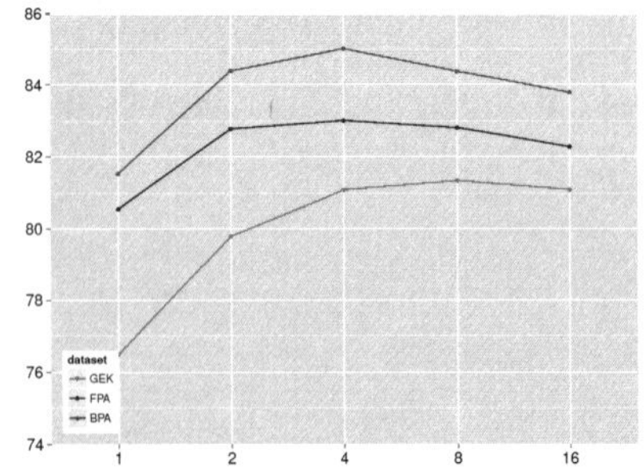

Figure 7: Window, syntagmatic, unreduced

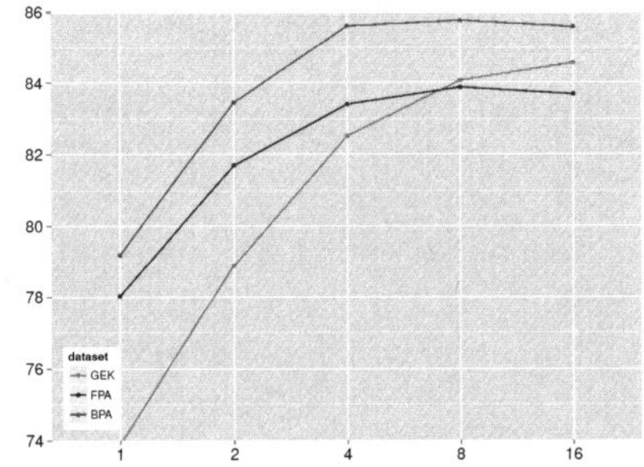

Figure 8: Window, syntagmatic, reduced

quickly for larger windows. With 50 or 100 dimensions skipped, performance improves up to a 4- or 8-word window. Our interpretation is that the first SVD dimensions capture general domain and topic information dominating the co-occurrence data; removing these dimensions reveals paradigmatic semantic relations even for larger windows. For syntagmatic relations without dimensionality reduction, a larger context window of 4 words is needed for FPA and BPA; a further increase of the window is detrimental. For the GEK dataset, performance peaks at 8 words, and decreases only minimally for even larger windows. Again, dimensionality reduction improves performance for large co-occurrence windows. For FPA and BPA, the optimum seems to be achieved with a window of 4–8 words; performance on GEK continues to increase up to 16 words, the largest window size considered in our experiments. Such patterns reflect differences in the nature of the semantic relations involved: smaller windows provide better contextual representations for paradigmatic relations while larger windows are needed to capture syntagmatic relations with bag-of-words DSMs (because co-occurring words then share a large portion of their context windows). Intermediate window sizes are sufficient for phrasal collocates (which are usually adjacent), while event-based relatedness (GEK) requires larger windows. Returning briefly to the slight preference shown by ANT for a larger window, we notice that ANT seems to be more similar to the syntagmatic relations than SYN and COH. This is in line with the observations of Justeson and Katz (1992) concerning the tendency of antonyms to co-occur (e.g., in coordinations such as *short and long*). Like synonyms, antonyms are interchangeable *in absentia*; but they also enter into syntagmatic patterns that are uncommon for synonyms.

We now focus on the parameters related to dimensionality reduction, namely the **number of latent dimensions** (figures 9 and 10) and the **number of skipped dimensions** (figures 11 and 12). These parameters represent an extension of the experiments conducted on the GEK dataset by Lapesa and Evert (2013). They have already been applied by Bullinaria and Levy (2012) to a different set of tasks, including the TOEFL multiple-choice synonymy task. In particular, Bullinaria and Levy found that discarding the initial SVD dimensions (with highest variance) leads to substantial improvements, especially in the TOEFL task. In our experiments, we found no difference between syntagmatic and paradigmatic relations wrt. the *number of latent dimensions*: the more, the better in both cases (900 dimensions). The *number of skipped dimensions*, however, shows some variability across the different relations. The results for SYN are in agreement with the findings of Bullinaria and Levy (2012) on TOEFL: skipping 50 or 100 initial dimensions improves performance. Skipping dimensions makes minimal difference

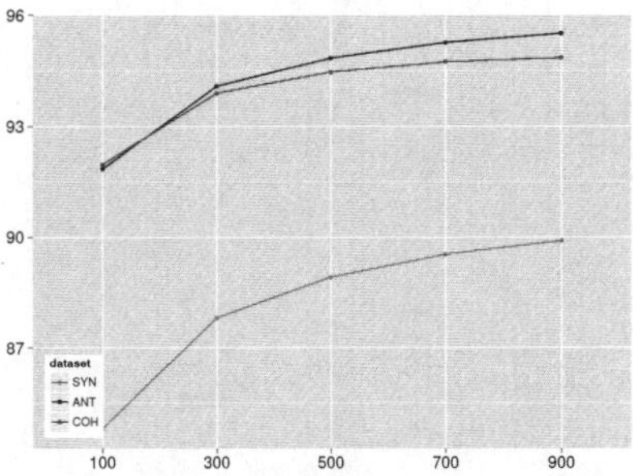

Figure 9: Latent dimensions, paradigmatic

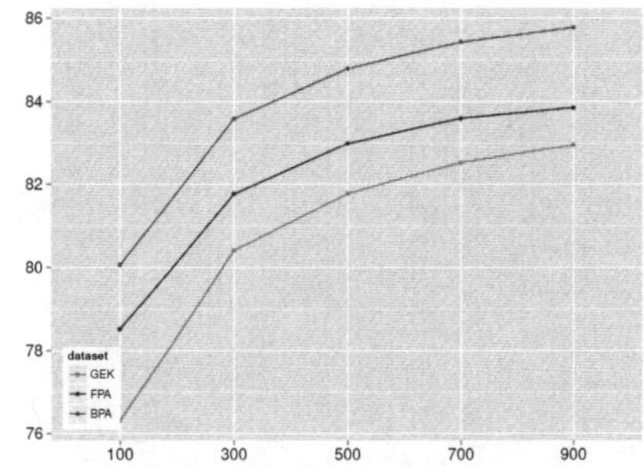

Figure 10: Latent dimensions, syntagmatic

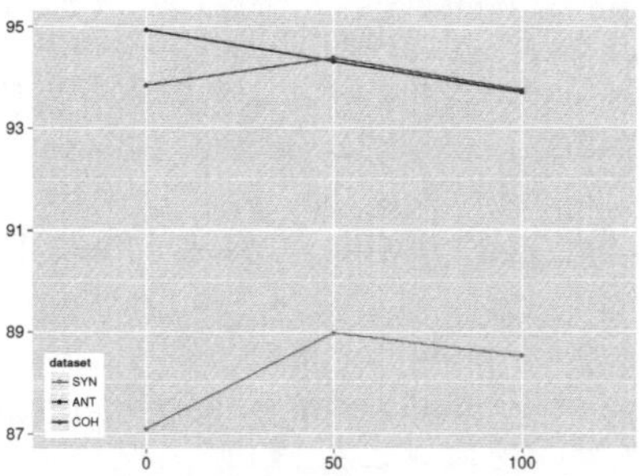

Figure 11: Skipped dimensions, paradigmatic

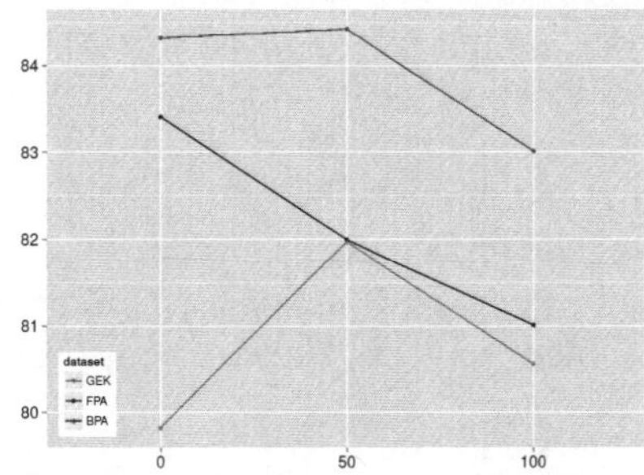

Figure 12: Skipped dimensions, syntagmatic

for COH (best choice is 50 dimensions), while the full range of reduced dimensions is necessary for ANT. Within syntagmatic relations, the full range of latent dimensions ensures good performance on phrasal associates (even if skipping 50 dimensions is not detrimental for BPA). GEK shows a pattern similar to SYN, with 50 skipped dimensions leading to a considerable improvement.

We now inspect the best values for the **relatedness index**. As shown in figure 13 for the unreduced runs and in figure 14 for the reduced runs, *neighbor rank* is consistently better than *distance* on all datasets. This is not surprising because, as discussed in section 3.2, our use of neighbor rank captures asymmetry and mirrors the experimental setting, in which targets are shown after primes. A further observation may be made relating to the degree of asymmetry of different relations. The unreduced setting in particular shows that syntagmatic relations are subject to stronger asymmetry effects than the paradigmatic ones, presumably due to the directional nature of the relations involved (phrasal associates and syntactic collocations). Among paradigmatic relations, antonyms appear to be the least asymmetric ones (because using neighbor rank instead of distance makes a comparatively small difference).

We conclude by briefly summarizing the optimal choices for the remaining parameters. The corresponding partial effects plots are not shown because of space constraints.

A very strong interaction between **score** and **transformation** characterizes all four settings (paradigmatic or syntagmatic datasets, reduced or unreduced experimental runs). Association measures outperform raw co-occurrence frequency. Measures based on significance tests (simple-ll, t-score, z-score) are better than Dice, and to a lesser extent, MI. Simple-ll is the best choice in combination with a logarithmic transformation for paradigmatic relations, z-score appears to be the best measure for syntagmatic relations in combination with a square root transformation. The difference is small, however, and *simple-ll with log transformation* works well across all datasets. Ongoing experiments with standard tasks show a similar pattern, suggesting that this combination of score and transformation parameters is appropriate for DSMs, regardless of the task involved.

The optimal **distance metric** is the *cosine distance*, consistently outperforming *Manhattan*. Concerning **source corpus**, *BNC* consistently yields the worst results, while *WaCkypedia* and *ukWaC* appear to be almost equivalent in the unreduced runs. The trade-off between quality and quantity appears to be strongly biased towards sheer corpus size in the case of distributional models. For syntagmatic relations and SVD-reduced models, *ukWaC* is clearly the best choice. This suggests that syntagmatic relations are better captured by features from a larger lexical inventory, combined with the abstraction performed by SVD.

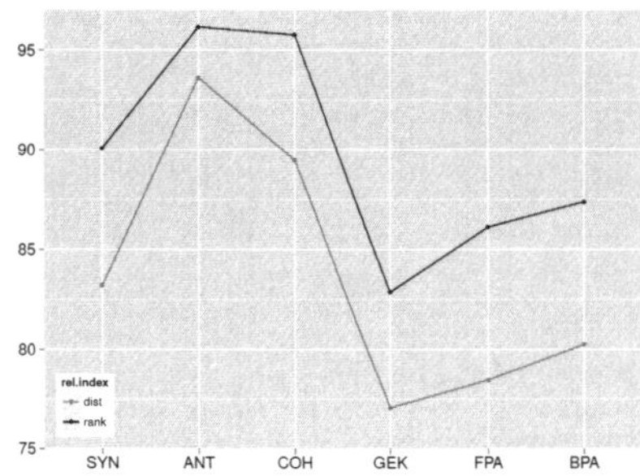

Figure 13: Relatedness index, unreduced

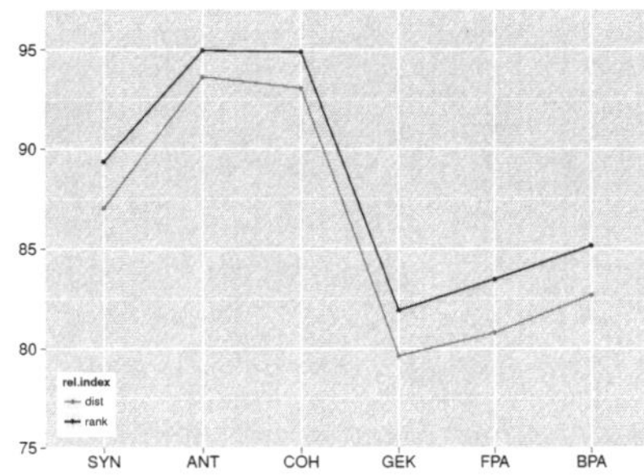

Figure 14: Relatedness index, reduced

Concerning minimally explanatory parameters, inspection of partial effect plots supported the choice of "unmarked" default values for **directionality of the context window** (i.e., *undirected*) and **criterion for context selection** (i.e., *frequency*), as well as an intermediate **number of context dimensions** (i.e., *50000* dimensions).

5.3 Best Settings

We conclude by comparing the performance achieved by our robust choice of optimal parameter values ("best setting") from section 5.2 with the performance of the best model for each dataset. For space constraints, the analysis of best settings focuses on the reduced experimental runs. Our best settings, shown in table 3, perform fairly well on the respective datasets[11].

dataset	corpus	win	score	transf	r.dim	d.sk	acc	best
GEK	ukwac	16	s-ll	log	900	50	96.0	97.0
FPA	ukwac	8	z-sc	root	900	0	93.0	98.6
BPA	ukwac	8	z-sc	root	900	0	95.5	98.9
SYN	ukwac	4	s-ll	log	900	50	96.3	99.0
COH	ukwac	4	s-ll	log	900	50	98.7	100
ANT	wacky	8	s-ll	log	900	0	100	100

Table 3: Best settings: datasets, parameter values, accuracy (*acc*), accuracy of the best model (*best*)

best setting	corpus	win	score	transf	r.dim	d.sk
Syntagmatic	ukwac	8	z-sc	root	900	0
Paradigmatic	ukwac	4	s-ll	log	900	50
General	ukwac	4	s-ll	log	900	0

Table 4: General best settings: parameter values

Dataset	Best Synt.	Best Para.	General
GEK	92.5	94.8	91.3
FPA	93.0	90.2	91.7
BPA	95.5	97.7	95.5
SYN	94.4	96.3	96.3
COH	99.3	98.7	98.7
ANT	99.2	99.2	99.2

Table 5: General best settings: accuracy

[11]Abbreviations in tables 3 and 4: win = window size; transf = transformation; z-sc = z-score; s-ll = simple-ll; r.dim = number of latent dimensions; d.sk = number of skipped dimensions. Parameters with fixed values for all datasets: number of context dimensions = 50k; direction = undirected; criterion = frequency; metric = cosine; relatedness index = rank.

As a next step, we identified parameter combinations that work well for all types of syntagmatic and paradigmatic relations, as well as an even more general setting that is suitable for paradigmatic and syntagmatic relations alike. Best settings are shown in table 4, their performance on each dataset is reported in table 5. General models achieve fairly good performance on all relations.

6 Conclusion

We presented a large-scale evaluation study of bag-of-words DSMs on a classification task derived from priming experiments. The leading theme of our study is a comparison between syntagmatic and paradigmatic relations in terms of the aspects of distributional similarity that characterize them. Our results show that second-order DSMs are capable of capturing both syntagmatic and paradigmatic relations, if parameters are properly tuned. Size of the co-occurrence window as well as parameters connected to dimensionality reduction play a key role in adapting DSMs to particular relations. Even if we do not address the more specific task of distinguishing between relations (e.g., synonyms vs. antonyms; see Scheible et al. (2013) and references therein), we believe that such applications may benefit from our detailed analyses on the effects of DSM parameters.

Ongoing and future work is concerned with the expansion of the evaluation setting to other classes of models (first-order models, dependency-based second-order models) and parameters (e.g., dimensionality reduction with Random Indexing).

Acknowledgments

We are grateful to Ken MacRae for providing us the GEK priming data and to the three reviewers. This research was funded by the DFG Collaborative Research Centre SFB 732 (Gabriella Lapesa) and the DFG Heisenberg Fellowship SCHU-2580/1-1 (Sabine Schulte im Walde).

References

Marco Baroni and Alessandro Lenci. 2010. Distributional memory: A general framework for corpus-based semantics. *Computational Linguistics*, 36(4):1–49.

Marco Baroni and Alessandro Lenci. 2011. How we BLESSed distributional semantic evaluation. In *Proceedings of the GEMS 2011 Workshop on GEometrical Models of Natural Language Semantics*, pages 1–10.

Marco Baroni and Roberto Zamparelli. 2010. Nouns are vectors, adjectives are matrices: Representing adjective-noun constructions in semantic space. In *Proceedings of the 2010 Conference on Empirical Methods in Natural Language Processing*, pages 1183–1193.

John A. Bullinaria and Joseph P. Levy. 2012. Extracting semantic representations from word cooccurrence statistics: stop-lists, stemming and svd. *Behavior Research Methods*, 44:890–907.

James Curran. 2003. *From distributional to semantic similarity*. Ph.D. thesis, Institute for Communicating and Collaborative Systems, School of Informatics, University of Edinburgh.

Philip Edmonds and Graeme Hirst. 2002. Near-synonymy and lexical choice. *Computational Linguistics*, 28(2):105–144.

Katrin Erk, Sebastian Padó, and Ulrike Padó. 2010. A flexible, corpus-driven model of regular and inverse selectional preferences. *Computational Linguistics*, 36(4):723–763.

Stefan Evert. 2008. Corpora and collocations. In Anke Lüdeling and Merja Kytö, editors, *Corpus Linguistics. An International Handbook*, chapter 58. Mouton de Gruyter, Berlin, New York.

Todd Ferretti, Ken McRae, and Ann Hatherell. 2001. Integrating verbs, situation schemas, and thematic role concepts. *Journal of Memory and Language*, 44(4):516–547.

John Fox. 2003. Effect displays in R for generalised linear models. *Journal of Statistical Software*, 8(15):1–27.

Nathan Halko, Per-Gunnar Martinsson, and Joel A. Tropp. 2009. Finding structure with randomness: Stochastic algorithms for constructing approximate matrix decompositions. Technical Report 2009-05, ACM, California Institute of Technology.

Mary Hare, Michael Jones, Caroline Thomson, Sarah Kelly, and Ken McRae. 2009. Activating event knowledge. *Cognition*, 111(2):151–167.

Zelig Harris. 1954. Distributional structure. *Word*, 10(23):146–162.

Amac Herdağdelen, Marco Baroni, and Katrin Erk. 2009. Measuring semantic relatedness with vector space models and random walks. In *Proceedings of the 2009 Workshop on Graph-based Methods for Natural Language Processing*, pages 50–53.

Keith A. Hutchison, David A. Balota, James H. Neely, Michael J. Cortese, Emily R. Cohen-Shikora, Chi-Shing Tse, Melvin J. Yap, Jesse J. Bengson, Dale Niemeyer, and Erin Buchanan. 2013. The semantic priming project. *Behavior Research Methods*, 45(4):1099–1114.

John. S. Justeson and Slava M. Katz. 1992. Redefining antonymy: The textual structure of a semantic relation. *Literary and Linguistic Computing*, 7(3):176–184.

Gabriella Lapesa and Stefan Evert. 2013. Evaluating neighbor rank and distance measures as predictors of semantic priming. In *Proceedings of the ACL Workshop on Cognitive Modeling and Computational Linguistics (CMCL 2013)*, pages 66–74.

Alessandro Lenci and Giulia Benotto. 2012. Identifying hypernyms in distributional semantic spaces. In *Proceedings of *SEM 2012: The First Joint Conference on Lexical and Computational Semantics – Volume 1*, pages 75–79.

Diana McCarthy and John Carroll. 2003. Disambiguating nouns, verbs and adjectives using automatically acquired selectional preferences. *Computational Linguistics*, 29(4):639–654.

Scott McDonald and Chris Brew. 2004. A distributional model of semantic context effects in lexical processing. In *Proceedings of the 42nd Annual Meeting of the Association for Computational Linguistics*, pages 17–24.

Ken McRae, Mary Hare, Jeffrey L. Elman, and Todd Ferretti. 2005. A basis for generating expectancies for verbs from nouns. *Memory & Cognition*, 33(7):1174–1184.

Sebastian Padó and Mirella Lapata. 2007. Dependency-based construction of semantic space models. *Computational Linguistics*, 33(2):161–199.

Yves Peirsman, Kris Heylen, and Dirk Speelman. 2008. Putting things in order. First and second order context models for the calculation of semantic similarity. In *JADT 2008: 9es Journées internationales d'Analyse statistique des Données Textuelles*.

Reinhard Rapp. 2002. The computation of word associations: Comparing syntagmatic and paradigmatic approaches. In *Proceedings of the 19th International Conference on Computational Linguistics - Volume 1*, pages 1–7.

Magnus Sahlgren. 2006. *The word-space model: Using distributional analysis to represent syntagmatic and paradigmatic relations between words in high-dimensional vector spaces*. Ph.D. thesis, University of Stockolm.

Magnus Sahlgren. 2008. The distributional hypothesis. *Rivista di Linguistica (Italian Journal of Linguistics)*, 20(1):33–53.

Silke Scheible, Sabine Schulte im Walde, and Sylvia Springorum. 2013. Uncovering Distributional Differences between Synonyms and Antonyms in a Word Space Model. In *Proceedings of the 6th International Joint Conference on Natural Language Processing*, pages 489—497.

Hinrich Schütze. 1998. Automatic word sense discrimination. *Computational Linguistics*, 27(1):97–123.

Peter D. Turney and Patrick Pantel. 2010. From frequency to meaning: Vector space models of semantics. *Journal of Artificial Intelligence Research*, 37:141–188.

Julie Weeds, David Weir, and Diana McCarthy. 2004. Characterising measures of lexical distributional similarity. In *Proceedings of the 20th International Conference of Computational Linguistics*, pages 1015–1021, Geneva, Switzerland.

Dead parrots make bad pets: Exploring modifier effects in noun phrases

Germán Kruszewski and **Marco Baroni**
Center for Mind/Brain Sciences (University of Trento, Italy)
(german.kruszewski|marco.baroni)@unitn.it

Abstract

Sometimes modifiers have a strong effect on core aspects of the meaning of the nouns they are attached to: A *parrot* is a desirable pet, but a *dead parrot* is, at the very least, a rather unusual household companion. In order to stimulate computational research into the impact of modification on phrase meaning, we collected and made available a large dataset containing subject ratings for a variety of noun phrases and the categories they might belong to. We propose to use *compositional distributional semantics* to model these data, experimenting with numerous distributional semantic spaces, phrase composition methods and asymmetric similarity measures. Our models capture a statistically significant portion of the data, although much work is still needed before we achieve a full computational account of modification effects.

1 Introduction

Not all modifiers are created equal. *Green* parrots have all essential qualities of parrots, but *dead* parrots don't. For example, as vocally argued by the disgruntled costumer in Monty Python's famous Dead Parrot Sketch,[1] dead parrots make rather poor pet birds. In modifier-head constructions (that, for the purpose of this article, we restrict to right-headed adjective-noun and noun-noun constructions), modifiers are not simply picking a subset of the denotation of the head they modify, but they are often *distorting* the properties of the head in a radical manner.

These *modifier effects* on phrase meaning have been studied extensively by theoretical linguists, who have focused primarily on the extreme case of *intensional* modifiers such as *fake*, *alleged* and *toy*, where the phrase denotes something that is no longer (or is not necessarily) a *head* (a *toy gun* is not a *gun*). See McNally (2013) for a recent review of the linguistic literature. Cognitive scientists have looked at modification phenomena within the general study of conceptual combination (see Chapter 12 of Murphy (2002) for an extensive review). The cognitive tradition has focused on how modification affects prototypicality: a *guppy* is the prototypical *pet fish*, but it is neither a typical *pet* nor a typical *fish* (Smith and Osherson, 1984). This line of research has highlighted how strong modification effects might be the rule, rather than the exception: Wisniewski (1997) reports that, when subjects were asked to provide the meaning for more than 200 novel modifier-head constructions, "70% [of the answers] involved the construal of a noun's referent as something other than the typical category named by the noun [head]." Indeed, recent research suggests that even the most stereotypical modifiers affect prototypicality, so that subjects are less willing to attribute to *quacking ducks* such obvious duck properties as *having webbed feet* (Connolly et al., 2007).

The impact of modification on phrase meaning is not only very interesting from a linguistic and cognitive perspective, but also important from a practical point of view, as it might affect expected entailment patterns: If *parrot* entails *pet*, then *lively parrot* also entails *pet*. However, as we saw above, *dead parrot* doesn't necessarily entail *pet* (at least not from the point of view of a disgruntled costumer who was just sold the corpse). Being able to track the impact that modifiers have on heads should thus have a positive effect on important tasks such as recognizing textual entailment, paraphrasing and anaphora resolution (Androutsopoulos and Malakasiotis, 2010; Dagan et

[1] http://en.wikipedia.org/wiki/Dead_Parrot_sketch

*Proceedings of the Third Joint Conference on Lexical and Computational Semantics (*SEM 2014)*, pages 171–181, Dublin, Ireland, August 23-24 2014.

al., 2009; Poesio et al., 2010).

Despite their theoretical and practical import, modification effects have been largely overlooked in computational linguistics, with the notable exception of Boleda et al. (2012; 2013), who only focused on the extreme case of intensional adjectives, studied a limited number of modifiers, and did not attempt to capture the graded nature of modification (a *dead parrot* is not a prototypical *animal*, but a *toy parrot* is not an *animal* at all).

This paper aims to stimulate computational research into modifier effects on phrase meaning in two ways. First, we introduce a new, large, publicly available data set of modifier-head phrases annotated with four kinds of modification-related subject ratings: whether the concept denoted by the phrase is an instance of the concept denoted by its head (is a *dead parrot* still a *parrot*?), to what extent it is a member of one of the larger categories the head belongs to (is it still a *pet*?), and typicality ratings for the same questions (how typical is a *dead parrot* as a *parrot*? and as a *pet*?).

Second, we present a first attempt to model the collected judgments computationally. We choose distributional semantics (Erk, 2012) as our frame of reference, as it produces continuous similarity scores, in line with the graded nature of the modification effects we are investigating. In particular, we look at the *compositional* extension of distributional semantics (Baroni, 2013), because we need representations not only for words, but also phrases, and we adopt the *asymmetric* similarity measures developed in the literature on lexical entailment (Kotlerman et al., 2010; Lenci and Benotto, 2012), because we are interested in an asymmetric relation (to what extent the concept denoted by the phrase is a good instance of the target class, and not *vice versa*). As far as we know, this is the first time these asymmetric measures are applied to composed representations (Baroni et al. (2012) experimented with entailment measures applied to phrase representations directly harvested from corpora, and not derived compositionally). We are thus also providing a novel evaluation of compositional models and asymmetric measures on a challenging task where they could potentially be very useful.[2]

[2]Connell and Ramscar (2001) showed good correlation of similarity scores produced by the LSA distributional semantic model with human category typicality judgments, however they did not consider phrases nor adopted an asymmetric measure to take directionality into account.

2 The Norwegian Blue Parrot data set

We introduce *Norwegian Blue Parrot* (NBP),[3] a new, large data set to explore modification effects. Given a **h**ead noun h and a **m**odifier adjective or noun m, NBP contains average membership and typicality ratings for the phrase mh both as an instance of h and as an instance of c (a broader **c**ategory h belongs to). As a control, we also present ratings for unmodified h as an instance of c (we will use them below to test similarity measures on their ability to capture the direction of the membership relation, and to zero in on the effect of modification vs. more general membership/typicality effects). We include, and indeed focus on, relations with broader categories because they are more prone to modification effects: Intuitively, a *dead parrot* is still a *parrot*, but it is, at the very least, an atypical *pet*. The statistics in Table 1, discussed below, confirm our intuition that subjects are more likely to assign lower scores with respect to a broader category than to the head category itself (although this is, no doubt, in part by construction, since we started constructing the dataset by mining examples where mh is atypical of c, not h). We collect both membership and typicality ratings because we expect them to have different implications for sound entailment. If x is not a member of class y, then x obviously does not entail y. However, if x is an atypical y, entailment still holds, but some typical properties of y might not carry over (e.g., in an anaphora resolution setting, we might still consider co-indexing *dead parrot* with *animal*, but not with *breathing creature*, despite the fact that *breathing* is a highly characteristic property of *animals*).

In order to make sure that NBP would contain a fair number of examples affected by strong modification effects, we first came up with a set of $\langle m, h, c\rangle$ tuples where, according to our own intuition, m makes h fairly atypical as an instance of c. For example, a *bottle* is a piece of *drinkware*. If we add the modifier *perfume*, we expect that, while subjects might still agree that a *perfume bottle* is a *bottle*, they should generally disagree on the statement that a *perfume bottle* belongs to the *drinkware* category. We refer to tuples of this sort (e.g., $\langle perfume, bottle, drinkware\rangle$) as *distorted* tuples in what follows.[4]

[3]Available from http://clic.cimec.unitn.it/composes/

[4]When creating the tuples, we also used some adjectives

We then constructed a number of tuples that should not display a strong modification effect. In particular, in order to insure that any atypical rating we obtained on the distorted tuples could not be explained away by characteristics of m or h alone (rather than by their combination), for each distorted tuple we constructed a few more tuples with the same h and c but a different m, that we did not expect to be strongly distorting (e.g., $\langle plastic, bottle, drinkware \rangle$). Similarly, for each distorted tuple we generated a few more with the same m, but combined with (the same or different) h and c on which the m should not exert a strong effect ($\langle perfume, bottle, container \rangle$). In total, NBP is based on 489 distorted tuples and 1938 more matching tuples.

We constructed NBP to insure that it would contain many tuples displaying strong modification effects, and highly comparable tuples that do not feature such effects. An alternative approach would have been to rate phrases that were randomly selected from a corpus. This would have led to a dataset reflecting a more realistic distribution of modification effects, but it would not have guaranteed, for the same number of pairs, a fair amount of distorted tuples and comparable controls. We leave the study of the natural distribution of modification strength in text to further work.

To find inspiration for the tuples, we looked into various databases containing concepts organized by category, namely BLESS (Baroni and Lenci, 2011), ConceptNet (Speer and Havasi, 2013) and WordNet (Fellbaum, 1998). We insured that all words in our tuples occurred at least 200 times in the large corpus we describe below (phrases were not filtered by frequency, due to data sparseness). Finally, when looking for tuples matching the distorted ones, we made sure that the mh phrases in the new tuples have similar Pointwise Mutual Information to the corresponding phrases in the distorted tuple (or, where the latter were not attested in the corpus, similar m and h frequencies). Finding meaningful combinations among unattested or infrequent phrases was not an easy task and there was not always a perfect candidate. However, the phrases selected in this way yielded challenging items for which there is little or no direct corpus evidence, so that compositional models are required to account for them.

that have been traditionally labeled as intensional by semanticists: *artificial*, *toy*, *former*.

From each source tuple (e.g., $\langle plastic, bottle, drinkware \rangle$), we generated 3 instance-class combinations to be rated: $mh \rightarrow c$ (*plastic bottle* $\rightarrow$ *drinkware*), $mh \rightarrow h$ (*plastic bottle* $\rightarrow$ *bottle*), $h \rightarrow c$ (*bottle* $\rightarrow$ *drinkware*), for a total of 5,849 pairs, that constitute the final NBP data set (2,417 $mh \rightarrow c$ pairs, 2,115 $mh \rightarrow h$ pairs and 1,317 $h \rightarrow c$ pairs).[5]

For each of these pairs, we collected both membership and typicality ratings through two surveys on the CrowdFlower platform.[6] Subjects came exclusively from English speaking countries and no special qualifications were required from them. Membership ratings were collected by asking subjects whether the instance is a member of the class (formulated as a yes/no question). In a separate study, we asked subjects to rate how typical the instance is as member of the class on a 7-point scale. For both questions, we collected 10 judgments per pair and report their averages in NBP. For both surveys, we added 48 control pairs with an expected answer (yes/no for membership, high/low range for typicality), that the subjects had to provide in order for their ratings to be included in the final set ("gold standard" items in crowd-sourcing parlance). These controls included highly prototypical pairs (*dog* $\rightarrow$ *animal*), possibly with stereotypical modifiers (*beautiful rose* $\rightarrow$ *flower*), and unrelated pairs (*biology* $\rightarrow$ *dance*), also possibly under modification (*popular magazine* $\rightarrow$ *animal*).

We asked for binary rather than graded membership judgments because these are more in line with commonsense intuitions about category membership (we might naturally speak of *sparrows* being more typical birds than *penguins*, but it is strange to say that they are "more birds"). The standard view in the psychology of concepts (Hampton, 1991) is that membership judgments are the product of a hard threshold we impose on the typicality scale (x is not y if the typicality of x as y is below a certain, subject-dependent threshold), although under certain experimental conditions subjects can also conceptualize membership as a graded property (Kalish, 1995).

Membership and typicality ratings, especially in borderline cases such as those we constructed, are the output of complex cognitive processes where large inter-subject differences are expected,

[5] There is a larger number of $mh \rightarrow c$ pairs because different tuples can lead to the same $mh \rightarrow h$ or $h \rightarrow c$ combinations.

[6] http://crowdflower.com/

measure	$mh \to c$	$mh \to h$	$h \to c$	tot.
memb.	0.84 (0.2)	0.97 (0.1)	0.88 (0.2)	0.89 (0.2)
typ.	5.45 (1.1)	6.29 (0.6)	5.81 (1.0)	5.84 (1.0)

Table 1: NBP summary statistics: Mean average ratings and their standard deviations across pairs, itemized by instance-class type and in total. Membership values range from 0 to 1, typicality values from 1 to 7.

so it doesn't make sense to worry about "inter-annotator agreement" in this context. Still, several sanity checks indicate that, overall, our subjects understood our questions as we meant them, and behaved in a reasonably coherent manner. First, both average membership and typicality, ratings are significantly lower ($p < 0.001$) for the $mh \to c$ pairs deriving from those tuples that we manually labeled as distorted than for the non-distorted ones. Moreover, for membership, in 86% of the cases at least 8 over 10 subjects gave the same response. For typicality, the observed average rating standard deviation across pairs (1.2) is significantly below what expected by chance ($p < 0.05$), based on a simulated random rating distribution. Membership and typicality ratings are highly correlated, but not identical ($r = 0.76$)

Table 1 reports mean membership and typicality scores in NBP. Both ratings are negatively skewed, that is, subjects had the tendency to respond assertively to the membership question and to give high typicality scores. This is not surprising: Because of the way NBP was constructed, there are about 4 tuples with no expected strong modification effect for each distorted tuple. Furthermore, except for the negative control items (not entered in NBP), our questions did not feature cases where a negative/low response would be entirely straightforward (of the "is a cat a building?" kind). We observe moreover that, in accordance with the intuition we discussed at the beginning of this section, the ratings are extremely high when the class is identical to the phrase head. On the other hand, the $mh \to c$ condition displays, as expected, the lowest averages, suggesting that this will be the most interesting type to model experimentally.

Table 2 presents a few example entries from NBP. The first block of the table illustrates cases with the highest possible membership and typicality scores. At the other extreme, the second block contains examples with very low membership and typicality. Interestingly, there are also cases, such

instance	*class*	*memb.*	*typ.*
top membership, top typicality			
gourmet soup	food	1.00	7.00
huge tiger	predator	1.00	7.00
sugared soda	drink	1.00	7.00
live fish	animal	1.00	7.00
Thai rice	rice	1.00	7.00
silver spoon	spoon	1.00	7.00
low membership, low typicality			
fatal shooting	sport	0.20	1.40
human egg	food	0.40	1.50
perfume bottle	drinkware	0.10	1.30
explosive vest	commodity	0.30	1.90
lemon water	chemical	0.20	1.60
creamy rice	bean	0.20	1.30
top membership, (relatively) low typicality			
sick tuna	tuna	1.00	3.20
explosive vest	vest	1.00	3.50
perforated sieve	tool	1.00	4.20
bottled oxygen	substance	1.00	4.30
grilled trout	creature	1.00	4.40
educational toy	amusement	1.00	4.50

Table 2: Instance-class pairs illustrating various combinations of membership and typicality ratings in NBP.

as the ones in the third block of the table, where all subjects agreed on class membership, but the typicality scores are relatively low (we did not find clear cases of the opposite pattern, and indeed we would have been surprised to find highly typical instances of a class not being treated as members of the class).

Some examples in Table 2 illustrate an important design choice we made in constructing NBP, namely, to ignore the issue of whether potential modification effects are actually due to the modifier and the category pertaining to different *word senses* of the head term. One might argue, for example, that *egg* has a *food* sense and a *reproductive vessel* sense. The *human* modifier picks the second sense, and so, obviously, *human eggs* are judged as bad instances of *food*. While we see the point of this objection, we think it's impossible to draw a clear-cut distinction between discrete word senses (even in the rather extreme egg case, the eggs we eat are reproductive vessels from a chicken point of view!). This has been long recognized in the linguistic and cognitive literature (Kilgarriff, 1997; Murphy, 2002), and even by the computational word sense disambiguation community, that is currently addressing the continuous nature of polysemy by shifting to the lexical-substitution-in-context task (McCarthy and Navigli, 2009). Context provides fundamental cues to disambiguating polysemous words, and noun modifiers typically act as important disambiguating contexts for the nouns. Thus, we think that it is more productive for computational systems to handle modifier-triggered disambiguation as a special case of the more general class of modification effects, than to engage in the quixotic pursuit to determine, *a priori*, what's the boundary between a word-sense and a "pure" modification effect. Note in Table 2 that *grilled trout* was unanimously rated by subjects as an instance of the *creature* category, despite the fact that the cooking-related *grilled* modifier cues a classic shift from an *animal* (and thus *creature*) sense to *food* (Copestake and Briscoe, 1995). Examples like this suggest that our agnosticism is warranted.

3 Methods

3.1 Composition models

We experiment with many ways to derive a phrase vector by combining the vectors of its constituents. Mitchell and Lapata (2010) proposed a set of simple models in which each component of the phrase vector is a function of the corresponding components of the constituent vectors. Given vectors $\vec{a}$ and $\vec{b}$, the weighted additive model (**wadd**) returns their weighted sum: $\vec{p} = w_1\vec{a} + w_2\vec{b}$. In the dilation model (**dil**), the output vector is obtained by decomposing one of the input vectors, say $\vec{b}$, into a vector parallel to $\vec{a}$ and its orthogonal counterpart, and then dilating only the parallel vector by a factor λ before re-combining. The corresponding formula is: $(\vec{a}\cdot\vec{a})\vec{b} + (\lambda - 1)(\vec{a}\cdot\vec{b})\vec{a}$. In our experiments, we stretch the head vector in the direction of the modifier (i.e., $\vec{a}$ is the modifier, $\vec{b}$ is the head). In the multiplicative model (**mult**), vectors are combined by component-wise multiplication, such that each phrase component p_i is given by: $p_i = a_i b_i$.

Guevara (2010) and Zanzotto et al. (2010) propose a full form of the additive model (**fulladd**), where the two constituent vectors are multiplied by weight matrices before being added, so that each phrase component is a weighted sum of *all* constituent components: $\vec{p} = W_1\vec{a} + W_2\vec{b}$.

Finally, the lexical function (**lexfunc**) model of Baroni and Zamparelli (2010) and Coecke et al. (2010) takes inspiration from formal semantics to characterize composition as function application. In particular, in modifier-head phrases, the modifier is treated as a linear function operating on the head vector. Given that linear functions can be expressed by matrices and their application by matrix-by-vector multiplication, the modifier is represented by a matrix A to be multiplied with the modifier vector $\vec{b}$, so that: $\vec{p} = A\vec{b}$.

We use the DISSECT toolkit[7] to estimate the parameters of the composition methods and derive phrase vectors. In particular, DISSECT finds optimal parameter settings by learning to approximate corpus-extracted phrase vector examples with least-squares methods (Dinu et al., 2013). We use as training examples all the modifier-head phrases that contain a modifier of interest and occur at least 50 times in our source corpus (see Section 3.3 below).

3.2 Asymmetric similarity measures

Several measures to identify word pairs that stand in an instance-class relationship by comparing their vectors have been proposed in the recent distributional semantics literature (Kotlerman et al., 2010; Lenci and Benotto, 2012; Weeds et al., 2004).[8] While the task of deciding if u is in class v is typically framed (also by distributional semanticists) in binary, yes-or-no terms, all proposed measures return a continuous numerical score.[9] Consequently, we conjecture that they might be well-suited to capture the graded notions of class membership and typicality we recorded in NBP.[10]

In what follows, we use $w_x(f)$ to denote the weight (value) of feature (dimension) f in the distributional vector of term x. F_x denotes the set of features (dimensions) in the vector of x such that $w_x(f) > t$, where t is a predefined threshold to decide whether a feature is active.[11] Importantly,

[7] `http://clic.cimec.unitn.it/composes/toolkit/`

[8] We speak of "instance-class relations" in a very broad and loose sense, to encompass classic relations such as hyponymy but also the fuzzier notion of lexical entailment.

[9] SVM classifiers have also been shown by Baroni et al. (2012) to be well-suited for entailment detection, but they do not naturally return continuous scores.

[10] Subjects had to answer a yes/no question concerning class membership, but by averaging their response we derive continuous membership scores.

[11] The obvious choice for t is 0. However, when working with the low-rank spaces described in Section 3.3 below, we set t to 0.1, since after SVD/NMF smoothing we observe

all measures assume non-negative values.

Most asymmetric measures proposed in the literature build upon the *distributional inclusion hypothesis*, stating that "if u is a semantically narrower term than v, then a significant number of salient distributional features of u is included in the feature vector of v as well" (Lenci and Benotto, 2012). In our terminology, u is the potential instance, and v is the class. We re-implement all the measures adopted by Lenci and Benotto, namely **weedsprec**, **cosweeds**, **clarkede** and **invcl** (see their paper for the original references):

$$weedsprec(u,v) = \frac{\sum_{f \in F_u \cap F_v} w_u(f)}{\sum_{f \in F_u} w_u(f)}$$

$$cosweeds(u,v) = \sqrt{weedsprec(u,v) \times cosine(u,v)}$$

$$clarkede(u,v) = \frac{\sum_{f \in F_u \cap F_v} \min(w_u(f), w_v(f))}{\sum_{f \in F_u} w_u(f)}$$

$$invcl(u,v) = \sqrt{clarkede(u,v) \times (1 - clarkede(u,v))}$$

The cosweeds formula combines weedsprec with the widely used symmetric *cosine* measure:

$$cosine(u,v) = \frac{\sum_{f \in F_u \cap F_v} w_u(f) \times w_v(f)}{\sqrt{\sum_{f \in F_u} w_u(f)^2} \times \sqrt{\sum_{f \in F_v} w_v(f)^2}}$$

Finally, we experiment with the carefully crafted **balapinc** measure of Kotlerman et al. (2010):

$$balapinc(u,v) = \sqrt{lin(u,v) \cdot apinc(u,v)}$$

where the *lin* term is computed as follows:

$$lin(u,v) = \frac{\sum_{f \in F_u \cap F_v} w_u(f) + w_v(f)}{\sum_{f \in F_u} w_u(f) + \sum_{f \in F_v} w_v(f)}$$

The balapinc score is the geometric average of a symmetric similarity measure (*lin*) and the strongly asymmetric *apinc* measure, that takes large values when dimensions with high values in the vector of the more specific term are also high in the vector of the more general term (refer to Kotlerman et al. (2010) for the apinc formula).

widespread low-frequency noise.

3.3 Distributional semantic spaces

We extract co-occurrence information from a corpus of about 2.8 billion words obtained by concatenating ukWaC,[12] Wikipedia[13] and the British National Corpus.[14] With DISSECT, we build co-occurrence vectors for the top 20K most frequent lemmas in the source corpus (plus any NBP term missing from this list). We treat the top 10K most frequent lemmas as context elements. We consider context windows of 2 and 20 words on the two sides of the targets. We weight the vectors by non-negative Pointwise Mutual Information and Local Mutual Information (Evert, 2005). We experiment with vectors in the resulting full-rank (10K-dimensional) semantic spaces as well as with vectors in spaces of ranks 100 and 300. Rank reduction is performed by applying the Singular Value Decomposition (Golub and Van Loan, 1996) or Non-negative Matrix Factorization (Lee and Seung, 2000). It is customary to represent the output of these operations directly in a dense low-dimensional space. However, the asymmetric similarity measures we use assume sparse vectors (or the "inclusion" criterion would be meaningless), so we project back the outcome of SVD and NMF to sparse 10K-dimensional but low-rank spaces. In total, we explore 20 distinct semantic spaces.

We also collect co-occurrence vectors for the phrases needed to estimate the composition method parameters (see Section 3.1 above). We use DISSECT's "peripheral space" option to project the phrase raw count vectors into the various spaces without affecting their structure.

Due to memory constraints, we restrict evaluation in the full-rank spaces to the *wadd* and *mult* models.

4 Experiments

Given the methods described above, the main question we want to answer is: Which combination of compositional model and asymmetric similarity measure yields a better fit for the data in the NBP dataset?

We start however with a sanity check on the ability of the measures to capture the *direction* of the instance-class membership relation. Even a measure that is good at capturing degrees of membership/typicality won't be of much practical use

[12] `http://wacky.sslmit.unibo.it`
[13] `http://en.wikipedia.org`
[14] `http://www.natcorp.ox.ac.uk`

clarkede	weedsprec	balapinc	cosweeds	invcl
		Low-rank spaces		
10	8	11	8	7
		Full-rank spaces		
2	4	4	4	2

Table 3: Number of spaces (over totals of 16 low-rank and 4 full-rank spaces) in which each measure was able to predict class membership direction significantly above chance.

if it is not able to tell us which item in a pair is the instance and which is the class.

Detecting membership direction As described in Section 2 above, NBP also contains single-word $h \rightarrow c$ pairs (*parrot*→ *pet*). We extracted the subset of those that all judges considered to be in the category membership relation, and we checked them manually to make sure that the direction was one-way only. This resulted in a set of 639 pairs where the membership relation holds unidirectionally. We tested all combination of semantic spaces (Section 3.3) and asymmetric similarity measures (Section 3.2) on the task of assigning a higher score to the pairs in the $h \rightarrow c$ (vs. $c \rightarrow h$) direction (e.g., ($score$(*parrot* $\rightarrow$ *pet*) $>$ $score$(*pet* $\rightarrow$ *parrot*)). Table 3 reports, for each measure, the number of spaces in which the measure was able to predict membership direction significantly better than chance (binomial test, $p < 0.05$). We report results on full- and low-rank (SVD, NMF) spaces separately since, as discussed above, for most composition models we can only use the latter. We observe that all measures are able to significantly detect directionality in at least some spaces. For all the analyses below, we exclude from further testing the space-measure combinations that failed to pass this sanity check, since they are clearly failing to capture properties pertaining to the instance-class relation (if a combination is not able to tell that it is a *parrot* that is a *pet*, and not *vice versa*, there is no point in asking if the same combination is able to model how typical a *dead parrot* is as a *pet*).

Modeling typicality ratings of $mh \rightarrow c$ pairs Next, for each of the remaining spaces, we first performed composition as described in Section 3.1 above to build the representations for the nominal phrases in the NBP dataset, and then computed asymmetric similarity scores for pairs made of a phrase and the corresponding potential class.

We computed the correlations between mean human membership or typicality ratings and the scores produced with each combination of composition model, similarity measure and space. The resulting performance profiles for membership and typicality are very highly correlated ($r =$ .99), and we thus report only the latter. We leave it to further work to devise measures that are more specifically tuned to capture membership or typicality.

Table 4 reports the top correlation coefficients between typicality judgments and scores of each $mh \rightarrow c$ pair (*dead parrot*→ *pet*) across spaces, organized by measures and composition methods. The best correlation is achieved with the weedsprec measure using the mult composition model in a full-rank space (precisely that of context window size 2 and ppmi weighting). Recall that mult returns the component-wise product of the vectors it combines. Thus, modification under mult is carried out by picking only those features of the head that are also present in the modifier, and enhancing them by a factor given by the modifier's feature value. The weedsprec measure is then given by the weighted proportion of active features in mh that are also active in c. Therefore, the more the modifier shares features with the parent category, the higher weedsprec will be. This might explain why weedsprec is a good fit for the mult model in measuring degrees of category typicality.

Looking at composition methods, there is no evidence that the more complex, matrix-based fuladd and lexfunc approaches are performing any better than the simple multiplicative and additive methods. Indeed, mult shows the most consistent overall performance, confirming the conclusion of Blacoe and Lapata (2012) that, at the present time, when it comes to composition, "simpler is better". A related point emerges from the comparison of the low- and full-rank results for mult and wadd. The smoothing process due to dimensionality reduction is quite disruptive for the current asymmetric measures, that are based on feature inclusion. This is a further reason to stick to simpler composition methods, that can be applied directly in the full-rank spaces.

Regarding the measures themselves, we see that cosweeds, that balances weedsprec with the classic cosine score, is the most robust, returning good

	clarkede	weedsprec	balapinc	cosweeds	invcl
	Low-rank spaces				
dil	9*	15*	16*	19*	8*
fulladd	17*	16*	12*	24*	−3
lexfunc	17*	12*	12*	27*	−2
mult	13*	19*	19*	29*	12*
wadd	14*	14*	16*	27*	−2
	Full-rank spaces				
mult	9*	**39***	**33***	**36***	**15***
wadd	**30***	34*	31*	35*	14*

Table 4: Percentage Pearson r between asymmetric similarity measures and $mh \rightarrow c$ typicality ratings. $*p < 0.001$

	clarkede	weedsprec	balapinc	cosweeds	invcl
	Low-rank spaces				
dil	5	−1	−1	−2	7*
fulladd	10*	7*	5+	7+	−2
lexfunc	**15***	9*	10*	18*	−2
mult	4+	14*	13*	15*	**9***
wadd	7+	7*	9*	12+	−2
	Full-rank spaces				
mult	1	**25***	**21***	**24***	5+
wadd	11*	18*	13*	20*	2

Table 5: Percentage Pearson r between asymmetric similarity measures and $mh \rightarrow c$ typicality ratings where $h \rightarrow c$ scores have been partialed out. $*p < 0.001$, $+p < 0.05$

results across all composition methods. On the other hand, the related clarkede and invcl measures turn out to be quite brittle.

The highly significant correlations show that the measures do capture to some extent the patterns of variance in the data. However, when considering potential practical applications, even the highest reported correlation (.39) is certainly not impressive, indicating that there is plenty of room for further research into developing better composition methods and/or membership/typicality measures.

Focusing on the modifier effect for $mh \rightarrow c$ pairs The typicality judgment for *dead parrot* as a *pet* is influenced by two factors: how typical *parrots* are as *pets*, and how much more or less typical *dead parrots* are as *pets*, as opposed to *parrots* in general. A good model must be able to capture both factors (and this is what we tested above). However, we are also interested in assessing to what extent the models are capturing the modification effectproper, as opposed to the overall degree of typicality of the h concept as member of the c category. To focus on the modification factor, we partialed out the $h \rightarrow c$ (*parrot→pet*) ratings from the $mh \rightarrow c$ (*dead parrot→pet*) ratings and from the corresponding model scores (that is, we correlated the residuals of $mh \rightarrow c$ ratings and model-produced scores after regressing the $h \rightarrow c$ ratings on both). The results are shown in Table 5. Correlations are lower overall, but the general picture from the previous analysis still holds, confirming that the computational models are (also) capturing modifier effects. Interestingly, wadd, dil and fulladd generally undergo larger performance drops than mult and lexfunc. Evidently, models like the latter, in which the modifier selects the relevant features from the head, are better suited to explain modification than the former, in which the modifier features are just added to those of the head by means of a linear combination.

Modeling typicality ratings of $mh \rightarrow h$ pairs We repeated the first analysis for pairs of the type $mh \rightarrow h$ (*dead parrot→ parrot*). The results, shown in Table 6, are lower than in the previous analysis. This is probably due to the fact that, as discussed in Section 2, when the very same concept is used as phrase head and category, judgments are subject to a strong ceiling effect, and none of our measures is designed to flatten out above a certain threshold. Indeed, if we measure the skewness of the typicality ratings,[15] we obtain that, while for $h \rightarrow c$ and $mh \rightarrow c$ the skewness is of -1.9 and -1.5, respectively, for $mh \rightarrow h$ it gets to -3.9.

In any case, the results confirm the brittleness of the clarkede and invcl measures. The linguistically motivated lexfunc model emerges here as a competitive alternative to the simpler models. Still, the best results are obtained with mult and cosweeds (on the full-rank, context window size 20, ppmi weighted space). Notably, weedsprec applied to a pair of the type $mh \rightarrow h$, where the phrase is constructed using the mult model, results in a constant value of 1, whatever the modifier and the head noun is. This is due to the fact that the features of a phrase composed using mult are a subset of the features of the head,[16] and in this case the head is the same as the category. Therefore, by definition, weedsprec yields a score of 1 for every pair, the variance is null and hence the correlation is unde-

[15] A skewness factor of 0 means that the distribution is balanced around the mean, while the more negative the coefficient is, the more the left tail is longer and the distribution is concentrated to the right (toward high typicality values in our case).

[16] In set notation: $F_u \cap F_v = F_u$ since $F_u \subseteq F_v$

	clarkede	weedsprec	balapinc	cosweeds	invcl
		Low-rank spaces			
dil	2	−1	−2	−3	4
fulladd	5+	5+	2	1	−1
lexfunc	**14***	8*	14*	17*	−1
mult	3	-	13*	15*	**5+**
wadd	6+	8*	7+	6	−3
		Full-rank spaces			
mult	−2	-	**18***	**19***	−2
wadd	7*	**13***	7*	12*	−2

Table 6: Percentage Pearson r between asymmetric similarity measures and $mh \rightarrow h$ typicality ratings. $^*p < 0.001$, $^+p < 0.05$

fined. As a consequence, in this case cosweeds, which is the geometric mean between weedsprec and cosine, reduces to cosine similarity! The latter might be effective in capturing the degree of similarity between the phrase and its potential category but, as a symmetric measure, it cannot, alone, provide a full account of category typicality effects.

5 Conclusion

We introduced the challenge of quantifying the impact of modification on the meaning of noun phrases to the computational linguistics community. We presented a new dataset that collects membership and typicality ratings for modifier-head phrases with respect to the category represented by the head as well as a broader category. Since accounting for modifier distortion requires semantic representations of phrases and modeling graded judgments, we consider this an ideal testbed for compositional distributional semantics.

In the interaction between compositional models and directional similarity measures, we have observed that simpler models yield better results. Specifically, mult and wadd are economical composition models than can be applied on full-rank spaces, which in turn work best with our similarity measures.

Psychologists studying modification effects in concept combination have proposed models that are usually quite complex, relying on hand-crafted feature definitions and making very strong assumptions about the combination process (see for example Cohen and Murphy (1984), Smith et al. (1988)). Some of these assumptions have led other researchers to argue that prototypes do not compose at all (Connolly et al., 2007). In contrast, the approach we borrow from distributional semantics, while only mildly successful for now, has the advantage of being very simple both in its construction and application, and in the assumptions that it makes.

Also notable is that we are putting under the same umbrella tasks that have been traditionally tackled separately. For example, among the effects present in the dataset, we can find both word sense disambiguation (see discussion at the end of Section 2) and what Murphy (2002) calls "knowledge effects" (e.g., a *plane* makes a very good *machine*, but a *paper plane* doesn't). Moreover, these effects can also interact (people know that a *human egg* is actually a single, small cell, and hence not even cannibals would consider it satisfactory food). We can thus explore the empirical question of whether all these related phenomena can be tackled together, with a single model accounting for all of them.

In conclusion, the challenge that we introduced brings together concept combination and non-subsective modification phenomena studied in psychology and theoretical linguistics, and tries to handle them with the standard machinery of computational linguistics. This challenge has proved quite difficult for current tools, but this is exactly what we expected in the first place. Our goal, from the outset, was to create a task that could help us delimiting the boundaries of computational methods for characterizing human concepts, while delimiting, at the same time, the notion of human concepts itself.

Acknowledgments

We acknowledge ERC 2011 Starting Independent Research Grant n. 283554 (COMPOSES).

References

Ion Androutsopoulos and Prodromos Malakasiotis. 2010. A survey of paraphrasing and textual entailment methods. *Journal of Artificial Intelligence Research*, 38:135–187.

Marco Baroni and Alessandro Lenci. 2011. How we BLESSed distributional semantic evaluation. In *Proceedings of the EMNLP GEMS Workshop*, pages 1–10, Edinburgh, UK.

Marco Baroni and Roberto Zamparelli. 2010. Nouns are vectors, adjectives are matrices: Representing adjective-noun constructions in semantic space. In *Proceedings of EMNLP*, pages 1183–1193, Boston, MA.

Marco Baroni, Raffaella Bernardi, Ngoc-Quynh Do, and Chung-Chieh Shan. 2012. Entailment above the word level in distributional semantics. In *Proceedings of EACL*, pages 23–32, Avignon, France.

Marco Baroni. 2013. Composition in distributional semantics. *Language and Linguistics Compass*, 7(10):511–522.

William Blacoe and Mirella Lapata. 2012. A comparison of vector-based representations for semantic composition. In *Proceedings of EMNLP*, pages 546–556, Jeju Island, Korea.

Gemma Boleda, Eva Maria Vecchi, Miquel Cornudella, and Louise McNally. 2012. First order vs. higher order modification in distributional semantics. In *Proceedings of EMNLP*, pages 1223–1233, Jeju Island, Korea.

Gemma Boleda, Marco Baroni, Louise McNally, and Nghia The Pham. 2013. Intensionality was only alleged: On adjective-noun composition in distributional semantics. In *Proceedings of IWCS*, pages 35–46, Potsdam, Germany.

Graham Chapman. 1989. *The complete Monty Python's flying circus : all the words*. Pantheon Books, New York.

Bob Coecke, Mehrnoosh Sadrzadeh, and Stephen Clark. 2010. Mathematical foundations for a compositional distributional model of meaning. *Linguistic Analysis*, 36:345–384.

Benjamin Cohen and Gregory L Murphy. 1984. Models of concepts. *Cognitive Science*, 8(1):27–58.

Louise Connell and Michael Ramscar. 2001. Using distributional measures to model typicality in categorization. In *Proceedings of CogSci*, pages 226–231, Edinburgh, UK.

Andrew Connolly, Jerry Fodor, Lila Gleitman, and Henry Gleitman. 2007. Why stereotypes don't even make good defaults. *Cognition*, 103(1):1–22.

Ann Copestake and Ted Briscoe. 1995. Semi-productive polysemy and sense extension. *Journal of Semantics*, 12:15–67.

Ido Dagan, Bill Dolan, Bernardo Magnini, and Dan Roth. 2009. Recognizing textual entailment: rationale, evaluation and approaches. *Natural Language Engineering*, 15:459–476.

Georgiana Dinu, Nghia The Pham, and Marco Baroni. 2013. General estimation and evaluation of compositional distributional semantic models. In *Proceedings of ACL Workshop on Continuous Vector Space Models and their Compositionality*, pages 50–58, Sofia, Bulgaria.

Katrin Erk. 2012. Vector space models of word meaning and phrase meaning: A survey. *Language and Linguistics Compass*, 6(10):635–653.

Stefan Evert. 2005. *The Statistics of Word Cooccurrences*. Ph.D dissertation, Stuttgart University.

Christiane Fellbaum, editor. 1998. *WordNet: An Electronic Lexical Database*. MIT Press, Cambridge, MA.

Gene Golub and Charles Van Loan. 1996. *Matrix Computations (3rd ed.)*. JHU Press, Baltimore, MD.

Emiliano Guevara. 2010. A regression model of adjective-noun compositionality in distributional semantics. In *Proceedings of GEMS*, pages 33–37, Uppsala, Sweden.

James Hampton. 1991. The combination of prototype concepts. In Paula Schwanenflugel, editor, *The psychology of word meanings*, pages 91–116. Erlbaum, Hillsdale, NJ.

Charles Kalish. 1995. Essentialism and graded membership in animal and artifact categories. *Memory and Cognition*, 23(3):335–353.

Adam Kilgarriff. 1997. I don't believe in word senses. *Computers and the Humanities*, 31:91–113.

Lili Kotlerman, Ido Dagan, Idan Szpektor, and Maayan Zhitomirsky-Geffet. 2010. Directional distributional similarity for lexical inference. *Natural Language Engineering*, 16(4):359–389.

Daniel Lee and Sebastian Seung. 2000. Algorithms for Non-negative Matrix Factorization. In *Proceedings of NIPS*, pages 556–562.

Alessandro Lenci and Giulia Benotto. 2012. Identifying hypernyms in distributional semantic spaces. In *Proceedings of *SEM*, pages 75–79, Montreal, Canada.

Diana McCarthy and Roberto Navigli. 2009. The English lexical substitution task. *Language Resources and Evaluation*, 43(2):139–159.

Louise McNally. 2013. Modification. In Maria Aloni and Paul Dekker, editors, *Cambridge Handbook of Semantics*. Cambridge University Press, Cambridge, UK. In press.

Jeff Mitchell and Mirella Lapata. 2010. Composition in distributional models of semantics. *Cognitive Science*, 34(8):1388–1429.

Gregory Murphy. 2002. *The Big Book of Concepts*. MIT Press, Cambridge, MA.

Massimo Poesio, Simone Ponzetto, and Yannick Versley. 2010. Computational models of anaphora resolution: A survey. `http://clic.cimec.unitn.it/massimo/Publications/lilt.pdf`.

Edward Smith and Daniel Osherson. 1984. Conceptual combination with prototype concepts. *Cognitive Science*, 8(4):337–361.

Edward E Smith, Daniel N Osherson, Lance J Rips, and Margaret Keane. 1988. Combining prototypes: A selective modification model. *Cognitive Science*, 12(4):485–527.

Robert Speer and Catherine Havasi. 2013. ConceptNet 5: A large semantic network for relational knowledge. In Iryna Gurevych and Jungi Kim, editors, *The People's Web Meets NLP*, pages 161–176. Springer, Berlin.

Julie Weeds, David Weir, and Diana McCarthy. 2004. Characterising measures of lexical distributional similarity. In *Proceedings of COLING*, pages 1015–1021, Geneva, Switzerland.

Edward Wisniewski. 1997. When concepts combine. *Psychonomic Bulletin & Review*, 4(2):167–183.

Fabio Zanzotto, Ioannis Korkontzelos, Francesca Falucchi, and Suresh Manandhar. 2010. Estimating linear models for compositional distributional semantics. In *Proceedings of COLING*, pages 1263–1271, Beijing, China.

Syntactic Transfer Patterns of German Particle Verbs and their Impact on Lexical Semantics

Stefan Bott **Sabine Schulte im Walde**
Institut für Maschinelle Sprachverabeitung
Universität Stuttgart
Pfaffenwaldring 5b, 70569 Stuttgart, Germany
{stefan.bott,schulte}@ims.uni-stuttgart.de

Abstract

German particle verbs, like *anblicken* (*to gaze at*) combine a base verb (*blicken*) with a particle (*an*) to form a special kind of Multi Word Expression. Particle verbs may share the semantics of the base verb and the particle to a variable degree. However, while syntactic subcategorization frames tend to be good predictor for the semantics of verbs in general (verbs that are similar in meaning also tend to have similar subcategorization frames and selectional preferences), there are regular changes in subcategorization frames by particle verbs with regard to the corresponding base verbs. This paper demonstrates that the syntactic behavior of particle verbs and base verbs together (modeling regular changes in subcategorization frames by particle verbs and corresponding base verbs) and applying clustering techniques allows us to distinguish particle verb meaning and shows the tight connection between transfer patterns and the semantic classes of particle verbs.

1 Introduction

In German, particle verbs (PVs), like *anblicken* in (1), are a highly productive class. PVs present challenges for a both theoretical analysis and their computational treatment. One of the central problems is the prediction of their meaning from their constituent parts: the base verb (BV, e.g. *blicken* in (1)) and the particle (e.g. *an*). Many PVs derive their meaning from the corresponding BVs – with a varying degree of transparency. It is often not clear, however, how to interpret the semantics of the particles and their contribution to the meaning of the PVs. Since particles never occur isolated, without the context of the verb, it is difficult to assign them a lexical semantic entry on their own. Even more, German particles are a notoriously ambiguous word class.

(1) Das Kind blickt seine Mutter an.
The child gazes his-acc mother PRT.
The child looks at his mother.

One way to approximate the meaning of particles is to group together the particle verbs which share the same particle into semantic groups (such as *anblicken, anstarren, anschauen* 'to stare/look at'), such that both the meaning of the PV and the meaning of the BV is similar in each group. This allows us to make inferences like "taking a BV from semantic group α and particle β, we will derive a PV from semantic group δ". Such groups can be established and they represent productive paradigms. Springorum et al. (2013) have shown in a generation experiment setup that subjects are able to associate a meaning to artificially created, previously unattested PVs and to construct example sentences for them.[1] Different subjects also agree to a large degree on the meaning they attribute to the newly formed lexical items.

But this approach also rises a series of questions, especially concerning the way in which such groups can be distinguished, both from a theoretical and a corpus-based perspective. For example, which kinds of linguistic features allow us to discriminate such semantic classes? In this paper we investigate the influence of syntax, which represents one of the possible feature sources. Syn-

[1]For example for the neologism *anlauschen*, referring to a partitive meaning of the particle, senentence like the following could be found: *Er hatte an der Wand angelauscht und wusste Bescheid.* ('He had listened at the wall and knew everything.')

*Proceedings of the Third Joint Conference on Lexical and Computational Semantics (*SEM 2014)*, pages 182–192,
Dublin, Ireland, August 23-24 2014.

tactic subcategorization frames tend to be good predictors for the semantics of verbs in general: verbs that are similar in meaning also tend to have similar subcategorization frames and selectional preferences (Schulte im Walde, 2000; Merlo and Stevenson, 2001; Korhonen et al., 2003; Schulte im Walde, 2006a; Joanis et al., 2008). But, as we will show below, PV-BV pairs tend to have a special behavior with respect to their subcategorization, even if their meanings are closely related. Because we are interested in pairs of PVs and their BVs, we thus have to look at pairs of subcategorization preferences, and rely on the concept of *syntactic transfer*. We use *syntactic transfer* as a technical term here, which we define as regular changes in subcategorization frames by PVs and corresponding BVs, e.g., the incorporation or addition of complements of PVs in comparison to their BVs (Stiebels, 1996; Lüdeling, 2001; Fleischer and Barz, 2012a). We claim that the syntactic behavior of PVs and BVs together allows us to distinguish semantic classes.

A better understanding of the nature of the connection between syntactic transfer patterns and semantic classes may be beneficial for both theoretical and computational linguistics. On the theoretical side we can hope to find new arguments to guide and justify lexical semantic classifications. We may also shed light on what particles actually mean, a topic which is not trivial by itself. In computational semantics, a better understanding of syntactic transfer patterns can potentially contribute to a better treatment of PVs in meaning-related areas, such as machine translation and information retrieval.

In sum, this paper makes the following contributions:

- We show that the meaning of verb particles can be modeled as classes of pairs of PVs and their corresponding BVs, where both PVs and BVs in each class are closely related in meaning. In addition, the PV-BV pairs in each class undergo the same syntactic transfers, i.e. the selectional preferences of PV-BV pairs within each class tend to be very similar, even if the subcategorization preferences may be different between PVs and BVs.
- We show that automatic clustering can replicate a gold standard classification of PV-BV pairs to a large degree when clustering only relies on syntax and the gold standard reflects semantic regularities.

The rest of this paper is organized as follows: In section 2 we describe the task and our goals. Here we also define the term *syntactic transfer pattern*, which is central to our discussion. Section 3 is dedicated to related work relevant for our study. In section 4 we describe the experimental setup, while sections 5 and 6 present the experiment results and discuss them.

2 Goal and Motivation

The work we describe here centers around the concept of semantic classes and syntactic transfer patterns. As concerning the semantic side, the PVs which share the same particle may be grouped into different classes according to their meaning. For example, among the PVs incorporating the particle *an* we find a group of verbs whose meanings center around the concept of *"to look at someone/something in manner X"*, *"to attach something somewhere in manner X"*, *"to make an unpleasant sound towards someone in a manner X"* and *"to start an action X on something which starts consuming it"*, as exemplified in (2) a-d.

(2) a. A blickt/schaut/starrt/stiert/ B an.
A looks/stares/gazes B PRT.
A looks/stares/gazes at B.

b. A klebt/heftet/schraubt/nagelt B an C an.
A glues/affixes/screws B at/onto C PRT.
A glues/affixes/screws B onto C.

c. A brüllt/faucht/bellt/meckert B an.
A roars/hisses/bleats B PRT.
A brawls/hisses/scolds at B.

d. A schneidet/bricht/reißt B an.
A cuts/breaks/tears B PRT.
A cuts/breaks/tears the first slice/piece of B.

Such semantic classes are not easy to define and they are also difficult to induce automatically. Although there is general agreement in the theoretical literature that such semantic classes for PVs exist (cf. Lechler and Roßdeutscher (2009), Kliche (2011) and Springorum (2011)) the agreement on the number and nature of such classes is not very high. For example, Springorum (2011) (who develops her analysis within Discourse Representation Theory (Kamp and Reyle, 1993)) distinguishes between 11 classes of PVs with the particle *an*, while Fleischer and Barz (2012b) only distinguish 3 major de-verbal classes, based on their *aktionsart*, which can be divided into some 9 minor classes.[2] It should be noted that all the PVs and BVs in (2) a-d are not only quite homogeneous in their *semantics*; they also form coherent *syntactic* classes. The PVs and BVs of these examples are quite similar in the way they typically select their syntactic complements. For example, the BVs of (2-a) typically take a PP argument that expresses the direction of gaze using a prepositional phrases with one of the prepositions *auf*, *zu*, *nach* or *in* subcategorizing a dative noun phrase. The corresponding PVs, however, typically express this semantic role by an accusative object. The type of change from the typical frame of a BV to the typical frame of a PV is an example of what we mean by a *syntactic transfer pattern*.

So, while similar syntactic behavior of two verbs in general may indicate that the verbs are also semantically similar, this is typically *not* the case for PV-BV pairs. Compare (1) to (3), which are nearly synonymous but (3) uses the BV *blicken* instead of the PV *anblicken* in (1). We can only induce the similarity of the PV and the BV if we take the syntactic transfer into consideration.

(3) a. Das Kind blickt zu seiner Mutter.
The child looks at his-dat mother.
b. Das Kind stiert/starrt/schaut zu
The child stares/stares/looks at
seiner Mutter.
his-dat Mother.

Looking at the class to which this PV belongs, all the variants of (3-b) are semantically very similar to (3-a). This also corresponds to a syntactic similarity: all the verbs of this group share the same preferred syntactic subcategorization frames. The dominant frame of theses verbs is "NPnom+PP-dat" (the head preposition of the PP may vary, but within well-defined limits). But this is not the case for the PV *anblicken* in (1). (1) is nearly synonymous to (3-a), but the PV in this example has a totally different frame, namely the simple transitive "NPnom+NP-acc". It may not come as a surprise that all of the verbs in (3-b) have PV counterparts (*anstieren*, *anstarren*, etc.), which all behave syntactically like *anblicken*.

In sum, we part from the hypothesis that there is a tight connection between transfer patterns and the semantic classes of PVs. There is only one more point to make: the classes shown in (2), could actually be seen as reflecting different meanings of the particle *an* itself.

3 Related Work

Particle verbs have been studied from the theoretical perspective and, to a more limited extend, from the aspect of the computational predictability of the degree of semantic compositionality (the transparency of their meaning with respect to the meaning of the base verb and the particle) and the semantic classifiabilty of PVs.

For English, there is work on the automatic extraction of PVs from corpora (Baldwin and Villavicencio, 2002; Baldwin, 2005; Villavicencio, 2005) and the determination of compositionality (McCarthy et al., 2003; Baldwin et al., 2003; Bannard, 2005).

To the best of our knowledge Aldinger (2004) is the first work that studies German PVs from a corpus based perspective, with an emphasis on the syntactic behavior and syntactic change. Schulte im Walde (2004), Schulte im Walde (2005) and Schulte im Walde (2006b) present preliminary distributional studies to explore salient features at the syntax-semantics interface that determine the semantic nearest neighbours of German PVs. Relying on the insights of those studies, Schulte im Walde (2006b) and Hartmann (2008) describe experiments which model the subcategorization transfer of German PVs with respect to their BVs in order to strengthen PV-BV distributional similarity. The main goal for them is to use transfer information in order to predict the degree of semantic compositionality of PVs. Kühner and Schulte im Walde (2010) use clustering to determine the degree of compositionality of German PVs, via common PV-BV cluster membership. They are, again, mainly interested in the assessment of compositionality, which is done on the basis of lexical information. They use syntactic information, but only as a filter and for lexical heads as cooccurrence features in order to limit the selected argument slots to certain syntactic functions. They conclude that the best results can be obtained with information stemming from direct objects and PP-objects. The incorporation of syntactic informa-

[2] The subdivision is, however not fully spelled out and only implicit in their description.

tion in the form of dependency arc labels (concatenated with the head nouns) does not yield satisfactory results, putting the syntactic transfer problem in evidence, again. They conclude that an incorporation of syntactic transfer information between BVs and PVs could possibly improve the results.

Based on a theoretical study (Springorum, 2011), which explains particle meanings in terms of Discourse Representation Theory (Kamp and Reyle, 1993), Springorum et al. (2012) show that four classes of PVs with the particle *an* can be classified automatically. They take a supervised approach using decision trees. The use of decision trees also allows them to manually inspect and analyze the decisions made by the classifier. As predictive features they use the head nouns of objects, generalized classes of these nouns and PP types.

The approach we take here is not fully comparable to any of the former approaches, since we try to derive a semantic classification BV-PP *pairs* in an unsupervised manner and we only use syntactic features, stemming from corpus instances of both the BVs and the PVs. In other words, we do not attempt to classify PVs, but we try to classify syntactic transfers and, by doing so, we identify syntactic transfer patterns which we hypothesize to have a close relation to semantic PV classes and the semantics of the particles.

4 Experimental Setup

4.1 Gold Standard Classification

For testing our hypothesis, we created a gold standard of 32 PVs, including 14 with the particle *an* and 18 with the particle *auf*. We concentrated on two particles here in order to have a small and controlled test bed which allows us to study the syntactic transfers.

We based the creation of the gold standard on the classification by Fleischer and Barz (2012b), but we further distinguished the classes based on the meanings of the BVs. For example, we grouped all the BVs with the meaning of '*looking in a manner X*' or '*tying X to Y in a manner Z*'. From these classes we selected those which had a clear subcategorization pattern for both the BVs and the PVs. We discarded such PVs where either the PV itself or its underlying BV was clearly ambiguous. The full gold standard can be seen in table 2. The table also lists the expected dominant subcategorization frames for the BVs and PVs of each category.

While the gold standard was based on theoretic considerations, we expected it to correlate with human intuitions. To test this, we presented the gold standard verbs to 6 human raters. These raters were all German native speakers with working practice in various areas of linguistics or language didactics. The raters were not directly asked to group PVs into categories. Instead the PVs were presented in pairs[3] and raters had to make a decision on whether or not the pairs belong to the same semantic category (even if they could not think of a name or description of that category). No pre-defined categories were given, nor were raters asked to provide a name or description for these categories. The annotators were asked to take the similarity of the BVs and the similarity of the PVs into consideration for their judgements. In order to avoid possible bias, the verbs were presented without given context. What is important here is that we did *not* ask them to take any syntactic criterion into consideration, the criterion we used for the initial compilation of the gold standard.

The inter-annotator agreement was substantial with a Fleiss' Kappa score of 0.68 (Fleiss, 1971).[4] As a measure of agreement between raters and the previously created gold standard, we performed pair-wise calculations between the ratings of each annotator and the gold standard. For the comparison, the gold standard was transformed into PV pairs and the value *true* was assigned if the two verbs of a pairs belonged to the same category, and *false* otherwise. We calculated the Kappa scores for each annotator and took the average of the agreement scores. Table 1 resumes the comparison. Values are given for the parts of the gold standard corresponding to PVs with *an* and *auf* separately and also for the gold standard as a whole.

It can clearly be seen that humans agreement with the gold standard is as high as the agreement among different annotators. This shows that the gold standard used here is a valid representation of human language intuition. Most importantly, the annotators did not use syntactic criteria

[3] All possible PV combinations were generated, but the PVs with *an* were kept separate from those with *auf* in order to avoid an unnecessary explosion of the number of pairs to be rated.

[4] One of the 6 raters showed less agreement with the other raters. If we eliminate this rater from the calculation of agreement, we achieve an even higher Kappa score of 0.76 and also agreement scores with the gold standard improved. Two of the annotators even achieved Kappa scores of over 0.80 when compared to the gold standard.

and still validated a gold standard whose creation was explicitly based on syntactic subcategorization frames. In other words: there is an apparent tight interrelation between syntax and semantics for PVs, at least in the sense that semantic distinctions can be used to predict different syntactic behaviour. The inverse case - predicting semantic classes from syntactic information - will be discussed below.

4.2 Corpus Data

We used a lemmatized and tagged version of the SdeWaC corpus (Faaß and Eckart, 2013), a web corpus of 880 million words. For linguistic preprocessing we used the MATE parser (Bohnet, 2010), which allowed us to extract syntactic subcategorization frames.

4.3 Feature Selection

For each PV-BV pair we extracted two parallel sets of features, one pertaining to the BV and one for the PV. This allows us to model the syntactic transfer. For example, we expected that an ideal transfer from a group of transitive BVs to a group of intransitive PVs should be reflected in high values for the features BV:transitive and PV:intransitive[5] and, in turn, low values for BV:intransitive and PV:transitive.

We had two ways of selecting the feature types: manually and automatically. For the manual feature selection we extracted only those features from the parsed frames which we already used in the creation of the gold standard and which are listed in table 2. This resulted in a small feature set of 30 features (15 features for PVs and BVs, respectively). For the automatic feature selection we simply used the *n* most frequent frames which could be observed in the corpus for the set of verbs of the gold standard.

From the syntactic dependency representation provided by the parser, we excluded subjects and modifiers (except for PP-modifiers) in the representation of subcat frames. We did not use information on subjects, because in German all verbs have subjects, which may be implicit in the case of subordinate clauses. We found that for this reason that with the representation of subjects in the extracted features no relevant information was gained, but some distortion was introduced. Modifiers in the MATE parser represent information which is too general to be good predictors. Based on theoretical considerations on the best lexicographic representation of verbs, we included PP-modifiers, however, because quantitative information on PP-adjuncts has proven successful next to that of PP-arguments (Schulte im Walde, 2006a; Joanis et al., 2008), and in addition the parser often distinguishes poorly between PP-modifiers and PP-arguments.

In order to create an idealized artificial upper bound, we also created a set of idealized "lexicographic" descriptions in the form of manually instantiated feature vectors and feature values, using the manually selected feature configuration we just described (and ultimately based on the gold standard description represented by table 2). These idealized vectors were also used for clustering experiments in order to estimate an upper bound.

4.4 Clustering Methods

For the clustering experiments we used two different clustering algorithms: K-means and Latent Semantic Classes (LSC). K-means is a standard flat, hard-clustering algorithm; we used the Weka implementation (Witten and Frank, 2005). LSC (Rooth, 1998; Rooth et al., 1999) is a two-dimensional soft-clustering algorithm which learns three probability distributions: one for the clusters, and one for the output probabilities of each element and for each feature type with regard to a cluster. The latter two (elements and features) correspond to the two dimensions of the clustering. In our case the elements are the PV-BV pairs, and the features are normalized counts of the subcategorization frames.

4.5 Evaluation

Our feature vectors are a combination of the feature vector for the BV and the feature vector for the PV of each PV-BV pair. Since the length of each vector depends on the base frequency of each verb we need to apply a feature normalization: we simply reduce each feature to its unit vector of length 1. Because the frequency ratio between BV and PV may vary strongly, we need to normalize PV vectors and BV vectors separately before they can be combined.

The vector combination for each PV-BV pair is done by simply adding the dimensions (and not the

[5]Note that *transitive* and *transitive* are only convenient abreviations for the labels *NPnom* and *NPnom+NPacc*, which are used in table2.

	an	auf	an+auf
Inter-annotator agreement	0.79	0.64	0.70
Average agreement between annotators and gold standard	0.73	0.74	0.73

Table 1: Inter-annotator agreement and comparison of the gold standard to the ratings of 6 human annotators (Fleiss' Kappa Scores).

Particle	Typical frames for the BV	Typical frames for the PV	Semantic Class	Verbs in Class	
an	NPnom +NPacc +PP-an	NPnom +NPacc +PP-an	locative/ relational tying	an|binden an|ketten	to tie at to chain at
	NPnom +PP-zu/in/ nach/auf	NPnom +NPacc	locative/ relational gaze	an|blicken an|gucken an|starren	to glance at to look at to stare at
	NPnom +NPacc +PP-mit	NPnom +NPacc +PP-mit	ingressive consump- tion	an|brechen an|reißen an|schneiden	start to break start to tear start to cut
	NPnom	NPnom +NPacc	locative/ relational sound	an|brüllen an|fauchen an|meckern	to roar at to hiss at to bleat at
	NPnom +NPacc +PP-an	NPnom +NPacc	locative/ relational fixation	an|heften an|kleben an|schrauben	to stick at to glue at to screw at
auf	NPnom	NPnom	locative blaze- bubble	auf|brodeln auf|flammen auf|lodern auf|spudeln	to bubble up to light up to blaze up to bubble up
	NPnom +PP-zu/in/ nach/auf	NPnom	locative gaze	auf|blicken auf|schauen auf|sehen	to glance up to look up to look up
	NPnom +NPacc	NPnom +NPacc	locative/ dimensional instigate	auf|hetzen auf|scheuchen	to instigate to rouse
	NPnom +NPacc +PP-auf	NPnom +NPacc	locative/ relational fixation	auf|heften auf|kleben auf|pressen	to staple on to glue on to press on
	NPnom	NPnom	ingressive sound	auf|brüllen auf|heulen auf|klingen auf|kreischen auf|schluchzen auf|stöhnen	suddenly roar suddenly howl suddenly sound suddenly scream suddenly sob suddenly moan

Table 2: The gold standard classes for the experiments, with subcategorization patterns.

		an			auf			an+auf		
		Purity	RI	ARI	Purity	RI	ARI	Purity	RI	ARI
	Human ratings		0.93			0.92			0.92	
K-means	idealized features (manually set)	0.83	0.91	0.70	0.88	0.92	0.72	0.93	0.97	8.2
	selected features (extracted)	**0.67**	**0.82**	**0.29**	0.75	**0.87**	0.52	0.46	0.88	0.32
	20 feat	0.58	0.74	0.18	0.69	0.69	0.40	0.43	0.88	0.14
	50 feat	**0.67**	0.80	0.20	0.75	0.83	0.38	0.43	0.90	0.19
	100 feat	**0.67**	0.79	0.18	0.75	0.83	0.40	0.49	0.90	*0.21*
	200 feat	0.58	0.74	0.13	**0.81**	0.86	0.52	0.43	0.88	0.18
LSC	selected features (extracted) Cutoff: 0.1	0.63	0.78	0.22	0.80	0.85	**0.55**	**0.85**	**0.92**	**0.59**

Table 3: Comparison of the results from different clustering methods and feature configurations.

dimension extensions) of the two vectors. In this way, each subcategorization frame is represented separately for the BV and the PV. For example, the vectors for the intransitive frame will be represented as *BV:intransitive* and *PV:intransitive*.

We evaluated the clusterings in terms of Purity (Manning et al., 2008), Rand Index and Adjusted Rand Index (Rand, 1971; Hubert and Arabie, 1985). Purity is a measure with values between 0 and 1 which captures the *purity* of individual clusters in terms of the ratio between the number of elements of the majority class in each cluster and the total of elements in the cluster. A perfect clustering will have a purity of 1. What Purity does not capture is the amount of clusters over which each target class is distributed. That means that also non-perfect clusters may achieve a Purity of 1 if there are more clusters than target classes. As long as the number of clusters is constant, however, purity is a good and intuitive approximation to clustering evaluation.

The Rand Index (RI) looks at pairs of elements and assesses whether they have been correctly placed in the same cluster (which is correct if they pertain to the same target class) or in different clusters (correct if they belong to different target classes). RI is sensitive to the number of non-empty clusters and can capture both the quality of individual clusters and the amount to which elements of target categories have been grouped together. RI looks as pair-wise decisions, which makes it also applicable to the human ratings described in section 4.1. The Adjusted Rand Index (ARI) is a version of RI which is corrected for chance. While RI has values between 0 and 1, ARI can have negative values; 1 still represents a perfect clustering.

The Adjusted Rand Index (ARI) is a version of RI which is corrected for chance. While RI has values between 0 and 1, ARI can have negative values; 1 still represents a perfect clustering.

We evaluated the clustering of the verbs with the particles *an* and *auf* separately from each other, since we have to expect that there is a different set of semantic classes for each verb particle. We also ran the same experiments for the gold standard as a whole (*an+auf*), in order to test if we could find some tendencies across clusters.

We set the number of clusters equal to the number of target categories from the gold standard. This gave us 5 clusters for both the *an*-set and the *auf*-set and 10 clusters for the classification of the whole gold standard.

Note that LSC is a soft clustering algorithm. For the evaluation of LSC clusters with respect to purity and RI and ARI, a conversion to hard clustering must be done. We did this conversion by simply applying a cutoff value for the output probabilities for cluster membership. We tried out various cut-off levels and found that for the sets of *an* and *auf* PVs the value of 0.1 gave a good trade-off between coverage (the total number of elements retained in all clusters) and ARI (cf also Table 4 below). This value is also the one used in Kühner and Schulte im Walde (2010).

5 Results

The comparison of the results from different methods can be seen in table 3. The strongest automatically obtained results are printed in bold face. The human rating scores are given in the first row and allow for a direct comparison between automatic clustering and human decisions.[6] The second row shows the artificial upper bound represented by the manually set feature vectors as lexicographic entries. Note that this is an *artificial* upper bound and not an experimental result, even if obtained by clustering.

The third row corresponds to the evaluation results for the manually selected corpus-based feature configuration used within K-means. They are to be compared with the following rows concerning the results based on automatically selected n most frequent features. The last row shows the results obtained with the LSC soft clustering algorithm, applying a cutoff of 0.1 output probability for cluster membership, again for the manually selected feature configuration. This result is not fully comparable to the rows above, which are obained with K-means or human ratings. Since LSC is a soft clustering algorithm, there is a trade-off between coverage and accuracy which depends on the cutoff point selected for the conversion into hard clusters.

Note that the Purity values are comparable among each other since the number of clusters was held constant. We always chose a number of clusters equal to the number of target categories (5 categories for *an*, 5 for *auf* and 10 for *an+auf*).

Table 4 shows the results for LSC clustering in more detail. The soft clusterings have to be converted to hard clusterings. Because of this the cut-off point within the conversion becomes an important parameter. We chose here cut-off points which correspond to the output probability of cluster-elements (e.g. PV-BV pairs) with regard to each cluster. The table shows a clear tendency towards better ARI scores when higher cutoff points are chosen. But this is counterbalanced by the fact that for higher cutoff points less elements are retained. Below a certain cutoff-point the total number of elements retaind is smaller than the target set of verbs in the gold standard.

[6]RI is a measure which is based on pair-wise clustering decisions, we were able to calculate these scores for the human ratings described in section 4.1. Since purity is not based on a pair-wise decision, it was not applicable to the human ratings. For the same reason ARI was also not adaptable to the human rating scenario.

6 Discussion

It is not surprising that the manually defined feature configuration in our "lexicographic" setting perform best. These results are also similar to those obtained by the human validation of the gold standard. They do not get perfect scores of 1 because of small lexicographic differences concerning individual entries. The automatic clustering results relying on corpus-based features are worse, as expected, but they still represent a very strong tendency to group together PV-BV pairs into semantic classes. We can achieve relatively high purity scores, thus demonstrating that our approach is generally valid.

Concerning the feature selection for the corpus-based data, the manually selected set seems to perform slightly better than the automatic feature selection settings. Moreover, the manual selection represents a more stable setting since automatic selection seems to vary with the number n of features. There appears to be no optimal setting for n which gives the best results for all sets. For the *an* set the local maximum is reached with the selection of the 50 or 100 most frequent subcat frames. The selection of more or less features leads to worse evaluation scores. For the *auf* set this local maximum is reach with much higher values for n. The manually created feature set, on the other hand, always results in a relatively good performance. This is also an expected result since the feature selection already contains human linguistic knowledge on which syntactic arguments represent the core set of the semantic roles which the verbs can realize.

It is apparently surprising that for the joint gold standard set *an+auf* LSC performs much better than K-means. But this high ARI value comes at the cost of a very low coverage. If we compare this value to table 4, it can be seen that the cutoff point of 0.1, which works very well for sets of *an* and *auf* is inadequate for the set *an+auf*: only 20 verbs are retained in the converted clusters while the target size is 32. While we can observe the general tendency of LSC to perform on a roughly comparable level to K-means, an exact comparison is hard to obtain with the used evaluation metrics. There are, nevertheless, possible problem settings where soft clusters are more adequate, which justifies to include LSC in this comparison.

	an		auf		an+auf	
Cutoff	ARI	n_{clust}	ARI	n_{clust}	ARI	n_{clust}
0.07	0.17	25	0.39	22	0.31	40
0.08	0.18	23	0.55	20	0.39	32
0.09	0.19	21	0.55	20	0.56	23
0.10	0.22	19	0.55	20	0.59	20
0.11	0.30	16	0.5	19	0.48	17
0.12	0.30	16	0.41	16	0.56	16
$n_{classes}$		14		18		32

Table 4: Evaluation with LSC using extracted selected features for different cutoff points (probabilities of class membership) when creating hard clusters from soft clusters. ($n_{classes}$ refers to the number of elements across target classes, n_{clust} refers to the number of elements across hard clusters.)

The class of *anketten/anbinden* tends to end up in singleton clusters, especially *anketten*. We first suspected that this is due to the fact that *anketten* is a relatively infrequent verb and is represented by a sparse vector. But a comparison to the human ratings reveals that human raters show a similar and quite consistent disagreement with the gold standad with respect to this the locative relational *tying* and *fixation* classes. All 6 raters judged *anheften* (a fixation verb) and *anbinden* (a tying verb) as pertaining to the same category, contrary to the gold standard. Interestingly, this fixation-tying distinction is the only one, where a majority of raters deviated in their judgements from the gold standard at the same point. On the other hand some of the raters were confused by the fact the class of *aufbrodeln* combines two different elements: water and fire. This did not affect the majority of raters, nor was the disagreement consistent, but it is reflected in the somewhat lower inter-annotator agreement for the *auf* set (cf. table 1). These findings strongly suggest that the problem should be located in the gold standard rather than in the clustering method.

Finally, is interesting to compare the automatic clustering results to the human ratings from section 4.1. The human annotation task was complementary to the automatic clustering because clustering was done on the basis of corpus-based purely syntactic features while for the human rating the annotators focused on purely semantic information. Apart from the expectably worse performance of an automatic clustering it can be concluded that both information from the semantic and the syntactic perspectives ultimately lead to the creation of quite similar clusters, which is probably the most important conclusion we can draw from the experiment.

7 Conclusion

In this paper we have shown that a pairwise clustering of particle verbs in combination with their base verbs can be done with success if syntactic subcategorization frames for PVs and BVs are taken as features separately. By combining the extracted subcategorization frame count from base verbs and particle verbs as separate dimensions in a common vector space, we are able to model syntactic transfer patterns. We can also show that within our setting we are able to replicate a gold standard classification with a reasonable degree of success when we apply various clustering algorithms. The gold standard by itself can be validated by human judgements to a high degree. Human judges based their annotations on semantic factors and still they converge largely with an automatic clustering which is purely based on syntactic subcategorization.

In future work we plan to adress the problem of finding correspondences between the syntactic subcategorization slots, hence model the syntactic transfer proper, and to investigate if the syntactic transfer information can be used to predict the degree of semantic compositionality of PVs.

Acknowledgements

This work was funded by the DFG Research Project "Distributional Approaches to Semantic Relatedness" (Stefan Bott, Sabine Schulte im Walde), and the DFG Heisenberg Fellowship SCHU-2580/1-1 (Sabine Schulte im Walde). We would also like to thank the participants of the human rating experiment.

References

Nadine Aldinger. 2004. Towards a Dynamic Lexicon: Predicting the Syntactic Argument Structure of Complex Verbs. In *Proceedings of the 4th International Conference on Language Resources and Evaluation*, Lisbon, Portugal.

Timothy Baldwin and Aline Villavicencio. 2002. Extracting the Unextractable: A Case Study on Verb Particles. In *Proceedings of the Sixth Conference on Computational Natural Language Learning*, pages 98–104, Taipei, Taiwan.

Timothy Baldwin, Colin Bannard, Takaaki Tanaka, and Dominic Widdows. 2003. An Empirical Model of Multiword Expression Decomposability. In *Proceedings of the ACL-2003 Workshop on Multiword Expressions: Analysis, Acquisition and Treatment*, pages 89–96, Sapporo, Japan.

Timothy Baldwin. 2005. Deep Lexical Acquisition of Verb–Particle Constructions. *Computer Speech and Language*, 19:398–414.

Collin Bannard. 2005. Learning about the Meaning of Verb–Particle Constructions from Corpora. *Computer Speech and Language*, 19:467–478.

Gertrud Faaß and Kerstin Eckart. 2013. SdeWaC – a Corpus of Parsable Sentences from the Web. In *Proceedings of the International Conference of the German Society for Computational Linguistics and Language Technology*, Darmstadt, Germany. To appear.

Wolfgang Fleischer and Irmhild Barz. 2012a. *Wortbildung der deutschen Gegenwartssprache*. de Gruyter.

Wolfgang Fleischer and Irmhild Barz. 2012b. *Wortbildung der deutschen Gegenwartssprache*. Walter de Gruyter, 4th edition.

Joseph L. Fleiss. 1971. Measuring nominal scale agreement among many raters. *Psychological Bulletin*, 76(5):378–382.

Silvana Hartmann. 2008. Einfluss syntaktischer und semantischer Subkategorisierung auf die Kompositionalität von Partikelverben. Studienarbeit. Institut für Maschinelle Sprachverarbeitung, Universität Stuttgart. Supervision: Sabine Schulte im Walde and Hans Kamp.

Lawrence Hubert and Phipps Arabie. 1985. Comparing Partitions. *Journal of Classification*, 2:193–218.

Eric Joanis, Suzanne Stevenson, and David James. 2008. A General Feature Space for Automatic Verb Classification. *Natural Language Engineering*, 14(3):337–367.

Hans Kamp and Uwe Reyle. 1993. *From discourse to logic: Introduction to modeltheoretic semantics of natural language, formal logic and discourse representation theory.* Number 42. Springer.

Fritz Kliche. 2011. Semantic Variants of German Particle Verbs with *"ab"*. *Leuvense Bijdragen*, 97:3–27.

Anna Korhonen, Yuval Krymolowski, and Zvika Marx. 2003. Clustering Polysemic Subcategorization Frame Distributions Semantically. In *Proceedings of the 41st Annual Meeting of the Association for Computational Linguistics*, pages 64–71, Sapporo, Japan.

Natalie Kühner and Sabine Schulte im Walde. 2010. Determining the Degree of Compositionality of German Particle Verbs by Clustering Approaches. In *Proceedings of the 10th Conference on Natural Language Processing*, pages 47–56, Saarbrücken, Germany.

Andrea Lechler and Antje Roßdeutscher. 2009. German Particle Verbs with *auf*. Reconstructing their Composition in a DRT-based Framework. *Linguistische Berichte*, 220.

Anke Lüdeling. 2001. *On German Particle Verbs and Similar Constructions in German*. Dissertations in Linguistics. CSLI Publications, Stanford, CA.

Christopher D Manning, Prabhakar Raghavan, and Hinrich Schütze. 2008. *Introduction to information retrieval*, volume 1. Cambridge university press Cambridge.

Diana McCarthy, Bill Keller, and John Carroll. 2003. Detecting a Continuum of Compositionality in Phrasal Verbs. In *Proceedings of the ACL-SIGLEX Workshop on Multiword Expressions: Analysis, Acquisition and Treatment*, Sapporo, Japan.

Paola Merlo and Suzanne Stevenson. 2001. Automatic Verb Classification Based on Statistical Distributions of Argument Structure. *Computational Linguistics*, 27(3):373–408.

William M. Rand. 1971. Objective Criteria for the Evaluation of Clustering Methods. *Journal of the American Statistical Association*, 66(336):846–850.

Mats Rooth, Stefan Riezler, Detlef Prescher, Glenn Carr oll, and Franz Beil. 1999. Inducing a Semantically Annotated Lexicon via EM-Based Clustering. In *Proceedings of the 37th Annual Meeting of the Association for Co mputational Linguistics*, Maryland, MD.

Mats Rooth. 1998. Two-Dimensional Clusters in Grammatical Relations. In *Inducing Lexicons with the EM Algorithm*, AIMS Report 4(3). Institut für Maschinelle Sprachverarbeitung, Universität Stuttgart.

Sabine Schulte im Walde. 2000. Clustering Verbs Semantically According to their Alternation Behaviour. In *Proceedings of the 18th International Conference on Computational Linguistics*, pages 747–753, Saarbrücken, Germany.

Sabine Schulte im Walde. 2004. Identification, Quantitative Description, and Preliminary Distributional Analysis of German Particle Verbs. In *Proceedings of the COLING Workshop on Enhancing and Using Electronic Dictionaries*, pages 85–88, Geneva, Switzerland.

Sabine Schulte im Walde. 2005. Exploring Features to Identify Semantic Nearest Neighbours: A Case Study on German Particle Verbs. In *Proceedings of the International Conference on Recent Advances in Natural Language Processing*, pages 608–614, Borovets, Bulgaria.

Sabine Schulte im Walde. 2006a. Experiments on the Automatic Induction of German Semantic Verb Classes. *Computational Linguistics*, 32(2):159–194.

Sabine Schulte im Walde. 2006b. The Syntax-Semantics Interface of German Particle Verbs. Panel discussion at the 3rd ACL-SIGSEM Workshop on Prepositions at the 11th Conference of the European Chapter of the Association for Computational Linguistics.

Sylvia Springorum, Sabine Schulte im Walde, and Antje Roßdeutscher. 2012. Automatic Classification of German *an* Particle Verbs. In *Proceedings of the 8th International Conference on Language Resources and Evaluation*, pages 73–80, Istanbul, Turkey.

Sylvia Springorum, Sabine Schulte im Walde, and Antje Roßdeutscher. 2013. Sentence Generation and Compositionality of Systematic Neologisms of German Particle Verbs. Talk at the 5th Conference on Quantitative Investigations in Theoretical Linguistics.

Sylvia Springorum. 2011. DRT-based Analysis of the German Verb Particle *"an"*. *Leuvense Bijdragen*, 97:80–105.

Barbara Stiebels. 1996. *Lexikalische Argumente und Adjunkte. Zum semantischen Beitrag von verbalen Präfixen und Partikeln*. Akademie Verlag, Berlin.

Aline Villavicencio. 2005. The Availability of Verb-Particle Constructions in Lexical Resources: How much is enough? *Computer Speech & Language*, 19(4):415–432.

Ian H. Witten and Eibe Frank. 2005. *Data Mining: Practical Machine Learning Tools and Techniques wi th Java Implementations*. Morgan Kaufmann.

Author Index